T0329672

M&A Information Technology Best Practices

M&A Information Technology Best Practices

Edited by

JANICE M. ROEHL-ANDERSON

WILEY

Library of Congress Cataloging-in-Publication Data:

M&A information technology best practices / Janice M. Roehl-Anderson, editor.
    pages cm. — (Wiley finance series)
  Includes index.
  ISBN 978-1-118-61757-1 (cloth) – ISBN 978-1-118-74095-8 (ePDF) –
ISBN 978-1-118-74106-1 (ePub) – ISBN 978-1-118-69202-8 (o-Book) 1. Information
technology–Management. 2. Consolidation and merger of corporations. 3. Business
enterprises. I. Roehl-Anderson, Janice M., editor.
  HD30.2.M3 2013
  004.068′1—dc23
                                                                    2013019139

Printed in the United States of America
10 9 8 7 6 5 4 3 2 1

Contents

Preface   **xv**

Acknowledgments   **xix**

PART I
Introduction

CHAPTER 1
Introduction to the IT Aspects of Mergers, Acquisitions, and Divestitures   **3**
Varun Joshi and Saurav Sharma

Role of IT in M&A   4
Due Diligence   6
Integration/Separation Planning   8
Integration/Separation Execution   16
Wrapping It Up   20

CHAPTER 2
The Role of IT in Mergers and Acquisitions   **23**
Peter Blatman and Eugene Lukac

Quest to Capture Synergies   24
Capturing the Benefits   26
Wrapping It Up   32

CHAPTER 3
Aligning Business and IT Strategy during Mergers, Acquisitions, and Divestitures   **35**
Jason Asper and Wes Protsman

The Business-Aligned Integration Model   36
Enterprise Blueprint and IT Alignment   38
IT's Role in Functional Blueprinting   39

Decision Making and Business Alignment   43
Business Alignment in Due Diligence   43
Wrapping It Up   44

CHAPTER 4
Mergers and Acquisitions IT Strategy, Approach, and Governance:
IT and Its Customers   **47**
Chris DeBeer and Michael H. Moore

Strategy   48
Approach   49
Governance   50
Finance   51
Operations   54
Human Resources   57
Information Technology   60
Wrapping It Up   66

PART II

Information Technology's Role in Mergers, Acquisitions,
and Divestitures

CHAPTER 5
IT Due Diligence Leading Practices   **69**
Mark Andrews and David Sternberg

Objectives and Complexities of IT Due Diligence   70
Areas of Investigation   72
Proprietary or Product Technology–Driven Due Diligence   76
Impact of Transaction Type on the Due Diligence
    Investigation   77
Investigation for Strategic Buyers versus Financial Buyers 78
Considerations of Planning IT Due Diligence   79
Considerations of Conducting IT Due Diligence   82
Considerations of Finalizing IT Due Diligence   86
Tying Due Diligence to the Next Steps in the Post-Merger
    Process   88
Wrapping It Up   88

CHAPTER 6
IT Infrastructure Aspects of Mergers, Acquisitions, and Divestitures **91**
Rick Kupcunas, Mike Trisko, Jeffry Sprengel,
   and Mushtaque Heera

   IT Infrastructure Blueprinting   91
   IT Infrastructure Planning   93
   IT Infrastructure Dependencies   100
   Wrapping It Up   102

CHAPTER 7
M&A IT and Synergies **105**
Jim Boland, Ronald Goldberg, Colin Hartnett, Sunil Rai,
   and Stephen Ronan

   IT's Role and Contribution to Synergy Capture   105
   Synergy Capture and Benefits Tracking during the Merger,
      Acquisition, and Divestiture Lifecycle   120
   Wrapping It Up   135

CHAPTER 8
Supporting Business Objectives with M&A-Aware Enterprise
Architecture **137**
Pavel Krumkachev, Shalva Nolen, Nitin Prabhakar,
   and Rajat Sharma

   Sources of IT-Related Synergies during M&A   137
   Post-Merger IT Integration Planning: The Model Makes
      the Difference   139
   M&A-Aware Enterprise Architecture Models   139
   Divestitures and the Enterprise Architecture Frameworks   143
   Wrapping It Up   144

CHAPTER 9
The Importance of a Tested IT Strategy and Approach for Mergers,
Acquisitions, and Divestitures **145**
Pavel Krumkachev, Shalva Nolen, Nitin Prabhakar,
   and Rajat Sharma

   M&A IT Organization and Strategy   145
   A Tested and Repeatable Approach for IT Integrations   149

A Tested and Repeatable Approach for IT Divestitures   152
Wrapping It Up   155

CHAPTER 10
Cloud Considerations for M&A IT Architecture   **157**
Mike Brown

Understanding Cloud Solutions   157
Types of Cloud Solutions   158
Cloud Solution: Potential Benefits   158
Opportunity during Post-M&A Integration   158
Cloud Solutions for Post-M&A Plug-and-Play IT
   Frameworks   159
Determining Suitability for Cloud Solutions   160
Assessing Cloud Migration Timing   160
Establishing a Cloud Strategy   162
Evaluating Cloud Providers   163
Cloud Solution Success Factors   164
Wrapping It Up   165

CHAPTER 11
Data Implications of Mergers and Acquisitions   **167**
Sascha Elsing

Criticality of Data Management in M&A Transactions   167
Data Governance and Organizational Considerations   167
Data Confidentiality, Privacy, Security, and Risk
   Management   168
Data Archiving Requirements   168
Data Management Road Map   169
Customer Data Considerations   172
Wrapping It Up   173

CHAPTER 12
Using M&A to Streamline the Applications Portfolio   **175**
Colin Whiteneck, Joydeep Mukherjee, Ted Veterano,
   and Venky Iyer

Overview of an Applications Rationalization Program   178
Achieving Cost Synergies through Applications
   Rationalization   178
Achieving Operational Synergies through Applications
   Rationalization   182

Technology and Cost Impact in a Divestiture Event — 188
Emerging Trends — 193
Best Practices for Applications Rationalization in an M&A
　Scenario — 194
Wrapping It Up — 198

CHAPTER 13
**Third-Party Contracts in M&A: Identifying and Managing Common
Implications** — **199**
*Christine McKay, Joseph Joy, Ramkumar Jayaraman,
　and Ninad Deshmukh*

Challenges Inherent in Different Types of M&A Transactions — 200
Typical Realities — 200
Primary Challenges — 204
Tackling Challenges — 206
Program Management — 215
Wrapping It Up — 217
Case Studies — 218
Lessons Learned — 221

CHAPTER 14
**M&A IT Architecture and Infrastructure: Developing and Delivering
Transition Services Agreements** — **225**
Olivier May and Kevin Charles

Plan Early and Resource Appropriately — 227
Foster Deal Team and Business Collaboration to Document
　Appropriately — 229
Price Services Conservatively — 231
Establish a Practical Governance Approach — 235
Plan Exits and Remove Stranded Costs — 247
Wrapping It Up — 250

CHAPTER 15
Day 1 Implications for IT Functions — **253**
Sejal Gala and Sandeep Dasharath

Top Day 1 Priorities for IT — 253
Wrapping It Up — 263

CHAPTER 16
Transition Services Agreement (TSA)—Untangling the Web   **265**
Simon Singh, Nikhil Uppal, and Jennie Miller

Key Considerations for Drafting an Effective TSA   267
Structuring the TSA   270
Managing TSAs   271
Governance of TSA Services through a Parallel Structure   273
Rationale for Accelerated Exit of a TSA   278
Key Considerations for TSA Exit   279
Wrapping It Up   281

CHAPTER 17
IT Risk, Security, and Controls in M&A: Identifying and Managing Common Considerations   **283**
David Caruso, Kelly Moynihan, John Clark, Jamie Fox, Joseph Joy, and Scott Kaufman

Understanding the IT Risk, Security, and Controls Current State   283
Practices for Managing IT Risk, Security, and Control Considerations   293
Wrapping It Up   301

PART III
The People Aspects of Mergers, Acquisitions, and Divestitures

CHAPTER 18
The Role of the CIO in Mergers, Acquisitions, and Divestitures   **305**
Irwin Goverman

The Double-Duty Role   305
The Internal Role   307
The External Role   314
Some Lessons Learned   317
Wrapping It Up   320

CHAPTER 19
The Role of CFO **321**
*Rich Rorem, Trevear Thomas, Nnamdi Lowrie, Heith
    Rothman, Venkat Swaminathan, Chelsea Gorr, Jenny Xu,
    and Mia Velasquez*

Strategist Face	324
Catalyst Face	329
Operator Face	332
Steward Face	338
Wrapping It Up	341

CHAPTER 20
Managing the People Side of IT M&A **345**
*Tammie Potvin, Don Miller, Suseela Kadiyala, Michael Proppe,
    Sarah Hindley, and Laurel Vickers*

Key Priority: Communicating for Impact	346
Merger Stages	348
Effective M&A Communication	351
Key Priority: Defining the Future-State IT Organization	352
Steps in M&A Organization Design	353
Key Priority: Assessing and Selecting IT Talent	358
Key Priority: Managing Change	363
Start with Your Leadership Team	363
Transition Employees	366
Consider Cultural Implications	367
Assess Integration Progress	369
Wrapping It Up	370

CHAPTER 21
**Planning for Business Process Changes Impacting
Information Technology** **373**
Blair Kin

Pre-Day 1 Planning	373
Day 1 Integration Imperatives	376
Long-Term Integration Requirements	380
Wrapping It Up	388

PART IV

M&A IT Project Governance, Testing, and Business Intelligence

CHAPTER 22
Integration Management Office Best Practices   **393**
David Lake and Mauro Schiavon

Roles and Responsibilities   393
Key Activities   395
Sample IMO Templates and Deliverables   398
Managing the Deal   398
Wrapping It Up   403

CHAPTER 23
IT Program Governance during the Deal   **405**
John Uccello

Establish Governance Model   405
Establish the Program Management Office   408
Execute the Plan   413
Wrapping It Up   415

CHAPTER 24
Important Role of Data in an M&A Transaction   **417**
Lynda Gibson, Anil Tondavadi, and Chris Vu

Current Challenges and Lost Opportunities   418
Top 10 Ways to Use Information Management to
    Improve M&A   419
Wrapping It Up   438

CHAPTER 25
Overview of Testing   **439**
Angela Mattix

Types of Testing   439
Testing Functions and Tools   443
Test Preparation Activities   444
Timing of Testing   446
Wrapping It Up   448

PART V
Conclusion

CHAPTER 26
Why Mergers, Acquisitions, and Divestitures Fail, and
Considerations to Help Avoid a Similar Fate   **451**
Nikhil Menon

   M&A Risks   452
   Common Pitfalls   453
   Critical Success Factors   455
   Wrapping It Up   457

CHAPTER 27
M&A IT Key Success Factors   **459**
Nadia Orawski and Luke Bates

   Key Success Factors   459
   Wrapping It Up   461

CHAPTER 28
M&A IT, Summing It All Up   **463**
Habeeb Dihu, Nadia Orawski, Justin Calvin, Luke Bates,
   Bryce Metro, and Eric Niederhelman

   Best Practices   464
   Best Practices to Be Considered Prior to the Deal   464
   M&A IT Strategy, Approach, and Governance Best Practices 467
   M&A IT Security and Privacy Implications Best Practices 472
   M&A IT and Synergies Best Practices   473
   M&A IT Contracts Best Practices   473
   M&A IT Organizational Implications Best Practices   475
   Best Practices to Consider in Order to Execute the Deal 477
   Lessons Learned   478
   Wrapping It Up   479

APPENDIX A
M&A IT Playbook Overview   **493**
Joseph Joy, Shalva Nolen, Simon Singh, and Nikhil Uppal

APPENDIX B
 Sample M&A IT Checklists   **509**
 Shalva Nolen, Sreekanth Gopinathan, and Devi Aradada

APPENDIX C
 M&A IT Sample Case Studies   **521**
 Manish Laad, Abhishek Mathur, and Prasanna Rajappa

About the Editor   **531**

About the Website   **533**

Index   **535**

Preface

One of the most important aspects of many executives' jobs can be making sure a merger, acquisition, or divestiture is successfully completed and anticipated benefits are realized. Additionally, these executives need to help ensure that the information technology (IT) aspects of the deal are appropriately addressed.

In 2012 alone, the global deal volume was over $2.6 trillion.[1] Given the increasing importance of IT over the past several years, there has been a significant amount of change in how systems impact the ultimate success (or failure) of a transaction. As a result, it is hard to stay abreast of the latest system trends and best practices[2] for mergers, acquisitions, and divestitures. This book is focused on providing executives with an understanding of some of the most important system-related areas that can impact a merger, an acquisition, or a divestiture.

THIS BOOK'S SETUP

This book has been written to serve as a guide to mergers, acquisitions, and divestitures for executives and their direct reports. It is written in nontechnical terms and focused on helping facilitate successful deals by appropriately leveraging the IT function throughout the transaction. In short, it is a guide to IT best practices for mergers, acquisitions, and divestitures.

This book is divided into the following parts:

- **Part I: Introduction (Chapters 1 to 4):** Many organizations can fail to successfully address the systems aspects of a merger, acquisition, or divestiture. This part includes a detailed discussion of the IT aspects of deals, the role of IT during those deals, how business and IT strategy can be aligned during a deal, and some key components of how IT needs to manage its operations during a deal.
- **Part II: Information Technology's Role in Mergers, Acquisitions, and Divestitures (Chapters 5 to 17):** Information technology generally plays a critical role in the successful completion of a deal. As a result, it is

important the IT area be included from deal conception to closure. In this part of the book the following key topics are discussed:

- The importance of conducting thorough IT due diligence prior to deal closure.
- Why it is important to assess and address the IT infrastructure (e.g., the hardware, software, and networks) prior to, during, and after the deal closes.
- How IT can help capture significant synergies, including rationalizing the applications portfolio.
- The importance of considering cloud computing as part of the deal, and why the data aspects of the transaction must be addressed up front.
- An overview of third-party contracts and why they need to be considered during any deal.
- Day 1 and Day 2 IT implications and the importance of transition services agreements (TSAs).

This part concludes with an overview of the IT-related risk, security, and control aspects of a merger, acquisition, or divestiture and why they need to be addressed.

- **Part III: The People Aspects of Mergers, Acquisitions, and Divestitures (Chapters 18 to 21):** One of the most important aspects of a merger, acquisition, or divestiture is addressing the people aspects of the deal. It is imperative for executives to understand the people-related components of these deals, whether they are the buyer or the seller. This part of the book contains overviews of and best practices related to the following aspects of these deals: the role of the CIO and CFO in mergers, acquisitions, and divestitures; an overview of how to manage the people side of the deal; and the importance of planning business process changes impacting IT.
- **Part IV: M&A IT Project Governance, Testing, and Business Intelligence (Chapters 22 to 25):** In this part, we review a number of topics critical to the success of a deal: program management office (PMO) best practices, the importance of strong IT governance during the deal, the business intelligence–related aspects of a deal, and the importance of testing the new systems.
- **Part V: Conclusion (Chapters 26 to 28):** This part of the book covers a number of topics that are important to any executive involved with a merger, acquisition, or divestiture: why deals fail and how to try to avoid a similar fate; the critical success factors for a merger, acquisition, or divestiture; and an overview of the key aspects the deals.

This book also includes valuable appendixes for readers as they embark on a merger, acquisition, or divestiture, including:

- Appendix A: An overview of an IT playbook that can be used to help guide the IT team during the deal.
- Appendix B: Sample IT checklists that can assist companies with making sure they are addressing the key aspects of a deal.
- Appendix C: Case studies.

Notes

1. "Headwinds Put Crimp on Global M&A Deals," Anapreeta Das and Dana Cimilluca *Wall Street Journal*, January 2, 2013.
2. "Best practices" represent the contributing authors' collective experience of what works in the real world and hundreds of years of their combined time facilitating the successful delivery of information technology projects.

Acknowledgments

Given the rapidly changing merger, acquisition, and divestiture environment, it was critical for the material in this book to be as timely and relevant as possible and also to represent the collective 200-plus years of experience of the contributing authors. The contributing authors, listed here in alphabetic order, wrote the chapters as follows:

Mark Andrews, Director, Deloitte Consulting LLP: Chapter 5, "IT Due Diligence Leading Practices"

Devi Aradada, Consultant, Deloitte Consulting LLP: Appendix B, "Sample M&A IT Checklists"

Jason Asper, Principal, Deloitte Consulting LLP: Chapter 3, "Aligning Business and IT Strategy during Mergers, Acquisitions, and Divestitures"

Luke Bates, Senior Consultant, Deloitte Consulting LLP: Chapter 27, "M&A IT Key Success Factors"; Chapter 28, "M&A IT, Summing It All Up"

Peter Blatman, Principal, Deloitte Consulting LLP: Chapter 2, "The Role of IT in Mergers and Acquisitions"

Jim Boland, Manager, Deloitte Consulting LLP: Chapter 7, "M&A IT and Synergies"

Mike Brown, Principal, Deloitte Consulting LLP: Chapter 10, "Cloud Considerations for M&A IT Architecture"

Justin Calvin, Manager, Deloitte Consulting LLP: Chapter 28, "M&A IT, Summing It All Up"

David Caruso, Manager, Deloitte Consulting LLP: Chapter 17, "IT Risk, Security, and Controls in M&A"

Kevin Charles, Senior Manager, Deloitte Consulting LLP: Chapter 14, "M&A IT Architecture and Infrastructure: Developing and Delivering Transition Services Agreements"

John Clark, Partner, AERS: Chapter 17, "IT Risk, Security, and Controls in M&A"

Sandeep Dasharath, Senior Consultant, Deloitte Consulting LLP: Chapter 15, "Day 1 Implications for IT Functions"

Chris DeBeer, Senior Manager, Deloitte Consulting LLP: Chapter 4, "Mergers and Acquisitions IT Strategy, Approach, and Governance: IT and Its Customers"

Ninad Deshmukh, Consultant, Deloitte Consulting LLP: Chapter 13, "Third-Party Contracts in M&A: Identifying and Managing Common Implications"

Habeeb Dihu, Senior Manager, Deloitte Consulting LLP: Chapter 28, "M&A IT, Summing It All Up"

Sascha Elsing, Director, Deloitte Consulting LLP: Chapter 11, "Data Implications of Mergers and Acquisitions"

Jamie Fox, Senior Manager, AERS: Chapter 17, "IT Risk, Security, and Controls in M&A"

Sejal Gala, Senior Manager, Deloitte Consulting LLP: Chapter 15, "Day 1 Implications for IT Functions"

Lynda Gibson, Director, Deloitte Consulting LLP: Chapter 24, "Important Role of Data in an M&A Transaction"

Ronald Goldberg, Principal, Deloitte Consulting LLP: Chapter 7, "M&A IT and Synergies"

Sreekanth Gopinathan, Senior Consultant, Deloitte Consulting LLP: Appendix B, "Sample M&A IT Checklists"

Chelsea Gorr, Manager, Deloitte Consulting LLP: Chapter 19, "The Role of CFO"

Irwin Goverman, Principal, Deloitte Consulting LLP: Chapter 18, "The Role of the CIO in Mergers, Acquisitions, and Divestitures"

Colin Hartnett, Principal, Deloitte Consulting LLP: Chapter 7, "M&A IT and Synergies"

Mushtaque Heera, Specialist Leader, Deloitte Consulting LLP: Chapter 6, "IT Infrastructure Aspects of Mergers, Acquisitions, and Divestitures"

Sarah Hindley, Principal, Deloitte Consulting LLP: Chapter 20, "Managing the People Side of IT M&A"

Venky Iyer, Specialist Leader, Deloitte Consulting LLP: Chapter 12, "Using M&A to Streamline the Applications Portfolio"

Ramkumar Jayaraman, Manager, Deloitte Consulting LLP: Chapter 13, "Third-Party Contracts in M&A: Identifying and Managing Common Implications"

Matthew A. Jones, Consultant, Deloitte Consulting LLP: Chapter 26, "Why Mergers, Acquisitions, and Divestitures Fail, and Considerations to Help Avoid a Similar Fate"

Varun Joshi, Senior Manager, Deloitte Consulting LLP: Chapter 1, "Introduction to the IT Aspects of Mergers, Acquisitions, and Divestitures"

Joseph Joy, Director, Deloitte Consulting LLP: Chapter 13, "Third-Party Contracts in M&A: Identifying and Managing Common Implications"; Chapter 17, "IT Risk, Security, and Controls in M&A"; Appendix A, "M&A IT Playbook Overview"

Suseela Kadiyala, Specialist Leader, Deloitte Consulting LLP: Chapter 20, "Managing the People Side of IT M&A"

Scott Kaufman, Business Analyst, Deloitte Consulting LLP: Chapter 17, "IT Risk, Security, and Controls in M&A"

Blair Kin, Senior Manager, Deloitte Consulting LLP: Chapter 21, "Planning for Business Process Changes Impacting Information Technology"

Pavel Krumkachev, Principal, Deloitte Consulting LLP: Chapter 8, "Supporting Business Objectives with M&A-Aware Enterprise Architecture"; Chapter 9, "The Importance of a Tested IT Strategy and Approach for Mergers, Acquisitions, and Divestitures"

Rick Kupcunas, Director, Deloitte Consulting LLP: Chapter 6, "IT Infrastructure Aspects of Mergers, Acquisitions, and Divestitures"

Manish Laad, Senior Manager, Deloitte Consulting LLP: Appendix C, "M&A IT Sample Case Studies"

David Lake, Senior Manager, Deloitte Consulting LLP: Chapter 22, "Integration Management Office Best Practices"

Nnamdi Lowrie, Principal, Deloitte Consulting LLP: Chapter 19, "The Role of CFO"

Eugene Lukac, Specialist Leader, Deloitte Consulting LLP: Chapter 2, "The Role of IT in Mergers and Acquisitions"

Abhishek Mathur, Manager, Deloitte Consulting LLP: Appendix C, "M&A IT Sample Case Studies"

Angela Mattix, Senior Manager, Deloitte Consulting LLP: Chapter 25, "Overview of Testing"

Olivier May, Principal, Deloitte Consulting LLP: Chapter 14, "M&A IT Architecture and Infrastructure: Developing and Delivering Transition Services Agreements"

Christine McKay, Specialist Leader, Deloitte Consulting LLP: Chapter 13, "Third-Party Contracts in M&A: Identifying and Managing Common Implications"

Nikhil Menon, Manager, Deloitte Consulting LLP: Chapter 26, "Why Mergers, Acquisitions, and Divestitures Fail, and Considerations to Help Avoid a Similar Fate"

Bryce Metro, Business Technology Analyst, Deloitte Consulting LLP: Chapter 28, "M&A IT, Summing It All Up"

Don Miller, Senior Manager, Deloitte Consulting LLP: Chapter 20, "Managing the People Side of IT M&A"

Jennie Miller, Consultant, Deloitte Consulting LLP: Chapter 16, "Transition Services Agreement (TSA)—Untangling the Web"

Michael H. Moore, Manager, Deloitte Consulting LLP: Chapter 4, "Mergers and Acquisitions IT Strategy, Approach, and Governance: IT and Its Customers"

Kelly Moynihan, Senior Consultant, AERS: Chapter 17, "IT Risk, Security, and Controls in M&A"

Joydeep Mukherjee, Senior Manager, Deloitte Consulting LLP: Chapter 12, "Using M&A to Streamline the Applications Portfolio"

Eric Niederhelman, Business Analyst, Deloitte Consulting LLP: Chapter 28, "M&A IT, Summing It All Up"

Shalva Nolen, Senior Manager, Deloitte Consulting LLP: Chapter 8, "Supporting Business Objectives with M&A-Aware Enterprise Architecture"; Chapter 9, "The Importance of a Tested IT Strategy and Approach for Mergers, Acquisitions, and Divestitures"; Appendix A, "M&A IT Playbook Overview"; Appendix B, "Sample M&A IT Checklists"

Nadia Orawski, Senior Manager, Deloitte Consulting LLP: Chapter 27, "M&A IT Key Success Factors"; Chapter 28, "M&A IT, Summing It All Up"

Tammie Potvin, Principal, Deloitte Consulting LLP: Chapter 20, "Managing the People Side of IT M&A"

Nitin Prabhakar, Specialist Leader, Deloitte Consulting LLP: Chapter 8, "Supporting Business Objectives with M&A-Aware Enterprise Architecture"; Chapter 9, "The Importance of a Tested IT Strategy and Approach for Mergers, Acquisitions, and Divestitures"

Michael Proppe, Manager, Deloitte Consulting LLP: Chapter 20, "Managing the People Side of IT M&A"

Wes Protsman, Specialist Leader, Deloitte Consulting LLP: Chapter 3, "Aligning Business and IT Strategy during Mergers, Acquisitions, and Divestitures"

Sunil Rai, Senior Manager, Deloitte Consulting LLP: Chapter 7, "M&A IT and Synergies"

Prasanna Rajappa, Senior Consultant, Deloitte Consulting LLP: Appendix C, "M&A IT Sample Case Studies"

Stephen Ronan, Manager, Deloitte Consulting LLP: Chapter 7, "M&A IT and Synergies"

Rich Rorem, Principal, Deloitte Consulting LLP: Chapter 19, "The Role of CFO"

Heith Rothman, Senior Manager, Deloitte Consulting LLP: Chapter 19, "The Role of CFO"

Mauro Schiavon, Senior Manager, Deloitte Consulting LLP: Chapter 22, "Integration Management Office Best Practices"

Rajat Sharma, Manager, Deloitte Consulting LLP: Chapter 8, "Supporting Business Objectives with M&A-Aware Enterprise Architecture"; Chapter 9, "The Importance of a Tested IT Strategy and Approach for Mergers, Acquisitions, and Divestitures"

Saurav Sharma, Manager, Deloitte Consulting LLP: Chapter 1, "Introduction to the IT Aspects of Mergers, Acquisitions, and Divestitures"

Simon Singh, Manager, Deloitte Consulting LLP: Chapter 16, "Transition Services Agreement (TSA)—Untangling the Web"; Appendix A, "M&A IT Playbook Overview"

Jeffry Sprengel, Specialist Leader, Deloitte Consulting LLP: Chapter 6, "IT Infrastructure Aspects of Mergers, Acquisitions, and Divestitures"

David Sternberg, Specialist Leader, Deloitte Consulting LLP: Chapter 5, "IT Due Diligence Leading Practices"

Venkat Swaminathan, Senior Manager, Deloitte Consulting LLP: Chapter 19, "The Role of CFO"

Trevear Thomas, Principal, Deloitte Consulting LLP: Chapter 19, "The Role of CFO"

Anil Tondavadi, Manager, Deloitte Consulting LLP: Chapter 24, "Important Role of Data in an M&A Transaction"

Mike Trisko, Specialist Leader, Deloitte Consulting LLP: Chapter 6, "IT Infrastructure Aspects of Mergers, Acquisitions, and Divestitures"

John Uccello, Senior Manager, Deloitte Consulting LLP: Chapter 23, "IT Program Governance during the Deal"

Nikhil Uppal, Consultant, Deloitte Consulting LLP: Chapter 16, "Transition Services Agreement (TSA)—Untangling the Web"; Appendix A, "M&A IT Playbook Overview"

Mia Velasquez, Business Analyst, Deloitte Consulting LLP: Chapter 19, "The Role of CFO"

Ted Veterano, Senior Manager, Deloitte Consulting LLP: Chapter 12, "Using M&A to Streamline the Applications Portfolio"

Laurel Vickers, Senior Manager, Deloitte Consulting LLP: Chapter 20, "Managing the People Side of IT M&A"

Chris Vu, Manager, Deloitte Consulting LLP: Chapter 24, "Important Role of Data in an M&A Transaction"

Colin Whiteneck, Manager, Deloitte Consulting LLP: Chapter 12, "Using M&A to Streamline the Applications Portfolio"

Jenny Xu, Senior Consultant, Deloitte Consulting LLP: Chapter 19, "The Role of CFO"

In addition, the following individuals should be acknowledged for their outstanding support:

- Janet Foutty, Deloitte Consulting LLP, who sponsored this book and provided guidance on its successful completion
- Mark Walsh and Asish Ramchandran, Deloitte Consulting LLP, who led our M&A and M&A IT practices and provided support and wisdom
- Mark Twomey and Suzanne Kounkel, Deloitte Consulting LLP, who were involved in building the eminence of the book
- Mark White, Deloitte Consulting LLP, who has coordinated the marketing plans for the book
- Tom Galizia, Deloitte Consulting LLP, who helped support the writing of the book
- Jared Faellaci, Deloitte Consulting LLP, who is involved with marketing the book
- Tony Scoles, Deloitte Consulting LLP, who provided outstanding legal support
- Heidi Boyer, Deloitte Consulting LLP, who coordinated the marketing of the book
- Eva Rowe, Deloitte Consulting LLP, who spent untold hours editing the book
- Rupen Patil, Deloitte Consulting LLP, who assisted with tracking the chapters

- Abhishck Singh, Deloitte Consulting LLP, who assisted with coordinating the development of the website materials
- Piper Sims, Deloitte Consulting LLP, from Deloitte's Nerve Center, who helped launch the book
- Danika Woods, Deloitte Consulting LLP, who assisted with preparing the book for publication

I am also indebted to the amazing folks at John Wiley & Sons, including:

- Sheck Cho, Executive Editor
- Stacey Rivera, Development Editor
- Helen Cho, Editorial Program Coordinator
- Kimberly Monroe-Hill, Senior Production Editor

Their ability to form the vision and guide the writing and editing of this book was beyond compare.

Introduction

Introduction to the IT Aspects of Mergers, Acquisitions, and Divestitures

Varun Joshi
Saurav Sharma

While many mergers and acquisitions (M&A) transactions fail to deliver value, a lesser-known but by some measures a more important fact is that the axis of value in mergers, acquisitions, and divestitures is more directly linked to getting information technology (IT) right than anything else. Information technology is generally the single biggest cost element in an M&A event (see Exhibit 1.1)—and can be the single biggest enabler of synergies. Getting IT involved early and often throughout the M&A lifecycle can be critical for effective execution and realization of benefits from a merger, acquisition, or divestiture.

Today, more than ever, the role of IT is under the lens as significant simultaneous disruptive forces are altering the technology landscape, and expectations are higher than ever from IT to enable changing business demand patterns. Disruptive technologies such as cloud computing, social media, mobility, and big data require a fundamental shift in the delivery and consumption of IT services. Business users now expect cheaper and more rapid deployment of technology to support business objectives through cloud computing and everything as a service (XaaS) platforms. Social technologies are enabling opportunities for collaboration, communication through social networks—the connected web of people and assets—and providing vehicles for discovering, growing, and propagating ideas and expertise. Mobility trends such as bring your own device (BYOD) are redefining mobile device management and enterprise security and privacy policies and procedures. Finally, through the application of big data, enterprises are looking to harness unstructured data formats that are not easily analyzed through existing business intelligence/analytics tool implementations.

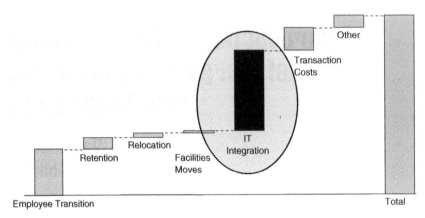

—————————————————— IT is the largest spend in an M&A event ——————————————

EXHIBIT 1.1   M&A Spend Distribution
Source: Deloitte Analysis

These disruptive trends provide IT organizations with new tools to add to their arsenals, and through their appropriate utilization IT organizations can increase the likelihood of achieving three critical goals of an M&A transaction:

1. Execute an issue-free Day 1.
2. Enable the realization of synergy targets.
3. Establish future-state platforms to support business growth.

ROLE OF IT IN M&A

While the drivers for M&A can be varied, at the most fundamental level an M&A transaction is largely about realization of business benefits through synergy capture—whether cost savings or growth/strategy enablement (or both). The heavy reliance on information technology (IT) for business operations, management information, and financial reporting in today's business environment makes IT a priority item in the M&A agenda. An M&A transaction can add a significant degree of complexity to preexisting and often complex IT environments. Integrating or carving out complex systems requires a very strong focus on IT. However, companies often neglect or give low priority to IT during the early stages of the M&A

lifecycle. The lack of focused IT involvement early on can have serious consequences, including:

- **Unexpected integration/divestiture costs.** IT-related activities are generally the largest cost items in a merger or divestiture. However, because IT is a secondary focus in most deals, the magnitude, complexity, and cost of these activities are often significantly underestimated.
- **Long delays in capturing benefits.** Many M&A deals expect significant synergies from economies of scale, cross-selling, consolidation of business back-office operations, and legacy system retirement. All of these synergies have one thing in common—they require major IT changes. Yet many companies put off developing an IT integration strategy and detailed IT plans until the deal is essentially closed. This delayed IT involvement can put IT in a reactive mode and make it virtually impossible for companies to achieve their aggressive goals.
- **Temporary IT solutions that are expensive, risky, and wasteful.** Because of the long lead times associated with IT, many companies are forced to develop and implement transition services agreements (TSAs) in order to close deals on schedule. While in some circumstances TSAs will be unavoidable, these short-term solutions for IT systems and business processes can be difficult and expensive to set up and can also increase security risks. To the extent IT has visibility early in the cycle, appropriate alternatives can be planned and developed so that TSAs are less comprehensive and complex in nature.

LOI signed	Deal signed (Day 0)	Deal closed (Day 1)
Due Diligence	Integration/Separation Planning	Integration/Separation Execution
• Getting the required information up front	• Aligning or separating systems and processes	• Effectively executing the acquisition or separation

EXHIBIT 1.2 M&A Lifecycle

In order to effectively partner with business stakeholders to achieve the desired goals of an M&A transaction, CIOs and IT executives must understand the M&A lifecycle (see Exhibit 1.2), the different types of M&A transactions, their impact on the IT function, and the contributions required from the IT organization.

Key milestones in the M&A lifecycle include:

- **LOI (letter of intent) signed.** Period of exclusivity; due diligence initiated.

- **Deal signed/announced (Day 0).** Period to obtain regulatory and shareholder approvals; integration/separation planning initiated.
- **Deal closed (Day 1).** Financial close of the transaction; integration/separation execution.

DUE DILIGENCE

No matter what the M&A agenda may be, due diligence is not an optional process. When done effectively, due diligence can help identify risks and opportunities. The risks include sources of instability requiring immediate action. Opportunities to reduce costs, to leverage resources or assets in new areas, and to improve IT effectiveness and increase business flexibility can be identified and pursued. During the due diligence process, decisions or actions that will be needed before there is any significant progress on the merger or separation can be identified. Expectations can also be set. For example, order-of-magnitude estimates of expected costs and anticipated benefits can be developed, and resources and timeframes required to address risks and issues and to capitalize on opportunities can be identified.

In our experience, the majority of transactions fail to achieve the required level of synergy due to inadequate focus on IT due diligence up front in the transaction cycle. Including IT in preannouncement due diligence and preparation can help with the early identification of potential synergies from the M&A transaction, empower business executives to take advantage of the important role IT plays in realizing M&A synergies, and support the collaboration of business leadership and IT in determining an effective integration or separation strategy. (See Chapter 5 for a more complete discussion of due diligence.)

Key Considerations for IT Due Diligence

One of the key objectives of IT due diligence is to review IT assets, processes/operations, and organization to build a quantitative and qualitative picture of the merged or separated entity. The due diligence process incudes questioning of knowledgeable personnel, competitive benchmark analysis, and an evaluation of IT documentation across the people, process, applications, and infrastructure domains (see Exhibit 1.3). This involves looking at the key attributes in each of the domains and identifying areas in which IT is a significant or critical element of the business plan. It enables companies to evaluate the effectiveness of IT systems and IT strategy, and identify factors that could be a barrier to achieving expected results.

EXHIBIT 1.3   Dimensions of IT Due Diligence

People, Process, and Spending	Applications	Infrastructure
▪ IT organization ▪ IT strategic planning and projects ▪ IT operating and capital expenditure ▪ User support (help desk, desk support) ▪ Security and disaster recovery	▪ Enterprise (ERP, financial reporting, consolidation, human resources, etc.) ▪ Specialized (revenue-generating portals, supply chain, manufacturing execution systems, distribution and logistics, safety, risk and compliance, etc.)	▪ Hardware (mainframes, servers, PCs, peripherals) ▪ Operating systems and databases ▪ Network ▪ Communication and interfaces to third-party providers (distributors, etc.)

From our experience, the application of the following IT due diligence best practices can significantly improve the odds of achieving expected M&A transaction benefits:

- **Assign senior IT executives to help with IT due diligence.** Make the seniormost member (CIO or designee) the key member in the IT due diligence team and involve the IT function in all phases of the M&A lifecycle, from preliminary due diligence to Day 1 and beyond until all key synergies have been captured.
- **Team IT with business.** For smooth functioning of M&A deals and to operate the program effectively, staff people from IT and from business areas to jointly drive planning and execution. This encourages collaboration and teamwork between IT and the business/functional areas, which is an effective strategy to foster a strong working relationship and sense of ownership.
- **Identify IT requirements before you sign the deal.** Insist the team identify IT investments that will be needed to achieve the expected short- and long-term benefits. Technology-related synergies often occur over multiple years. Also, it is essential to develop order-of-magnitude estimates for these critical IT projects to validate the magnitude and timing of the expected benefits.
- **Make IT costs and timing part of deal valuation.** Make IT investments a mandatory part of your valuation model, and include estimated costs for IT projects that are required for capturing the expected short- and long-term business synergies, as well as costs for software licensing and TSAs.
- **Get a head start on IT projects.** "Clean teams" are groups of specialists who are given special access to restricted information before the deal is

complete. They can provide an early start on time-critical IT activities. For example, clean teams can be used to compare business and data models, assess the impact of the deal on the company's future IT landscape, and conduct detailed scoping and planning.

■ **Get your priorities straight.** Every deal has an impact on IT, and it is essential to immediately inventory and assess IT projects (even those not directly related to the deal) to verify that they are still required and align with the company's future direction. Priority should be given to IT projects that (1) link to critical Day 1 requirements, (2) enable or accelerate large synergy opportunities, or (3) are essential to implementing the company's future strategic initiatives.

■ **Keep the pressure on.** An effective Day 1 is only the beginning. IT projects that are critical to synergy capture and to long-term deal results often require many months to complete. To maintain critical momentum for an integration or divestiture, it is vital that management stays focused on related projects until the majority of benefits have been captured.

A well-executed IT due diligence effort should result in a baseline understanding of anticipated costs as well as a high-level action plan to mitigate identified risks, resolve specific/identified issues, and capitalize on major opportunities.

INTEGRATION/SEPARATION PLANNING

The old adage "Those who fail to plan, plan to fail" is particularly applicable to M&A transactions. IT integrations or separations are typically complex, resource-intensive initiatives that should be closely aligned with the overall business integration or separation effort. This type of activity requires significant time and staff and must be done in addition to the day-to-day activities of the IT function required to keep the business running effectively. As a result, the normal IT activity combined with effectively executing M&A transaction-related tasks can put significant levels of stress on an IT function. Exhibit 1.4 shows the specific focus areas that should be considered during the planning phase.

Selection of the appropriate integration or separation model is a critical aspect of planning the IT effort to support an M&A transaction. The model chosen is dependent on the goals of the new entity and is based on the M&A objective driving the deal.

EXHIBIT 1.4 Integration/Separation Planning

LOI signed

Deal signed (Day 0)

Deal closed (Day 1)

Due Diligence

Integration/Separation Planning

Integration/Separation Execution

IT Integration/Separation Planning and Governance

IT Day 1 and End-State Blueprinting

IT Synergy Analysis Planning

IT TSA Strategy and Planning

Integration Models In general, there are four models that can be applied to post-merger integration of most M&A transactions (see Exhibit 1.5).

See Chapters 8 and 9 for detailed discussion of these four models.

Separation Models Typically there are six models that can be applied to IT systems separation or carve-outs, as shown in Exhibit 1.6.

IT Day 1 and End-State Blueprinting

Blueprinting helps address the organizational, functional, and technical requirements for Day 1 and the end state. These requirements will drive projects, milestones, and timetables (for example, Day 1, Day 1 + 30, Day 1 + 90). A structured integration blueprinting approach can enable IT and the business to rapidly identify cross-functional requirements at the operational level. Blueprinting should start with the end in mind and work backward to Day 1. The two key phases in the blueprinting phase include:

- **End state.** What does IT look like today, and what will it look like when the integration or divestiture is complete? How long will it take to reach the end state (organization, infrastructure, applications, service delivery model)? What value will be captured as a result of the integration or divestiture?
- **Day 1.** What is absolutely essential for meeting Day 1? These requirements should be highly focused on keeping the business running, removing uncertainty for stakeholders, complying with regulatory requirements, and delivering the Day 1 must-haves. Some typical examples of Day 1 requirements include:
  - Keep the business running. The company must be able to take orders, invoice the customers, and deliver product.
  - Comply with federal, legal, and regulatory requirements. On Day 1, licenses must be transferred, applied for, or in place, and contracts must be assigned. Finance has to be able to produce consolidated financial reports.
  - Deliver Day 1 must-haves. IT has to establish e-mail connectivity, voice mail, and some level of file transfer capability.

Exhibit 1.7 is an example of a blueprint of IT strategies for Day 1 and the end state.

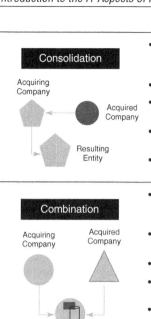

Consolidation Acquiring Company Acquired Company Resulting Entity	• Calls for the rapid and efficient conversion of one company to the strategy, structure, processes, and systems of the acquiring company. • Processes and systems adopted from parent company. • Significant resources dedicated to integrating operations. • Easiest path toward achieving aggressive synergy targets. • Parent company's compliance standards will dominate the acquired entity.
Combination Acquiring Company Acquired Company Resulting Entity	• Means selecting best processes, structures, and systems from each company to form an optimized operating model. • Processes and tools are fine-tuned and optimized using best practices from either company. • Hybrid approach used in governance structure. • Significant resources dedicated to integrating operations. • Best path toward achieving aggressive synergy targets.
Transformation Acquiring Company Acquired Company Resulting Entity	• Entails synthesizing disparate organizational and technology pieces into a new whole. • Significant people, process, and technology impact. • Significant planning. • More deliberate focus on execution. • Extensive use of internal and external resources. • Complex change management characteristics.
Resulting Entity Acquired Company Acquiring Company	• Supports individual companies or business units in retaining their unique capabilities and cultures. • Minimal standardization outside of contracts consolidation and financial reporting roll up Holding company controls the operating companies using a "portfolio" model. • Governance limited to management control, performance targets and expectations.

EXHIBIT 1.5   Integration Models

EXHIBIT 1.6 Separation Models

Model	Advantages	Disadvantages
Clone and go ■ Set up a copy of production/application on a separate instance; operational Day 1	■ Time-efficient solution; incorporates flexibility needed for moving divestiture	■ Sensitive data might be exposed to the buyer
Clone, vitiate, and go ■ Clone copy, clean out sensitive data (legal and competitive), release for production use	■ Competitively sensitive data is masked from the buyer; incorporates flexibility, is operational Day 1	■ Requires more time than clone and go
Copy, configure, and load ■ Create a configuration-only copy of application, then load relevant master and transactional data onto new/separate instance	■ Outcome is predictable; know-how for doing this is widely available	■ Longest timeline, scope needs to be static; more expensive
Extract and go ■ Extract data from production systems, put in flat file, and hand over to buyer	■ Quick and easy for seller; low-cost option	■ Potentially nonviable option for the buyer (may not have an operational business on Day 1); significant pressure on buyer to keep the business operational during the transition
Give and go ■ Hand off production system to buyer	■ Buyer is operational Day 1 with a system that is familiar; users are comfortable; seller costs drop immediately	■ Deal will involve personnel; seller will no longer have access to historical data; potentially sensitive data will be left in the system
Hybrid ■ Choose different techniques for different application suites	■ Overall risk may be better managed; more options to effectively get to Day 1	■ Requires detailed planning early on for each suite; business participation is increased

EXHIBIT 1.7   IT Blueprint Sample

	Process/Subprocess Strategy			Technology (Application)	
Subfunction	Day 1 Strategy	Day 1 to Day 2 Exit Strategy	Application	Day 1 Strategy	Day 1 to Day 2 Exit Strategy
Example: HR— Organization Design and Structure	▓ Performed manually by buyer	▓ N/A	▓ Human resource information system (HRIS)	▓ Transferred to buyer on Day 1	▓ N/A
Example: Finance— Fixed Assets	▓ Continue to use same processes and systems ▓ Identify assets migrating to buyer and book value	▓ Migrate to buyer systems and processes ▓ Train fixed assets resources	▓ Asset manager	▓ Transition services agreement (TSA)	▓ Develop data separation plan from seller system ▓ Migrate information to buyer system

IT Synergy Analysis Planning

In most M&A events, companies expect synergy—a business value that comes from the fact that the two entities are (or should be) more valuable together than apart. Synergy comes from various sources, such as reduced operating costs, reduced risks, increased market share, or the ability to enter or create a new market. Synergies are captured by sharing overhead functions, integrating operations, jointly creating new capabilities, and exploiting economies of scale. The objective of synergy analysis planning is to lay the foundation for accelerating benefits realization from the integration. (See Chapter 7 for a more in-depth discussion of synergies.)

EXHIBIT 1.8   Key Phases in IT Synergy Capture Analysis

Exhibit 1.8 shows the following key steps involved in performing IT synergy capture analysis:

▓ **Develop IT cost baseline.**   The first step in synergy analysis planning is developing an IT cost baseline by reviewing various cost sources as well as the due diligence analysis to develop a common view for cost. Cost baselines are developed at the regional and functional level. This step also involves identifying best practice synergy opportunities, using benchmarks to compare the baseline.

- **Conduct top-down target setting.** This step involves identifying high-level synergy initiatives and communicating a range of savings at the functional/regional level. High-level synergy initiatives are identified by function, and potential savings are estimated using best practice benchmarks. The identified synergy targets are reviewed with management to communicate synergy ranges to functional/regional teams.
- **Develop bottom-up synergy commitments.** This step involves taking the high-level synergy targets and developing detailed initiatives that match or exceed targets. Validate IT cost baselines alignment. Detailed project plans are developed and reviewed with management.
- **Create tracking tools and processes.** Processes and tools necessary to track and prioritize synergy initiatives on an ongoing basis are developed. A central repository should be developed for managing all IT projects across regions/functions along with the high-level process for tracking synergies.

IT TSA Strategy and Planning

Identifying and carving out the pieces in a divestiture can be a complex and time-consuming process, particularly when the affected people, processes, and systems are deeply integrated within the seller's business, or when services and infrastructure are shared across multiple business units. During the planning process, participants from the affected business units on both sides must think through the transition period from Day 1 (financial close) to Day 2 (full separation/exit) to determine the strategy for each business process, associated applications, and underlying infrastructure. Depending on the strategy, it may be beneficial for certain services to be covered under a transition services agreement (TSA). A TSA is a legal agreement, separate from the separation and purchase agreement, in which the buyer agrees to pay the seller for certain services to support the divested business for a defined period of time. TSAs are most often used in carve-outs where the buyer lacks the necessary information technology capabilities or capacity to support the business on its own. For instance, many private equity (PE) firms rely on TSAs until they can identify and engage an IT outsourcing vendor. TSAs are also often necessary when the deal closes faster than the buyer's organization can respond. (See Chapters 14 and 16 for detailed discussion of TSAs.)

Exhibit 1.9 shows an illustrative timeline for establishing TSAs and the key activities involved.

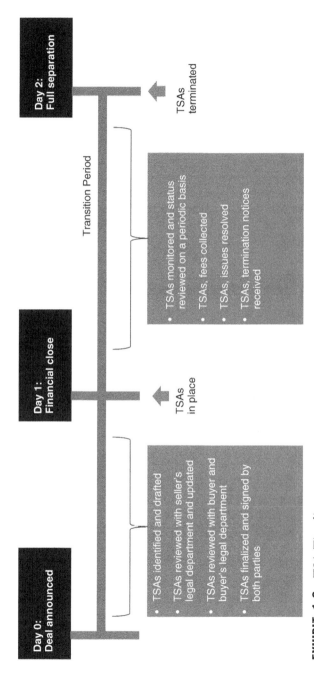

EXHIBIT 1.9 TSA Timelines
Copyright © 2012 Deloitte Development LLC

INTEGRATION/SEPARATION EXECUTION

Execution priorities focus on process and technology integration or separation in order to realize synergy benefits driving the M&A transaction. The emphasis is on effectively and efficiently reaching the end state (organization, infrastructure, applications, service delivery model) while capturing synergy targets. Typically, experience breeds effectiveness, and companies that have participated in multiple M&A transactions often fare better than companies that are undergoing the process for the first time. The execution of the IT integration or separation process is where third-party advice and assistance can often be extremely valuable, especially to companies that are attempting post-merger IT integration or divestiture IT carve-out for the first time, or that lack a series of deals to draw upon. Exhibit 1.10 shows the specific focus areas that should be considered during the execution phase.

IT Integration/Separation Program Management

A detailed, developed, and defined program structure and decision-making mechanism are critical to control all aspects of the execution. An IT program management office (PMO) should be established to manage overall integration or carve out activities and provide overall day-to-day direction. The PMO should also drive detailed IT blueprint and work plan development and execution, and provide common tools and templates for all IT working teams to capture functional plans and synergies through center of excellence (COE) and playbooks. Exhibit 1.11 shows an illustrative governance structure to drive IT integration or separation program management.

IT Blueprint Design Execution

The execution phase is where the rubber meets the road. Execution of M&A transactions can be extremely complex due to the fluidity of the decision making, the need for speed, and the change aspects imposed on the organization due to the M&A event. Having a well-defined program structure and framework for execution is critical for removing uncertainty from some of the controllable elements.

Integration will typically translate into decisions to retire, replace, consolidate, or upgrade applications and associated platforms. Exhibit 1.12 highlights a framework that can be adopted to execute IT integration.

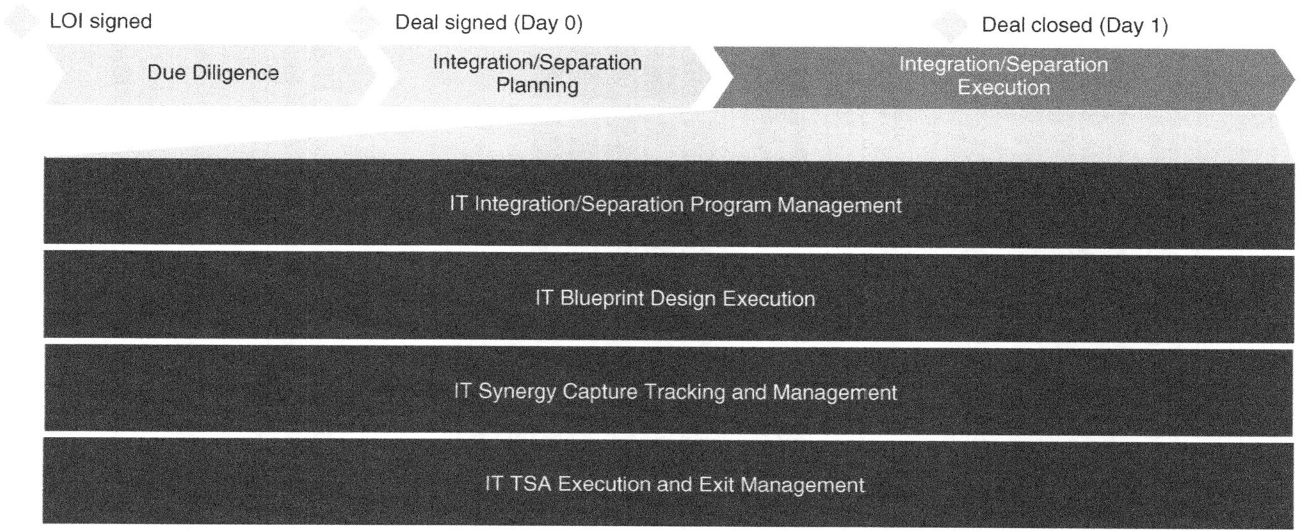

EXHIBIT 1.10 Integration/Separation Execution

The figure shows a process flow with the following phases across the top:
- LOI signed
- Deal signed (Day 0)
- Deal closed (Day 1)

Phases: Due Diligence → Integration/Separation Planning → Integration/Separation Execution

Execution workstreams:
- IT Integration/Separation Program Management
- IT Blueprint Design Execution
- IT Synergy Capture Tracking and Management
- IT TSA Execution and Exit Management

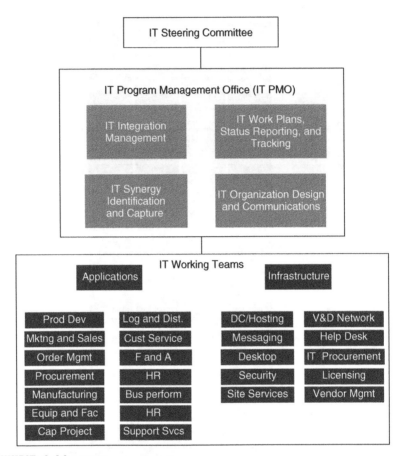

EXHIBIT 1.11   IT Governance Structure

An objective during the execution phase is to tie the IT initiatives to the synergy targets so they will enable and have a full cross-functional view of the risks and dependencies across the organization.

IT Synergy Capture Tracking and Management

An objective of synergy capture tracking is to establish a formal mechanism for tracking the capture of synergy targets. The two specific focus areas in this process are:

1. **Establish tracking organization.** The IT PMO should set up an IT synergy tracking function to achieve stated synergy targets and prioritize

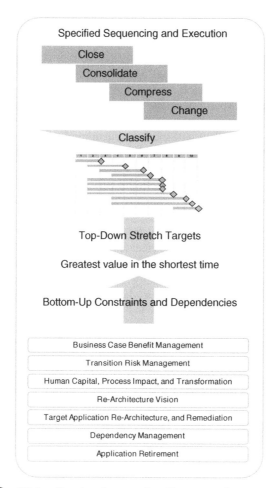

EXHIBIT 1.12　IT Application Integration Framework

as necessary. This function will work closely with the finance department to capture financial data from IT projects and help ensure that financial metrics and targets are being met.

2. **Track synergies.** The IT synergy function is responsible for providing executive management an ongoing view of achieved milestones and targets. This involves developing executive dashboards to highlight initiatives by region, function, and total. These dashboards also track critical milestones and achievements and enable reporting of synergy achievement status.

IT TSA Execution and Exit Management

Once the deal closes and the TSAs go into effect, it is important to continually track and manage the services that are being performed. It is also critical to keep track of the migration activities and related step-down in services. The relationship between buyer and seller will inevitably change once the deal has closed, regardless of how well they might have worked together leading up to Day 1. Sellers will focus on cleaning up the bits and pieces the divestiture left behind, and then quickly shift their attention to their retained businesses and other priorities. Buyers may find themselves wrestling with unanticipated service costs and struggling to capture the anticipated and expected integration synergies as quickly as possible.

A well-defined TSA management structure (see Exhibit 1.13) is a critical component for jointly managing service levels after Day 1. Companies should identify and assign a service coordinator to manage their part of the overall relationship. This profile is similar to the vendor manager profile that currently exists in many organizations. They do not need to delve deeply into the details of day-to-day operations; rather, they need a holistic view of the services being provided and an understanding of the overall requirements. Their job is to monitor the services being delivered against the TSA and to keep the separation activities on track. Retention of key transition resources is another important issue. Sellers will generally want to get on with their business by shifting people to new assignments as quickly as possible. To maintain adequate staffing and performance during the transition, buyers must specify in the TSA exactly which key resources and groups will be retained to execute the contracted or required services.

WRAPPING IT UP

In order to effectively partner with business stakeholders, CIOs and IT executives must understand the M&A lifecycle and the contributions required from the IT organization. IT integrations or separations are generally complex, resource-intensive initiatives that need to be closely aligned with the overall business integration effort. A detailed and defined program management structure and decision-making mechanism are critical to control all aspects of the execution. The IT PMO should drive detailed IT blueprint and work plan development and execution, and provide common tools and templates for all IT working teams. Given the high fluidity and speed involved in a transaction, a well-orchestrated PMO provides the much-needed structure to ensure that cross-work-stream dependencies and risks

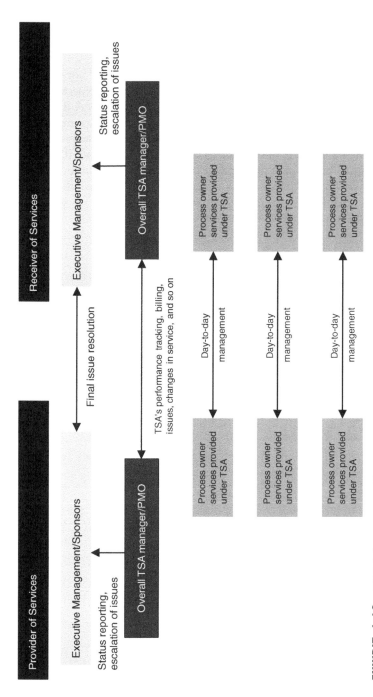

EXHIBIT 1.13 TSA Management Structure

are identified, escalated, and resolved in an expeditious manner. Based on the M&A objective, selection of the appropriate integration or separation model is a critical aspect of planning and executing the IT effort to support an M&A transaction.

Merger, acquisition, and divestiture transactions are not easy. They are fraught with pitfalls and roadblocks to achieving the expected benefits. CIOs have the license to get involved up front in the M&A lifecycle and have the obligation to educate other C-suite executives on the importance of giving IT a head start. Having IT involved up front in the deal is absolutely critical to helping ensure the overall success of the transaction. It enables the IT function to better plan and budget for the costs to achieve. Regardless of the size and complexity of an integration or a divestiture, the IT team's speed and effectiveness are likely to have a major impact on whether the deal ultimately achieves the expected results.

CHAPTER 2

The Role of IT in Mergers and Acquisitions

Peter Blatman
Eugene Lukac

The rationale frequently behind prospective mergers and acquisitions (M&A) transactions is the expectation of specific business benefits such as increased market share, reduced joint operating costs, and a more integrated value chain. These potential M&A-related benefits are usually directly linked to anticipated synergies, including, but not limited to, shared overhead, economies of scale, cross-fertilization, greater market access, and operational integration. What is sometimes overlooked or underestimated is the crucial importance of effective information technology (IT) integration in achieving anticipated synergies. Examples include:

- **Shared overhead.** Reduction of IT support costs through consolidation of IT platforms.
- **Economies of scale.** Shared IT procurement and maintenance.
- **Cross-fertilization.** Mining of joint customer and vendor database information.
- **Operational integration.** Integrated purchasing, production/manufacturing, forecasting, and logistics systems.

Evidence of the importance of IT to achieving M&A-related benefits is reflected in numerous market studies over the past 10 years that indicate 50 to 70 percent of M&A transactions fail to ultimately create incremental shareholder value.[1] While there are many reasons for the low rate of success, failed post-merger integration stands out as the most common root cause.

This chapter addresses the essential role IT should play in the full cycle of M&A activities, from pre-merger integration planning to post-merger integration, with the goal of increasing shareholder value from the deal. It discusses four basic IT integration models, defined as preservation, combination, consolidation, and transformation, and how they can be applied by both business and IT across the four pillars of M&A:

1. **Strategy.** Picking the appropriate integration model.
2. **Due diligence.** Getting the necessary information up front.
3. **Post-merger integration planning.** Aligning systems and processes.
4. **Execution.** Effectively implementing the merger or acquisition.

Research, data, and practical experience gained from extensive M&A-related efforts support the importance of closely aligning IT and M&A processes to maintain post-transaction momentum and to increase the potential of achieving the defined business goals of the transaction.

QUEST TO CAPTURE SYNERGIES

Synergy. The word is overused, to be sure, but it has real meaning for companies engaging in a merger or acquisition process. Synergy is defined as "a mutually advantageous conjunction or compatibility of distinct business participants or elements (as resources or efforts)."[2] Creating these advantageous conjunctions and compatibilities can have significant benefits for companies pursuing M&A activities. Some potential benefits include:

- Increased market share.
- Expanded technical and management capabilities.
- Reduced costs through economies of scale.
- Improved market position.
- Diversification.
- Integration along the value chain.

These benefits have one thing in common: they are realized through effective planning and execution of pre- and post-merger activities—especially the integration of the merging entities' IT processes and systems.

Exhibit 2.1 depicts how properly integrated IT processes and systems can help achieve anticipated synergies post-M&A.

Failing at the Quest: What Goes Wrong

One of the most frequent causes of failure to achieve expected M&A-related benefits is poor planning and execution of the merger project. Poor IT integration, especially the integration of disparate IT architectures, can be extremely detrimental.

	Reduce Costs	Increase Market Share	Enter or Create New Markets
Shared Overhead	• Eliminate duplicate Information system (IS) roles and functions • Reduce support costs through standardization		
Economies of scale	• Common technologies, platforms, and systems • Combined IT procurement	• State-of-the-art scheduling, forecasting, or yield management • Global systems	• Combined electronic delivery channel infrastructure
Cross-Fertilization	• Groupware • Intranets • Workflow	• Customer database • Data mining	• Selling derivative information • Channel innovation
Operational Integration	• Integrated operational systems (e.g., production, forecasting, and logistics) • Work flow engine	• Order-entry or customer-facing systems • Data warehouse • Internet presence	• Truly integrated products and services
Synthesis of Capabilities	• Computer-aided design (CAD) • IT technology transfer	• Uncommitted product and customer models	• Cross-industry business models • Content/context/conduit

EXHIBIT 2.1 How an Effective Information Technology Integration Can Help Achieve Three Types of Benefits

Source: Deloitte

Applications, data, and infrastructure should enable efficient and effective business processes. Without effective planning and execution of a well-aimed IT integration strategy, the capture of sought-after synergies between the acquiring and acquired companies will likely fall short of expectations.

In a recent effort to quantify the relationship between IT integration and the achievement of the intended M&A benefits, Deloitte Consulting LLP conducted a survey[3] of over 50 M&A (including divestiture projects) transactions from 2005 to 2007 to test the following hypothesis:

> *The lack of attention to pre-merger strategy setting, IT due diligence, [and] post-merger IT planning and execution, as well as poor IT/business coordination, are dominant factors in explaining the [low] empirical rate of M&A success.*

The findings were consistent with this hypothesis. The survey results suggest that while IT typically has limited impact on the valuation of the deal, early involvement of IT in due diligence is critical to the effective identification of synergies and the effectiveness of subsequent post-merger planning and execution.

While the data with respect to the role of IT integration and its impact on the results of M&A transactions are not conclusive, when taken together with anecdotal evidence, the hypothesis is compelling. The available evidence points to a straightforward approach to M&A deals that can significantly improve the odds of achieving the expected benefits.

CAPTURING THE BENEFITS

Capturing M&A benefits requires a straightforward approach that starts with the recognition that IT activities should be closely aligned with business activities during the M&A process. As highlighted earlier, there are four dimensions to an M&A transaction:

1. Strategy
2. Due diligence
3. Post-merger IT integration planning
4. Execution

These dimensions apply to IT as well as business activities. How well companies navigate each of these dimensions during the M&A process— especially as they apply to IT integration—will play a large part in determining whether the merger or acquisition ultimately achieves the expected benefits.

Strategy

Companies vary in their motivations to pursue M&A deals. Some are pioneers. The reasoning for the merger is to combine two (or more) entities to create a better future. These companies are most likely to have the desire to seek out synergies as their main motivation for the combination. Others are talent scouts. Often in this scenario, the acquiring or larger entity wants to acquire knowledge or capabilities that it does not have. These companies also desire to create synergies with the combination. Then there are the consolidators. These companies seek mainly operating value from the merger or acquisition. Finally, there are the revenue hunters. These companies desire operating value from the combination, but their main motivation is growth in revenue.

These differing agendas are the dominant drivers of post-merger integration focus, complexity, and intensity. The more synergies the companies seek, the more complex the post-merger integration is likely to be. Companies that set a high level of ambition and expectation for post-merger synergy should place significant focus on external stakeholder management and integration management as the merger or acquisition progresses.

Whatever the strategy chosen, there are critical success factors (CSFs) that can help improve the odds of achieving the expected benefits. They are:

- Ensure that the business is accountable for setting the IT integration strategy.
- Make the integration strategy explicit—consolidation, transformation, combination, or preservation; each has specific critical success factors and risks.
- Set realistic targets and concrete performance measures for meeting the targets—as well as consequences for not meeting them.

Addressing these IT-related CSFs can assist organizations with achieving their M&A goals.

Due Diligence

No matter the merger agenda, due diligence is *not* an optional process. Performing due diligence, especially with regard to information systems compatibility and integration issues, is absolutely critical. When correctly performed, due diligence can help identify risks and opportunities. The risks include sources of instability requiring immediate action. Opportunities to reduce costs, to leverage resources or assets in new areas, and to improve IT effectiveness and increase business flexibility can be identified and pursued.

Moreover, during the due diligence process, decisions or actions that will be needed before there is any significant progress on the merger or acquisition can be identified. Expectations can also be set. For example, order-of-magnitude estimates of expected costs and anticipated benefits can be developed, and resources and timeframes required to address risks and issues and to capitalize on opportunities can be identified. Finally, due diligence should confirm how much (or how little) compatibility there is between IT architectures and assets of the merging entities.

As with the process of setting the strategy, there are CSFs in performing due diligence that will help improve the odds of achieving the expected benefits. They are:

- Form an IT integration team early in the due diligence process.
- Get the appropriate people on the team—both internally and externally. These people should have cross-functional knowledge and experience, and be able to see the big picture going forward.
- Set a broad due diligence scope—from assessing the IT environment to assessing risk and identifying potential synergies.
- Set the baseline—the knowledge base that must be in place to move forward with the M&A process.

The bottom line is that IT due diligence should result in a high-level action plan to mitigate identified risks, resolve key issues, and capitalize on major opportunities.

Post-Merger Integration Planning—the Model Makes the Difference

Once due diligence is finished, the results can be used to push forward with post-merger integration planning. When two companies merge, or when one acquires the other, there are a myriad of scenarios in which the combination can occur. In general, there are four models or approaches that can be applied to post-merger integration of most M&A transactions:

1. **Consolidation.** Calls for the rapid and efficient conversion of one company to the strategy, structure, processes, and systems of the acquiring company.

2. **Combination.** Means selecting the most effective processes, structures, and systems from each company to form an efficient operating model for the new entity.
3. **Transformation.** Entails synthesizing disparate organizational and technology pieces into a new whole.
4. **Preservation.** Supports individual companies or business units in retaining their individual capabilities and cultures.

The approach a company chooses is dependent on its goals for the new entity. More specifically, M&A business objectives usually reflect the acquiring company's acquisition profile and business agenda, as discussed previously in the "Strategy" section.

Exhibit 2.2 depicts how the adopted integration approach should match the business objectives and acquisition profile.

Reason for Acquisition		Approach			
		Consolidation	Combination	Transformation	Preservation
Consolidator	Capture efficiencies	✔	?	✘	✘
	Open new geographic markets	✔	?	✘	?
Revenue Hunter	Open new market segments	✘	✔	?	?
	Acquire new products	✘	✔	✘	?
	Buy into new distribution channels	✘	✔	✘	?
Talent Scout	Acquire expertise	✘	?	✘	✔
	Buy new or superior technology	✘	✔	?	?
Pioneer	Develop a new business model	✘	?	✔	✘

✔ A Key Objective	✘ Not Usually a Key Objective	? A Possible Objective

EXHIBIT 2.2 The Integration Approach Should Match the Acquisition Profile
Source: Deloitte

Key questions to ask when choosing a model include:

- What are the main business objectives of the merger or acquisition (e.g., growth, market positioning, cost savings)?
- What key benefits are expected from the transaction?
- What approach to business integration is required to realize these benefits?
- What approach to IT integration is required to realize these benefits?

- In what ways can IT help the business realize its goals for the transaction?
- What opportunities exist to use technology to position the business for future growth and change?

For each model, the critical success factors (CSFs), as well as the causes of potential failure, are strikingly different. Exhibit 2.3 depicts some of these critical success factors and potential causes of failure.

In addition to CSFs for each integration model, there are CSFs for the overall integration that will help improve the odds of achieving the expected benefits. They are:

- Facilitate close integration between the IT integration planning and business process and organization planning.
- Appoint a full-time project manager under an IT integration program management office (PMO) linked to a companywide PMO.
- Decide the future state of the IT organization, processes, and architecture.
- Create specific project plans based on which integration strategy is chosen.
- Create and maintain a broad communication plan that keeps everyone in the loop.

Having the right model makes a significant difference in the ultimate success (or failure) of the transaction.

Execution

Each of the four post-merger IT integration approaches has associated execution priorities and management issues that must be addressed. The execution priorities focus on process and technology integration. The management issues include leadership and cultural blending challenges. For example, with a consolidation approach to IT integration, the focus is on risk management for process issues and on data conversion for technology issues. With a combination approach, the process focus is on systems evaluation and the technology focus is on systems integration. With a transformation approach, the process emphasis is on innovation; the technology emphasis is on the overall IT architecture. Finally, with a preservation approach, stakeholder management is the focal point of process issues, while communication between business units is key for technology concerns.

Management issues can be challenging, even in the smoothest of M&A transactions. The blending of organizations and cultures is not easy, because

	Consolidation	Combination	Transformation	Preservation
Success Factors	• Detailed implementation plans • Rapid systems conversion • Uniform and consistent implementation	• True collaboration • Commitment to preserving the most valuable parts of both organizations • Proficiency at synthesizing disparate systems and technologies	• Compelling vision of new organization • Unwavering focus and committed leadership • Substantial expertise in change management	• Protection of autonomy; prevention of chaos • Restrained management involvement • Rigorous operational monitoring
Causes of Failure	• Squandering exploitable assets • Alienating key people • Overlooking possible synergies	• Long-drawn-out assessment exercises • Unresolved issues • Inefficient or complex patchwork of systems	• Organizational resistance to change • Unrealistic goals • Failing to balance long-term solutions and short-term benefits	• Excessive inefficiency • Unnecessary duplication • Missed cost and operational synergies

EXHIBIT 2.3 Success Factors and Causes of M&A Failure

Source: Deloitte

no matter the industry, no two companies evolve in quite the same manner. Each will each have its own leadership style and culture. To facilitate the transition to the newly merged entity, each post-merger IT integration approach will have to deal with different management and cultural issues. For example, the typical leadership style in a consolidation approach to IT integration is an authoritarian approach that imposes the will of the acquiring company onto the company being acquired. The culture of the acquiring company is also imposed (as much as possible) on the new entity. In a combination approach, the leadership is more collegial and there is a knitting together of corporate cultures. In a transformation approach, there is often inspirational leadership that seeks out new ideas and synergies more than with any of the other approaches; there is often a new corporate culture that is sculpted from select parts of the prior cultures. With a preservation approach, the leadership style is most effectively described as respectful, with leaders of both companies retaining autonomy and with the cultures of both companies remaining largely unchanged.

Why all the discussion about leadership styles and process issues? Because these issues directly affect how smoothly (or not) the post-merger IT integration will proceed.

As with the other three dimensions of post-merger success, there are CSFs for the execution of IT integration that will help improve the odds of achieving the expected benefits. They are:

- Execute the post-merger integration in a timely manner. The longer it takes, the lower the realized value from the transaction.
- Develop, track, and report on project performance metrics.
- Measure and publish realized benefits. This will establish goodwill in the newly merged entity going forward.

The ultimate success of an M&A transaction depends on executing a well-chosen strategy based on thorough due diligence and planning.

WRAPPING IT UP

The M&A transaction process can be challenging. It is fraught with pitfalls and roadblocks to achieving the expected benefits that must be carefully navigated and overcome with skill and care to achieve the goal of one new (hopefully) improved organization from two separate, distinctly different companies. While there are many hurdles that must be surmounted in any M&A transaction, the one that most frequently poses a challenge is how to plan for and execute the post-merger IT systems integration.

Consequently, proper selection and execution of a postclose IT integration plan in a timely manner can help achieve anticipated synergies from the M&A transaction. Our experience indicates that the better the postclose planning and execution, the better to overall merger results, and that a key attribute to effective postclose integration is a high level of integration between IT and the business.

To achieve this, effective IT due diligence and speed of integration are critical. Any post-merger integration approach chosen should be guided by the M&A business objectives, and the selected approach (consolidation, combination, transformation, or preservation) should match the business objectives and acquisition profile. Each of these approaches has its individual characteristics, success factors, and potential causes of failure and should be selected with a full understanding of which approach most effectively fits the particular M&A transaction and which would work well with the IT integration issues uncovered in the due diligence process. Each approach should be executed in a timely manner to realize the expected value from the transaction, and benefits should be tracked and championed throughout the new organization to promote acceptance of a transition to the new culture.

To improve the odds of achieving the expected benefits, it is very important to consider the four pillars of M&A:

1. **Set the strategy.** Develop and carry out the IT and business integration strategies in parallel.
2. **Do not skip on the due diligence.** Form an IT integration team early on and cast a broad net to identify potential issues and roadblocks to success.
3. **Plan the post-merger IT integration.** Closely align IT integration planning and execution with business planning and execution.
4. **Execute the postclose IT integration speedily.** Execute fast and nimbly. The longer it takes, the lower the realized value.

Following this path won't ensure that the expected benefits are achieved—nothing is guaranteed. However, proper planning and execution of post-merger IT integration can make the process easier and more effective to increase the likelihood of achieving the expected benefits in the long run. That's a win-win deal.

Notes

1. Bloor Research, November 2007; "Solving the Merger Mystery, Maximizing the Payoff of Mergers & Acquisitions," Deloitte, 2000;

Robert F. Bruner, "Does M&A Pay?" chap. 3 in *Applied Mergers and Acquisitions* (Hoboken, NJ: John Wiley & Sons, 2004).

2. Merriam-Webster's Online Dictionary, www.m-w.com/dictionary/synergy.

3. Deloitte Consulting LLP, 2008 internal study.

CHAPTER 3

Aligning Business and IT Strategy during Mergers, Acquisitions, and Divestitures

Jason Asper
Wes Protsman

The previous chapter highlights the essential role of information technology (IT) in mergers and acquisitions (M&A) and discusses its important role in delivering against the deal objectives.

Often, this role can be overwhelming to both IT executives and business leaders, due to the complexity of the IT environment, as well as the timeline and cost commitments involved in execution. The IT complexity spans business applications and data management as well as infrastructure elements such as data centers, telephony, networks, security, and end-user support.

Acquisitions are completed for many reasons (see Exhibit 2.2 in the previous chapter), but in most cases, the driver can broadly be described with the objective to capture incremental business value. This business value, defined most often as synergies, is frequently dependent on IT.

Given the role of IT as a key enabler to this business value creation, as well as a source of value in itself, IT has three key objectives in M&A:

1. Enabling the business synergies and value creation.
2. Effectively integrating IT and driving IT synergies.
3. Stabilizing the IT function as it adapts to significant change.

Often, IT's first and most important function is to enable the business synergies critical to the deal. This key objective must parallel with IT function-specific synergy capture and integration, as well as IT stabilization activities during the course of the integration.

Given that IT can often be the most expensive and, at the same time, one of the most critical enablers of value creation in a deal, it is important for the IT M&A strategy and planning effort to align with the business.

Specific aspects of this book focus on IT M&A frameworks and synergy enablement. This chapter is concerned with the priority to support the business in M&A and enable synergy achievement. The main focus is on acquisition integration, though many of the concepts are relevant to the broader M&A context.

THE BUSINESS-ALIGNED INTEGRATION MODEL

In Chapter 2, we introduced four models or approaches that can be applied to a post-merger integration context. Further, we highlighted the importance of aligning the integration approach with the strategic intent of the acquisition.

Exhibit 3.1 revisits these models and evaluates them based on two fundamental characteristics, highlighting two key business acquisition objectives for each approach:

1. The degree of similarity among the merger partners' business model, or the amount of overlap in products, customers, distribution channels, and geographies.
2. The degree of similarity among business operations or functional capabilities.

In selecting the most effective integration approach, business executives must, of course, evaluate the strategic intent of the acquisition, as well as the similarity with the existing businesses. Here are two brief examples:

1. If the acquired business model is similar to the acquirer, the preferred option may likely be a consolidation strategy, particularly if the acquirer is much larger than the target. This allows the acquirer to expand its business and product lines and to leverage its existing operational infrastructure.
2. Conversely, if the acquired business is much different from the acquirer, the acquirer's existing operations may not support the new business effectively. This situation may lend itself to a transformation strategy focused on retaining best-of-breed capabilities, or a preservation strategy if autonomy and innovation are critical.

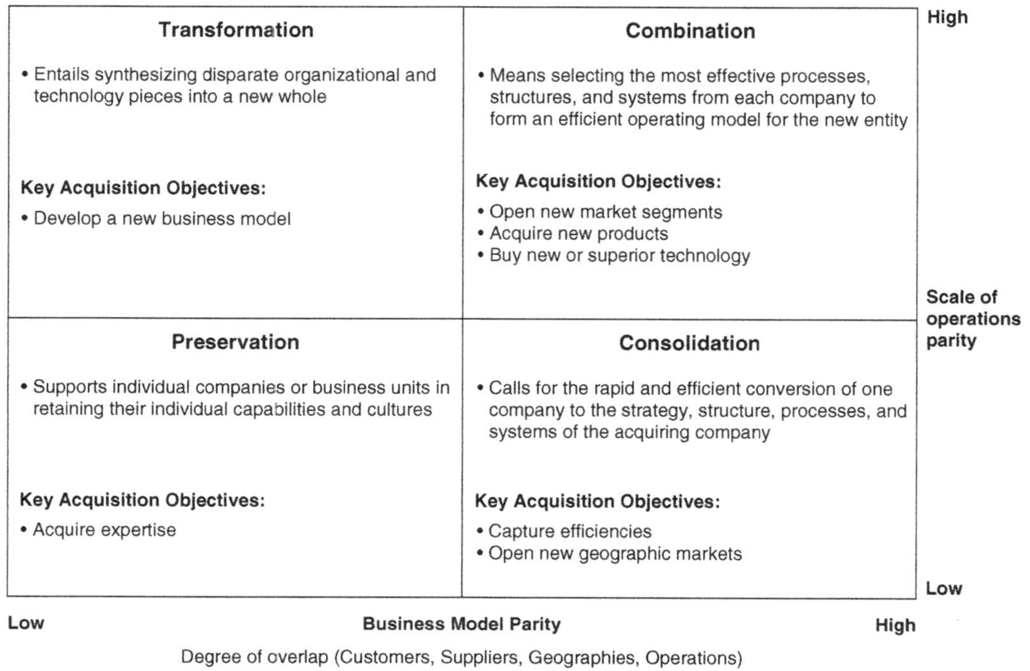

	Business Model Parity — Low	**Business Model Parity** — High	Scale of operations parity
High	**Transformation** • Entails synthesizing disparate organizational and technology pieces into a new whole **Key Acquisition Objectives:** • Develop a new business model	**Combination** • Means selecting the most effective processes, structures, and systems from each company to form an efficient operating model for the new entity **Key Acquisition Objectives:** • Open new market segments • Acquire new products • Buy new or superior technology	High
Low	**Preservation** • Supports individual companies or business units in retaining their individual capabilities and cultures **Key Acquisition Objectives:** • Acquire expertise	**Consolidation** • Calls for the rapid and efficient conversion of one company to the strategy, structure, processes, and systems of the acquiring company **Key Acquisition Objectives:** • Capture efficiencies • Open new geographic markets	Low

Business Model Parity

Degree of overlap (Customers, Suppliers, Geographies, Operations)

EXHIBIT 3.1 Business Integration Models

In practice, an acquisition, depending on the size, may require multiple models for different product lines or business units within the acquired company. For example, an acquisition of a company may provide for a new business unit that serves to extend the acquirer's existing business and aligns well operationally, but the same acquisition also may provide for a separate, additional business unit (or product line) that does not align well with the acquirer's operations. In such a case, a consolidation strategy may be appropriately applied to the complementary business unit (or product line), and a preservation or combination strategy might be applied to the business unit (or product line) that is not as complementary.

Further, the acquiring company may also define an integration strategy or approach that changes over time. For example, a preservation strategy might be appropriate for Day 1 and for an interim period, to allow for continued innovation and growth of a strategic product line, with a longer-term transformation strategy intended after two or three years.

In each of the cases, the business integration approach has key implications for IT and sets the context for the IT M&A strategy and planning. These examples also highlight the importance of the alignment between the business and IT. In short, the IT mission in M&A is to understand the business integration model and to plan accordingly to support the business and deliver the intended value of the deal.

A practical method is described in the following section, one that aligns the business and the IT integration planning effort in support of the deal value creation. This practical method starts with the creation of an enterprise blueprint that incorporates and further defines the business integration model.

ENTERPRISE BLUEPRINT AND IT ALIGNMENT

We have discussed the various integration models and the importance of the alignment of the IT plan with the overall strategic intent of the deal. The problem in many failed integrations is not that the company lacked the capabilities to manage a large-scale transformation. Rather, it's that the company failed to develop an enterprise blueprint for the newly combined entity—a clear end-state vision for how the new entity will operate after the integration.

An enterprise blueprint is a definitive statement of how the new company should operate in order to achieve the business rationale for the deal and further the combined company's overall strategy. It should answer a number of key questions that help specify the operating model and capabilities the combined company needs to possess in order to deliver value to customers, employees, and shareholders. (See Exhibit 3.2.)[1]

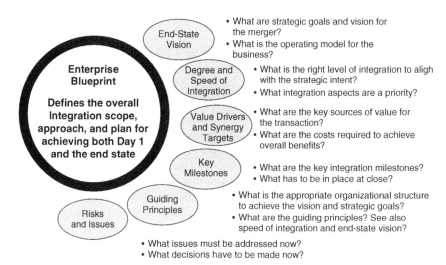

EXHIBIT 3.2 Enterprise Blueprint to Align IT Integration Planning

An enterprise blueprint is needed to help the functional integration teams stay aligned with the overall deal strategy, thereby enhancing and accelerating synergy capture. An enterprise blueprint will also guide the development of functional blueprints, which represent more detailed descriptions of how each function should operate to deliver the expected value of the deal.

For IT, the enterprise blueprint can help define the IT integration strategy that will most effectively meet the end-state vision of the business. For example, an enterprise blueprint that outlines the intent to keep the acquired business as a separate entity—to maintain the integrity of its innovation expertise (preservation strategy)—provides the basis for a distinct IT integration model. In this case, the IT integration strategy would mirror and support the business integration approach, likely resulting in a plan to integrate core IT infrastructure and operations with minimal or no impact to the supporting operating business systems.

In conclusion, as an IT executive leader in M&A, it is imperative that you and your team thoroughly understand the business strategy and work with the leadership team to validate the enterprise blueprint. All IT acquisition activities should be explicitly supportive of the business acquisition objectives, and there should be a clear line of sight from acquisition activities to the business objectives.

IT'S ROLE IN FUNCTIONAL BLUEPRINTING

As the integration effort is launched, the goal of each functional team leader is to develop a set of functional blueprints that align with the enterprise blueprint and thus with the business integration model (combination, transformation, etc.).

The functional blueprint should start at a high level, with a focus on the end state and success factors. Further iterations should then work down through the key elements and requirements of the function to carry out key process areas to support the new business and should follow through to define the activities, road map, charters, and project plans, as well as costs, to achieve the desired results. (See Exhibit 3.3.)

The IT integration team should be represented as a strategic partner in each of the functional blueprint sessions. The most effective blueprinting approach is carried out through a number of workshops in which IT participates as a key business partner to refine the requirements and make sure the integration plans for applications, data, and infrastructure align with the business requirements and targeted timelines.

IT's involvement in the workshop and functional blueprinting process is to capture requirements but also to support the business in planning most effectively for the desired processes given the current entity's IT applications and tools. IT may also take an active role in providing a view of enabling or new technologies that can create incremental value for the business, but must also consider the cost and return on investment of doing so relative to the deal model.

Exhibit 3.4 shows representative functional and IT requirement and dependency areas that may arise during the functional blueprinting process. To highlight an example, as the finance department develops its functional blueprint, the team will likely be focused on Day 1 priorities, such as consolidation and financial reporting. In post-Day 1 blueprint planning, the finance team may define activities such as legal entity consolidation, financial systems migration, and shared services consolidation.

To realize both of these short-term and longer-term integration objectives, IT will likely have a significant role to play as the underlying enterprise resource planning systems and supporting financial systems need to be modified, consolidated, or integrated to support the business changes—often a complex and time-consuming process.

Beyond supporting the business and functional teams, the IT department should also create a functional blueprint. The IT functional blueprint will describe both the applications and infrastructure that IT supplies to the business, as well as the way in which IT services the business. While much of the IT blueprint will be determined through support of the other functional blueprints, the IT functional team should develop its blueprint to meet both the business and IT objectives.

The end result of the blueprinting process should be an integrated and aligned IT and business/functional road map, which will serve as the

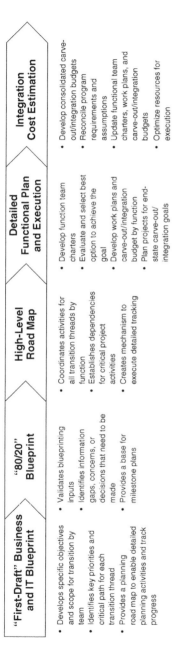

"First-Draft" Business and IT Blueprint

- Develops specific objectives and scope for transition by team
- Identifies key priorities and critical path for each transition thread
- Provides a planning road map to enable detailed planning activities and track progress

"80/20" Blueprint

- Validates blueprinting inputs
- Identifies information gaps, concerns, or decisions that need to be made
- Provides a base for milestone plans

High-Level Road Map

- Coordinates activities for all transition threads by function
- Establishes dependencies for critical project activities
- Creates mechanism to execute detailed tracking

Detailed Functional Plan and Execution

- Develop function team charters
- Evaluate and select best option to achieve the goal
- Develop work plans and carve-out/integration budget by function
- Plan projects for end-state carve-out/integration goals

Integration Cost Estimation

- Develop consolidated carve-out/integration budgets
- Reconcile program requirements and assumptions
- Update functional team charters, work plans, and carve-out/integration budgets
- Optimize resources for execution

Requirements definition workshops accelerate the alignment of required business and IT capabilities and actions

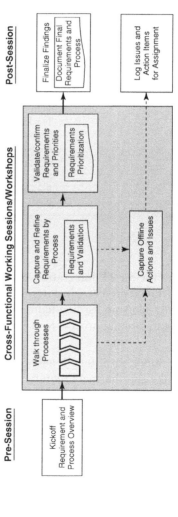

Pre-Session

Kickoff Requirement and Process Overview

Cross-Functional Working Sessions/Workshops

Walk through Processes

Capture and Refine Requirements by Process
- Requirements and Validation

Capture Offline Actions and Issues

Validate/confirm Requirements and Priorities
- Requirements Prioritization

Post-Session

Finalize Findings
- Document Final Requirements and Process

Log Issues and Action Items for Assignment

EXHIBIT 3.3 Functional Blueprinting Process

EXHIBIT 3.4 Representative IT and Functional Requirement and Dependency Areas

Function	Representative IT Dependency Areas
Finance	Consolidations systems strategy Financial systems Legal entity structure and tax model Shared services integration
Human Resources	Human resources systems and employee data Payroll and time management systems Performance management and training systems
Commercial	Go-to-market model and channel consolidations Customer relationship management systems Websites and branding capabilities
Operations and Supply Chain	Manufacturing and operations systems Third-party providers and integration Tracking and tracing capabilities Consolidation and optimization Procurement and sourcing spend leverage
Other	Quality processes and execution Import/export systems and third-party integration Research and development systems consolidation Real estate and facilities

baseline for the IT integration program and will be leveraged to develop more detailed project schedules, resource plans, and integration costs.

The following list highlights a few of the critical success factors in the blueprint planning process for IT and business alignment:

- Identify critical functional needs that drive value to the deal up front.
- Make sure business requirements are documented, vetted, and agreed upon.
- Conduct periodic joint design and blueprint reviews (align business and IT requirements).
- Communicate IT integration blueprint timelines and highlight impacts to functional blueprints.
- Keep track of critical dependencies to support continued alignment.

In conclusion, business and IT alignment in integration planning is critical to successful M&A integration. Whether the deal is an M&A integration or a carve-out/separation, the success factors for IT and business alignment during the blueprint phase are the same and should be considered in each transaction.

DECISION MAKING AND BUSINESS ALIGNMENT

In M&A, it is important for an IT leader to make efficient decisions and make sure there is alignment with the business. Often, IT and business executives responsible for an M&A deal are challenged with how to make decisions in light of the complexity of integration and tight timelines.

The first aspect of decision making in M&A is to make sure there is a clear decision governance structure in place, with roles and responsibilities defined. If the broader integration program is established in a well-organized manner, it should provide for the decision governance structure to escalate and attain critical integration decisions across the businesses, functions, and regions. This model can be expanded upon and leveraged by the IT team to drive critical decisions.

The second aspect in M&A decision making is an efficient decision-making methodology. For IT, the decision-making methodology should begin with business and IT alignment up front and should provide for aligned decision criteria. This alignment will allow for more efficient, quicker decision making and will support a more fact-based approach.

In many cases in M&A, the most effective decision-making methodology is referred to as "adopt and go" and involves quickly selecting the process, systems, and policy that best suit the new combined company, leveraging existing capabilities. The methodology is supported by agreed-on decision-making criteria such as the following:

Representative "Adopt and Go" Decision Criteria
- Business strategy alignment
- Cost reduction and efficiencies
- Cost to achieve or implement
- Customer experience
- Employee experience
- Time to implement
- Implementation risk
- Change management

The complexity of M&A and lack of decisions can be destructive to deal value and can be the cause of failure over time. Through the use of a simple methodology such as adopt and go, the IT integration and business teams can work quickly to make decisions to guide the integration and achieve success.

BUSINESS ALIGNMENT IN DUE DILIGENCE

Much of this chapter has been devoted to planning and executing the key IT aspects of M&A integration. It is imperative to recognize the importance of

IT in the due diligence process, as well as the importance of IT and business alignment.

Similar to the IT integration planning effort, the understanding of the intended business integration strategy is equally important for the IT due diligence efforts. Further, consistent with integration, IT is required to play a dual role in assessing the risks and opportunities with the business as well as within IT. In evaluating both opportunities and risks related to the business, the team should focus on those areas that will enable the business integration and intended value. The following list highlights some representative business and risk-based questions:

- What systems and capabilities are critical to supporting the deal value?
- Do the applications and technologies adequately support the business today?
- Are mission-critical technologies stable and reliable?
- Are adequate provisions in place to facilitate business continuity?
- Are procedures and capabilities evident to protect the company's data from unauthorized disclosure?

Consider the case where a potential target with strong manufacturing capabilities is supported by an antiquated manufacturing execution system (MES). Certainly, this would be a critical deal factor, as it could create operational risk for ongoing business and may be detrimental to the business case as a result of the required investment to bring the MES to a more stable and up-to-date state.

Of course, IT diligence will involve assessment beyond the afore-mentioned identified business-related questions, expanding to a broader assessment of IT risks and opportunities; however, this chapter attempts to highlight the importance of alignment between the business and IT during the IT diligence process.

WRAPPING IT UP

IT can often be the most complex and costly aspect of any integration and, at the same time, one of the most critical enablers of success overall. IT's role in M&A is to simultaneously address the requirements of the business to enable synergies while delivering on IT-specific opportunities. This is both the challenge and the opportunity for IT in the M&A process.

IT's main focus is to enable the business synergies critical to the deal. To do this effectively, it is imperative that the integration approach (strategy) as well as the planning process and approach are aligned and coordinated jointly across IT and the business. Much of this book provides a framework for IT to be successful in M&A. This chapter serves to highlight the importance of IT and business alignment and to provide some concepts and tools for consideration in the planning process.

To summarize, the key success factors to consider include:

- Understand the strategic intent and enterprise blueprint. Make it a priority to understand the strategic value drivers, operating model, and key integration guiding principles. Begin this process in due diligence.
- Align the IT integration plan with the enterprise blueprint. Focus on building an end-state IT blueprint that aligns with the business integration vision and intended business operating model.
- Develop an iterative blueprint process to capture IT requirements. Execute an iterative functional blueprint process and work closely with the functions to define requirements, establish dependencies, and align timelines.
- Develop an efficient and business-aligned decision-making methodology. Establish the governance structure, methodology, and decision criteria in conjunction with the business, and consider the adopt-and-go methodology to quickly make decisions to support the integration.

The concept of IT and business alignment is not a new topic, but the importance of it in an M&A context is critical. Each of these success factors, as well as the concepts in this chapter, serves to support business and IT alignment throughout the M&A planning process to enable deal success.

Note

1. "Set Your Sights on the M&A Endgame: How an Enterprise Blueprint Can Help You Navigate Multiple M&A Challenges," Deloitte Consulting LLP, 2007.

CHAPTER 4

Mergers and Acquisitions IT Strategy, Approach, and Governance

IT and Its Customers

Chris DeBeer
Michael H. Moore

Mergers, acquisitions, and divestitures are often some of the most unsettling activities that many functions and their staffs face in the life of a company. There generally are many communications from leadership extolling the virtues of the combination, but the fact remains that many of the changes to come are unknown and that there is a lot of work to come before the "new normal" is realized.

Information technology (IT) is, oftentimes, one of the functions most affected as a result of a merger or acquisition, and, in turn, affects many of the other functions as well. Changes to IT systems and applications—such as e-mail, human capital management (HCM), customer relationship management (CRM), and enterprise resource planning (ERP)—may be some of the first and most noticeable changes to many of the people across the new company or organization (NewCo). Working to make sure system changes cause the least amount of disruption possible and benefit from the effectiveness of NewCo needs to be a top priority of senior management in all functions, not just IT.

Effectively linking strategy, approach, and governance is difficult in stand-alone organizations; maintaining the linkages between these three areas becomes even more challenging during a merger or acquisition. In this chapter we lay out the key components of IT integration as it relates to four key functional areas—finance, operations, human resources (HR), and information technology (IT)—and how leading organizations can link strategy, approach, and governance within and across each function.

STRATEGY

In order to limit or reduce disruption and increase or improve effectiveness, the pre- and post-merger integration activities of IT need to be aligned with the company's overall strategy for integration. There are three primary integration strategies that companies pursuing mergers or acquisitions generally adopt:

1. **Full integration.** This IT integration strategy is most often pursued by companies doing mergers or acquisitions within industries or segments in which they already operate and are pursuing either geographic expansion or new products and services that are closely related to those they already offer. Synergies between the two organizations can be significant in terms of overlapping systems and how the systems are structured to support the business (e.g., airline mergers). Technology integration generally involves the combined entity operating on the same or single platform of applications for e-mail, HCM, CRM, and ERP.

2. **Partial integration.** Those companies that are merging with or acquiring companies in geographic areas that are significantly removed from their current base of operations or pursuing a diversification strategy around products or services unrelated to their current offerings may choose a strategy of partial IT integration. Synergies between organizations may not be significant, and the structures of the systems and setup may be significantly divergent geographically or in how they support the business. Integrating select systems and back-office applications such as e-mail and HCM are generally pursued for the synergies they represent, but if the geographic or language differences warrant, different CRM and ERP applications may remain in place and not be integrated.

3. **Minimal integration.** Holding companies and those organizations that conduct mergers and acquisitions as part of a portfolio strategy are most likely to minimally integrate IT. Synergies are not material between organizations, and the ownership of both organizations may, in fact, be the only thing that they have in common in some cases. IT integration may be only for financial reporting purposes, with few systems, including e-mail, HCM, CRM, and ERP, integrated. While this integration strategy produces little synergy or savings in terms of systems, the ability to divest the acquired organization is much easier down the road.

IT leadership should be required to align its strategy with that of the overall organization and define the synergies and timing of the IT integration that will occur as part of the merger or acquisition and get buy-in from the other functions' leaders for the systems and applications that affect each. (For more information on IT-related integration models, see Chapters 3 and 22.)

APPROACH

As soon as a potential transaction is identified, IT should begin work with leaders across the organization to assess the IT capabilities of the potential acquisition or merger partner. The due diligence leading practices in Chapter 5 provides a good starting point for this assessment.

Once the due diligence is finished and an inventory of the potential acquisition or merger partner is complete, the next step is to determine what the key objectives for NewCo are for each of the four main functional areas (finance, operations, human resources, and information technology). The synergies targeted for each functional area should be mapped out and a systems impact analysis performed for each of the goals identified. For example, in an airline merger, the way the customers make reservations and select seat assignments is a critical area of integration, so the booking and reservation system integration will be one of the top-priority items in any merger or acquisition in that industry.

After the synergies and systems impact are determined for each of the functional categories, the IT integration activities associated with each function and the timing of those activities can be mapped out and prioritized. See Exhibit 4.1.

We have identified the four main functional areas of finance, operations, human resources, and information technology that, at a minimum, need to be addressed in any merger or acquisition. Each of these functions can have a critical impact on the success or failure of the enterprise, and leadership should take steps to make sure the IT integration for these functions follows

EXHIBIT 4.1 Timing Matrix

	−60 Days	−30 Days	+90 Days	+180 Days
Finance				
Operations				
Human Resources				
Information Technology				

the overall strategy of the organization. While there are industries where other specific functions should be considered and are critical to results (for example, in health care the clinical functions should be separated and evaluated), the same approach outlined in this chapter can be applied to those areas.

For each of the four functional areas, there are specific considerations and subareas that should be evaluated during a merger or acquisition. Using the timing matrix as a guide, organizations can determine how the overall strategic goals map to the tactical needs of each and what IT systems and applications should be addressed and when. This can create important links between strategy, approach, and ongoing governance to define the new normal as it relates to IT systems and applications.

GOVERNANCE

Governance of both the people and the process to assess capabilities, define synergies, and implement IT integration in the combined organization is critical to the objectives and results of any merger or acquisition. Creating a governance structure that involves, at a minimum, key stakeholders from across the combined organizations in each of the four functions should be the determined before the transaction closes in order to begin the integration process quickly once the deal closes.

Senior leaders across the organization should work to achieve the targeted IT integration as soon as possible for several reasons. The first reason is to get NewCo operating in the new normal as quickly as possible to increase and improve the benefits and synergies of the combination. The second is to reduce the anxiety and uncertainty of staff and have them focus on their roles in helping the new combined organization achieve its goals and objectives. It is critical that the leadership of NewCo act quickly to implement the changes from people, process, and technology standpoints. Most of the strategic and operational changes that are envisioned should be in place after the first six months.

The governance structure that an organization chooses will be somewhat defined by the type of integration strategy it is pursuing. Those organizations with a full integration strategy may choose to define an official post-merger integration (PMI) IT steering committee made up of representatives from across the four main factions that meets frequently during the period of integration after the deal closes. Those pursuing partial integration may only have leaders from those functions selected for integration in a working group format, and minimally integrated organizations may not organize a formal governance structure for IT integration.

Whatever governance structure is selected, there should be clearly documented decision paths and "the buck stops here" decision makers assigned. Staff within NewCo will be looking for leadership during the transition and need to know to whom to escalate issues and who will be empowered to make decisions during the execution of the integration plan.

While IT integration may not be the primary driver of a merger or acquisition, it is almost always listed as one of the key areas for rationalization and review. By starting early and committing resources to finish quickly, IT integration can become a key enabler of success for the new organization.

FINANCE

Finance is one of the key functional areas involved in and affected by any merger or acquisition. From the evaluation and assessment of financing to projecting the future cash flows and synergy scenarios, the finance staff ends up burning a lot of midnight oil leading up to the close of any transaction. However, closing is just the start for the finance staff, and having a plan for the integration of both the processes and the systems should be one of the top PMI priorities of the CFO and the finance staff.

Using the systems impact analysis developed with IT, the finance staff can begin to execute on the activities they've prioritized in the timing matrix for each subarea that follows.

Accounting

Financial Consolidation Financial consolidation and reporting will be a priority for NewCo. If the merger or acquisition is international in nature, general ledgers that are denominated in foreign currencies will need to be translated and the different accounting treatments required in each country—for example, U.S. generally accepted accounting principles (GAAP) versus International Financial Reporting Standards (IFRS)—need to be assessed so that a consolidated set of financial statements is produced at the close of the first month as a combined organization. Based on the integration strategy selected, there are three options that organizations can select:

1. **Consolidate in ERP.** This approach is most often used by companies pursuing a full integration strategy. The ERP system is set up in such a

way that business units can be defined and ledgers and subledgers set up to support the financial consolidation and reporting activities. Fully integrating a merger or new acquisition into the ERP system requires a significant investment in time and resources and may require significant process changes for the merged or acquired entity. There are significant long-term benefits and potential synergies from being on a single ERP platform that have to be balanced against the investment before this approach is taken.

2. **Consolidate in a third-party system.** Several third-party software packages from software vendors, such as SAP and Oracle, are designed specifically to support financial consolidation outside of the ERP system. These systems have several advantages in that they generally require an export of the trial balance from the general ledger of the merged or acquired entity and some up-front mapping to make sure that a complete financial picture is being captured. This approach also requires investments in potentially new systems and training of resources within the new entity and within the parent finance organization.

3. **Consolidate in a spreadsheet.** While widespread, this approach is the least recommended and most prone to error. A manual effort is required to consolidate the financials, and significant work is needed on an ongoing basis by the finance staff across the organization to reconcile and review the results, as changes to any of the subsidiary general ledgers may not be automatically captured. This approach also does not provide sufficient security, controls, or audit trails.

Financial Policies and Procedures   Establishing effective financial controls, policies, and procedures for the new firm should be completed shortly after closing, including defining an enterprise-wide authorization matrix, as well and defining and disseminating financial policies and procedures for revenue recognition and billing. Any policies and any work flow or security provisions required in systems will need to be identified and coordinated with IT.

Payroll Processing   Making sure everyone still gets paid once the deal closes is a critical consideration that should be addressed and managed by the accounting department in close coordination with human resources. The funding for payroll and the banks that will be used, particularly in an international organization, needs to be planned carefully. If the organization will be consolidating its banking relationships, then coordination with treasury will be critical. IT should work with the treasury and accounting departments to identify interfaces with external service providers, particularly those that provide payroll and cash clearing for NewCo.

Statutory Reporting and Compliance   If NewCo is publicly traded, then additional considerations around statutory reporting and filing should be considered along with any specific rule sets that apply. Sarbanes-Oxley also requires compliance across several systems that affect the general ledger and other process controls that IT will need to be involved with to make sure NewCo is following the regulations consistently.

Tax   Depending on where NewCo operates geographically, there may be several different tax and governmental entities that need to be paid on widely divergent schedules. Having a clear idea of what countries and tax jurisdictions NewCo has liabilities in and how the accounting systems will manage the calculation and accrual of those liabilities needs to be addressed as part of the overall consolidation and reporting strategy.

Financial Planning and Analysis

In the heat of a merger or acquisition, many plans and forecasts are made on how the combined organization will achieve both revenue and cost synergies. Linking the plans made leading up to, and serving as the basis for, the acquisition to the actual operating results of the combined organization should be the top priority for any financial planning and analysis (FP&A) department after a deal.

Budgeting and Forecasting   Budgeting and forecasting provide the critical link between what was planned to happen as part of the merger or acquisition and what actually happens once the deal closes. New budgets should be built out for the combined organization with the synergies that were planned built into the numbers. This may be the first time that many of the operation managers will see what the expectations of leadership are under the new normal, and by playing an active role in developing the new budget, leaders can get buy-in from across the organization.

Reporting and Analysis   Technology plays a critical role around reporting in NewCo by helping to get the organization's master data defined, including the entity structure that shows how financials will be consolidated, ways product and/or services hierarchies will be defined, and how they will keep track of the markets and customers that NewCo will serve. If NewCo doesn't take the time to create common definitions and build the synergies it assumed as a basis for the combination into its operating budget, it has little or no chance of achieving those synergies, much less understanding in a timely manner when course corrections may need to be made.

Treasury and Cash Management

As mentioned in the earlier subsection on payroll processing, the treasury department serves an important role in the combined organization and will need the support of IT to be effective. Having a clear idea of where the cash is and how it is being used can make or break NewCo.

Treasury Systems   Integration of the treasury function can dramatically improve the visibility in the cash available to NewCo and should be one of the top priorities for investment after integration. There are four key areas of treasury automation that should be prioritized:

1. Treasury workstation:
   - Enables process standardization and efficiencies.
   - Leverages ERP data from accounts payable (A/P) and accounts receivable (A/R).
   - Integrates treasury transactions and reporting.
2. SWIFT connectivity—The Society for Worldwide Interbank Financial Telecommunication (SWIFT) provides a network that enables financial institutions worldwide to send and receive information about financial transactions in a secure, standardized, and reliable environment.
   - Provides a single pipeline for all financial messaging.
   - Allows real-time visibility of global cash positions.
   - Is bank agnostic.
3. XML format—Extensible markup language (XML) defines a set of rules for encoding documents in a format that is both human-readable and machine-readable. This language emphasizes simplicity and usability.
   - Is the International Organization for Standardization (ISO) standard format among financial institutions.
   - Enables rich information content.
4. Electronic bank account management (eBAM):
   - Streamlines open/close account processes globally.
   - Eases management of bank mandates globally.

OPERATIONS

The term *operations* can have many meanings depending on the company and the industry in which you operate. While finance, human resources, and information technology are largely focused on the internal workings of NewCo, the operations element of the firm typically has more of an external component and deals with suppliers as well as customers or clients of the organization. In this section, we cover manufacturing, supply chain, marketing, and sales.

Information technology plays an important role in facilitating and coordinating the connection between the purchase of materials to manufacture the goods that are eventually sold to and purchased by the customers of NewCo. The enterprise resource planning (ERP) systems at NewCo play a central role in making this connection, and the integration strategy the new organization's leadership chooses will have a significant impact on the success or failure of the combined organization.

As stated in the introduction to this chapter, for those organizations that are merging with or acquiring an organization that is closely related to the existing business, it is common to choose a full integration strategy in order to leverage, manage, and improve the synergies around the combination of departments such as manufacturing and supply chain as well as marketing and sales. The IT area will play a critical role in making sure the systems are set up and operating quickly to leverage, increase, and improve the synergies in these areas.

Manufacturing and Supply Chain

Information technology plays a central role in managing and maintaining the ERP system and its various subsystems that support manufacturing and the supply chain. During a merger or acquisition, obtaining the synergies that result from the increased purchasing power is a critical synergy the management will be watching.

Procure to Pay Procure to pay (PTP) encompasses the supply chain and sourcing functions and capabilities of the ERP system within NewCo. If NewCo is pursuing full integration, then the PTP staff will need to understand quickly what the existing contracts and standing orders for material are in order to develop a plan to negotiate potentially better prices for the increased volume from existing suppliers or to evaluate new suppliers based on the overall volume and geographic needs of the combined organization.

IT can support this effort by working with the PTP staff by integrating the merged entity or acquisition into the existing contract lifecycle management (CLM) system, if any, or proposing a new one if none exists. Based on the work effort involved in rationalizing and managing the large number of contracts across two organizations, a merger or acquisition is an opportune time to get NewCo's house in order around the supply chain and contracts.

Plan to Make   Plan to make (PTM) covers the people and processes associated with the planning and production of the goods or services that NewCo provides. There are several elements around PTM, including demand planning, production planning, and optimization as well as warehousing and distribution. Each of these elements leverages systems that need to be integrated with and optimized based on how NewCo will best serve its customers. Leveraging the timing matrix developed and approved by leadership IT can prioritize how best to integrate and manage these elements.

- **Demand planning.** Understanding how much of NewCo's products will be required when and where is critical to developing the production plan to make those products. IT should understand the different types of products that NewCo makes and how to integrate those products, including any synergies that are expected as a result of cross-selling, into a centralized demand plan. If the products are very divergent, then multiple demand plans may be required and multiple systems needed to support each.
- **Production planning and optimization.** Once the demand planning is complete, the integration with the order entry system and the production plan will need to be completed. This can be a daunting task, particularly for those organizations that have global customers and manufacturing. Information technology personnel should work with PTM leadership to understand how best to integrate these components and validate the timing matrix.
- **Warehousing and distribution.** Finished goods and work-in-progress inventories eat up valuable working capital for NewCo, and optimizing the stock of both will be something that finance, PTP, and PTM leadership need to manage. While excess inventory eats up working capital, stock-outs and shortages reduce cash flow and alienate customers. IT must work with functional leadership to keep the systems and capabilities of NewCo aligned with NewCo's business model.

Marketing and Sales

Marketing, trade promotion management, and sales are key areas of rationalization and optimization, as they are highly visible to NewCo's customers. In fact, the benefits and synergies on the revenue side of the ledger are often larger than the cost-saving synergies predicted. Technology has a central role to play in this aspect of the merger or acquisition by helping maintain and sustain the customer relationship management (CRM) system or systems that NewCo will use.

Master data management (MDM) plays a central role in this integration, particularly around the maintenance and management of a customer master data (CMD). Understanding who NewCo's customers are, and having their addresses, preferences, and related information such as contract and payment information, gives the marketing and sales staff the ability to better serve existing customers with NewCo's products, but also to identify and convert new customers. The integration of CMD can be extensive and include elements from many other functions, including PTP, PTM, and finance.

Marketing Having accurate CMD allows the marketing department to more efficiently and effectively target NewCo's combined customer list and can dramatically improve the revenue synergies of the new organization. Cross-marketing of products and services to new and existing customers becomes difficult, if not impossible, without an accurate set of data on the customers that each of the previously independent organizations served. Technology can assist in this process by converting and/or integrating the CRM system at NewCo in addition to the rationalization and integration of the CMD data across the enterprise.

Sales The sales and channel strategy of NewCo will also need input from the IT staff. Data on the volume and profitability of each channel or representative will need to come from the business intelligence (BI) system of NewCo, and getting that information integrated with ERP and CRM will be required. Sales staff are particularly avid consumers of data, as data relate to their quotas and commissions, which will need to be tracked and managed. By leveraging quantitative data provided by IT, NewCo's leaders will be better able to make informed decisions on how to manage their sales strategies effectively.

HUMAN RESOURCES

Human resources (HR) is one of the key functional areas involved in and affected by any merger or acquisition. From the establishment of a new corporate organizational chart to rationalization of job roles and levels and succession planning, human resources staff has a significant workload leading up to the close of any transaction.

Human resources is central to developing the answers employees will be looking for as soon as, and sometimes sooner than, the transaction is announced. Employees will want basic questions answered (for example: Does my position still exist? What is the new reporting structure? Will

I need to relocate?). Answering these questions as quickly as possible, or at a minimum providing a timeline indicating when information will be made available, is a key success factor in managing talent during a tumultuous period for the new organization. In the absence of information communicated by leadership, uncertainty and rumor will fill the void. (See Chapter 20 for a detailed discussion of the human aspects of mergers, acquisitions, and divestitures.)

From the beginning of the transaction and continuing through steady-state operation, human resources activity is organized in three main threads: talent management, talent acquisition, and talent rationalization. These three areas are critical to the effective transition of the business through an acquisition or a divestiture, and each requires a well-thought-out strategy, approach, and controls.

Talent Management

Payroll   Avoiding an interruption to payroll or expense reimbursement will limit the impact of the transaction on employees. Frequently, a one-time event impacting a payroll run will be required. Switching to a new payroll schedule (for example, weekly to biweekly) is common. It is also common for expense reimbursement schedules to be impacted and the cutoff date for submissions to be brought forward or pushed back to support IT activity. For both payroll and expenses it is important for the impacts to be communicated as early as possible to allow employees to plan accordingly and take action. A leading practice is communicating at regular intervals, such as four weeks prior, two weeks prior, and the week leading up to the event, to keep employees informed.

Benefits   As part of an employee's complete compensation package, benefits also require a strategy and approach. Clearly communicating information on options available to replace current health benefits or additional financial benefits—for example, 401(k) and matching contributions—will assist employees in making decisions and will reduce confusion and related questions. Options should be analyzed early in the transaction by human resources and the details provided to employees as early as possible. In most cases, benefits information is made available to employees on an internal website accessible to new employees as soon as system access is granted. Health benefits typically switch immediately or are retained without changes until the next scheduled open-enrollment period.

Security Roles and Responsibilities   The human resources division manages the roles and responsibilities definitions within an organization. All employees must be mapped to an appropriate role and responsibility. The rules associated with roles and responsibilities govern not only approval authority and allowable activity, but also system access and physical access to facilities. These definitions should be assessed and updated if the corporate structure has changed. Changes will require an impact analysis to validate if new security or separation of duties issues have been created. Internal audit generally is involved in this analysis, and an automated tool is frequently used to determine whether security issues have been created in an ERP system.

Talent Acquisition

It is commonplace for the M&A transaction to generate new resource needs. A change in the scale of operations in the newly combined entity may require resources with different skill sets (for example, experience managing a much larger business). Technology changes, such as transitioning to a new ERP system, may require the acquisition of new skill sets to support business operations. Recruiting activities have long lead times, particularly for niche skills. It is critical that the human resources group work with all internal customers to identify needs early, create staffing plans that align with approved budgets, and begin the recruiting process.

Talent Rationalization

Retention   Frequently, the value of the resources themselves is a factor in the valuation of an organization and a driver for the M&A activity. Retaining these resources is a critical success factor. The resources can be divided into two groups. The first group of employees included in a retention strategy is key to the long-term success of the organization. Top contributors, thought leaders, and those deemed to have significant growth potential within the new organization should be identified. The second group of employees included in a retention strategy is key to the short-term success of the M&A activity. These resources include employees with specific legacy system knowledge or accumulated "tribal" knowledge of key business processes. These resources are valuable during the transition period in support of business process reengineering, system cutover, and data conversion activities. Those resources needed only for the transitional period are frequently offered retention packages to secure their participation and include payouts tied to the achievement of major integration or divestiture milestones.

Assessment   Merger and acquisition activity provides organizations with an opportunity to assess resources across the organization. Typically these assessments focus on current performance levels, value to the organization, and the ability to be promoted in the future. The assessment provides a set of criteria that enable human resources to make informed staffing decisions, identify key resources for long- and short-term needs, and determine where recruiting efforts need to be focused. This assessment activity is a key input into decisions on who will retain their positions and who will be part of a staffing reduction if one is planned.

Succession Planning   When the transaction is announced, immediate changes to the corporate leadership structure will be communicated. Significant effort on the part of human resources will have been invested to reach this point. Human resources, in conjunction with a board of directors, will develop immediate, near-term, and long-term succession plans.

Immediate plans are announced as part of the transaction or soon after. Near-term planning focuses on the integration period, beginning with the initial announcement, continuing through integration activity, and ending when steady-state operations are reached. Long-term succession planning is an ongoing activity continually assessed and updated by human resources, company leadership, and the board of directors.

Both internal and external resources should be considered to match the skill set, expertise, and character required fill any open position. Human resources also needs to take into consideration the fact that the resources required to successfully manage the business during the transitional period may differ from those required during steady-state operations. Internal successors are, in many ways, lower-risk than outsiders since they generally have deep knowledge of current operations and known track records. However, outside resources are frequently selected to fill leadership roles based on their ability to bring new skill sets or an external perspective to positions.

INFORMATION TECHNOLOGY

Working closely with representatives from all business units is key to successfully creating the information technology strategy, approach, and governance within and across each function. As mentioned earlier in this chapter, IT customers span the entire organization and possess vastly different business requirements supported by technical components managed by IT. The technology department is the facilitator and enabler of the systems and application integration across the organization, and activity is driven by the needs of the individual business functions and by the overall corporate strategy (that is, full, partial, or minimal integration). Other corporate-wide mandates that drive activity in this area include direction on process redesign, application rationalization, and synergy goal achievement.

In a divestiture, significant planning and effort will be required to produce a transition services agreement (TSA) to guarantee access to key business-support services while replacement capabilities are being built. Each area of the business needs to be consulted during the development of these agreements to define what business functions need to be supported, for what duration, and at what level of service. The TSA, which looks and functions much like an outsourcing contract, needs to be drafted to make sure no interruptions in key services take place while both entities perform the activities required to allow complete stand-alone operations. The TSA will clearly define the scope of services, performance standards, service-level agreements, and fees. The TSA will be valid for a set period of time and will frequently contain large penalties if services need to be extended. Proper analysis and planning are key to reducing additional cost in this area. (See Chapters 14 and 16 for detailed discussion of TSAs.)

In a merger, the approach to integrating the process and technology aspects of the two formerly separate entities presents a much more complex set of problems driven by the need to combine multiple organizations. Having a clear strategy communicated by leadership will assist IT in developing the appropriate systems integration plan, approach, and governance.

Regardless of the type of M&A transaction, the IT tasks are typically complex and require a broad set of project management tools (for example, project plan, issues log, readiness assessments, and phase approval gates) that provide the structure required to complete the project on schedule. Focusing on the details for each task, such as dependencies, resources, and timing, will allow IT to build a comprehensive plan to manage M&A activity. It is important to maintain the involvement of cross-functional resources whenever changes are required to the plan to help ensure that all affected parties are included in any resolution decisions. The structure and rigor implemented to support task completion facilitates on-time completion of activities and the early identification of issues.

Within the three primary integration strategies (described earlier in this chapter), further guidance will be provided by leadership to form a framework to make IT and functional decisions. Organizations generally adopt one of the following three approaches to managing changes to processes and supporting technology:

1. Adopting the acquiring organization's processes and supporting technology:
   - This is the most common approach where the acquiring organization is significantly larger than the acquired entity.
   - Emphasis in this approach is on the successful conversion of MDM and transactional data.
2. Adopting the acquired organization's processes and supporting technology:
   - Though less frequently seen, this approach is adopted when the transaction involves two entities closer in scale where the smaller entity has implemented processes or technologies that provide a significant strategic business advantage.
   - Again, the emphasis in this approach is on the successful conversion of MDM and transactional data.
3. Adopting a best-of-breed approach:
   - Organizations will, at times, view the M&A activity as an opportunity to completely reevaluate business process and supporting technology.
   - This effort begins with business process reengineering activity and developing a new set of process flows, followed by an assessment of the technology required to support the to-be state.

The first two options provide clearer paths and shorter timelines to complete integration activity compared to the best-of-breed approach. The best-of-breed approach provides an opportunity for the organization to reevaluate every aspect of how the new entity will operate.

Architecture, Databases, and Networking

IT Infrastructure   IT should determine how best to support business processes in an environment that differs significantly from the current state based on the addition of a significant numbers of new users and the need to manage an entirely new set of applications. An analysis of the current infrastructure, including existing telecommunications, network, storage, applications, and disaster recovery capabilities, generally is required. Generating accurate data on existing capabilities will allow IT to identify gaps between current and future state and to begin related planning activity. Data from this analysis, in combination with to-be process documentation, will provide data required by IT to develop architecture and infrastructure plans to support to-be business processes. It is important to begin this activity as early as possible to account for the lead times, which can be months, required to update the foundational elements needed to support integration and operations activity.

Conversely, this same assessment in a divestiture situation will allow IT to identify where excess capacity now exists. That surplus could be retained to support future growth or allow IT to downsize and reduce cost. (See Chapter 14, which contains an overview of M&A-related infrastructure topics.)

Instance Management   Over the course of an M&A engagement, IT will be called upon to provide environments to support a wide range of project activities, including development, integration testing, user acceptance, training, and configuration. Providing these instances at the time they are required and in a state that supports the intended activity (for example, configured, required data staged, interfaces enabled) is key to keeping to the project timeline and to the overall success of the project. If an automated configuration management tool is not being used, the time required for functional resources to update the environment should be factored into the schedule.

If the instances are externally hosted, significant costs may be incurred on a per-instance basis. The instance management plan should take this cost impact into account and not include any instances that are not supporting a specific business activity.

Server and Network Management   Merger and acquisition activity will impact data volumes across the organizations. The technology department should assess the current capacity of key infrastructure components, such as servers and network, to determine whether the needs of the business can be met. Available capacity in the future state should include capacity sufficient to support ongoing operations, with excess capacity available to manage spikes in demand. Changes to the number of users, transactional volume, application footprint, and even geographical location will drive infrastructure requirements.

Lead times to plan and execute infrastructure changes can be weeks or months long depending on the scale of the activity and whether the capabilities are managed in-house or externally. Identifying significant changes early in the integration process allows IT to begin work on infrastructure changes, enabling the IT transition tasks to be completed in the shortest possible timeframe with the smallest negative business impact.

Application Administration

Rationalization Strategy   After the completion of a merger transaction, IT will find itself in a situation where two different applications are in use to accomplish the same task or support the same process, such as payroll. Organizing this "Noah's Ark" of applications is a much easier task to complete if a framework is in place to support the decision-making process. Corporate strategy and guidance, combined with a set of evaluation criteria, will provide structure and consistency in rationalizing these applications. Some examples of criteria frequently used to support application rationalization decisions are:

- Business criticality of the application.
- Applicability to current and future processes.
- Operational supportability and sustainability.
- Vendor viability assessment.
- Usage, maintenance, and licensing cost.
- Compatibility with current ERP.

Chapter 12 has an in-depth analysis of applications rationalization strategies.

Application Support   Application support strategy and approach are driven by a number of factors, including integration strategy, process reengineering, and application rationalization. The factors will drive the number and type of applications that require IT support. Technology personnel needs to work closely with human resources to provide recruiting information to fill any gaps in application knowledge required to support new applications. Additionally, the current staffing levels for existing applications need to be analyzed to help ensure the workload generated by additional uses is manageable and service-level commitments can be met. Last, the support systems used by IT to log and resolve issues should be assessed to determine whether projected increases in volume are supportable or improvements to the systems are required.

Communications

The following IT-related components support high-visibility areas, and any issues will be readily apparent: telephony, portals and websites, and e-mail. It is critical for IT to effectively plan, manage, and execute updates to these communications-related systems. IT should work closely with business representation, particularly on customer-facing elements, to help ensure that mission-critical systems are ready to support business processes and facilitate customer interaction.

Telephony Inbound customer instructions provided via interactive voice response (IVR) should be updated to provide direction to both new and existing customers. If support calls are handled through a single number, the call tree should be updated to route calls to appropriate support groups. Standard recordings providing general information (for example, hours of operation) need to be updated to reflect any name changes to the new entity.

Portals and Web The internal and external web presence of the new entity needs to be updated to support the needs of both customers and employees. Externally, the web pages should include any rebranding or changes to visual identity and provide clear instructions to support customer inquiries. Internally, the web pages frequently include information dedicated to transition support, providing new employees with links to onboarding procedures, corporate policies, and benefits information.

Depending on the complexity of the websites and the volume of data involved, a gradual process of combining web content will be implemented to transition to a single website over time. Once the transition is complete, the older website is mapped to the new website where all customer interaction is managed.

E-Mail Many individuals' day-to-day business lives are e-mail-centric. Transitioning acquired employees to new e-mail addresses should be a seamless process and involves the coordination of human resources and IT. To maintain business continuity and mitigate the impact of this change on customers, old e-mail addresses generally remain functional for a period of time determined by the organization.

If executed properly, the management of IT components in an M&A transaction will largely go unnoticed by most of the organization. Paychecks will arrive, e-mails will be delivered, and system-supported transactions will be processed as if nothing has changed. If not properly planned, tracked, managed, and executed, the business impact will be highly visible and have significant detrimental impact on business operations. It is critical that IT includes all internal customers in the planning, approach definition, execution, and management of M&A activity. Understanding the requirements from these groups will enable IT to provide the supporting infrastructure and applications required to effectively operate the future state of the new organization.

WRAPPING IT UP

The success of the merger, acquisition, or divestiture activity is dependent on the organization developing an effective management framework that provides structure during a period of great change and upheaval within the organization. This framework should contain a well-thought-out strategy, a clearly defined approach, and governance mechanisms that provide sufficient rigor. During steady-state operations, organizations find developing this type of management framework and maintaining the linkages between the components to be difficult. The importance of having these elements in place is magnified during the execution of M&A activity.

Each of the four key functional areas—finance, operations, HR, and IT—has a significant impact on the overall success of the transaction. While IT frequently is the function most affected as a result of merger or acquisition, it is important to keep finance, operations, and HR fully involved in the planning and execution of the transaction. The transaction should never be viewed as an IT-only endeavor.

The coordination between IT and all of its customers can facilitate a seamless transition, whether that includes the addition of a new company or the divestiture of a business unit. The changes required to IT systems and applications—such as e-mail, human capital management (HCM), customer relationship management (CRM), and enterprise resource planning (ERP)—are driven by the needs of each internal organization. The effective planning and execution of M&A-driven IT tasks cannot be completed in a vacuum, without contributions from resources across the organization.

If a company does not align its approach to post-merger integration with its overall strategy, the benefits or synergies that were planned have a limited chance of being realized. IT integration may never be the primary driver of a merger or acquisition, but it is almost always listed as one of the key areas for rationalization and review. It takes hard work to make sure IT strategy is aligned with corporate strategy, but it can be a key enabler and positive differentiator in mergers and acquisitions.

The coordination among IT, finance, operations, and HR and the implementation of strategy, approach, and governance components are critical success factors in completing an M&A transition. If executed properly, these elements work in concert to help make sure the business-driven system changes cause the least amount of disruption possible and optimize the effectiveness of the new combined organization.

Information Technology's Role in Mergers, Acquisitions, and Divestitures

CHAPTER 5

IT Due Diligence Leading Practices

Mark Andrews
David Sternberg

Executing an M&A IT due diligence assessment is the same as performing a typical IT assessment, right? No. In fact, there are a number of challenges that are faced during the M&A cycle that an IT department would not normally experience during a typical IT assessment project. A due diligence project usually operates at an accelerated pace with a fixed deadline and with limited information at the team's disposal. In these circumstances, a well-defined process is a must in order to allow the team to handle curveballs as they are thrown.

Another consideration is how much firepower management needs to throw at the process. The decision could take away from the IT department's ability to keep the lights on. However, reduced IT involvement in the pre-deal process can be extremely costly in the long term. Potential buyers that overlook, or minimize, IT due diligence during a proposed transaction often pay a high price later on through unexpected conversion costs, consolidation methods, or environment improvements. Of course, no one wants to overspend on IT due diligence (or anything else for that matter), especially when the IT environment will be quickly replaced or changed.

The focus of this chapter is to help an IT department understand and address the processes, and nuances, involved in an IT due diligence assessment and arrive at an applicable balance of effort, cost, and speed. Discussion topics include:

- Objectives and complexities of IT due diligence.
- Areas of investigation.
- Considerations of planning IT due diligence.
- Considerations of conducting IT due diligence.
- Considerations of finalizing IT due diligence.
- Connecting due diligence findings to the next steps in the post-merger process.

OBJECTIVES AND COMPLEXITIES OF IT DUE DILIGENCE

The primary objective of an IT due diligence assessment is to understand those matters (risks or issues) that can have a material impact on the value of the target business and that need to be accounted for by the buyer prior to acquisition (and often planned for or addressed post-acquisition), such as:

- Identification of previously unknown or undisclosed risks and opportunities (e.g., departing intellectual property [IP]).
- Onetime IT costs to integrate the acquisition (e.g., setting up an ERP replacement system).
- Impact of the acquisition on recurring IT costs to run the business (e.g., maintenance costs of ERP licenses and support).
- Evaluation of opportunities such as IT-enabled synergies (e.g., rationalization of similar applications).

In addition to these specific points, IT due diligence provides an opportunity to collect information that can accelerate post-merger (or post-transaction) activities should the deal be completed—including critical Day 1 tasks and midterm and end-state visions. IT generally has the highest cost to achieve post-merger benefits; additionally, the majority of planned synergies in many deals are dependent upon the successful completion of a post-transaction IT initiative. So a lack of information discovered during the pre-deal process could make or break a deal.

Conducting IT due diligence is a complex and demanding activity. The difficulty of the work will depend on a number of factors, such as deal timeline, complexity of the buyer's and seller's IT environment, post-merger strategy, and transaction context (e.g., a carve-out transaction is typically more challenging due to shared resources and systems between the target business unit and the parent company). Additionally, IT due diligence can be challenging simply because of the short timeframe to conduct analysis, the lack of available information, and having little or no access to the target's IT management team. For these reasons, many traditional IT assessment methods and approaches may not be applicable to the IT due diligence process.

The level of effort and the number of resources required to conduct a due diligence assessment can be estimated more effectively by understanding potential project characteristics and complexities, including those identified in Exhibit 5.1.

Although the focus of this chapter is primarily geared toward buy-side due diligence activities (due diligence performed by the buying company on a particular target company), many of the same attributes can translate to IT-related sell-side due diligence (due diligence activities conducted from the seller company's perspective). That being said, if the IT due diligence team is

EXHIBIT 5.1 Potential Project Characteristics and Associated Complexities

Criteria		Considerations That Can Impact Level of Complexity
Deal Type	Full acquisition	Dependencies on the other factors noted below (often full acquisitions are a more straightforward deal type).
	Joint venture	Greater coordination may be required when both parties are performing due diligence assessments at the same time.
		Future integration road map may be unclear, resulting in more complex cost/synergy estimate analysis.
		Post-transaction reporting requirements and plans need to be accounted for.
	Carve-out	Identification of shared resources (which may need to be replaced) and their associated replacement costs.
		Could be a requirement for transition services agreements (TSAs). (See Chapters 14 and 16 for additional information on TSAs.)
Integration Requirements	Target entity is planned to be integrated into buyer's environment (or vice versa)	IT resources and systems may require rationalization.
		Thorough system scalability assessments may be required (because users may be transferred to an existing buyer or seller system).
		Future integration road map may be unclear, resulting in more complex cost/synergy estimate analysis.
Target Size	Not significant in comparison to buyer	Less time may be required to review and finalize disposition because of smaller IT footprint.
		May affect integration requirements (may be more likely to choose buyer's systems).
	Significant in comparison to buyer	Time requirements may be greater because there is more information to review.
		May affect integration requirements (may be more difficult to determine if buyer's systems will be the end-state platforms).
IT Landscape	Low complexity	May allow for quicker dispositions.
	High complexity	Level of interdependencies between systems and processes may require more time.
		May require support from buyer subject matter advisers or external resources.
Timing	Sufficient time	More time allows for a greater ability to drill down into concerning areas.
	Limited time	Quickly need to assess what is most important to deal team, and drive toward finding the most critical issues that could affect the deal.

on the sell side, many activities can be performed before the buyer interacts with the seller. These activities should include the collection and preparation of data room documentation, including a determination of what level of detail should be shared with the buyer. Careful data preparation provides confidence to potential buyers because it shows that the target company has mature documentation and processes and is being transparent and willing to share information. Overall, appropriate data preparation can accelerate the IT due diligence process for the benefit of all.

AREAS OF INVESTIGATION

IT due diligence requires the review and analysis of several aspects of the IT domain, which are illustrated in Exhibit 5.2. Typically, approximately 80 percent of the due diligence effort may be placed on people, process, and spending; applications; and infrastructure. The remaining 20 percent generally is tailored to the particular situation or some out-of-the-ordinary feature(s) of the buyer and/or target. The analysis scope may then be further refined based on the type of buyer (strategic vs. financial), deal type (full purchase, carve-out, or joint venture), level of integration required, or due diligence scope (back office vs. proprietary technology). In this last aspect, proprietary technology due diligence focuses on assessing custom-developed systems that are either a main driver of company revenues or directly supporting a company's core services.

People, Process, and Spending

Understand the organization that supports business operations, the standard policies and procedures that guide IT delivery, the IT strategy, and the historical and expected costs for IT maintenance and delivery.

Exhibit 5.3 summarizes specific areas to investigate and common findings across the people, process, and spending aspects of the IT domain.

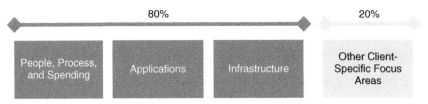

EXHIBIT 5.2   Areas of IT Due Diligence Investigation
Copyright © 2012 Deloitte Development LLC

EXHIBIT 5.3 People, Process, and Spending: Illustrative Areas of Investigation and Findings

Topic	Illustrative Areas of Investigation	Illustrative Findings
Operating Model	Is IT managed to deliver value to the business?	Lean IT organization that will require expansion to suitably support future growth plans.
	Is the IT organization sufficient to support the current business and expected growth?	
	What is the mix of staff skills and experience? Are there any areas where IT staff support is limited?	Staff to proactively target for retention post-transaction.
	Is there sufficient redundancy or cross-training on critical knowledge areas?	Areas where institutional knowledge has been lost or is at risk.
	Are there succession plans for staff?	
	Is IT leadership capable and well suited for successfully driving the company's IT strategy and operation?	IT skills are not aligned with current/future requirements.
	Are there planned or anticipated changes to the company's operating model?	Staff turnover is abnormally high.
		Lack of a dedicated leader.
Vendors and Contracts	What services are provided by external vendors?	Noncurrent software licenses.
	What contingency plans are in place if the vendor needs to be replaced?	Expired contracts.
	Does each vendor sufficiently meet company needs, and are their rates competitive?	Contracts that are nontransferable.
	How well are strategic vendor relationships managed?	
	How flexible are the current vendor contracts?	
	Are all software licenses current?	
Processes and Controls	Are the IT processes and controls well defined and documented?	Lack of disaster recovery and other documented processes.
	Are IT processes sufficient for supporting proper alignment with company strategy and effective management of company IT?	Processes are not comprehensive.
	Do company policies and controls promote compliance with industry and regulatory standards (e.g., HIPAA, PCI)?	Audits have uncovered critical issues that have not been remediated.
	What security/privacy protocols are in place at the company?	IT operations are not monitored or not run in an effective and efficient manner.
	Have there been any historical security breaches? Are policies in place to deal with breaches?	
	How often are IT operations metrics reviewed?	

(*Continued*)

EXHIBIT 5.3 (*Continued*)

Topic	Illustrative Areas of Investigation	Illustrative Findings
IT Strategy and Projects	How well do planned initiatives align with business needs? What enhancements or changes to IT are planned or needed? What projects do not align with buyer's post-transaction integration plans, IT environment, or IT strategy?	Lack of an IT road map. Projects that do not add business value. Planned or in-flight projects that may need to be placed on hold or deferred until the transaction and integration have been completed.
IT Spending	Does the technology spend seem reasonable and appropriate? What future investments in company IT are planned or may be needed? Have there been any significant variances in the operating budget year-over-year? Have there been any unusual or unexpected costs related to software or infrastructure that have occurred recently?	Capital expenditures and operating expenditures are disproportionate to comparative companies or historical trends. Unexplained variances in year-over-year costs.

Applications

A company's application landscape—in particular business/operations systems—is central to running a company's operations. Therefore, significant effort should be spent on this aspect of the IT domain during the due diligence effort. Understand how applications support the company's business, dependencies on other applications (internal and external), any risks that could prevent the systems from effectively supporting the future business model, and any investment required to mitigate those risks.

Exhibit 5.4 summarizes areas to investigate and common findings across the application aspect of the IT domain.

Infrastructure

Exhibit 5.5 summarizes areas to investigate and common findings with respect to the company's infrastructure.

EXHIBIT 5.4 Applications: Illustrative Areas of Investigation and Findings

Topic	Illustrative Areas of Investigation	Illustrative Findings
Application Landscape	What are the major IT applications used to support the business? What business functionality is supported by each system, and are there any areas where system support is lacking (i.e., require manual processes)? What system interfaces and dependencies are in place, and how complex are they? What is the level of system stability, availability, and scalability?	Frequent system availability or reliability issues. Complex application suites. System is not readily scalable. System has known security holes. Noncompliant IT systems. Significant level of user complaints. Buildup of technical debt.
Commercial Applications	What version of each application is in use, and what other underlying technology is required? What license, maintenance, and support agreements are there for each application? What is the level of customization?	Obsolete applications. Significant number of systems customizations that make it difficult to maintain or upgrade the system.
Custom-Developed Applications	What technology is used to develop each system? What software development process and coding practices are in place? What is the level of scalability, reliability, maintainability, and security of the systems? Does the system support the required functionality to have parity with comparative systems? Does the system design and architecture support the preceding attributes of the system?	Obsolete technologies that constrain system performance or enhancement options. Poorly documented systems and other maintainability problems. System is unlikely to have the capability to scale to future business requirements. System has a significant level of technical debt that may need a significant effort to mitigate.
Ad Hoc Tools	Are any business processes supported by ad hoc tools (e.g., Excel spreadsheets)?	Business process limitations that require system enhancement investments to support business growth or more efficient operations. Data inconsistencies due to manual data entry errors.

EXHIBIT 5.5   Infrastructure: Illustrative Areas of Investigation and Findings

Topic	Illustrative Areas of Investigation	Illustrative Findings
Data Center, Servers, Workstations, Telecommunications, Networks, and Other Devices	What is the state of the data center environment (HVAC, power, backup power, backup generator, etc.)? What level of excess capacity is in the data center? What is the composition of the company's IT asset inventory (including existing assets, useful life, and refresh/replacement expectations)? What type of network connections and bandwidth does the company have? What is the current utilization of servers, storage, and network capacity?	Obsolete servers, workstations, network appliances. Historical lack of investment in infrastructure. Future infrastructure investment requirements to maintain technology currency or support expected growth.
Infrastructure Management	How does the company support system availability and performance monitoring? What is the level of redundancy in servers, storage, network, and data center HVAC and power? Does the company have established data backup and disaster recovery procedures? What information security mechanisms are in place at the company?	Limited or no disaster recovery capability. Reliability issues. No redundancy in data center or data backups. Insecure data center.

PROPRIETARY OR PRODUCT TECHNOLOGY–DRIVEN DUE DILIGENCE

With the proliferation of companies whose core operations *are* their IT systems, there is an increasing number of IT due diligence efforts focused on assessing proprietary technology. The overall evaluation areas in a proprietary due diligence are the same as those covered previously, but with additional depth of analysis and specific measures focused on assessing the architecture, maintainability, reliability, scalability, and security of the

---

• **Product strategy** and product value versus select competitors.

• **Organizational effectiveness and maturity** of product management, development, and support teams.

• **Functionality** of the system is appropriate within the industry domain.

• **Architecture**—the design of both the software and hardware components of the system that enable reliability, scalability, and maintainability.

• **Reliability** and the impact to the client (and the company) of the software and/or services becoming unstable.

• **Scalability** and the ability to add new customers and clients as the business expands.

• **Maintainability** and the level of complexity (and resulting cost) to incorporate bug fixes and enhancements.

• **Age/viability** of underlying software, system, and service environments.

EXHIBIT 5.6   Proprietary Technology Considerations

custom platforms that the company delivers to its clients. In addition to these more technical characteristics of proprietary technology, the due diligence team should investigate the functionality of the platform and assess whether it provides parity against its market competitors. If any of the factors noted in Exhibit 5.6 are found to be inadequate, the platform may require significant time and resources to bring it back to the level necessary to drive business operations effectively.

IMPACT OF TRANSACTION TYPE ON THE DUE DILIGENCE INVESTIGATION

As illustrated in Exhibit 5.7, transaction type also plays a role in determining relevant investigation areas. For special transaction types, such as carve-outs or joint ventures, due diligence analysis is still required across each of the IT investigation domains. However, the buyer should consider additional situation-specific areas such as shared seller resources or systems and transition support requirements.

EXHIBIT 5.7 Transaction Type: Illustrative Areas of Investigation and Findings

Topic	Illustrative Areas of Investigation	Illustrative Findings
Carve-Out: Separation and Stand-Up	What staff, applications, and infrastructure are provided by or shared with the parent? What is planned for inclusion with the transaction? Which licenses cannot transfer with the transaction? What interfaces will need to be disentangled? What transition services are being contemplated and for what length of time? What are the estimated onetime investment and recurring costs for a stand-alone IT environment?	Shared resources will need to be replaced. Specific human resources will not accompany the transaction, resulting in a loss of operational efficiency (due to lack of IP). The seller has not fully vetted out TSAs to be offered. There is a significant difference between the seller's estimated costs and the buyer's estimated costs.
Joint Venture	What is the expected breakdown of IT responsibilities, systems, and funding from each partner going forward? Are there IT systems and processes present with one organization that have better functionality, scalability, and other attributes that align with the deal team's future strategy?	Organization support and future IT strategy expectations do not align. Post-transaction reporting requirements have not been determined between the two entities.

INVESTIGATION FOR STRATEGIC BUYERS VERSUS FINANCIAL BUYERS

Overall, the due diligence team should focus on the same areas regardless of whether they are supporting a financial buyer or a strategic buyer. However, the team's lens should be different.

Strategic buyers tend to be more interested in the details of the target company's IT environment, since they will have to decide whether to operate the environment on a stand-alone basis post-merger or to integrate it into their existing organization. In the event an integrated environment is chosen, the team will need to document the specifics of each aspect of the IT domain (organization, processes, applications, and infrastructure). They will also need to determine potential synergies between buyer and target IT environments, including the rationalization of resources, processes, and systems, which should all be evaluated in more detail during the post-merger phase.

Financial buyers are typically interested in making an investment that has a defined exit strategy (with the hope of making a profit). Oftentimes, a financial buyer will be fairly hands-off with the ongoing management of the target company, and, as a result, the buyer may care more about the short-term financial risks of the investment than the longer-term issues. For financial buyers, the team might perform an initial high-level review across each aspect of the IT domain, followed by a more targeted assessment in the specific areas that appear to have significant risk or cost impacts (including opportunities to gain cost efficiencies through IT investment).

CONSIDERATIONS OF PLANNING IT DUE DILIGENCE

Before the team starts down the path of determining any risks or opportunities in the IT environment, consider the following practices that can help promote a more effective due diligence effort.

Prepare in Advance

As already noted, M&A due diligence efforts tend to move very quickly. Fortunately, IT due diligence assessments share many of the same elements across projects. As a result, the advance preparation of detailed document templates and question sets is both feasible and beneficial. Not only can these templates expedite the creation of more customized documents, but they can also promote consistency across future projects. As new information is gathered, the due diligence team should enhance its template library to strengthen its due diligence process and capabilities.

By their nature, due diligence efforts have high levels of unpredictability. Much of this volatility stems from the fact that the target company and deal team have their own priorities, objectives, and other requirements that are unknown to the due diligence team. In addition, these groups' goals could even be in conflict with each other. This can result in the characteristics of the due diligence assessment (including information needs and deadlines) changing throughout the project. For instance, the target may not send important follow-up information in a timely manner, and, at the same time, the deal team is asking for your final disposition in an hour! Although not all situations have one solution, having a consistent process and governance model can enable due diligence practitioners to prepare for the expected issues and handle complications as gracefully as possible.

Pick the Right Team

Choose a team comprising the following individuals:

- *Core team members* who combine strong general IT knowledge with an understanding of process, considerations, and approach required to make M&A due diligence and transactions a success.
- *Subject matter advisers (SMAs)* who supplement the core team with deeper expertise in an IT or industry subject area that is critical to the transaction.
- *Strategic buyer-side IT leadership* should be actively (and promptly) engaged with the due diligence team, especially for buyers looking to integrate the target into the buyer's organization.

Team members (especially the core team) should be aware of, or at least prepped regarding, the particular expectations of an M&A project—including extreme responsiveness, precision, and flexibility.

The core team will need to seek out subject matter advisers (SMAs) for those areas that require deeper expertise. For instance, if a target company uses an ERP technology that the core team is not familiar with, that may be a good opportunity to bring in an adviser. Core team members are the glue that holds the IT project together. Even if there is an SMA on the team, it is generally a good idea for the core team to have some level of understanding of the subject matter (even if it is an introductory lesson on the Internet!). SMAs may not be familiar with M&A concepts, and this context is important in providing an appropriate disposition. The goal is to have the best team for the job.

Often IT leadership is forced to work reactively during the M&A cycle. In fact, they may be presented with integration timeframes and synergy targets that were established without their involvement. Without the appropriate IT leadership oversight, the many complexities of post-merger activities and costs can be vastly underestimated. Involving buyer IT leadership (especially for strategic buyers) brings several benefits to the due diligence team, such as providing the deal team insight into future IT integration plans (which helps drive more directed and effective evaluation) and providing a source that can identify and vet integration and synergy scenarios.

Understand the Project Context

Although due diligence projects may follow a similar framework, many different attributes of the deal (identified earlier in Exhibit 5.1) can affect where the due diligence team should focus their efforts. For example, deal type (full purchase, carve-out, or joint venture) and planned level of integration can affect the level of separation and transition considerations (including required transition services) and/or synergies between target and buyer IT. It is therefore important for the due diligence team to properly understand project context and to ask situation-appropriate questions.

Establish Expectations Up Front

The fast pace and high expectations of a due diligence effort leave less room for error than the team may see on other types of IT projects. Consequently, the IT due diligence team leader should set expectations up front with both the IT due diligence team and the deal team. Setting these expectations will help stakeholders move forward in a coordinated fashion in regard to the process and deliverables.

The IT due diligence team leader should work with each team member to confirm members' project roles and responsibilities (e.g., topics to cover, deliverable responsibility), and discuss any relevant information provided from the deal team (or other information sources).

In addition, the due diligence team leader should work with the deal team to confirm the business rationale, transaction objectives, and due diligence priorities, and may ask questions such as:

- Will the target company plan to be integrated (to some extent) into the buyer's organization (or one of its subsidiaries), or will it operate in a stand-alone environment?
- What is the transaction timeline, and when will the investment committee require the due diligence disposition?
- What is the proposed timeline of the postclose activities?
- What are the preliminary expectations regarding the integration or rationalization of target IT staff, applications, and infrastructure (if this is an integration project)?

Use Benchmarks (When Appropriate)

Given limited access to data, IT costs estimates should be compiled with a focus on critical domains. The IT due diligence team can leverage benchmarks to rapidly assess these focal areas and help estimate these costs. However, the team should utilize benchmarks with care, as factors unique to each organization's specific situation can significantly impact a company's actual spending needs.

CONSIDERATIONS OF CONDUCTING IT DUE DILIGENCE

Each IT due diligence step builds upon itself with the ultimate intent of gaining as much significant information as possible. Although the due diligence team may never obtain all of the required information (even in the best of circumstances), the conducting phase, the heart of the due diligence process, will help the team to reach a final disposition. The team should consider the upcoming items as they address this phase.

Perform Initial Research on the Target Company

Initial research allows the IT due diligence team to establish a basic foundation of knowledge and to develop preliminary project assumptions and hypotheses. In fact, these assumptions and hypotheses, along with other gaps in specific information, will form the basis for upcoming data requests and interviews.

When a due diligence project is first initiated, the data room, or document repository where target company data files are stored, may not be available or may have limited documentation. As a result, the IT due diligence team may also need to explore the following sources for potential information about the target:

- Company website (including investor relations and annual reporting for public companies).
- IT job listings for the company (these may give insight into the technologies used at the company).
- News and analyst research articles.
- Social networking and media sites (the company may post information or the due diligence team may be able to gather information regarding IT staff).

Develop a Concise Data Request

A data request is a concise document that can be used to gain access to resources and information required for the due diligence process. Items contained in the data request document should be limited to information that has not yet been asked of or proactively provided by the target company to date (to the extent possible). The due diligence team should develop an initial data request (for items such as those in Exhibit 5.8) with the intent of gaining a high-level understanding of the target's IT environment. Supplemental data requests should have targeted, specific questions.

> - Provide information on the IT organization, including outsourced vendor relationships.
> - Provide a description of the IT strategy and any documented IT policies and processes (data retention, performance monitoring, risk/control, etc.) in place within the organization.
> - Provide an inventory of software applications, including primary business functionality, version and licenses, customization, platform/architecture, level of scalability and redundancy, and hosting and support arrangements.
> - Provide an application architecture diagram showing the interfaces between the applications (and modules) in use.
> - Provide a summary-level inventory of infrastructure components (servers, workstations, networking, etc.) showing location, age, current utilization, and expected replacement dates.
> - Provide the company's disaster recovery plan.

EXHIBIT 5.8   Initial Data Request

Because the deal process generally is highly confidential, a limited number of target company staff (such as the CIO) may be involved in the project. As a result, the due diligence team should be sensitive to the fact that these individuals may be constrained in the information they can ask from people unaware of the transaction (in order to avoid suspicion that "something is going on").

Also, the due diligence team should limit going back to the target with multiple requests—the seller can become overwhelmed and even ultimately unresponsive. If it is already available, the team should follow the data request process set up by the deal team so that requests are promptly sent to the target. If data requests are not being responded to in a timely fashion, the due diligence team should escalate this concern to the deal team. Keep in mind that a lack of data could also be a sign that the IT environment is not very mature.

Review the Data Room

When the due diligence team is granted access to the data room (permission should always be confirmed with the deal team), the folder structure will typically be partitioned into different functions, often including financials, human resources, legal, and, of course, information technology. Although most IT data may reside in folders labeled "Information Technology," the due diligence team should check other folders in the data room where critical IT documents may reside (see Exhibit 5.9). For instance, IT budgets may be in the "Finance" folder. The team should check the data room frequently for updates, as documents may come in a sporadic fashion. One day the team

Finance	• IT budgets • Historical IT expenses • Fixed asset inventory • Audit controls
HR	• IT organization charts • Target employee count • Employee locations • IT CVs • IT job responsibilities • Employee roster (often with salary)
Legal	• IT contracts (applications, infrastructure, services, etc.) • Intellectual property inventory
Real Estate	• Data center locations
Other	• Confident information memorandum • Management presentations • Business process narratives

EXHIBIT 5.9   Sources of "Hidden" IT Information

may receive 20 documents; the next day, nothing. If the target's data room has the ability to send alerts when new files are added, the team should take advantage of this feature.

After reviewing the data room, the due diligence team should capture its initial findings and questions for the target in a draft summary document. This document can be updated as the due diligence project progresses and act as a base for the final report.

Develop a Comprehensive Interview Process

The interview process enables the IT due diligence team to follow up on questions they have developed after reviewing available documentation. The due diligence team should request access to the highest-ranking IT officer of the target company and any other IT members who can provide an understanding of the IT environment. It is the responsibility of the target company to provide the appropriate resources in order for the acquirer to make a determination of risks. As noted earlier, the target may limit the number of employees who are aware of a pending transaction. IT individuals who are "over the fence" (i.e., aware of the transaction), such as the CIO, may not have full knowledge of all operational workings of each IT area. In this case, some questions may need to be followed up in a supplemental data request so that these questions can be asked under cover.

Preparing interview questions in advance is essential and can have a direct impact on the entire tone of the meeting. If the team is prepared, they may be able to more quickly think of follow-up questions to the target company's initial responses. The questions asked should be subtle unless the interviewee is being evasive. For example, instead of asking, "Does your department deliver value to the business?" the team should ask more focused questions such as, "Have you had any challenges meeting business requirements or know of challenges that may develop in the near future?" Questions should be concise (although, time permitting, open-ended questions should be used so as not to "lead the witness") and should be prioritized because time with the target management team is usually limited. In addition, the interview process provides an opportunity to create a positive impression on the target about the acquirer and can help to identify initial cultural differences between the two entities.

Similar to creating data requests, the due diligence team should develop a high-level agenda for the initial meeting with the target IT management team, which can set the stage for asking a broader set of questions. In follow-up meetings, the agenda should be more focused. For consistency, it often makes sense to use similar agenda topics in line with the team's earlier data request. Again, to limit the frustration of the target management team, the due diligence team should avoid asking the same questions repeatedly—unless they believe there is a need for further clarification.

Meetings can be either over the phone or in person. In-person meetings are often preferred, because the due diligence team can see the person's reactions to their questions. Although ideal, these types of meetings are not always possible. The team should consider the following factors when deciding whether an in-person meeting is required:

- Availability of due diligence team and target personnel.
- Size of the project.
- Budgetary constraints.
- Any discovered risks that require additional tactile/visual due diligence, such as a complicated proprietary tool that requires whiteboarding.
- An IT data center review.

When going to an on-site target location, the due diligence team must be sensitive to the extreme confidentiality required. This includes items such as:

- Having a cover story when arriving.
- Not talking about the deal (or any related information) in shared corridors or elevators.
- Not wearing anything with a buyer's logo.

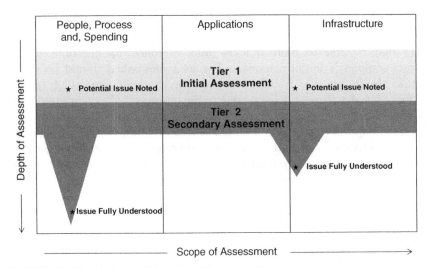

EXHIBIT 5.10   Utilize a Tiered and Iterative Process

To be more cost effective, a tiered approach should be applied to the conducting phase, as illustrated in Exhibit 5.10.

In this case, the due diligence team performed a high-level initial assessment (Tier 1) across all aspects of the target's IT environment. During that assessment, they found two potential issues (could be risks or opportunities). Tier 2 involved going down another layer across all aspects of the environment (which is typical, but not always warranted), as well as more vigorous effort around the perceived areas of potential risk. This methodology can be used repeatedly (each tier drilling down on potential issues) until the due diligence team is familiar with the target's IT environment and fully comprehends each area of potential risk and opportunity.

From a tactical perspective and depending on the project timeline (dictated by the deal team), several data requests and conversations with the target management team may be required. The sizes of the shaded areas of Exhibit 5.10 represent effort (or expense) associated with each tier of the assessment. So, using this approach can identify potential issues at a deeper level with the least amount of exertion.

CONSIDERATIONS OF FINALIZING IT DUE DILIGENCE

When compiling the final IT due diligence report, the team should consider the findings from any IT due diligence interviews, advice from advisers, information identified in the data room, and any cost estimation performed. The magnitudes of significant risks and opportunities should be assessed based on these findings. As part of the initial preparation for this report, the due diligence team should understand what the deal team is expecting and prioritize findings as appropriate. It is not uncommon for these requirements to change—one day the deal team may want just a high-level summary, and the next day they may want detailed information.

As part of the due diligence team's analysis, the deal team will want to understand if there are any significant onetime costs that impact the more immediate deal valuation, and also those costs that could affect the IT environment post-merger (both onetime and recurring costs).

Due to the multiple variables associated with cost estimation, it is not practical for the due diligence team to identify exact costs of matters discovered during IT due diligence. Examples of reasons why variations in cost occur include vendor pricing, level of functionality, level of quality, discount rates applied, and other factors. Therefore, cost estimates provided to the deal team should be order-of-magnitude ranges. To help with cost analysis efforts, there are multiple resources that the IT due diligence team should consider utilizing, such as IT core team member experience, adviser experience, vendor websites or discussions, benchmarks, and other Internet sources. As this can be a fairly extensive process, the team should allow adequate time to prepare and research the different elements of its IT cost model.

If the deal is a complete purchase, estimates should focus on any onetime or recurring costs to mitigate risks or opportunities found during the due diligence process. If the deal is a carve-out, the due diligence team's estimates should also include replacing resources, systems, and services performed by the parent company that are not planned to accompany the transaction.

If the transaction involves establishing a joint venture or any level of integration between the two entities, the due diligence team should develop a preliminary IT integration approach in line with the deal team's future business strategy. Based on this information, the team should provide an estimate of incremental onetime or recurring IT costs associated with the integration efforts, as well as any costs that may be rationalized (i.e., synergies).

When providing cost estimates (and regardless of deal type), it is essential for the due diligence team to document assumptions and to have a deep understanding of how the estimates may change if the assumptions do not hold true.

Finally, as part of its due diligence report, the team should include any open matters that need further investigation in the next phases of the project (if the deal moves forward).

TYING DUE DILIGENCE TO THE NEXT STEPS IN THE POST-MERGER PROCESS

Up to this point, this chapter has predominantly provided details on the due diligence process. But, how does the due diligence process tie to post-transaction activities (i.e., the next steps once a deal has been signed)?

Findings from the IT due diligence process will often reduce the surprises (i.e., costs) encountered during the postsigning phase of the project. Additional information may be discovered after the official due diligence phase has been completed; therefore, all assumptions and crucial decisions made during the due diligence phase should be revisited and validated.

To accelerate the post-transaction planning process, information that the team identified during the due diligence process should be mapped to the buyer's post-transaction plan. To aid in this mapping exercise, the buyer should consider including the due diligence team in the process. These individuals can provide valuable assistance to the broader team based on their historical knowledge of the target company's IT environment.

Exhibit 5.11 provides a list of due diligence outputs that can be tied to the next steps in the M&A process.

WRAPPING IT UP

IT due diligence is a vital step in identifying specific risks and opportunities associated with large-scale M&A transactions. Because of the various characteristics and nuances specific to these types of projects, corporate IT organizations cannot rely on the same processes they use to manage a non-M&A IT assessment. To be most effective, the IT due diligence team should understand the deal's objectives and context, have a defined process in place, and have the ability to translate the due diligence findings into appropriate post-transaction plans.

Furthermore, although it may not be immediately clear whether the transaction will move forward, deal teams should include the IT due diligence team as early as possible in the process. Analyzing the IT environment, identifying cost concerns, and addressing questions related to the post-transaction phase earlier in the process can mitigate many typical issues identified in less prepared M&A projects.

EXHIBIT 5.11 Opportunities to Leverage Due Diligence Outputs

IT Domain	Opportunity to Leverage Due Diligence Outputs
Strategy, Process, and Controls	Identify alternative IT processes and/or IT strategy (target company's vs. buyer's processes) for NewCo.
	Identify pool of controls (e.g., regulatory, vulnerability, and audit) that may need to be implemented for new company (NewCo).
	Identify current leading practices in place that could be leveraged by the buyer's organization.
	Identify critical IT support activities that need to be prioritized.
	Identify existing communication channels used within the existing IT organization that could be continued at NewCo.
	Carve-out: Identify how separation of IT environment might impact IT and business teams.
	Joint venture: Identify level of post-transaction reporting that will be required between the two entities.
Organization, Vendors, and Contracts	Identify need to hire new staff or the pool of existing staff that could be retained.
	Define high-level plan to transition from current IT operating model to end-state operating model vision.
	Identify need to contract with new vendors or retain existing vendors (for integration projects or ongoing support).
	Identify the pool of contracts that could be utilized in NewCo.
	Identify contracts that may need to be renegotiated, have termination costs, or have transfer costs.
	Carve-out: Identify critical resources and develop retention plan to limit disruption to business.
	Joint venture and carve-out: For all required contracts going forward, define the preferred options in terms of services provided and costs associated.
Budgeting and Projects	Identify order of magnitude of onetime and recurring costs to integrate the new organization.
	Identify potential projects that may continue after close.
	Identify potential new projects to be launched after close (e.g., due to gaps or issues identified during due diligence or due to stand-alone company or joint venture structure set up).
Applications	Identify the pool of applications that could be implemented at NewCo (target company's applications vs. buyer's applications).
	Identify the need to purchase any new application licenses.
	Identify applications that will require new or existing interfaces to other entities.
	Identify at a high level what systems and associated data could be integrated into the buyer's existing systems.
	Carve-out: Identify at a high level what systems and associated data will need to be separated from the target's parent company; identify any potential data separation issues.

(Continued)

EXHIBIT 5.11   (*Continued*)

IT Domain	Opportunity to Leverage Due Diligence Outputs
Infrastructure	Identify need for a new data center or ability to use an existing data center (target company's vs. buyer's data center).
	Identify underlying infrastructure required to support the target's applications.
	Identify the need to purchase new telecommunications equipment.
	Identify NewCo bandwidth requirements.
	Identify the need to purchase new workstations, cell phones, and so on.
	Identify at a high level what systems could be integrated into the buyer's existing systems.
	Carve-out: Identify at a high level what systems will need to be separated from the target's parent company.

References

Andrews, James M. 2010. "How Critical Is Information Technology to My Deal? (And How Much Should I Spend to Understand It?)." Deloitte.

Sternberg, David. 2012. "In IT Due Diligence, Scrutinize Proprietary Software." CIO Journal, *Wall Street Journal*, September 12.

IT Infrastructure Aspects of Mergers, Acquisitions, and Divestitures

Rick Kupcunas
Mike Trisko
Jeffry Sprengel
Mushtaque Heera

In many cases, when an organization is going through a merger, acquisition, or divestiture, the IT infrastructure will go through significant and rapid transformation. (Note: The IT infrastructure generally consists of hardware, networks, data center, and phone services. See the upcoming list for more component examples.) Several services the IT infrastructure supports will be high priorities for integration and/or separation by the time the transaction closes. A large number of synergies can often be quickly gained by combining, consolidating, and streamlining IT infrastructure assets and services.

The rapid transformation brought about by the transaction can be challenging for many organizations. For divestiture transactions, is also common for the IT infrastructure area to have one of the largest numbers of transition services agreements (TSAs) because of long lead times to fully transition and separate all of the IT infrastructure services. (See Chapters 14 and 16 for additional information on TSAs.) One of the contributing factors to this is the large number of dependencies among IT infrastructure, other IT functions, and each of the business functions.

IT INFRASTRUCTURE BLUEPRINTING

The first order of business when preparing for a merger, acquisition, or divestiture is to gather an inventory of all of the IT infrastructure components that are being transitioned from the seller to the buyer, and determine high-level target states for Day 1 and the end state. This process is referred to as IT infrastructure blueprinting and typically begins during the due diligence phase; once the deal has been signed with proper nondisclosure agreements in place, more detailed inventories can be shared and further planning can proceed.

Each business is different and will have its own IT infrastructure asset and service footprint. Typical IT infrastructure assets and services to consider include (but are not limited to):

- Data centers
- Hosting services
- Disaster recovery infrastructure and services
- Servers (both physical and virtual)
- Mainframes
- Storage infrastructure (e.g., storage area network [SAN])
- Databases and data infrastructure
- Backup or tape infrastructure
- Managed print services
- Batch processing
- Software licensing
- Hardware maintenance agreements
- Wide area network (WAN)
- Local area network (LAN)
- Internet services
- Web services (e.g., domain names)
- E-mail and messaging services
- Active directory
- Call center infrastructure
- Desktop and laptop computers
- Mobile devices (e.g., tablets, smartphones, cell phones)
- Telephony (e.g., voice over Internet protocol [VoIP], traditional private branch exchange [PBX])
- Help desk services

Based on the inventory gathered, high-level separation or integration strategies can be developed, and key milestones can be determined for the transition of each set of assets and services. It is critical to develop a crystal-clear vision of two key points during the transition—Day 1 and the desired end state—from each organization's perspective. For the merged entity, the end state represents the IT infrastructure architecture, services, organization, and operating model as it will exist after all integration activities are complete. For the seller of a carve-out, the end state represents the IT infrastructure as it will exist when all separation activities and TSAs are ended, with the buyer and the seller completely separate and independent.

The end state can vary based on the structure of the deal and the type of organization acquiring the business. For example, a private equity organization acquiring a business unit may require that an independent IT infrastructure be stood up along with all staff and services required to operate the business unit as an independent entity. If instead two companies are merging, the desired state may be a single, integrated IT infrastructure serving the needs of both companies.

IT INFRASTRUCTURE PLANNING

Once there is agreement on the desired state of the IT infrastructure for both Day 1 and the end state, plans can be created for each of the necessary projects to achieve those target states. Initially the focus should be on the creation of detailed project plans to achieve the objectives for Day 1; these plans should also enable migration toward the end state. While in the ideal case the Day 1 state and the end state would be the same, in many cases the team must prioritize what can be completed by Day 1 and what will need to be deferred to a transitional period after the transaction closes. (See Exhibit 6.1.)

Network, E-Mail/Messaging, Active Directory

Following are some key considerations for the major IT infrastructure components typically involved in merger, acquisition, and divestiture transactions regarding network, email/messaging, and active directory.

Network   Exhibit 6.2 shows the solution options for Day 1 concerning the network in a variety of circumstances (no TSA versus TSA).

Network Migration Lessons Learned   The following lists some of the key lessons learned related to network migrations:

- Plan early for security and access requirements between the two organizations—planning, procurement, testing, and implementation of secured, restricted access is often a critical path effort.
- When firewall rules will be required during a transitional period, consolidate accountability for firewall rule management with a single team that works with IT and business units to manage changes.
- Order and procure any new or changed dedicated circuits as early as possible, especially for international locations, some of which can have particularly long procurement lead times.

Day 1		Network Solution Options	Messaging Solution Options	Application Solution Options	Active Directory Solution Options
No TSA	Seller	Separation to stand-alone infrastructure	Migrate data to stand-alone system	Clone and Go (Give and Go) / Extract and Go	Migrate data to stand-alone AD
	Buyer	Separate to buyer infrastructure	Migrate data to buyer mail system	Clone and vitiate / New build	Migrate data to stand-alone AD
TSA	Seller	Restricted Access (TSA gateway)	Restricted Access (TSA gateway)	Restricted Access (TSA gateway)	Restricted Access (TSA gateway)
	Buyer	As-Is access	As-Is access	As-Is access	As-Is access

EXHIBIT 6.1 Functional Planning and Execution: IT Solutions under TSA Considerations from Divested Entity's Perspective

Source: Deloitte

Day 1		Data Center Solution Options	Mainframe Solution Options	Vendor Management/ Contracts Solution Options	Security Solution Options
No TSA	Seller	Separate DC Assets and infrastructure (including DR, owned or hosted)	Clone and Go (Give and Go)	Retain As-is (opportunity for renegotiating Teams and conditions)	Separate Access
	Buyer		Extract and Go		
	Seller	Separate to Buyer DC Infrastructure (including DR, owned or hosted)	Clone and vitiate	Transfer to buyer (opportunity for renegotiating terms and conditions)	Separate Access
	Buyer		New build		
TSA	Seller	Restricted access (TSA gateway)	Restricted access (TSA gateway)	Acquire New or Replacement service, App (phase out legacy)	Restricted Access (TSA gateway)
	Buyer	As-Is Access	As-Is Access	Negotiate New Contracts for Same Service, App	As-Is Access

EXHIBIT 6.1 (*Continued*)

Day 1	Solution	Solution Description	Considerations
No TSA	**Separation to Stand-alone Infrastructure**	▪ Company establishes stand-alone infrastructure. ▪ Typically appropriate if buyer does not have infrastructure in new locations.	▪ Timeline—Full separation typically requires long implementation time that is feasible by Day 1 only with extensive pre-planning. ▪ Risk—Lowest-risk option to seller. ▪ Dependencies—Typically requires most other IT-dependent services to be cutover before Day 1.
	Separate to Buyer Infrastructure	▪ Buyer integrates businesses on to Buyer network by Day 1.	▪ Typically a Day 2 and not Day 1 option; this is because buyer security typically will not allow the business they are acquiring access to buyer network before Day 1.
TSA	**Restricted Access**	▪ Seller provides sold business with restricted access to internal network.	▪ Timeline—Achievable by Day 1 with sufficient planning and early ordering of necessary equipment and circuits if necessary. ▪ Risk—While there is some risk, this is typically an acceptable security and risk compromise. ▪ Dependencies—Critical dependency is firewall rule collection and testing across all sites.
	As-Is Access	▪ Seller provides sold business with as-is and unrestricted access to internal services, data and information.	▪ Timeline—Often measure of last resort if timeline between Day 0 and Day 1 is extremely short. ▪ Risk—High risk to seller due to open-third party access to internal services, data, and information. ▪ Dependencies—Limited, as seller leave access as-is.

EXHIBIT 6.2 Network—Day 1 Solution Options

Source: Deloitte

E-Mail/Messaging Service   Exhibit 6.3 shows the solution options for Day 1 regarding e-mail/messaging service in a variety of circumstances (no TSA versus TSA).

E-Mail/Messaging Service Lessons Learned   The following are some of the key lessons learned related to e-mail/messaging services:

- Understand any applicable regulatory, compliance, and security requirements about third-party usage of e-mail—timing of e-mail migrations and allowable TSAs are often limited by rules and associated risks surrounding the use of e-mail services after Day 1.
- Communicate early between both organizations about the desired Day 1 state for e-mail and calendaring; such a simple thing as having everyone on a single e-mail and calendaring system on or around Day 1 enables good communication, makes employees feel like part of the new company, and helps establish the new company brand.
- Consider offering e-mail forwarding and/or auto-reply services for a period of time following Day 1 to minimize disruption in communications to customers and partners.
- For large user bases, multiple waves of e-mail migration may be required—consider how to group users across business function or geography to minimize business disruption during the transition.
- Think through how historical and archived e-mail will be treated after the Day 1 close—if a company has high volumes of e-mail data either stored centrally or distributed on PCs, it may require a significant effort to migrate to the new messaging platform.

Active Directory   Exhibit 6.4 shows the solution options for Day 1 regarding the active directory in a variety of circumstances (no TSA versus TSA).

Active Directory Lessons Learned   The following are some of the key lessons learned related to active directory access:

- Understand applicable regulatory, compliance, and security requirements about third-party usage of the active directory. Active directory access can present a significant security risk; as a result, timing of migrations and allowable TSAs are often limited.
- Establish a clear and detailed up-front vision for how the active directory domains, privileges, and the like will be integrated, including harmonizing naming schemes and structures.

Day 1	Solution	Solution Description	Considerations
No TSA	**Migrate Data to Stand-alone System**	▪ Company establishes stand-alone infrastructure. ▪ Typically appropriate if buyer does not have comparable infrastructure.	▪ Timeline—Requires long lead time—usually over 6 months. ▪ Risk—Lowest-risk option to seller. ▪ Dependencies—Sold company may does not have skills to stand up or support new mail system and seller will have to offer support through internal or third-party resources.
	Migrate Data to Buyer Mail System	▪ Buyer moves acquired company to buyer mail system by Day 1.	▪ Typically occurs right after Day 1 because buyer and regulatory authorities may have concern regarding sold business access to buyer systems before Day 1. ▪ Dependency—While affected users may not have access to seller's mail system, a TSA will typically needed for mail forwarding.
TSA	**Restricted Access**	▪ Seller provides sold business with restricted access to messaging system via firewall restrictions.	▪ Timeline—Achievable by Day 1 with at least 30 days before close to define and test firewall rules. ▪ Risk—Typically viewed as very-high-risk solution especially if large number of users; nature of firewall rules means that access is wide and risk to seller is appreciable. ▪ Dependencies—Continued use of seller's system after Day 1 requires the implementation of a disclaimer notifying senders that users are no longer a part of the seller's organization.
	As-Is Access	▪ Seller provides sold business with as-is and unrestricted access to mail system with no firewall rules.	▪ Timeline— Often measure of last resort if timeline between Day 0 and Day 1 is extremely short. ▪ Risk—High-risk option. ▪ Dependencies—Limited as leave access as-is; requires implementation of a disclaimer notifying senders that users are no longer a part of the seller's organization.

EXHIBIT 6.3 E-Mail/Messaging Service—Day 1 Solution Options

Source: Deloitte

Day 1	Solution	Solution Description	Considerations
No TSA	**Migrate Data to Stand-alone AD**	▪ Company establishes stand-alone infrastructure.	▪ Timeline—Long lead time project due to equipment orders and systematic migration of users over weekends; server migration is typically after user migration. ▪ Risk—Lowest-risk option to seller if migrated by Day 1; trust between existing and new domain may need to be established to migrate data. ▪ Dependencies—Seller and buyer need to make decision who will perform the migration because migration tools typically need domain level access to both domains.
TSA	**Restrict Access**	▪ Seller provides sold business with restricted access active directory by either setting up Domain Controllers on buyer side of the network or ensuring Domain Controllers contain only transferred users.	▪ Timeline—Achievable by Day 1 with sufficient planning and early ordering of necessary equipment and circuits if necessary. ▪ Post Day 1 effort—Trust typically cannot be allowed between seller and buyer active directory, as this needs review of how migration will be performed. ▪ Risk—While there is some risk, this is typically an acceptable security and risk compromise. ▪ Dependencies—Critical dependency is firewall rule collection and testing across all sites.
	As-Is Access	▪ Seller provides sold business with as-is and unrestricted access to internal services, data and information. ▪ Migrate to buyer or stand alone AD after Day 1.	▪ Timeline—Often measure of last resort if timeline between Day 0 and Day 1 is extremely short. ▪ Post Day 1 effort—Trust typically cannot be allowed between seller and buyer active directory, as this needs review of how migration will be performed. ▪ Risk—High risk to seller due to open third party access to internal services, data and information. ▪ Dependencies—Limited as leave access as-is.

EXHIBIT 6.4 Active Directory Access—Day 1 Solution Options
Source: Deloitte

IT INFRASTRUCTURE DEPENDENCIES

Transitioning an IT infrastructure to a new organization in a merger, acquisition, or divestiture is typically a very large and complex undertaking, and often has to be completed on an aggressive schedule to achieve the desired synergies that drove the reason for the transaction. Complicating matters further, plans need to be agreed upon across the organizations on both sides of the transaction. Accomplishing the required objectives with a program with a challenging mix of size, complexity, risk, and urgency makes it critical for the IT infrastructure organization and project team to stay tightly coordinated with other teams and business functions. Some of the critical dependencies that should be considered when planning an IT infrastructure separation or integration are discussed next.

IT Applications

Almost every element of the IT infrastructure is tied to providing IT application services to end users, customers, and partners. While the IT infrastructure team is busy planning the transition of infrastructure components toward the end-state vision, the IT applications team is going through a very similar exercise for each IT application being transitioned or changed. The IT infrastructure, applications, and database teams need to closely coordinate their plans and stay in constant communication from initial requirements gathering through the final cut over and transition to ongoing support. (See Exhibit 6.5.) Note that due to the long timeline to separate infrastructure, most sellers provide a TSA with firewalled access.

Real Estate and Facilities

It is important for the IT infrastructure team to understand the vision and schedule for how each location and facility will be transitioned to the target end state. It is common that some facilities may be combined, closed, or expanded for the merged organization. Each facility change can include a number of IT infrastructure impacts, ranging from simple user provisioning and access to complex data center consolidation programs.

For organizations with global footprints, each country may have different requirements that can affect the IT infrastructure transition. For example, some countries have specific requirements about where certain types of data can be hosted, which could in some cases be in conflict with the desired real estate/facility strategy. Countries may also have business

Due to the long timeline to separate infrastructure, most sellers provide a TSA with firewalled access

Day 1	Solution	Solution Description	Considerations
No TSA	**Clone and Go (Give and Go)**	▪ Seller transfers ownership of appropriate portions of client application portfolio to buyer.	▪ Timeline—Achievable by Day 1 with sufficient planning and execution. ▪ Dependencies—For carve-out scenarios, critical dependency is separation of sold business data.
	Extract and Go	▪ Seller extracts and transfers data to buyer for loading onto its systems.	▪ Timeline—Achievable by Day 1 with sufficient planning and execution. ▪ Dependencies—Critical dependency is new system readiness.
	Clone and Vitiate	▪ Seller copies production onto a separate instance production clone.	▪ Timeline—Achievable by Day 1 with sufficient planning and execution. ▪ Dependencies—Critical dependency is separation of data.
	New Build	▪ Company establishes stand-alone infrastructure.	▪ Timeline—Achievable by Day 1 with sufficient planning and execution. ▪ Risk—Lowest-risk option to seller.
TSA	**Restricted Access**	▪ Seller provides sold business with restricted access to applications.	▪ Timeline—Achievable by Day 1 with sufficient planning and execution. ▪ Risk—While there is some risk, this is typically an acceptable security and risk compromise. ▪ Dependencies—Critical dependency is application information and access collection.
	As-Is Access	▪ Seller provides sold business with as-is and unrestricted access to internal services, data, and information.	▪ Timeline—Often measure of last resort if timeline between Day 0 and Day 1 is extremely short. ▪ Risk—High risk to seller due to open third-party access to internal services, data, and information. ▪ Dependencies—Limited, as seller leaves access as-is.

EXHIBIT 6.5 Application Access—Day 1 Solution Options
Source: Deloitte

licensing or other requirements that may need to be renegotiated or reestablished for the merged enterprise. Doing so may be very time-consuming and may require the IT infrastructure team to adjust their transition plans according to those country-specific conditions.

Contracts

Software licensing, hardware maintenance agreements, and other IT contracts were originally agreed and written in the names of the original companies. As the IT infrastructure is transitioned to the new entity, the team needs to stay in close, constant communication with whichever function is handling contract transitions. Some contracts may include right to use (RTU) clauses that allow a third-party company to continue using their software for up to one year past the close of the transaction; others may have shorter timeframes, special provisions for how licenses can be transferred, or no provisions at all relating to M&A scenarios. In many cases, the IT infrastructure team may need to purchase additional licenses as systems are transitioned, cloned, or separated, in which case contract licensing can be a critical dependency.

Regulatory, Compliance, and IT Security

IT security and regulatory/compliance issues take on a heightened importance given the third-party status between the buyer and seller. There can be a number of restrictions about what can be done before or after Day 1 that may never have come up on prior IT projects. IT infrastructure staff often have privileged access to many systems, and in some cases may need to be held back from transition to buyer control if data, applications, or IT infrastructure components have not been fully separated. Security and regulatory/compliance functions also may need to approve and sign off on IT infrastructure separation or integration strategies and plans, and in some cases may need to be changed or expanded to address security or regulatory/compliance needs.

WRAPPING IT UP

One of the largest obstacles in mergers, acquisitions, and divestitures is how to segregate or integrate enterprise infrastructure and applications to support the organizations that are to be combined or divested. Separation or integration of the IT infrastructure is almost always a critical path effort in the overall M&A program.

Having a detailed, broad, and well-planned infrastructure and a skilled and experienced project team are key to the rapid changes required to support M&A activities. However, even more important is the need to build a system that is scalable to allow for both growth and consolidation of the underlying infrastructure.

To prepare for a possible merger or acquisition, the organizations' infrastructures should be designed in such a way that the combined infrastructure operates as a single cohesive unit to increase, improve, and leverage the synergies of the different business units. With respect to a divestiture, a subset of the infrastructure should be created that allows the divested organization to operate independently of the source infrastructure. To accomplish this objective, the architecture should be designed in a way to allow for the creation of an infrastructure to still operate the divested organization without reliance on the master organization's infrastructure, applications, and data.

CHAPTER 7

M&A IT and Synergies

Jim Boland
Ronald Goldberg
Colin Hartnett
Sunil Rai
Stephen Ronan

IT'S ROLE AND CONTRIBUTION TO SYNERGY CAPTURE

Merger, acquisition, and divestiture transactions can be times of great stress and great opportunity for the information technology (IT) organization. In today's business world, IT will be on the front line of any M&A transaction, and its leadership must be ready, willing, and able to:

- Think and act strategically and dispassionately about where transaction synergies can be achieved.
- Work collaboratively with the leadership team in creating the vision for, identifying, and capturing the synergies.

Information technology personnel see firsthand the impact of the process efficiencies and inefficiencies across the company. This chapter focuses on IT's role in identifying, developing, and capturing these synergies in the M&A transition.

IT's Unique Position in Synergies Identification

The IT function in most organizations is truly a hub and engine of business activity. Visions and plans of products and services to be created, product designs, product development, sales, orders, shipments, bills, customers, vendors, purchases, payments, human resource allocations, payroll, financials, budgets, and business plans are captured, tracked, and coordinated on a variety of computer platforms, and most, if not all, of these are maintained by the IT organization. The CIOs and VPs of IT who see this have an opportunity, especially during M&A transactions, to create value, efficiencies, and control, while minimizing cost for the organization.

Part of the IT function's responsibility is to help ensure that data created, maintained, and used to run the business are clearly understood as the data are passed from system to system. The data should be processed correctly within each system and securely controlled from inception to usage and storage. Based on this and the business-as-usual processes, IT leadership has at its fingertips a set of charts of where efficiencies and inefficiencies may exist. These charts are typically in the form of one or all of the following:

- System architecture diagrams showing simplified views of the data flowing from system to system throughout the company's application architecture. These are sometimes structured in such a way to show organizational "swim lanes" that identify where in the organization data pass from one group to another. While some of these swim-lane handoffs are necessary and normal, excessive handoffs can be a source of inefficiency because of reconciliations, storage, and the need to reformat data in the handoffs.
- Business process diagrams showing how the company's business processes are accomplished, usually indicating where controls may exist. These diagrams are also frequently organized in an organization swim-lane structure, which can be invaluable in understanding inefficiencies (see Exhibit 7.1).
- Logical and physical data architecture diagrams or entity relationship diagrams (ERDs) explaining how data entities relate to other data entities, and, in the physical model, places where data redundancy could be eliminated.
- Technical infrastructure diagrams showing servers, physical data transport mechanisms, data storage mediums, and network and cloud infrastructure. Evaluation of the technical infrastructure can help identify cost savings through infrastructure consolidation and through use of the cloud as appropriate (see Chapter 10 for more details on the cloud).

By analyzing these views of the merged or acquired businesses, as well as their underlying IT support, a company's IT leadership can identify the signatures of inefficient information processing patterns, which typically are:

- **Functional redundancy.** These are processes where the same business process is performed differently, or multiple applications enable the same business processes across the organization.

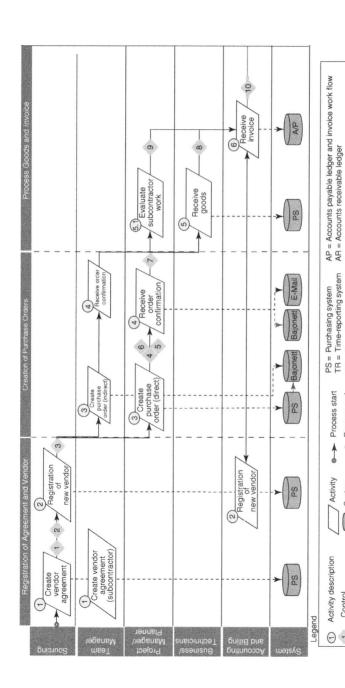

EXHIBIT 7.1 Sample Business Process Flow Diagram

107

▪ **Repetitive cycles on the same source data.** These are processing cycles where multiple processes, organizations, and/or individuals need to manipulate, adjust, or transform data before it can be used.
▪ **Significant manual intervention.** These are processing points where data is manually manipulated to adjust for specific situations.
▪ **Overcontrolled processing.** These are processing points where data is checked, reported on, or confirmed without an apparent reason for the activity. These are frequently vestiges of control activities that are no longer necessary.
▪ **Processes that are enabled by out-of-date technology.** While legacy systems can be efficient processing engines, these are typically less flexible in accommodating change or merging of business processes.

Exhibit 7.2 is an example of a current-state systems architecture diagram of a communications equipment manufacturer that is a result of the aforementioned inefficiencies.

A thorough and targeted review of the aforementioned documentation can uncover numerous inefficient information processing patterns that can be targeted for M&A synergies. In addition to such types of inefficient information processing patterns, there is typically opportunity for synergy in the technical assets of the combined entity. Technology leadership should use this opportunity to leverage high-potential, more flexible system assets more heavily and to sunset the inflexible and low-potential assets. Examples of more flexible system assets include:

▪ Customer relationship management (CRM) systems
▪ Call center systems
▪ Product development lifecycle management systems
▪ Enterprise resource planning (ERP) systems
▪ Master data management (MDM) systems
▪ Financial consolidation management systems

Exhibit 7.3 is an example of a future-state systems architecture diagram of a communications equipment manufacturer that addresses many of the efficiencies in current-state processing.

While IT leadership sponsors the synergies identification analysis, it is important to recognize that there is a human element as well to locating synergies. As with other company leadership during the M&A transaction period, it is important for IT leadership to recognize that achieving synergies will likely involve changing employees' work patterns and job roles. This may, fortunately or unfortunately, render them redundant in the organization. While this is the case in almost all M&A transactions, it is also critically important that the IT function in particular remains intact for

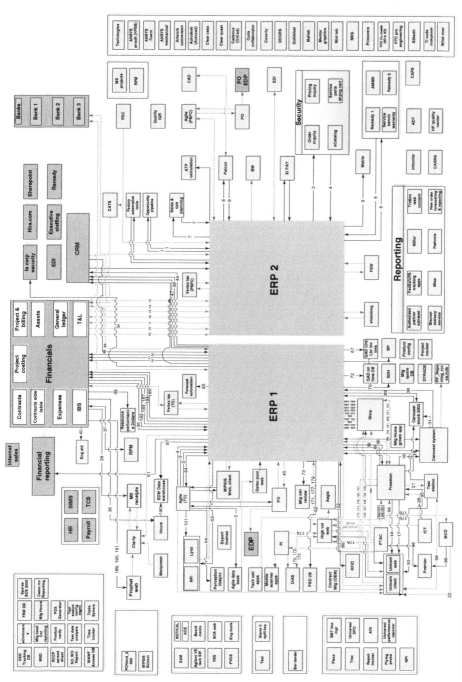

EXHIBIT 7.2 Example of Current-State Systems Architecture Diagram Prior to Integration

109

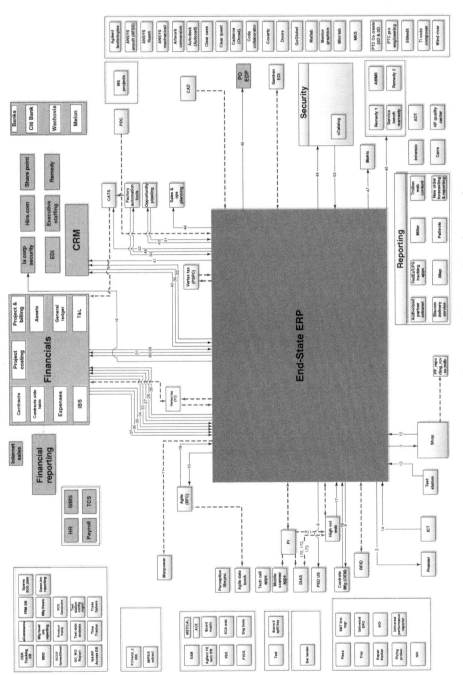

EXHIBIT 7.3 Example of Future-State Systems Architecture Diagram Post-integration

the transaction period to support business-as-usual processing as well as necessary system changes and conversions.

As with any change, the best way to address fears and concerns about the transition, as well as the opportunities involved with it, is to communicate regularly, honestly, and concisely the information and messages that can be disseminated. Very often, the M&A transaction program management office (PMO) will be responsible for implementing a communications plan for the flow of such information. However, it is also important for IT leadership to maintain additional communication with its own employees in the IT function. Keeping the IT staff well informed typically helps to stave off any unnecessary voluntary IT employee turnover during the transaction period. We discuss this topic more in the next section on M&A IT organizational implications.

Of additional concern during the M&A cycle is the natural potential bias in the synergies analysis. The team of individuals performing the synergy identification within IT will be charged with identifying opportunities that will have challenging impacts. It is IT leadership's role to make sure this analysis is detailed and balanced across all areas. This means that even if the synergies could significantly change or eliminate the permanent job roles of those involved in analysis, the review must be objective and fair. Therefore, an effective way for IT leadership to lead during this period is to recognize and communicate that change through synergies realization will occur, and it is the team's job to create the most efficient, flexible, and cost-effective operating model through the transaction.

IT as a Business Partner in Synergies Identification and Planning

The IT function is uniquely positioned to visualize potential synergies. The IT function can also be a catalyst for the planning and realization of these synergies. The IT function typically houses the organization's most experienced project management talent, structured analysis capability, and the know-how to think cross-functionally about where and how data are sourced, how it is processed, and how it is used. Because these capabilities tend to be more prevalent in IT, IT has an obligation to leverage these talents in the synergy identification, the synergy realization planning, and the execution and project management of synergy attainment. Technology leadership should use the capabilities available to it to seize the opportunity in front of it. As with any project, a structured approach is called for, and the IT leadership typically can assist with the planning tools and approaches it has available in its toolbox and is familiar with to employ. It is also recommended that the organization leverage tools and approaches specifically for the M&A transactions.

For companies contemplating merger, acquisition, or divestiture activity, one of the primary criteria for identifying and achieving synergies is how additional shareholder value can be created. Increasing shareholder value is typically the number one expected outcome for all involved in identifying the transaction, structuring it, closing the deal, and realizing meaningful benefits is what ultimately determines whether it is a success. Identifying synergies is a step in which it is invaluable to obtain external assistance from individuals and firms that have helped other companies identify and achieve synergies. Along with "been there, done that" experience, such firms have databases of business process frameworks tailored by industry, potential synergies, and structured methodologies for achieving synergies. All of this will be critical in rapidly identifying and achieving the highest value, lowest cost synergies.

It is essential to begin the synergies identification and planning process with a structured and disciplined approach to identify and prioritize M&A synergies, plan activities necessary for their implementation, and track the synergy benefits over the course of the transaction and through the first several business cycles. A structured approach for achieving these benefits in most, if not all, M&A transactions is discussed next.

Day 0—Begin with the End in Mind After the merger, acquisition, or divestiture deal is announced, the M&A team should focus on identifying potential synergies and developing business process and systems visions of the post-transaction end state. This model should include consideration for capturing and tracking expected benefits. During this phase of the transaction, an M&A road map is established by the PMO with assistance of IT and other functions impacted. Synergies are identified through structured brainstorming sessions to identify potential synergies, what-if analysis on the synergies, and finally, development of the vision business process and systems models.

Day 1—Nothing Can Happen without a Successful Launch Companies undertaking a merger, acquisition, or divestiture will typically invest a considerable amount of time and resources in driving to a successful Day 1. Day 1 is defined as the first day the merging or separating entities conduct business as one or separate entities. These entities' goal for Day 1 is to deliver a stable baseline business and to identify, but not necessarily immediately capture, the benefits resulting from the transaction. To achieve the projected shareholder value, these same companies will rigorously manage the planning efforts up to and beyond Day 1 to avoid disruptions and keep business and customer-facing operations running smoothly.

Day 2—Realize the Benefits with Patient, but Persistent Plan Execution and Benefits Tracking Day 2 is when the real fun typically begins. Day 2 is defined as the point in time when the deal vision is ultimately realized. This is when the company's business functions are integrated or separated and synergies are realized. A lesson learned from numerous transactions is that the synergies are not only about Day 1. While the Day 1 priorities center on stabilizing the business and planning to capture operational and financial benefits, the Day 2 priorities focus on truly unlocking the value inherent to the deal. The typical transaction approach identifies and targets benefits realization during Day 0 and Day 1. However, achieving the desired goals of an M&A transaction frequently does not occur, and can't occur until Day 2. The key to this success comes back in the Day 0 work where the synergies are defined.

The more complex an M&A transaction is (that is, the more geographies in scope, the more parties involved, the more significant the organization functional changes, the more politics) the greater the effort required to reach a successful Day 2. However, regardless of the transaction's complexity, common change themes that emerge include the necessity for customer operations to acquire different core competencies, shifts in geographic coverage, conflicting philosophies regarding direct sales and channel operations, and supply chain realignment and vendor rationalization. Sorting through these changes calls for the use of a common value language to talk about value-creation and tracking the benefits for a company during Day 2. The challenges of bringing two or more businesses, cultures, processes and priorities together make up the majority of the effort the transaction team will need to exert.

A common value language used by the authors is the Enterprise Value Map (EVM) (see Exhibit 7.4). This is a Deloitte & Touche proprietary tool that provides a practical way to link shareholder value and what clients can do in their various functions to influence it. It provides a framework to standardize how everyone talks about value and benefits to the business as part of a transaction. The common value language tool is easy to understand, works well for all levels of the combined organization, and gives the transaction team a basis from which to identify synergies, go after them, and measure the benefits achieved.

Enterprise Value Map is a variation of a model known as the DuPont Model. Developed in 1919, the DuPont Model serves as a simple way to measure return on equity (ROE). Multiplying net profit margin, asset turnover, and the equity multiplier provides an ROE and can show a company's profitability and potential for growth in comparison to its competitors in the same industry. The EVM approach measures the same

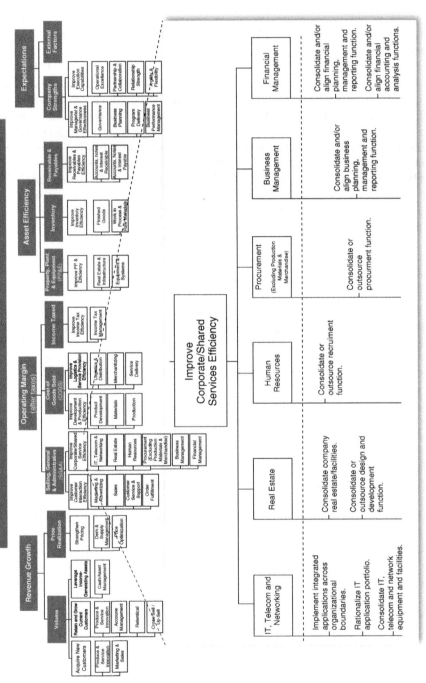

EXHIBIT 7.4 Enterprise Value Map with Explosion of One Improvement Area (i.e., "Improve Corporate / Shared Service Efficiency")

components of financial performance while incorporating a tactical layer of operational levers that drive desired financial improvements.

What the EVM shows is that the link between financial targets and operational improvement opportunities can serve as the common language throughout an M&A transaction. Synergies can be developed top-down by targeting improvement opportunities to address a specific financial area, or they can be developed bottom-up by highlighting synergies and the resulting financial impact. Either way, EVM provides a company's management a simple structure to talk about synergies and depict the areas where an M&A transaction synergy will improve shareholder value, since that's the goal.

An example of an organization where the EVM framework put to use is a global chemicals company that was struggling with a disparate environment of various business systems. This U.S.-based company, having recently acquired a business in the United Kingdom with nonstandardized business processes, systems, or useful operational reporting, the acquiring company faced the daunting challenge of integrating the new entity into its own patchwork of processes and systems. And of course, geographic, cultural, and strategic differences between the two entities only added to the complexity of the effort.

In this case, one of the key synergies identified was the opportunity to move to a single, global common set of business processes enabled by a single ERP platform. The team's value assessment for developing and implementing this synergy opportunity relied heavily on utilizing a common value language. The process of bringing people from different businesses, countries, sites, and process areas together required a structured way to capture and analyze all of this information. The EVM framework served that purpose. In this example, the company's executives debated business strategy while standing in front of a literally poster-sized EVM.

Those strategic priorities then served as guiding principles for the executives to embark on more detailed operational improvement discussions. With IT management contributing its insights across process areas, the EVM focused discussions on what generated the most value in the combined business. Using the EVM, the participants in this activity recognized synergies regardless of their individual roles in the organization.

While organizations involved in M&A transactions typically will resist change, as we all naturally do, bringing thought leaders together from the combined businesses to identify synergies and improvement opportunities can be a very effective way to bridge this resistance and begin to have the organizations work as one.

So how do we identify synergies?

Details of Synergy Identification

Tactically, workshops tend to be a highly effective vehicle for identifying potential synergies. When structuring synergy opportunity workshops as a business leader, keep these guidelines in mind:

- Group workshop participants into common, typically end-to-end process areas, and schedule workshops based on these areas. A tested way to do this utilizes the EVM approach or the other available business process or systems process frameworks described previously in this chapter, to facilitate strategic, operational, and technical improvement opportunities.
- Gather process area subject matter specialists from different business units and geographies together for the workshops. If the organization has a large global presence, regional workshops may be needed to make this work successfully.
- Encourage in-person participation, which is far more valuable than telephone participation. Use videoconferencing as a backup plan.
- Select the right individuals who have an understanding of the process details, but are not "buried in the weeds" of the current-state environment. Visioning for what is possible is critical. Hanging on to the past because "we've always done it that way" will yield suboptimal results.

Once the workshops are planned, the next step is to develop a structure to identify and capture synergy opportunities in the workshops. When doing this, consider the following four-part workshop approach:

1. Review strategic objectives of the M&A transaction strategy with workshop participants. This is a great way to level-set the participants on what is most important. Use the EVM approach or similar tools to jump-start the discussion regarding where there might be synergies. Keep the participants out of the details of their jobs; get them thinking about the future vision of the business. Step through each of the business processes of the merged area participants.

    Considerations: Try using the EVM or similar tools to align the strategic objectives of the organization with financial benchmarks. This is a great way to visually link the high-level M&A transaction strategy with the discrete metrics used to judge the success of each synergy opportunity.

    What to avoid: Avoid facilitating too much discussion on the structure of the EVM or the process and systems modeling tools. These tools simply structure the conversation, making sure that the content covered is broad enough. They are not intended to build an academically perfect value model for the organization.

2. Identify synergies. Ask questions of the participants regarding how each of them believes the merged entity could save money, perform processes more efficiently or effectively, reduce cycle times, and increase output. The answers to these questions will typically become the synergy opportunities.

   Considerations: Use a tested framework to step through the business process areas. Tools such as EVM, business process models, process maturity models, or IT services frameworks can help to keep participants on the same page.

   What to avoid: Don't assume that specific areas have more synergy opportunities and others have less. This is a time to consider synergy opportunities across the entire organization.

3. Confirm the scope of synergy identified by defining which business units, geographies, processes, and technologies are in the scope of the synergy identification. Be very clear. This will help focus on tangible synergies, while confirming that the necessary areas of the business have been addressed in the workshops.

   Considerations: Again use a tested framework to define the scope of discussion.

   What to avoid: Do not debate what should be in the scope. If something is questionable, park the open question with an action item to confirm it, and assume it is not in the scope. Focus the group's time on the areas that clearly drive the most business value and will continue to drive the most value as a result of the M&A transaction.

4. Flush out the key performance indicators (KPIs), as well as the current challenges and risks for each synergy opportunity identified. A very strong facilitator should promote everyone's involvement to cover the full scope of discussion. The facilitator should also take time to probe into areas that may present the largest opportunities for the business. Utilize a predefined template (see Exhibit 7.5 for an example of synergy opportunity template used by a global engineered materials manufacturer) to capture each of the critical pieces of information. And don't let the participants disburse it until they have come to agreement on the top-priority opportunities, estimating relative benefit value if possible.

   Considerations: Document workshop discussions in real time on a projector or similar device. This helps everyone in the room confirm the details when they are fresh and helps everyone remain focused on the discussion.

   What to avoid: Do not waste time wordsmithing the specifics of the opportunity. This can take the discussion off-course. Capture the idea and move on.

Standardize Transaction and Reporting Processes

Opportunity Description	Benefit Description
The current environment requires accounting and shared services to follow different processes and use different systems to perform what should be standardized routine transactions (e.g., A/P, A/R, journal entries, inter-company transactions, and more). This multi-process/system environment drives significant complexity in the month and quarter-end closing process. Source data are not easily available for reconciliation and analysis purposes; in some cases (e.g., incorrectly costed intercompany transactions), if errors are discovered, they cannot be corrected, which can result in increased duties and customs cost to the business. Key elements of this opportunity include: • Consolidation of all transaction processing into one ERP system. • Simplification of intercompany transactions and month-end reconciliation process. • Analysis and drill-down capabilities to evaluate source data to support reconciliation process and for responding to audit requests for information; accessibility to this capability beyond finance puts analysis capabilities directly in the hands of decision makers (i.e., less reliance on finance to reconcile, run reports, etc, means the business can do this more directly).	• Consolidate personnel support processes for three different systems to one system. • Reduce head count of shared services center for both transaction processing and month-end close support. • Reduce manual effort required to collect and analyze source data during reconciliation process. Reduce effort to complete intercompany reconciliation process. • Reduce inflated costs from inaccurate markups. • More effective and efficient ability to manage growing business while minimizing errors/resource complexity. • Reduce audit fees resulting from effort required to audit current complex transactional processes due to multisystem environment. • Reduced cost/effort required to complete IT audits. • Provide capability to conform to various reporting regulations across global business environment; today this is complex and labor-intensive due to multi-ERP landscape. • Reduced IT costs required to maintain complex system interfaces. • Speed of analysis of results. • Provides the opportunity to cross-train shared services resources, reducing staffing complexity and cost.

	Action Required to Obtain Benefit
	• Standardized master data, including single chart of accounts. • Integrate businesses into single ERP solution. • Standardization of processes with data management (e.g., way to charge costs/transfer order). • Consolidation of resources in shared services center and corporate finance.

Value Map Alignment	Process KPIs	Key Functional Requirements	Anticipated Benefit (H, M, L)

• Operating margin
  ➤ SG&A
• Expectations
  ➤ Improve management and governance effectiveness.
  ➤ Business performance management.
	• Closing checklist adherence.
	• Number of manual journal entries.
		• Standardized master data, including single (common) chart of accounts across all businesses.	• High

EXHIBIT 7.5 Sample Value-Creating Synergy Opportunity Template

Quantifying and Detailing Synergy Benefits, Cost Estimates, and Risks

Once potential synergies have been identified, the next step is to detail and quantify the benefits, costs, and risks in addressing each synergy opportunity. Tactically, smaller and more targeted breakout groups of the synergy benefit workshop attendees tend to be the preferred vehicle to accomplish this. These smaller groups can focus specifically on quantifying the benefits, costs, and risks, as well as updating the synergy opportunity template.

The highlighted sections of the template may require additional calculations, which are typically performed and maintained in spreadsheet models to support the numbers. Members of the team should focus on the anticipated benefits, costs to obtain the benefits, and key performance indicators (KPI) for each opportunity. Clearly, individual subject matter specialists will measure their business performance in different parts of the business differently. Therefore, it is important to gain insights on which KPIs can most effectively measure business performance and relate those specifically to the synergy benefits. These will serve as the benefit-tracking mechanism through the project lifecycle and beyond.

Quantifying the costs and risks of each synergy opportunity requires careful consideration of what it will really take to implement and achieve the synergy. On the surface, achieving synergy benefits may sound simple, but in reality it is not. This is why it is critical that the costs of doing so from an organization, business process, and technology change perspective be estimated properly to help ensure the opportunity is clearly evaluated and the synergy benefit timing projected (Day 1 and Day 2).

Exhibit 7.6 provides a starter set of how to consider synergy opportunity costs and risks.

EXHIBIT 7.6 Synergy Opportunity Challenges, Descriptions, and Considerations

Opportunity Challenges	Descriptions	Considerations
Cost	Acquisition costs	Supports cash flow analysis
	Implementation/integration costs	Offsets program costs
	Support costs	
Business Disruption	Best and brightest removed from business-as-usual roles	Provides best thinking into future state design
	Resources taken away from other growth and cost savings initiatives	Serves as change management tool
		Keeps benefits front of mind for project team
Risk	Implementation/integration risk	Allows for focus on priority items
	Business disruption risk	Enables risk versus benefit value analysis
	Financial risk	Serves as communication tool throughout organization
	Cultural and morale risk	

Once the synergy opportunity templates and supporting details have been completed and agreed to by the workshop participants, the transaction team generally summarizes the approach, scope, potential synergy benefits, costs, and risks in an executive report provided to the merged organization's senior leadership. This group evaluates and approves each of the synergy opportunities, and directs the transaction team to develop more formalized charters, plans, and staffing as necessary to implement and achieve the synergy benefits.

SYNERGY CAPTURE AND BENEFITS TRACKING DURING THE MERGER, ACQUISITION, AND DIVESTITURE LIFECYCLE

M&A synergies may begin long before the transaction date and accrue for years to come. Like reverberations from a stone dropped in a pond, the synergies may build on top of each other. The IT department has a critical role in understanding how these synergies can be captured and establishing the mechanisms for capturing them. The remainder of this chapter focuses on how, when, and where synergies are captured during the M&A lifecycle. It also describes demonstrated processes for identifying IT benefits that are aligned to business and M&A strategies. With these opportunities defined, we create a mechanism for measuring realization of these benefits once the merger or acquisition has been stabilized on Day 1.

IT's Role on the Synergy Capture Team

The pervasive use of IT across the enterprise makes the IT function critical to any major initiative, including mergers and acquisitions. Typically many synergy areas end up falling into the IT space or require considerable support from IT for their realization. Hence, IT should be an important voice on the synergy capture team right from the start: from synergy identification, analysis, and capture to benefits tracking. In many M&A transactions, IT stands alone and jointly as a key stream of work. This role also requires suitable senior IT leadership representation on the synergy capture team.

The IT synergy goals of most transactions are driven from the transaction structure—merger of equals versus absorption of a smaller operation. Transaction structure is a critical determinant, among other factors, to decide on the IT-related synergy capture goals. In addition, IT typically has other key focus areas that should be ably represented on the synergy capture team for the successful consummation of a deal, as follows:

■ **Continuity of support to key constituencies.** A smooth Day 1 experience is critical for the key stakeholders—customers, employees, suppliers, and operations. The IT area has a significant role in the ability to design and drive this experience. It has to be close to restructuring decisions on any assets or businesses that have to be divested as a result of the deal and whether these assets will be sold, will be spun off, or will have to be held separately. These are critical factors based on which IT may need to plan on addressing issues related to supporting processes and underlying applications.

■ **Talent retention.** Experience suggests that key employees begin to receive external job inquiries within days or weeks of an M&A announcement. Successful transaction consummation and synergy capture require that IT is able to retain the key employees from both organizations for all of the long-term technologies and applications. IT should provide the current roster of IT organization skills and experience as well as the anticipated supply of qualified IT resources to meet future integration demands (both internal staff and externally contracted resources) and work with the broader synergy capture team to align on the synergy goals for these.

■ **IT strategy and application direction.** Though the transaction structure often dictates the broad direction for the new enterprise's IT strategy, one should generally expect to see variations. This is especially true in a merger of equals, where such decisions should be made on the merit of individual solutions and broad architectural implications. The technology department has a critical role to play in deciding which of the current technologies from the legacy organizations support the key business needs and objectives as well as appropriate financial and operational controls. It is expected to provide a perspective on the availability, stability, reliability, scalability, and flexibility of in-use technologies (for example, Oracle versus Microsoft versus IBM), as well as to profile in-flight IT projects currently supporting the legacy IT strategy. The choice of technologies should suitably blend in with the long-term application decisions. Big areas, such as ERP integration, often yield considerable synergies for the new enterprise. However, because of their complex nature, they also require an extra amount of care and focus right from synergy capture target setting down to actual integration execution.

■ **IT standards.** Adherence to various IT standards is a considerable driver of IT costs. In any M&A transaction where the focus on costs is extraordinarily high, it is best to not address cost issues while deciding on synergies. The IT area should drive the definition of future-state standards in areas such as IT architecture, application development, change management, deployment, network infrastructure, desktop configuration, database environment, help desk, security, disaster recovery, program management, project management, vendor management, IT procurement, and financial management.

- **IT vendor sourcing.** Vendor sourcing is a common area for most cost-reduction strategies, and M&A is no different in that respect. Especially related to IT integration across the two organizations, there are likely to be significant deviations in the sourcing strategies where questions such as these will need to be answered: How is IT sourcing products and services (pricing, terms, conditions, service levels, etc.) and managing supplier relationships and contracts? What elements of the IT environment are outsourced? To what extent will vendor contracts support future requirements? IT leadership has a significant role on the synergy capture team to address this question for the future enterprise.

- **IT infrastructure.** This is typically one of the biggest areas of IT spending. Organizations have used multiple levers to manage and control this cost, like consolidated data centers, aligning on technology standards, outsourcing the infrastructure, using hosted providers, and, most recently, the adoption of cloud-based services. Merging entities may have a mix of these, and likely not one answer may be the right one for the merged enterprise. Since this can be an important area for future savings, IT should have an important voice in deciding about this from a synergy standpoint. There are also other linked questions that will need to be addressed in due course with these decisions: To what extent is equipment up-to-date? What percentage of the capacity is currently utilized? Are there applications limitations due to current platforms? What is the level of compliance with architectural standards? What system management and asset management tools are used?

It is crucial that IT leadership, owners of key strategic systems, and owners of systems that will be significantly impacted due to the transaction are suitably represented on the synergy capture team. In many of the typical M&A transactions, the synergy capture team is a subteam who reports to the overall M&A PMO, of which IT is one of the key work streams. So if the specific situation does not dictate the presence of key IT system owners on the synergy capture team, there should be a vehicle in the overall governance structure to include their inputs for synergy capture. Governance is critical during overall M&A and is covered in earlier sections in this book in more detail.

The synergy capture teams have an important goal of setting common direction, aiding overall technology direction for the new enterprise, and creating compelling arguments and deadlines to allow the constituents from the merging organizations to meaningfully support the integration. During this, IT's role on the team has to be central for its wider relevance and success to the integration.

Planning Synergy Achievement

Success in synergy capture is a result of series of successful steps: identifying the right kind of synergies, establishing targets that are ambitious yet achievable, planning for the achievement of these targets, and measuring against the execution toward these targets (and exceeding them). In this chapter and the previous one, we have described the importance of identifying the synergies and establishing targets against them, and IT's central role in this process. Here we will discuss how *planning* early and properly is the next crucial component of making this story successful.

As discussed in the previous chapter, once the benefit opportunities are identified, the next step is to calculate the associated value to the business. Like any other goal, it is crucial for synergy goals to be measurable in a clear and concise manner. At the end of synergy identification, certain business leaders are usually aligned to each benefit area. However, stepping into an M&A situation changes the dynamic, and typically these leaders find it hard to envision a new world much different from the current one.

On top of that, these leaders should estimate the value of the improvements (or synergies), and commit themselves to delivering that value to the shareholders. This commitment, of course, has the potential to drive nonproductive behaviors, such as arguing against previously agreed-to opportunities and sandbagging, or lowering the expectations of what a project can do for the business to limit the pressure to deliver. On the flip side, there are also business leaders who are well versed in the game and are eager to inflate benefits to help prioritize their projects to the top of the list.

Typically, most M&A transactions bring to light many, if not all, of these situations. That can make it extremely hard to push further on synergy capture. Therefore, an effective way to get people over their natural concerns and disbeliefs is to present them with facts and plan for benefit achievement through a strong and transparent program governance organization. Relying on benchmarks to put the current business in context of the company's industry, its competition, or its acquisition target is important for developing the right agreement on goals.

Synergy planning should run through a series of logical steps to manage against these challenges typical of the M&A cycle (see Exhibit 7.7).

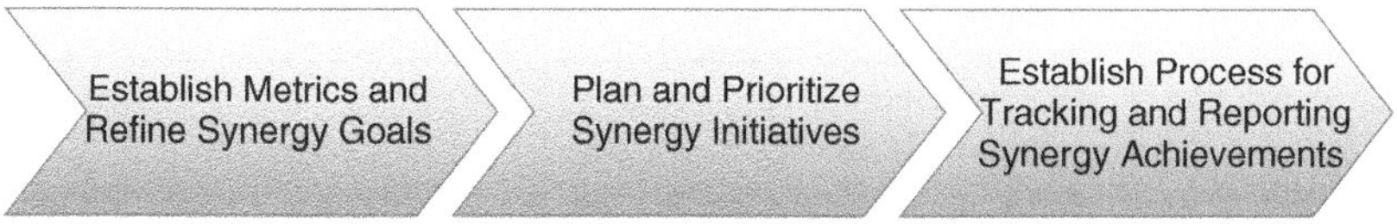

EXHIBIT 7.7 Synergy Planning Approach

Establish Metrics and Refine Synergy Goals   The refinement of synergy goals established earlier and the further drilling down to the KPIs helps to better understand the realization potential of synergies identified. However, it is very important for all on a synergy capture team to understand that the goals established earlier are sacrosanct, with flexibility only for refinements and adding specificity to them. Planning is not an opportunity to debate the goals established earlier in the process to serve individual causes. Rather, it is an opportunity to validate the goals, refine where required (subject to tolerances, of course), and make them more specific.

One of the first steps in this process is to agree on the KPIs or metrics to track synergies. KPIs are the link between operational performance and financial results. The recommended uses of standard models like EVM or DuPont help bring these out in a transparent manner for everyone. Benchmarks can support this KPI target setting, but ultimately what is important is that the business leader agrees to a percentage improvement in performance. KPIs are the variables that will drive any specific benefit calculation.

Metrics ranging from macroeconomic indicators to process-level measures are tracked and reported to gain insight into a company's integration performance. These metrics vary by stage in the integration process (initiation, planning, and execution), and should be balanced between forward-looking or leading or backward-looking or lagging. It is recommended to have a mix of qualitative and quantitative metrics. Also, it is important to have metrics that show both a leading and also a lagging effect of changes.

Samples of the metrics for a transaction are included in Exhibit 7.8 for reference.

Additional examples of metrics that may be used in synergy planning are included in Exhibit 7.9 for reference.

EXHIBIT 7.8   Sample of Metrics for Increasing Asset Utilization

Metric	Description	Baseline	Projected
KPI	Constrained asset capacity	100%	105%
Fixed variables	Annual revenue from constrained assets	$200M	$250M
	Average marginal income	62%	65%
Annual cash flow	Incremental gross margin from increased capacity	$130M	$137M
Project annual improvement			$7M

EXHIBIT 7.9 Sample of Metrics and Change in Focus during the Integration Program

Initiate *Measure Efficiency*	Plan *Measure Readiness*	Execute *Measure Performance*

Measures of Complexity
Number of integration teams
Number of data requests
  submitted
Number of clean team
  members
Number of clean team
  projects
Measure of Fragmentation
Number of employee
  integration team members
Measure of Capacity
Number of full-time
  employees (FTEs) on team
Measures of Progress
Number of data requests
  complete
Percentage of data requests
  complete
	Total Synergies
	Percentage of goal
	  committed
	Cost of achieving synergies
	Workforce Reduction
	Severance costs
	Staff-up head count required
	  based on location strategy
	Total workforce cost
	Total cost of workforce as
	  percentage of expense
	Average salary cost per
	  employee
	**Organizational Design
	Efficiency**
	Span of control
	Number of layers
	Percentage of voluntary
	  turnover
		Finance
		Expense/revenue
		High-performing employee
		  retention
		Monthly close days
		Number of legal entities
		  unconsolidated
		Number of manual journal
		  entries
		Human Resources
		Expense/revenue
		Total cost of the workforce
		Benefits as a percentage of
		  total cost of the workforce
		High-performing employee
		  retention
		Number of employees to HR
		  staff
		Employee satisfaction
		Information Technology
		Expense/revenue
		Percentage of acquired
		  company data network
		  integrated into the
		  company model
		Percentage of laptops with
		  company-approved image
		Total number of applications
		  retired
		Percentage of applications
		  integrated onto common
		  company infrastructure

Typically IT can contribute to metric establishment through multiple means, such as:

- Providing estimates for IT-focused synergy areas—often a very significant area for synergy capture.
- Leveraging its role as the guardian of process documentation.
- Serving as an enabler of business intelligence to provide baseline metrics currently captured.

EXHIBIT 7.10   Sample Steps to Build Out Metrics and Synergy Plan

Recommend Metrics	Definition (Metric and Goal Definition)	Source and Frequency	Baseline Established	Process Test and Calculations	First Review
Week 1	Week 2	Week 3	Week 4	Week 5	Week 6

Identifying the metrics for each work stream to track during execution is only the first step in a vigilant and structured performance measurement process. Our experience suggests that moving teams from the identification step to the monitoring step requires a multistep process. This process will likely take two weeks to complete. So start this effort early, so you can be fully enabled to track performance on Day 1. Exhibit 7.10 is a recent example of the steps a company took and the elapsed time of teach step to move the teams from identification to tracking in a global M&A transaction.

Plan and Prioritize Synergy Initiatives   Having established the metrics and refined the goals, it is important to prioritize them and lay them out in a road map that can be easily communicated to others. The road map depicts the initiatives needed to obtain the planned benefits and synergies. The road map should include Day 0, Day 1, and Day 2, as well as all of the associated people, process, and technology initiatives needed to support the synergy goals. Once complete, the synergy plan will include the integration road map and all of the associated costs and benefits.

Building the road map requires prioritization across the business. However, more often than not, different business leaders will have their own ideas for prioritization. Managing all of those expectations within a constrained resource pool is often a big challenge. So, a simple guideline to adopt during such situations as this is to prioritize those opportunities that deliver the most value to the business. A road map based on benefit realization will generally have positive reactions from key stakeholders because of how it clearly and methodically offsets project costs and expedites big wins for the business. IT as the guardian of data and process documentation can play a significant role in this process.

There will normally be dependencies that restrict the ability to simply sort by benefit value and start checking off the list. This is the art in road map design. Strategic considerations, organizational limitations, or technical barriers may all play a role in how your company sequences its initiatives. Once again, a workshop approach to flush these out is recommended. Things that emerge from such workshops will often be better accepted. However, occasionally the outputs might surprise some.

As an example, one company prioritized a zero-dollar-value HR system implementation ahead of a high-value supply chain planning solution because one of the organizational limitations was a lack of visibility to the global head count of the combined entity. In other instances, acquiring companies have delayed high-value opportunities given the need to get basic financial visibility into the new business they have acquired.

Whatever the reason, having an objective and transparent prioritization process run by the right synergy capture team under the sponsorship of the overall M&A PMO, and supported actively by the executive leadership, is the way to gain acceptance and move forward successfully.

To take this concept one step further, some key IT-specific guiding principles to adopt in the synergy planning and road map process are:

- Start synergy analysis with a broad baseline of full-time employees (FTEs), expenses, and assets. In order to develop an appropriate synergy road map, you must align the plan to the revised operating model.
- Endeavor to achieve the quickest and highest-impact synergies from canceling redundant, noncore, or nonstrategic projects, but remember to back out any revenue- or expense-reduction commitments based on the programs.
- Remember that application consolidation and associated legacy application retirement are often difficult, time-consuming, and costly, but typically offer some of the highest rates of return.
- Factor retention bonuses into integration program costs to account for this cost since FTE synergy candidates may be required for integration project support.
- Drive synergy planning down to specific projects and embed synergy commitments, cost to achieve, and milestones into operational budgets and objectives.
- Control the scope for Day 1. Mandatory requirements are quite limited. Balance trade-offs among speed, risk, and cost.
- Bifurcate planning and release management into Day 1 and Day 2 paths. Investigate work-arounds for short-term requirements that may be challenging to implement on Day 1 (e.g., active directory integration).
- Demands for IT integration cost estimates and resource requirements will likely outpace development of functional strategies, decision making, and detailed requirement development. Take the lead and liberty to establish the required management processes, escalation process, and accelerators to make things happen quickly.
- Specifically confirm that IT programs are scoped and timed to synchronize with the business commitments on synergy attainment, whether they be either revenue or expense reduction.

- Establish clear timelines, processes, templates, and resource assignments for integration requirements identification, prioritization, and management. Make noncompliance visible to all.
- Champion regularly scheduled integration workshops to drive cross-functional team alignment. Clearly document decisions, action items, and interdependencies, as well as issues and risks along the way; make sure to include business partners and IT integration leaders during the workshops.
- Gather and prioritize requirements by function and determine the respective implications for each supported business process (for example, order-to-cash, procure-to-pay, account-to-report, and hire-to-retire processes).

Our experience indicates that an integration road map with a focused synergy section following this approach, with adherence to the guidelines, will be more readily actionable and accepted by the wider business teams during the M&A (see Exhibit 7.11).

Establish Process for Tracking and Reporting Synergy Achievements   A synergy road map serves as the foundation for tracking of benefits. However, effective measurement of benefits also requires a detailed and repeatable process. This process should align with and be sanctioned by the M&A PMO.

Three key steps in establishing the process for tracking and reporting synergy achievements are:

1. **Socialize synergy road map.** Communicate the synergy road map to the M&A integration teams and external stakeholders. This, however, should be a carefully weighted communication as there will be obvious synergy areas that should not be communicated widely. Hence, we recommend gaining explicit executive approval on the synergy road map, leveraging the M&A PMO, and developing structured communication channels for socializing the road map.
2. **Develop detailed work plans and checklists.** The synergy road map and included initiatives should be supported by detailed work and resource plans. These plans should be included in the program-level initiative planning activities. We suggest that it is also important to validate the detailed plans and that can be accomplished with the resource commitments for the overall M&A program. In addition, the synergy capture team should develop synergy capture checklists, which make it easier to track synergy achievement (see sample in Exhibit 7.12).
3. **Meeting cadence and data capture plans.** The synergy tracking should be an integral part of the overall integration program cadence. We

Sample Road Map

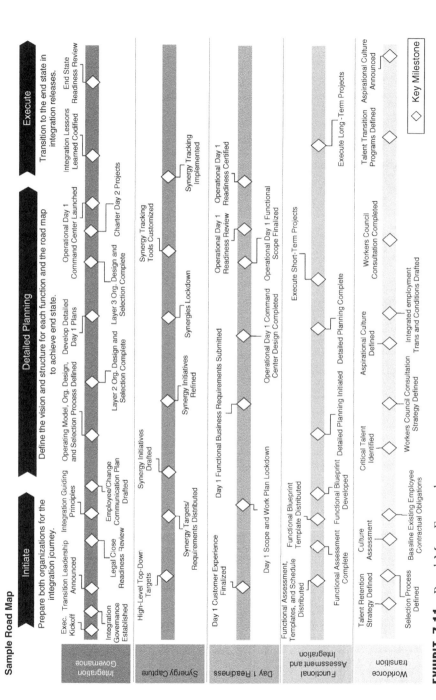

EXHIBIT 7.11 Road Map Example

Business Unit/ Function: Group
Workstream: INFORMATION TECHNOLOGY
Owner: Work Stream Owner
Day 1: XX
Report Date: xx

Last Updated: xx
0

Task ID	Description of Task/Action	Joint Activity with Target (Yes/No)	Accountability	Dependency	Priority	Timing (+/−) Days	Due Date	Status	Completion Date	Comments
	Synergy Tasks									
	Develop a Day 1 IT vision and distribute to all relevant stakeholders.	No		None	Day 1 mandatory	95		Green		
	Agree on synergy targets.	No		None		95		Green		
	Align synergy targets.	No		None	Day 1 mandatory	101		Green		
	Identify IT contacts for each delivery area (technical and divisional) to support Day 1 and Integration activities.	No		None	Day 1 mandatory	101		Green		
	Infrastructure consolidation.	No		None	Day 1 mandatory	101		Green		
	Vendor sourcing rationalization.	No		None	Day 1 mandatory	101		Green		
	Technology platform consolidation.	No		None	Day 1 mandatory	94		Green		
	ERP application migration.	Yes		None	Day 1 mandatory	87		Green		
	CRM application migration.	Yes		None	Day 1 mandatory	87		Green		
	Set up IT PMO and agree on reporting and governance approach for the IT plan.	Yes		None	Day 1 mandatory	87		Green		
	Obtain detailed IT budgets for both Opex and Capex (pre Day 1) for Day 1 IT delivery.	No		None	Day 1 mandatory	87		Green		
	Drawn-down budget set up with WBS and cost center codes for Day 1 delivery activities.	No		None	Day 1 mandatory	87		Green		

EXHIBIT 7.12 Sample Synergy Capture Checklist

suggest leveraging the existing program status reporting tools, with any requisite enhancement to allow for capture of synergy data. This is the preferred way to go, and it allows synergy tracking to become part of the program governance DNA, preventing it from becoming an activity unto itself. Additionally, synergy tracking data sheets and dashboards should be established as part of the overall synergy planning process to share, and view, the results.

Exhibit 7.13 provides an example of a tool we have used to capture synergy results.

Overall, establishing a believable synergy plan will serve as the building block that carries the synergy goals established earlier in the process to successful value execution and, it is hoped, to the overall success of the deal.

Value Execution

After the value plan is established, the integration should track its progress not only against the projected timeline and milestones, but also against the benefits targets set forth earlier on in the road map. Integrating value tracking into day-to-day project activities is what will focus the team on the benefits realization part of the program. Projects are typically most successful when management can integrate value into the integration's framework. There are many ways to track and incentivize value execution, but we will focus on the following four:

1. Integrate value into team culture.
2. Establish value-driven traceability.
3. Establish value ownership.
4. Define and manage to KPIs.

Make Value Tracking Part of the Project Team's Culture   When defining, measuring, and tracking value are an integral part of the program's culture, then ownership and stewardship of the benefits become easier to manage. There are many ways to influence the culture of the team, but there are a few tactical steps managers can take to formalize the cultural elements they would like the team to adopt.

Considerations   First, include the program's overall value goals in the project charter and include specific value areas in each work stream's vision statement. These should be documented in such a way that each project team member reads and understands them when beginning to work on the project. The charter and goals should continue to be referenced when

Synergy Financial Impact Template

				Include in Consolidation:	**Yes**
Benefit FIT Title: (must be unique)	Rationalize IT Application Portfolio	ValuePlan Cross Reference:		Benefit FIT Number:	FIT_001
Client Sponsor:		FIT Author:		Team Name:	
Core Process:		Subprocess:		Location:	
Description:	Client X can reduce IT spend by reducing the number of applications used to support core financial processing and business intelligence. Costs include program conversion and interface costs, and benefits will include decrease in license and support spend.				

Financial Assumptions (Update Category: One-Time/Recurring and Year of Benefit for accurate financial results)

				EVM Assumptions
Category:	(-) SG&A Expenses-->Information Technology	Year of Benefit/Starting Year:	Year 0	Improvement Lever: (This information is required for the EVM Alignment Report).
One-Time/Recurring:	Recurring	If one-time, split over how many years:		

	Baseline	Projected Performance		Change (should not = 0)	
		Low	High	Low	High
Key Metric Description (e.g. A = transactions/FTE)					
A = Total annual support license cost (all financial applications)		-	-	-	-
B = Direct support FTEs		-	-	-	-
D = Annual external support/hosting cost (annual)		-	-	-	-
E = Hardware costs (annual)		-	-	-	-
F = Annual business continuity costs (sum of hardware and location costs)		-	-	-	-
G = Location/data center costs (annual)		-	-	-	-
H = Cost avoidance		-	-	-	-
Fixed Variables Description (e.g. B = yearly salary/FTE, C = transactions/year)	Baseline				
C = Average cost per support personnel (salary and benefits)					
Misc. Calculations Description (e.g. describe interim equation if required)	Baseline	Low	High	Low	High
Direct support savings = B3C					
Total license costs = A					
External support cost = D					
Hardware costs = E					
Business continuity costs = F					
Data center/co-location costs = G					
Annual Cash Flow Calc. Description (e.g. D=C/ATFES to perform transactions)	Baseline	Low	High	Low	High
H = G+F+E+D+A+(B×C)					

Projected Annual Improvement

Projection Option	Year 0	Year 1	Year 2	Year 3	Year 4	Year 5
% of Annual Realization for Year	100%	100%	100%	100%	100%	100%
Low	Projected Yearly Improvement	-	-	-	-	-

Projected Annual Improvement

	Year 6	Year 7	Year 8	Year 9	Year 10	Sum of 10 Years
% of Annual Realization for Year	100%	100%	100%	100%	100%	
Projected Yearly Improvement	-	-	-	-	-	

Actual Annual Improvement

Actual Yearly Improvement	Year 0	Year 1	Year 2	Year 3	Year 4	Year 5
	Year 6	Year 7	Year 8	Year 9	Year 10	Sum of 10 Years

Support for Projected Key Metric (e.g., justify it)

Notes:

EXHIBIT 7.13 Synergy Capture Data Sheets

making key decisions, as well as at logical milestones during the execution of the road map.

Second, include value tracking in the project's management and implementation methodology. This includes building value-specific activities and milestones into the project plan, the high-level project road map, and establishing value criteria for all stage gates. In addition, make sure to build status reports and issues and risk tracking mechanisms that incorporate the specific impact to value drivers. These reports should highlight the magnitude of each impact by helping the team ensure they make decisions for their respective work streams that can improve the synergies realized.

What to Avoid   One of the primary inhibitors to value recognition we often see is allowing the team to fall into a project rhythm that is more focused on the tactical technology tasks (that is, the "what" and the "how"), rather than the strategic goal of those activities (that is, the "why"). We find that regularly tying back project activities to discrete aspects of the EVM will pull the team out of the weeds and reorient them toward the big picture. We also find that the weekly status meetings and periodic project-wide meetings are often the logical times to do this.

Establish Value-Driver Traceability   Once the value drivers are defined, each should be traced to discrete capabilities, behaviors, and results. We suggest that each of these be owned by one or more work streams during the integration. Tracing work stream goals and deliverables to these value drivers will likely improve the project's ability to achieve them and will enhance their auditability during, and after, the transaction.

Considerations   Integrating value traceability into the project delivery life-cycle can mirror familiar management tools (for example, requirements traceability and testing results tracking) and create the necessary linkages between the future-state technology and process ecosystem and their targeted outcomes. As the project team tracks business requirements they will also be tracking their solution's ability to meet the value targets.

Each driver must have an appropriate enabler in the future-state platform that can be used to prioritize project activities such as risk tracking, testing, and issue resolution. Integrating value into the project's priority definitions will keep it as part of all project conversations and allow the project managers to make informed decisions on where to direct scarce project resources.

What to Avoid   Avoid trying to trace *all* project activities down to a value-driver level. Many project activities and requirements are enabling components of the overall solution, so trying to trace them all the way back to a value driver will result in unnecessary overhead and administrative effort for the project team. We do not recommend this. Instead, identify the value drivers that are likely to have the greatest impact and make sure they are traced.

Additionally, take a holistic approach to working through the overall value of the project. Certain combinations of value drivers are likely to be more productive in the aggregate than others. Focusing too much on individual drivers in each work stream will often result in less value being unlocked over the long term.

Establish Overall and Work Stream Value Ownership   In our experience, benefit tracking is a PMO-owned responsibility. As such, a lead who sits in the office of project management should assume ownership for establishing value-tracking methodologies and KPIs and be responsible for integrating the project's value goals across all work streams.

Considerations   Establish a value lead and, depending on the size and complexity of the M&A integration, possibly consider creating a team that assumes responsibility for tracking value and making sure it is integrated into the overall solution. The value lead will own the establishment of PMO policies and procedures as well as value-tracking methods. He or she will also help ensure each team understands and is compliant with project standards in these areas.

This lead should also be responsible for integrating value goals across the work streams and for connecting the overall solution (i.e., people, process, and technology), making sure the desired amount of aggregate value is unlocked. This will mean the lead should prioritize issues and conflicts across the work streams as well as be able to balance high- and low-value functions and processes into the best integrated solution for the organization.

What to Avoid   Work stream leads play an important role in defining, tracking, and testing the value for his or her area. However, these activities should not be delegated entirely to the work stream leads, since we often see conflicts arise and the project is likely to end up suboptimizing the overall solution in the interest of the most influential, or loudest, party.

Establish Clear, Achievable KPIs for Each Value Driver   The KPIs will play two important roles in the integration. First, they will provide timely feedback to the PMO and to the sponsoring executives on the progress made toward enabling each key value driver. Well-structured project analytics will allow each stakeholder to focus on the progress that stakeholder's area is making and provide project managers with metrics on which to base key project decisions. Second, the KPIs will allow the business to track and measure the results of the project throughout the entire road map—from value expectations through value realization. Our experience dictates that establishing strong KPIs or metrics up front will greatly enhance the ability to define and communicate the program's value over time.

Considerations First, establish project KPIs. This activity should be completed during the planning phase, and the data for these KPIs should be enabled in the project management system. This information may be a combination of data sourced from project plans, issues and risk lists, and status reports. The status dashboards should integrate these KPIs into their regular status reporting cadence, and their generation should be automated as much as possible.

Second, identify the KPIs that will be used by the business on an ongoing basis to track value realization following Day 1, and build the data requirements and dashboard features for these KPIs into the system design. Our experience shows that identifying these early in the project will help ensure that the correct data relationships are built into the processes and the systems that will allow the KPIs to be automatically generated.

What to Avoid Manually intensive processes to track and gather KPI data will make it more difficult for the business to make a long-term commitment to tracking project results. The greater the automation, the more likely the business will monitor the value going forward. So, to provide a sustainable business solution as part of the M&A integration, we suggest avoiding manual work-arounds, multiple manual reports, or decentralized data collection. While these mechanisms may seem like a palatable work-around for Day 1, they are likely to deteriorate over the long term of the project.

Additionally, do not wait until go-live to closely look at reporting and tracking requirements. Although they are not likely to be valuable for several months after Day 1, the relationships, processes, and system requirements to gather and calculate the correct metrics should be established up front. If not, there are likely to be technical and possibly process-related changes required to enable them. These challenges have demonstrated to be, in our experience, significantly more cumbersome to implement in an active, production environment.

WRAPPING IT UP

IT can and should have a leadership role in the identification and realization of synergies from an M&A transaction. From the technical architecture to data and process governance and to management reporting tools, the IT function is at the heart of any organization's operations. This position provides a platform to collaborate with leaders across the business and share expertise on how systems can be effectively used to realize synergies and where other improvement opportunities may exist.

It is through these improvement opportunities that IT can lead the organization in a structured process to identify, plan, and capture transaction synergies. To accomplish this, IT should speak in business terms, translating people, process, and technology synergies into a common value language. With the organization aligned to the synergies at hand, defining improvement metrics and a process to track them throughout the M&A lifecycle is critical.

Synergies will be found across the organization, but IT's leadership of the organization through a process of prioritizing initiatives, creating a plan to implement them, and achieving the associated benefits is a true attribute of successful M&A transactions. This value plan then serves as a road map to guide day-to-day activities, keeping the common goal top of mind across the organization: achieving transaction value targets.

Supporting Business Objectives with M&A-Aware Enterprise Architecture

Pavel Krumkachev
Shalva Nolen
Nitin Prabhakar
Rajat Sharma

Mergers and acquisitions (M&A) are transforming companies, creating opportunities, and revolutionizing whole industries in many corners of the business world. However, many M&A transactions fall far short of their goals and often fail because of a lack of planning and an inability to execute on post-merger integration. This is evident in the area of information technology (IT), where understanding and planning for the impact of deals on IT can make or break an organization's M&A strategy and the synergies realized.

Based on our collective experience of conducting IT due diligence, preclose planning, postclose execution, and synergy tracking, we have identified specific components of an "M&A-aware" enterprise architecture that can be proactively established by companies in advance of an M&A event. When implemented correctly, these options can help increase the projected merger synergies, accelerate the time to achieve these synergies, and help reduce the cost of M&A transactions.

SOURCES OF IT-RELATED SYNERGIES DURING M&A

The corporate IT environments consist of the technical components required to support the many applications and services needed by a company. These components include, but are not limited to:

- Data centers (including disaster recovery sites).
- Network and network equipment (switches, routers, etc.).

■ Computers (servers, PCs, laptops) and mobile devices.
■ Phone systems.
■ Enterprise and departmental applications hosted internally.
■ Outsourced applications (e.g., cloud-based and software as a service applications).

There is a wide range of merger synergy opportunities within IT during an M&A event. As an example, data center consolidation is one way to efficiently enhance IT-related synergies as part of a merger. As companies are combined, an opportunity exists to combine infrastructure components into a single data center or set of data centers. Server virtualization and virtual storage arrays provide the opportunity to use excess capacity of one entity to host the combined applications and services portfolio with a decrease in overall cost.

The same principle applies to the network requirements for the new entity. In the case of a merger or an acquisition, the acquiring company's network should be built out to handle the additional capacity required by the combined organization. Once again, the total capacity required by the combined organization should be less than the sum of the parts.

Standardizing hardware (computers, mobile devices, etc.) and software used by employees provides another opportunity to realize cost savings. Standardization of these items can lead to reduced license and support costs and provide leverage with vendors to reduce purchase prices of equipment and services. IT infrastructure synergies typically will have significant up-front costs associated with achieving a reduced run rate. Care should be taken to do a cost-benefit analysis of where it makes sense to conduct a cost rationalization exercise on the infrastructure components. This should be kept in line with the IT operating model and the business strategic direction.

Similar to hardware and infrastructure, consolidation and standardization of enterprise and departmental applications can yield significant cost savings. In fact, enterprise application consolidation is often the driver of synergies in other areas of IT (e.g., infrastructure, maintenance, and support). Enterprise applications are therefore a logical starting point for planning an M&A-aware enterprise architecture and are the primary focus of the architecture options discussed further in this chapter.

It is important to mention that divestitures generally do not provide the same opportunities to leverage economies of scale with respect to the IT. The divesting entity should instead realize IT cost reductions as the business unit is removed from the parent company's environment; however, the divested entity will incur costs associated with its own, separate infrastructure. The advantage for the divested entity is the opportunity to move to new, more efficient infrastructure components and leverage commoditized IT services offered by various outsourcing vendors, services that may not have been available when the original infrastructure was created.

POST-MERGER IT INTEGRATION PLANNING: THE MODEL MAKES THE DIFFERENCE

The IT operating model is part of the overall business operating model, and necessarily the two should align in order to achieve the company's goals and strategic vision. M&A transactions are usually material changes to the company's overall operating model. Any such material change should trigger a review of the IT operating model to understand if IT is capable of supporting the new entity, particularly changes following a merger, acquisition, or divestiture, which typically results in a change in the company size along with the change in the business model.

Each M&A transaction is different, but most companies will broadly end up in one of four classic operating models following the M&A transaction. These models are:

1. Portfolio
2. Revenue capture
3. Cost saving
4. Consolidation

These are discussed in detail further in this chapter. The IT operating model should align to the changed business model in order to support the business's goals for the transaction. More detail on the four operating models and the implications for IT follows.

M&A-AWARE ENTERPRISE ARCHITECTURE MODELS

Depending on the operating model being proposed for the merger, IT can become either an enabler of synergy capture or one of the primary sources of planned synergies. Generally, most mergers fall into one of four future-state operating models, each with its own set of IT implications. Important questions to ask when choosing a model include:

- What are the main business objectives of the merger or acquisition (e.g., growth, market positioning, or cost savings)?
- What approach to business integration is required to realize these benefits?
- What level of IT integration is required to realize these benefits?
- In what ways can IT help the business realize its goals for the transaction?
- What opportunities exist to use current technology to position the business for future growth and change?

Portfolio Integration Model

This model aims to support each company as an individual entity with different capabilities and cultures. The business imperatives of this model are to achieve purchasing economies of scale and preserve competitive advantages and the differentiation of each organization.

Critical success factors:

- Focus on retaining individual capabilities across business units and IT organizations.
- Limit management involvement to protect autonomy and niche subject matter expertise.
- Monitor operations across all portfolio entities.

Characteristics and challenges:

- Reduced IT migration and integration effort.
- Some benefits from purchasing economies and standard risk management and security policies.
- IT organizations stay essentially the same.

Considerations for building an M&A-aware enterprise architecture:

- Integrate only the highest-level processes and systems required to run the business.
- Standardize and consolidate procurement/purchasing applications as well as security access control tools ahead of M&A event.
- Consolidated financial reporting is typically the biggest challenge; implement a flexible finance consolidation tool and a scalable business intelligence environment.

Revenue Capture Integration Model

Combine only "revenue capture-centric" processes and applications (e.g., sales channels). The business imperatives of this model are to open new distribution channels, open new market segments, capture revenue synergies, and preserve the competitive advantages and uniqueness of each company.

Critical success factors:

- Develop detailed implementation plans if new technology components are deployed to enable revenue-capture synergies.
- Deploy strong access control mechanisms to support multiple users across various sales channels.
- Ensure sell-side business processes are consistent and standardized.

Characteristics and challenges:

- Complex decisions about which systems to keep and which to abandon.
- Data migration from abandoned applications.
- Significant application integration effort.
- Significant economies from application and infrastructure rationalization.

Considerations for building an M&A-aware enterprise architecture:

- Prioritize integration of customer-facing sales and marketing applications (e.g., web storefronts, point of sale, customer relationship management) to accelerate revenue capture through cross-selling and up-selling to the expanded customer base.
- Leverage reusable services and open protocols (e.g., XML, Simple Object Access Protocol [SOAP]) to establish plug-and-play environments for applications that will not be immediately consolidated.
- Externalize customer data to a centralized repository in order to make it easily accessible to newly integrated sales tools for cross-selling and up-selling.
- Leverage composite application technologies to quickly combine existing and acquired order-capture applications and provide a single user interface for the sales force and customer service representatives.

Cost-Saving Integration Model

Combine only "cost synergy-centric" processes and applications (e.g., shared services). The business imperatives of this model are to realize cost-saving synergies, capture efficiencies, and achieve economies of scale.

Critical success factors:

- True collaboration and commitment to preserving most valuable parts of both organizations.
- Access to tools and methodologies to select best-of-breed solutions when required.

Characteristics and challenges:

- Complex in-or-out decisions to be made for overlapping shared services functions and applications.
- Significant work to integrate surviving back-office systems to operational and customer-facing applications.
- Significant economies from application and infrastructure rationalization.

Considerations for building an M&A-aware enterprise architecture:

- Prioritize integration of back-office applications (e.g., financials, human resources) to help accelerate cost synergy capture.
- Externalize item and vendor master data ahead of M&A activity to an external data store. This will help create a plug-and-play transactional environment for front-office applications, which are not immediately consolidated.
- Invest in flexible service-oriented architecture (SOA)–based middleware to avoid having to build custom and redundant integrations to new systems.

Consolidation Integration Model

Convert one organization to the same processes and systems of the other. The business imperatives of this model are to realize cost-saving synergies as well as revenue synergies, standardize global processes, and improve control and visibility over business operations.

Critical success factors:

- Focus on business case and return on investment (ROI) analysis prior to initiation of multiyear projects.
- Track synergy targets closely and implement governance procedures for funding and prioritizing IT-driven projects.

Characteristics and challenges:

- Data migration from all of target's systems into acquirer's systems (or vice versa), except for highly unique systems.
- Consolidation of enterprise resource planning (ERP) and non-ERP applications.
- Significant economies from application and infrastructure rationalization.
- Single IT organization.

Considerations for building an M&A-aware enterprise architecture:

- Highly customized architecture can significantly slow down consolidation of enterprise applications. Enforce the use of industry-standard processes and plain-vanilla functionality in order to make post-merger consolidation more straightforward.
- Keep current with the newest technology platforms by upgrading to the latest version of enterprise applications. Consolidating enterprise

systems from the same generation (e.g., client server versus mainframe) requires less time for design, testing, and end-user adoption.

■ Migration of data presents the biggest challenge during ERP consolidation. Invest in data-cleansing and data-consistency management tools. When appropriately deployed, these tools can quickly identify potential issues and reduce the risks related to data integrity and quality.

DIVESTITURES AND THE ENTERPRISE ARCHITECTURE FRAMEWORKS

Divestitures pose a whole new set of challenges that IT usually needs to address in a timely manner. Based on the current operating model of the organization and the scope of carve-out for the new entity, the IT systems affected could have several interdependencies. This tight coupling of processes and IT systems is addressed by carefully selecting the length of the transition services agreement and defining a clear blueprint of the future state.

This carve-out process for IT is about identifying the various systems that are interdependent, documenting the impact of the divestiture, prioritizing alternatives to replace or transition, and striking a right balance between the estimated cost and the expected value.

As part of the identification process, an enterprise-wide view of the IT assets is compiled. This includes data centers, technology assets, third-party applications, and associated contractual obligations for licenses and subscriptions. Once the level of interdependence and the associated impact of separation are identified, an IT enterprise architecture strategy consistent with the goals of the divestiture can be finalized. The four approaches that follow represent four typical divestiture scenarios based on the impact on the parent company and the interdependencies with the new divested company.

1. **Outsource and simplify.** For functional processes and IT assets where there is a low level of impact on the business and interdependence between the parent and the new company is limited, a low one-time investment with a focus on third-party outsourcing may be sufficient. The divestiture also provides an opportunity to simplify the operations and leverage the core competencies of the outsourcing service provider.

2. **Clone and replicate.** An enterprise architecture model focused primarily on replication from the parent company is applicable for functional areas between the two entities where there is a low impact and a high level of interdependencies. One example of this model would be the case of portals where salespeople are managing various opportunities at the same client.

3. **Carve out and go.** In the case of critical, high-impact business functions that will be completely independent at each of the divested entities, the enterprise architecture strategy is primarily focused on identifying the level of overlap and implementing that functionality in separate systems by migration and conversion of data. Hosted HR shared service providers at the parent company could easily carve out a separate instance for the new company.
4. **Transition and innovate.** A new entity that has a high level of inter-dependence and impact on the parent company should carefully plan the transition and focus on building those IT capabilities on a priority basis. These differentiating capabilities should be closely aligned to new business goals and growing the new independent company.

WRAPPING IT UP

An M&A-aware enterprise architecture can help IT become either an enabler of synergy capture or a primary source of synergies. For instance, in the "revenue capture" operating model scenario, the business may wish to achieve revenue-related synergies by combining the sales channels of both merging companies. IT, in this case, can focus primarily on consolidating and integrating synergy-specific applications (e.g., dealer systems and web sales channels). Here, IT becomes an enabler of synergy capture, without which the business objectives may not be met. In the "consolidation" scenario, in contrast, IT-related cost savings are a significant portion of planned synergies after the merger. An accelerated consolidation of IT staff, applications, and infrastructure under this model is, therefore, critically important to effective synergy capture.

The Importance of a Tested IT Strategy and Approach for Mergers, Acquisitions, and Divestitures

Pavel Krumkachev
Shalva Nolen
Nitin Prabhakar
Rajat Sharma

M&A IT ORGANIZATION AND STRATEGY

Merger and acquisition events are so varied and dynamic, and the nature of each transaction generally so unique, that they require a comprehensive strategy and focused preparation to guide IT organizations as they plan for future M&A scenarios. Described here are some specific guiding principles that can be used to develop an effective strategy for an IT organization and the IT resources it maintains to execute the integration of an acquired entity effectively. These principles encompass the development of a flexible and open IT function. They effectively help establish an IT ecosystem that allows acquiring companies to easily integrate new IT components from acquired companies and operate them to support the newly combined businesses. This strategy comprises the following five components, which are then each described in the sections that follow:

1. Increase IT-enabled business value by tightly aligning M&A business goals and IT priorities.
2. Design an enterprise architecture to support effective M&A IT integration.
3. Structure IT organizations to minimize impact from M&A deals.
4. Streamline IT funding and governance processes.
5. Build IT capabilities to support and execute an M&A transaction.

Increase IT-Enabled Business Value by Tightly Aligning M&A Business Goals and IT Priorities

It has become almost a cliché: The business complains that IT doesn't deliver; IT says that the business doesn't understand how difficult it is to implement some of the business's requests. The business claims IT is unreliable; IT claims the business is unreasonable. During a merger or an acquisition, the CIO can help bridge that gap by understanding the rationale behind the deal and the business's future direction, and determining how IT can most effectively support the strategy. In a merger, many business functions will be combined (for example, the new organization may not need two sales forces, two warehouse managers, two HR departments, and two accounting departments). When one of the two is eliminated, its IT systems frequently are also rationalized. In addition, the merger itself may lead to the discontinuance of some operations and their IT support.

A merger provides an opportunity for IT to reevaluate the service levels provided to the business. The IT department may be able to fine-tune its outputs without adversely impacting business performance by delivering services selectively—say, only to engineering or only to administrative services—based on need rather than companywide. The business strategy for any merger or acquisition will often determine post-merger business operating requirements, which, in turn, will help determine the scope and degree of business process integration (e.g., tightly vs. loosely) for the combined company. Further, IT integration requirements are driven largely by the business process integration requirement. Finally, and perhaps most importantly, the energy and expectations brought about by a merger give the CIO the opportunity to engage business leaders in strategic discussions aimed at improving business results from the use of existing or proposed capabilities.

Design an Enterprise Architecture to Support Effective M&A IT Integration

An open and flexible enterprise application architecture is one key to the effective execution of an integration strategy for IT applications and infrastructure.

Most long-term enterprise architecture design methodologies require detailed modeling of an organization's entire technology and network infrastructure. However, an enterprise architecture design in an M&A context analyzes the business activities and related technology dependencies only within the overlapping areas of the two businesses. In other words, it is intended to provide better information where it's needed faster. Proactive planning and implementation of an M&A-aware enterprise architecture can be a major accelerator of post-merger integration activities and can help businesses more quickly realize planned synergies during the integration of people, processes, and systems. (See Chapter 8 for a review of four potential M&A-aware models.) The detailed models identified as part of the M&A-aware enterprise architecture approach need to be aligned with the target operating model of a combined business and can bring flexibility and consistency at multiple tiers:

- At the business tier, the enterprise architecture strategy provides a business-centric view of the merging entities from a functional perspective. A graphical representation of various functional areas such as HR, payroll, finance, and marketing easily helps identify the overlap and potential synergies between the two companies.
- At the information tier, the enterprise architecture defines information models that accommodate new and existing business processes. It also provides information on the various data stores and functional data entities that need to be involved as part of the integration.
- At the application tier, the enterprise architecture provides information on the application landscape that details ERP applications that exist at the merging entities, boundary applications, and hosted services supporting the companies.

Implementing an open and flexible M&A-aware enterprise architecture can help a business accelerate the post-merger integration activities and more rapidly achieve synergy targets related to IT.

Structure IT Organizations to Minimize Impact from M&A Deals

Information technology readiness is dependent on many factors; there is no one element that is common to all acquisition scenarios. Technology organizational profiles can vary greatly, from a loosely knit conglomerate of dissimilar entities supporting heterogeneous platforms to a tightly focused group intent on unifying disparate IT applications and infrastructure and aligning them with an overarching strategic IT-enabled business vision. Some of the key areas to consider for a nimble and flexible IT organization include the following:

- **Organization structure.** Common organization structures are by function, by business units or departments, or by geographic locations. Regardless of the IT organization's structure, the roles and responsibilities between internal IT departments and business functions should be clearly defined, and the structure should be aligned with the overall business objectives. A decentralized IT organization, with dedicated IT support for each business unit or department, will lend itself more easily to an M&A-aware structure, with the retention of knowledge of IT systems and infrastructure within the business units.

▪ **Outsourcing.** Outsourcing is an integral part of any IT operation. Many companies now rely on outsourcing relationships for numerous critical services, from application maintenance to telecommunications and data network support. To stay M&A aware on the outsourcing operation, an IT organization should be familiar with the terms and conditions of the outsourcing contracts and should try to negotiate contracts in a way that is flexible and easy to terminate or change in the event of a merger or an acquisition.

▪ **Empowered leadership.** IT leaders, who are being asked to lead M&A initiatives, need to have the right level of authority, tools, and executive-level support in order to be effective in their roles. These leaders also need direct access to company executives for rapid escalation and decision making when quick action is required. This access can help prevent corporate red tape from slowing down the post-merger integration work.

Streamline IT Funding and Governance Processes

Regardless of the transaction size or desired degree of integration, every deal has an impact on IT. Since IT resources and funding generally are limited, it is essential to immediately inventory and assess all IT projects (even those not directly related to the deal) to verify they are still required and align with the company's future direction. Priority should be given to IT projects that (1) link to critical Day 1 requirements, (2) enable or accelerate large synergy opportunities, or (3) are essential to implementing the company's future strategic initiatives.

IT should be an integral part of a predeal due diligence process and should have a say in the budget and effort estimates related to the integration. Many IT integration initiatives exceed their planned budgets simply because CIOs and their staff are not consulted before a deal is finalized.

The enterprise IT governance model is another important factor. Some effective IT organizations are organized around decentralized IT, with key business and IT roles existing at the line of business or business unit level. Though decentralization may increase the cost of IT operations, it usually facilitates a quicker IT decision-making process and can simplify the integration or divestiture of the IT organization through an M&A transaction.

Build IT Capabilities to Support and Execute an M&A Transaction

Even with appropriate planning for the M&A transaction, the IT organization must still be able to execute the plans effectively. Typically, experience breeds effectiveness, and companies that have participated in multiple M&A transactions often fare better than companies that are undergoing the process for the first time. The execution of the IT integration process is where third-party integration advice and assistance can often be extremely valuable, especially to companies that are attempting post-merger IT integration for the first time, or that lack the experience of a series of deals to draw upon.

Companies that frequently undertake major M&A initiatives should also consider building a strong bench of IT specialists who can be made available to work on the M&A IT integration projects. These centers of excellence can help ensure organizations are ready to rapidly address the merger, integration, or divestiture. Often, the top performers get called upon to work on strategic and urgent M&A initiatives; however, no backfill resource capacity exists to perform the day-to-day responsibilities of IT staff.

A TESTED AND REPEATABLE APPROACH FOR IT INTEGRATIONS

Applying the set of industry leading principles during each phase of an IT integration is a tested approach to effectively integrating the acquired company from an IT perspective.

Due Diligence

The predeal due diligence phase can be where the success or failure of the merger or acquisition is determined. The probability of success frequently is tied to the amount of time and effort expended understanding the target company and the synergies to be realized as a result of the deal. This is also true from an IT perspective, as IT enables merger synergies and provides significant opportunities for cost reduction. Unfortunately, IT is often overlooked during the due diligence process, and this can result in surprise costs, integration delays, and a failure to achieve the anticipated synergies. For a successful integration that achieves the planned synergies, IT and the business should be aligned, and this should occur early in the M&A lifecycle.

The key objectives for IT during the due diligence phase are to identify any IT risks and IT synergy opportunities while developing an understanding of the target's IT function, including the IT architecture, IT operations, IT financials, and the IT organization. To fully assess these areas properly requires that some members of the due diligence team have IT expertise. They also need to understand the acquiring company's IT function in order to identify and accurately estimate the value of the IT synergy opportunities. Because IT enables the business synergies, any missed risks or areas of significant effort during IT due diligence can result in problems in achieving the synergy targets.

Experience does make a difference in effectively executing an IT due diligence effort. Organizations attempting a due diligence effort for the first time should consider getting assistance from a third party to help them as they build that experience. Even organizations that have gone through multiple M&A transactions might need to seek assistance while building experience in the IT due diligence arena if this has not been a focus in the past.

An effective IT due diligence effort is a key component in ultimately achieving IT integration success and is the basis for the next step in the time-tested approach. (See Chapter 5 for a more detailed analysis of the IT due diligence process and why it can be so important to the ultimate success of deals.)

Integration Planning

A major reason acquisitions fail to achieve the anticipated value is ineffective integration planning and execution. The business integration approach will be driven by the reasons for the acquisition. The IT integration approach should, in turn, be highly dependent on the business approach, and thus the two must be closely aligned. The business and IT should conduct joint kickoff and planning sessions, and IT needs to work with the business to understand how the business requirements impact IT and vice versa. Typically, this sort of collaboration is facilitated using a joint business/IT blueprinting effort. During this effort, business function and IT leads from both companies collaboratively make decisions on what the future-state blueprint of people, processes, and systems will look like for the combined company.

The key objectives for IT during the integration planning phase are to develop the IT strategy and vision for the combined entity and to create a strategic plan for the IT piece of the integration. No two M&A transactions are the same, so thoughtful planning is required to address the particular intricacies of any given deal. Having an open and flexible enterprise application and infrastructure architecture and a nimble and flexible IT organization facilitates bringing in new components from the target company and then operating the combined IT systems to support the newly combined business.

The integration planning team should be identified early and ideally would contain those who participated in the IT due diligence effort for continuity. Furthermore, if possible, the team should contain resources from both the buyer's and the acquired company's IT function who are knowledgeable about their respective IT systems and processes and can help develop a plan that would successfully integrate the acquired company while minimizing disruption for either business.

The IT integration plan needs to address the IT architecture, including the future-state application and infrastructure architectures and the enterprise architecture standards. The plan also needs to address the strategy and vision for the future-state IT organization and IT operating model. The integration plan needs to keep in mind the key principles in the M&A IT strategy so that changes to the IT organization, operating model, and architecture will result in an IT function that continues to be able to support the business's M&A needs.

When developing the plan, the IT integration planning team also needs to develop plans for dealing with third-party vendors and their contracts and licenses. Furthermore, the team needs to review plans for any in-flight IT projects at both the buyer and the acquired company and address these projects in the plan. The planning team also needs to consider how to track planned synergies as part of the IT integration plan. A critical part of the plan focuses on the activities that are needed to get to Day 1, while the remainder of the plan addresses those integration initiatives that will conclude post-Day 1.

Once the IT integration plan is complete, the work toward moving into the transition phase and implementing the plan begins.

Transition

The key objectives of the transition phase are to execute the plan that was developed in the previous phase. As preparations for the integration move out of planning and transition toward Day 1, IT and the business should conduct periodic joint design and integration plan reviews so that they remain aligned on the business and IT requirements and track all critical dependencies. IT and the business should also be aligned for the testing effort with the business resources being fully involved in testing and responsible for sign-off on the results. Finally, the business and IT should conduct joint Day 1 readiness and cut-over planning sessions so the Day 1 transition goes as smoothly as possible.

Even a perfect IT integration plan is worthless if the IT organization doesn't have the necessary capabilities to execute the plan effectively. The IT function needs to have the processes and tools in place to execute the M&A IT activities. Furthermore, the value of experience cannot be underestimated. If the organization is undergoing the process for the first time, management should seriously consider getting advice and guidance from an experienced third party that can point out an effective way to navigate the obstacles that frequently occur.

Postclose Integration Phase

The key objective of the postclose phase is to complete the IT integration projects as quickly as possible to achieve the anticipated deal synergies as soon as feasible. Just because a successful Day 1 was achieved doesn't mean that the need for business-IT alignment is eliminated. This is when the real work begins to capture the integration-related synergies, and our experience has shown that the sooner the projects to capture these synergies are completed, the more successful the integration is. Moreover, this postclose period is also when additional IT synergies are identified that hadn't been considered previously. With full access to the target's systems and IT team members, more accurate information is available to determine rationalization opportunities for applications, infrastructure, contracts, and the IT organization.

A TESTED AND REPEATABLE APPROACH FOR IT DIVESTITURES

On the other side of the IT integration coin lies IT divestiture. Divestures can include carve-outs, spin-offs, liquidations, split-offs, exchanges, and tracking stocks. The separation type selected is based on a valuation analysis and potential acquirers. As with IT integrations, applying the key principles in the M&A IT framework during each phase of an IT divestiture is a demonstrated approach to effective IT separation.

Detailed Due Diligence

As with mergers or acquisitions, the predeal due diligence phase is also where the success or failure of most divestitures can be determined. Success is tied to the effort expended maximizing the perceived value of the assets to potential buyers. For a successful divestiture that achieves the deal's value capture, IT and the business need to be aligned; ideally, this will occur early in the M&A lifecycle.

The key objectives for the divesting company's IT divestiture team during the due diligence phase are to assess the current IT function, including the IT architecture, IT operations, IT financials, and the IT organization, and address any issues that would help improve the perceived value of the business to buyers. As part of this assessment, the team should also identify the cost-reduction opportunities for the organization that will remain. The IT divestiture team would also be responsible for supporting the due diligence effort and pulling together the information on the IT function to be shared with the potential buyers during their due diligence efforts.

Separation Planning

As with IT integrations, failing to plan will likely lead to problems in achieving a clean IT separation for the divested business. The IT separation approach will be highly dependent on the business approach, and the two should be closely aligned. The business and IT should conduct joint kickoff and planning sessions, and IT should work with the business to understand the how the business requirements impact IT and vice versa.

The key objectives of the IT divestiture planning phase are to plan the IT separation process in order to capture the expected IT divestiture value and mitigate the risk. The IT divestiture planning team should work with the business and the other functions to develop a cross-functional separation plan that is consistent with the business's operational and strategic objectives. The IT separation plan should also make sure the divested entity can continue its business without interruptions in applications, systems, or network availability. Furthermore, the plan should address the divested business's access to the software licenses it needs to operate on Day 1. During this planning phase, the IT divestiture team should also develop a data management strategy that provides the divested business access to its data and that protects access to the parent company's sensitive data that is not part of the deal.

The IT divestiture plan should also address the parent company's IT architecture, including the future-state application and infrastructure architectures and the enterprise architecture standards. The plan also should address the strategy and vision for the parent company's future-state IT organization and IT operating model.

One aspect of IT divestiture planning that differs significantly from IT integration planning is the need to plan for the development, management, and support of transition services agreements (TSAs). Supporting the TSAs can have a major impact on the IT organization, as this should be done in addition to activities to support the parent company's remaining IT systems. (See Chapters 14 and 16 for more information on TSAs.)

As with the IT integration plan, a critical part of the plan focuses on the activities that are needed to get to Day 1, while the remainder of the plan addresses those IT divestiture initiatives that will conclude post-Day 1. Some of those activities that will conclude post-Day 1 are postdivestiture IT cost-reduction activities, such as removing unnecessary infrastructure. The IT separation plan should keep in mind the key principles in the M&A IT framework so that changes to the IT organization, operating model, and architecture still result in an IT function that continues to be able to support the business's future M&A needs.

Once the IT separation plan is complete, the work toward moving into the transition phase and implementing the plan begins.

Transition

The key objectives of the transition phase are to execute the plan that was developed in the previous phase to achieve an issue-free Day 1 separation. As with integrations, when preparations for the IT separation move out of planning and transition toward Day 1, IT and the business should conduct regular joint design and integration plan reviews so that they remain aligned on the business and IT requirements and any dependencies. Also similar to an acquisition, IT and the business should also be aligned for the testing effort. The business resources should conduct acceptance testing, and the business should be responsible for sign-off. Finally, the business and IT should conduct joint Day 1 readiness and cut-over planning sessions so that Day 1 separation is as issue-free as possible.

Just as with an acquisition, the IT function needs to have the processes and tools in place to effectively execute the IT separation activities, and experience with previous deals can make a big difference. Organizations undergoing the process for the first time should consider getting advice and guidance from an experienced third party.

Postclose Separation Phase

The key objective of the postclose separation phase is to provide support to the divested business through the TSAs and to complete the IT cost-reduction projects as quickly as possible to achieve the anticipated savings as soon as feasible. The divesting company should strive to end the TSAs as quickly as possible.

WRAPPING IT UP

Using the aforementioned approach to IT integrations and divestitures can help an organization in its efforts to effectively complete the IT integration or IT separation activities that support its goals for a given M&A transaction. Applying the key guiding principles of the M&A IT strategy within each phase of the M&A lifecycle is part of a time-tested, structured approach to capture the value of an M&A deal and prepare an IT organization to effectively support future M&A activity.

CHAPTER 10

Cloud Considerations for M&A IT Architecture

Mike Brown

Organizations in the midst of mergers and acquisitions (M&A) activity will go through a rapid transformation, and post-merger synergies can be gained by consolidating and streamlining IT capabilities. Organizations that are evaluating how to address IT in a post-M&A environment should consider how cloud solutions can affect their architecture. This evaluation may include both assessing current cloud solutions that are in place and determining how cloud solutions can contribute to the target future state.

Used appropriately, cloud solutions can provide solutions that are more scalable and agile, and that enable innovation. They can also reduce the skills required internally and the time that internal resources need to spend on operational and administrative tasks. In addition, cloud computing can allow organizations going through post-M&A integration to redeploy IT resources toward value-added activities such as enabling business innovation.

Licensed applications that are installed and maintained in an enterprise's dedicated infrastructure may have a higher total cost of ownership than cloud-based applications or infrastructure used "as a service," and may be more difficult and costly to adapt to changing business needs.

UNDERSTANDING CLOUD SOLUTIONS

For purposes of this discussion, cloud solutions are identified by the following:

- **Vendor (external) clouds, either public clouds or virtual private clouds.** Public cloud infrastructure consists of vendor-provided services that can be accessed across the Internet using systems in one or more data centers, shared among multiple customers, and with varying degrees of data privacy controls. Internal private clouds are not addressed directly here, but follow many of the same principles.

- **On demand.** Provides almost immediate access to IT applications and services, platforms, or a pool of hardware resources that can be allocated and provisioned on demand.
- **Scalable and elastic.** Provides the ability to dynamically provision and deprovision, and automatically scale capacity up or down.
- **Pay as you use.** Vendor-provided cloud services are not licensed products or purchasable assets. Services are billed by user, quantity of resources consumed, or similar consumption-based metrics.

These characteristics distinguish cloud solutions from traditional hosting, where a hosting provider allocates dedicated hardware to a single customer, which is used to deliver solutions the customer has licensed.

TYPES OF CLOUD SOLUTIONS

Cloud solutions are typically categorized as the following:

- Infrastructure as a service (IaaS) refers to virtualized infrastructure (database, servers, network, and storage) delivered as a service.
- Platform as a service (PaaS) refers to platforms and tools for development, testing, and deployment, delivered as a subscription service.
- Software as a service (SaaS) refers to applications delivered as a subscription service, for both consumers and businesses.

CLOUD SOLUTION: POTENTIAL BENEFITS

More organizations are evaluating cloud options first, because of the benefits of cloud solutions. This shift toward evaluating cloud options first results from the potential benefits that cloud solutions can provide. The potential benefits that organizations can realize through cloud solutions are shown in Exhibit 10.1.

OPPORTUNITY DURING POST-M&A INTEGRATION

Post-M&A integration provides a rare opportunity for organizations to make significant steps forward in their IT strategy. This opportunity can be realized by leveraging cloud solutions as appropriate to standardize and simplify IT solutions and improve business alignment. Post-M&A cloud benefits can include:

- Development of repeatable approaches and standards for architecture, tools, and applications. These repeatable approaches and standards can

EXHIBIT 10.1 Potential Cloud Benefits

Category	Description
Business Agility	Enables greater organizational agility to respond to the marketplace and competitive dynamics.
Access	Provides users with access to all users regardless of location.
IT Value	Allows resources to shift from operational items to supporting business initiatives.
Cost Management	Can reduce resources needed to support and maintain in-house hardware and infrastructure.
	May reduce capital expenditure (capex) commitments and overall IT spend.
Increased Flexibility	Reduces time to develop, test, and deploy applications and environments.
Upgradability	Reduces time and costs to upgrade software since there are fewer instances of the software and they are more standardized.
	Minimizes downtime and increases operational efficiency.
Elasticity	Can allocate resources to specific services or processes based on fluctuating demand.

result in reduced license costs, reduced infrastructure complexity costs, reduced training and development costs, and reduced application defect and error rates.

- Implementation of SaaS solutions that can provide products better tailored to specific requirements and industries and reduce the IT infrastructure support required.
- Standardization of PaaS solutions that can reduce the number of development platforms that need to be supported, improve version control, and provide the opportunity to more easily test modules before purchase.
- Deployment of IaaS to standardize environment architectures, improve service level agreement (SLA) compliance, enhance disaster recovery, and provide scalability as business needs change.

CLOUD SOLUTIONS FOR POST-M&A PLUG-AND-PLAY IT FRAMEWORKS

As discussed in this book, most mergers fall into one of four future operating state models. Cloud solutions can be a strategic component of each of these operating models, as shown in Exhibit 10.2.

EXHIBIT 10.2   Cloud Solution Considerations by Operating Model

M&A Plug-and-Play Operating Model	Cloud Computing Considerations
Portfolio Model	IaaS solutions can expedite the consolidation of IT infrastructure, expediting the decommissioning of legacy data centers, reducing the IT skill sets required, and allowing IT resources to focus on business activities rather than IT infrastructure tasks.
Revenue Capture	IaaS solutions can expedite IT consolidation. SaaS applications around customer-facing and sales and marketing solutions can provide a strategic platform for revenue channel applications. PaaS solutions may provide a tool for creating composite applications to meet different requirements around revenue channel solutions.
Cost Saving	IaaS solutions can expedite IT consolidation. SaaS applications can provide strategic solutions for various shared service and back-office applications (for example, human resources and financials). PaaS solutions may provide a tool for creating composite applications and integration logic to plug in various applications.
Consolidation	IaaS solutions can expedite IT consolidation. SaaS applications can meet many application consolidation needs; consideration would need to be given to less mature cloud areas such as ERP.

DETERMINING SUITABILITY FOR CLOUD SOLUTIONS

Once an IT framework and operating model are determined, organizations should evaluate which capabilities will leverage cloud solutions. There are a number of characteristics that determine which capabilities are most suitable for cloud solutions, as shown in Exhibit 10.3. The level of suitability is a subjective assessment that depends on numerous factors, including the criteria shown in the exhibit.

Based on these criteria, some general conclusions can be made about the cloud suitability of various capabilities. This suitability can vary based on specific situations, and can change over time as cloud capabilities mature. Exhibit 10.4 contains examples of the types of applications or IT areas and their potential applicability to a cloud environment.

ASSESSING CLOUD MIGRATION TIMING

While many organizations consider cloud solutions to be a key part of their IT strategy, many have only partially realized this strategy. This is a

EXHIBIT 10.3 Cloud Computing Suitability Criteria

Suitability Criteria	Characteristic Implying Low Cloud Suitability	Characteristic Implying High Cloud Suitability
Scalability	No scalability requirements	High scalability requirements
Integration Complexity	High integration complexity	Limited integration complexity
Security and Privacy	High security and privacy requirements	Limited security and privacy requirements
Elasticity	No elasticity requirements	High elasticity requirements
Maturity in Cloud	Nonexistent cloud solutions	Enterprise-ready cloud solutions
Business Criticality	High business criticality/mission-critical application	Low business criticality
Governance and Compliance Requirements	Stringent governance and compliance requirements	Limited governance and compliance requirements
High-Performance Computing	High performance computing requirements	Limited high performance computing requirements
Data Transfers	Very large data transfers	Low-volume data transfers
SLA/Availability	Stringent SLA and availability requirements	Low to medium SLA and availability requirements
Ubiquitous Access	Not available as a web service	All functionality available as a web service (for example, can be accessed on-site, on a mobile device)

EXHIBIT 10.4 Sample Application/IT Area Cloud Applicability

Workloads Ready for Cloud Adoption	Workloads Transitioning toward Cloud	Workloads Being Evaluated for Cloud Adoption	Workloads Not Ready for Cloud Adoption
▪ Collaboration ▪ Infrastructure storage ▪ Workplace, desktop, and devices ▪ Development and testing ▪ Infrastructure computation and storage ▪ Customer-facing applications ▪ Workforce/HR applications	▪ Analytics industry applications ▪ Business processes ▪ Disaster recovery ▪ Financials and procurement applications	▪ Information-intensive workloads ▪ Isolated workloads ▪ Mature workloads ▪ Preproduction systems ▪ Batch processing ▪ Business intelligence and analytics ▪ Identity management	▪ Sensitive data ▪ Highly customized workloads ▪ Not yet virtualized third-party software ▪ Complex processes and transactions ▪ Regulation-sensitive workloads ▪ Enterprise resource planning and manufacturing solutions

result of several factors that drive cloud migration timing. In a post-M&A environment, some of the key factors to consider are:

- Migration effort and cost required.
- End-of-life schedule for servers.
- Software license renewal schedule.
- Skill sets required to support various current applications and technologies (scarce or readily available).
- Risks in current environments (for example, availability, support, and stability).
- Business requirements not being met by current solutions.
- Availability of funds for migration.

Once these factors have been considered, the timing for cloud migration can be determined. Post-M&A integration provides an opportunity to make a substantial transition to cloud solutions. However, cloud migration timing may occur over a significant period of time. As a result, post-merger cloud migration timing generally should be part of an overall cloud strategy.

ESTABLISHING A CLOUD STRATEGY

Since leveraging cloud solutions is a continuous process, it is important to establish a cloud computing strategy. A cloud strategy provides for a multiyear process and plan to achieve a strategic vision and long-term objectives. A good strategy is not meant to be a single major action, but a series of planned steps executed over a multiyear period, comprising a strategic direction. These steps are then executed in stages, with planned milestones and decision points to allow for strategic course correction and adjustment.

An organization's cloud strategy should be based on business-driven considerations:

- Key business and IT functional capabilities and workloads, rather than primarily by IT infrastructure services.
- Impacts to business models and processes.
- The anticipated future evolution of cloud computing capabilities and alignment with expected business and technology disruptive changes.
- The impact of cloud computing on current and emerging IT architectures, and how they will change with the adoption of cloud services.
- The core set of functional capabilities, and the trade-offs of leveraging leading vendor applications and technologies.

A typical cloud strategy initially emphasizes one of two approaches: either SaaS/PaaS solutions or a migration to IaaS services. In some cases, the initial approach emphasis can vary by capability.

- **SaaS/PaaS strategy.** This approach initially leverages certain capabilities from leading specialized applications (SaaS) and development platform (PaaS) service providers, and has a limited focus on infrastructure (IaaS). This can include migration of edge functions such as marketing, salesforce automation, HR, and some IT operations tasks. Organizations with this approach then typically continue this strategy with a deeper focus on core operational and ERP applications over a longer term.
- **IaaS strategy.** This approach initially focuses on migrating existing applications and systems to an IaaS architecture with limited migration to SaaS/PaaS cloud solutions. This strategy focuses on shifting on-premises software currently in use in a manner similar to traditional hosting approaches. This approach can avoid maintaining on-premises hardware and architectures. However, the organization generally would retain responsibility for software maintenance and upgrades/patching.

EVALUATING CLOUD PROVIDERS

Once a cloud strategy has been developed, it is necessary to determine which cloud providers to utilize. This is an important consideration, as organizations have a closer relationship with cloud providers than they typically have with software vendors. This close relationship occurs because the cloud providers are typically providing the software, product support, operational support, upgrades, and expertise in using their solutions.

Based on this close relationship, evaluating cloud providers is a key activity. In addition, these cloud providers should be evaluated on a broader set of criteria than typical software providers. A list follows of some of the areas to consider when evaluating cloud vendors. These areas apply in a post-M&A integration environment when evaluating whether to retain an existing cloud solution or when evaluating a cloud solution for a future organizational standard. In addition to specific considerations based on the solution requirements, some general areas to investigate include:

- Current client base and applicability to your organization.
- Typical client profile.
- Migration costs and effort.

- Service level agreements (SLAs) and materiality of incentives for cloud vendor to meet SLAs.
- Historical uptime percentage.
- Scheduled outage frequency and duration.
- Process, pricing, and options to adjust for peak loads.
- Ability to reduce costs after peak load has passed.
- Incremental costs associated with storage, bandwidth, and users.
- Data location and data privacy compliance (for example, whether your organization has specific European Union data privacy requirements).
- Third-party software licenses provided or required.
- For SaaS solutions:
  - Number of nonproduction environments provided.
  - Cost for additional environments.
  - Cost, time, and process to copy environments or restore from backup snapshots.
- Process, effort, and costs to migrate off of the vendor's cloud environment.
- Integration with external and on-premises identity management and middleware tools.
- Data encryption capabilities on transfer among cloud vendor and other systems.
- Impact of cloud environment on support of applications (for example, if the cloud environment operating system and architecture are certified for the applications being deployed).

CLOUD SOLUTION SUCCESS FACTORS

Effectively implementing a cloud strategy requires a new approach to IT. For an organization to effectively leverage cloud solutions, some of the critical success factors are:

- Implement appropriate cloud governance and risk management processes and guidelines.
- Identify key business processes and capabilities that rely on on-premises applications.
- Consolidate application and infrastructure platforms as needed to support cloud offerings.
- Assess the current operating model and how effectively it can support the adoption of cloud services and technologies.
- Reduce the architectural complexity of the IT environment.

- Design for scalability and allow for management capabilities that will horizontally scale the application workload.
- Structure interapplication component communications to be as efficient as possible.
- Adopt standardized cloud platforms in a phased manner, with functionality, flexibility, implementation time, and overall costs that compare favorably to alternatives.
- Make sure the chosen cloud technology allows for ongoing development and test operations along with running the production environment.
- Validate that the technical performance levels meet the required balance of reliability, capacity, and disaster recovery capability.
- Review data controls, security, privacy, and compliance requirements, particularly for data that is being stored in new physical locations or accessed by new users.

It is important for all of these factors to be reviewed during the implementation. Additionally, there are other factors that may be specific to your organization that should be considered.

WRAPPING IT UP

Cloud computing is transforming how IT operates and supports business objectives. Organizations that are going through mergers and acquisitions activity can particularly benefit from cloud solutions. These organizations are also well positioned to take advantage of these solutions.

To effectively leverage cloud solutions, it is important to establish a cloud strategy. This strategy will help facilitate having a cloud solution integrate with the organization's IT operating model and framework. Once a cloud strategy is established, execution of that strategy requires effective evaluation of cloud providers and implementation of new processes, standards, and governance. With these success factors in place, cloud solutions can help drive more agility to meet business requirements, better scalability, and higher-value use of IT resources.

CHAPTER 11

Data Implications of Mergers and Acquisitions

Sascha Elsing

CRITICALITY OF DATA MANAGEMENT IN M&A TRANSACTIONS

Speed is of the essence in merger and divestiture programs, and data integration or separation is often complicated and time-consuming enough to fall on the critical path. Additionally, data quality problems can have highly detrimental impacts on business operations and can put the success of the entire transaction at risk. Customer data integration offers one important way of achieving benefits out of a merger if done broadly and in a timely manner. This chapter contains some key governance and organizational considerations critical for data management, as well as recommendations on data confidentiality, privacy, security, risk, and archiving. It also provides a step-by-step road map for data integration and separation projects, as well as a summary of customer data considerations.

DATA GOVERNANCE AND ORGANIZATIONAL CONSIDERATIONS

Given the value data has to most organizations and how easily it can become corrupted and lost in a transaction, it is critical to put resources in charge of protecting this asset. At a minimum, there should be clear ownership of *each data domain* by two types of business resources:

1. A data steward, who has a deep understanding of the data, including its business meaning, quality, suppliers, consumers, and applicable business rules.

2. An executive owner, who helps ensure the recommendations developed by the data steward receive appropriate consideration at the leadership level, relative to other priorities.

It is equally critical to dedicate the right IT resources to the management and protection of the data asset. At a minimum, companies should consider assigning a team of architects, application specialists, and information security experts to manage each data domain. This team should support the business data steward with analysis and recommendations and also proactively manage the data asset from an IT perspective.

Depending on the size of the organization, the circumstances of the transaction, and the number of distinct data domains, it is sometimes helpful to establish an enterprise-wide data management and protection committee, which is responsible for the overall coordination and alignment of data-related activities.

DATA CONFIDENTIALITY, PRIVACY, SECURITY, AND RISK MANAGEMENT

M&A transactions typically raise additional data protection requirements beyond the standard confidentiality, privacy, security, and audit controls required in a steady state. For example, commercially sensitive data that is shared before the close of a merger is typically subject to special temporary confidentiality requirements. Similarly, divestitures often raise special restrictions on data that cannot be physically deleted.

This may require careful planning, implementation, and monitoring of additional data safeguards. For example, a so-called clean room may have to be established, where sensitive data can be analyzed and tests can be conducted without releasing data to the larger enterprise. Another common data protection approach is the masking (i.e., automated alteration or deletion) of sensitive data.

Aggressive timelines, as well as evolving processes and organizational structures, frequently tempt personnel to improvise and take shortcuts when it comes to data management. It is therefore advisable to counteract this proactively—for example, by placing special emphasis on definition, communication, and monitoring of roles, responsibilities, and controls.

DATA ARCHIVING REQUIREMENTS

Regulatory and business requirements for data archiving demand special attention during M&A transactions. It is critical that archived data is preserved in a format that can be accessed independently of any applications that may become inaccessible as part of the transaction. This may require development of special processes or retention of applications for the sole purpose of access to archived data. Divestitures often raise the challenge of separating archived data or implementing controls that reliably restrict access to any parts of the archived data that cannot be easily deleted.

DATA MANAGEMENT ROAD MAP

Key data management activities differ from transaction to transaction. In particular, mergers and acquisitions aim at data integration, whereas divestitures aim at data separation. Another important differentiator is the planned business and application cut-over strategy, which should be selected with data considerations in mind. Specifically, if legacy systems will continue to run in parallel for a period of time, data management aims at data synchronization across systems (for example, using middleware), whereas if systems are being consolidated, data management aims at data standardization and migration. The following pages outline the key steps that are generally required.

Identification of Data Assets

It is critical to identify and catalog all data assets as early as possible. Depending on the existing documentation in place, this can be a very time-consuming and involved process. Structured data contained in major applications tend to be well known. However, most organizations also have numerous applications and information repositories that are not as easily identified. These may include data managed by individual departments or sometimes even by single employees, such as spreadsheets. They may also include data managed by third parties (for example, agencies) or in cloud-based applications not managed by IT. Other data types often missed include big or unstructured data, such as images and documents, as well as certain hard-to-derive data stored only in analytical repositories, such as aggregate data in data warehouses.

In order to avoid gaps or redundancies and to achieve a consistent outcome, the data identification activity should be carefully managed by a data architecture team, which may gather the information through documentation reviews and interviews. It is advisable to organize the inventory around applications and data domains, such as customer, order, product, or supplier.

Assignment of Data Owners

Many data assets have multiple stakeholders and lack clear ownership by a business data steward and an executive owner. In order to manage the data asset effectively and reliably throughout the transaction, it is recommended to establish clear ownership for each data asset from both a business and an IT perspective.

Data Prioritization Based on Value and Risk

To make sure management attention and organizational resources are directed at the most important data assets, it is advisable to prioritize data assets from both a value and a risk perspective. This assessment can typically be done by the data owners with facilitation from IT.

Data Definition

Planning and design of data integration or separation activities are dependent on a detailed understanding of each data asset, as typically documented in data dictionaries. Important information includes descriptions of each data element (at the table and field level), including what the data mean (particularly important for code values), how the data are updated, where the data are consumed, what business rules apply, how historical data may differ from recent data (for example, due to past system or process changes), what volumes exist, how the data are archived and purged, and what confidentiality or privacy classifications apply. If reliable data dictionaries are missing, then their creation should be prioritized based on value and risk of the data asset.

Data Quality Assessment

Data quality should be one of the most important considerations when planning for data integration or separation. It tends to be hard to measure and difficult to express, but it can have an enormous impact on business operations and profitability. It is, therefore, critical to assess and document the quality of each data asset involved in an M&A transaction. Key questions include: How complete are the data? How consistent are the data? How many duplicates exist? How up-to-date are the data? How much of the data is corrupted? Answering these questions typically requires a two-pronged approach: data profiling (there are tools and third-party services for this) and discussions with the business users updating and using the data. It should also be documented whether there are any ongoing projects or trends that are expected to have a material impact on the data in the near term.

Data Mapping

If data are to be integrated from multiple sources, such as two organizations involved in a merger or an acquisition, it is necessary to map out which data elements in one organization correspond to which data elements in the other organization. This is most commonly done by listing the corresponding application, table, and field names and noting any differences between the data (for example, how the code values in one system relate to the code values in the other system).

Data Requirements Definition

The data requirements definition should specify which data should be integrated or separated, when (relative to the overall transaction timeline), and according to which rules. It must align with the planned business and application cut-over strategy (which business processes will use which applications when and for what). For example, if systems are to run in parallel for a period of time, then the data requirements definition should elaborate on the data mapping by specifying which data are to be synchronized according to which rules, such as timing, conflict resolution, and data cleansing needs. Special consideration should be given to the management of in-flight transactions (for example, open orders).

Any targeted data quality improvements should be described in detail. This typically requires balancing the value of the improvements against available time and resources. While it is recommended to bring data across that are as clean as possible, some cleansing objectives may be better left for data quality projects after the integration is complete.

In a divestiture scenario, the data requirements definition would primarily specify the criteria according to which data are to be separated.

Data Solution Implementation

Once the data requirements have been defined, IT typically follows an accelerated systems development lifecycle (SDLC) to implement the processes required. Typical solutions for data integration are based on middleware (primarily for ongoing synchronization of time-sensitive and lower-volume data) and extract, transform, load (ETL) tools (typical for bulk loads of high-volume and less time-sensitive data). Ongoing synchronizations also frequently leverage master data management (MDM) tools. Basic data cleansing can be accomplished using middleware, ETL, and MDM tools, but complex requirements frequently necessitate specialized data cleansing tools or use of third-party cleansing service providers, who often perform tasks such as language translation, standardization, deduplication, cleansing, enrichment, and validation. Many data integration or separation efforts also include substantial manual efforts to handle transformation tasks low in volume or hard to automate.

Similar to other data integration or conversion projects, testing typically involves five key types of activities:

1. Quantitative checks, such as using counts and checksums to compare source systems, target systems, and reject logs.
2. Qualitative checks, such as sampling and manual review of data in source systems, target systems, and reject logs.
3. Functional checks to confirm that the data can be accessed and processed by the target system and any downstream systems into which it might flow from there.
4. Performance checks to identify any required tuning of the target system or underlying infrastructure to accommodate the larger data and transaction volumes.
5. Cut-over execution checks (for example, mock or practice conversions) to confirm and practice the actual cut-over process.

In a divestiture scenario, it is often also necessary to separate archived data, analytical data (for example, data warehouses), and unstructured data, a task that is typically much more complicated than the separation of structured data in live systems.

Post-Execution Data Assessment and Audit

Once the planned processes have been executed and the data have been integrated or separated, it is recommended to assess the results (using quantitative and qualitative checks). Depending on the type of data asset, it may also be necessary to conduct a formal audit to assess compliance matters.

CUSTOMER DATA CONSIDERATIONS

Customer data integration offers one important way of achieving benefits out of a merger or an acquisition if done comprehensively and in a timely manner. Combining customer data from two organizations offers the opportunity to obtain a more comprehensive picture (360-degree view) of shared customers, and it can increase the total number of customer records available for marketing and analytics. This can lead to competitive advantages in marketing, sales, and customer service.

It should be noted, however, that merging customer data can be particularly challenging. Some of the complications include:

- Business customers are typically represented by complex account hierarchies that are often maintained manually and hence complicated to reconcile using automated processes. This frequently necessitates the use of third-party service providers, who maintain databases of businesses. In addition, business customers may have different terms, such as payment terms, in each organization. This often requires complex business rules in order to merge the data.
- Consumer data tends to be difficult to deduplicate, since the same person may be represented differently in each organization (for example, use of nicknames and abbreviations, variations in spelling and addresses).

WRAPPING IT UP

Data management is one of the key challenges for businesses and IT during M&A transactions, primarily since data integration and separation can be very complicated and time-consuming. Critical success factors include early identification and analysis of data assets, effective data governance and ownership, as well as a focus on compliance and data quality.

Using M&A to Streamline the Applications Portfolio

Colin Whiteneck
Joydeep Mukherjee
Ted Veterano
Venky Iyer

New market drivers and business opportunities such as mergers, acquisitions, and divestitures are continually impacting the way IT can support and drive the business. A regularly evolving applications portfolio strategy can enable CIOs to position IT to support and leverage technology enablers for business efficiency. CIOs are continuously looking to streamline the applications footprint to:

- Support mergers, acquisitions, and divestures and help achieve synergy targets.
- Position IT as a business partner in addition to being a business enabler.
- Respond to newer technologies.
- Improving IT cost run rates.

Exhibit 12.1 outlines the drivers that contribute to rationalizing the applications footprint.

An M&A transaction is a disruptive event that can be leveraged to streamline the applications portfolio. No matter whether the transaction is an acquisition, a merger, or even a divestiture, applications rationalization can help to accomplish the following:

- Attain operational and cost synergies.
- Reduce stranded costs left with the seller after a divestiture.
- Standardize, streamline, and simplify the applications portfolio.

New market drivers and business opportunities are impacting the way IT should support and drive the business.

An applications portfolio strategy (APS) is designed to ensure that IT supports business strategy and imperatives.

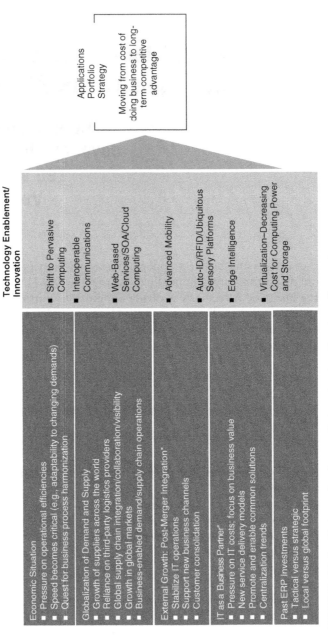

EXHIBIT 12.1 Drivers for Streamlining the Applications Footprint

*Driven by M&A events

Source: Deloitte

"Four Cs" are a simple approach to solving the complex problem of applications rationalization and simplification.

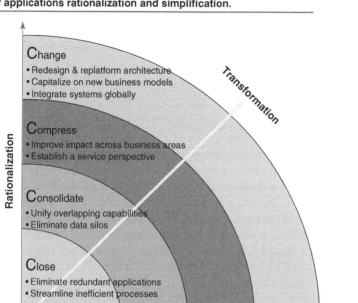

EXHIBIT 12.2 The Four Cs of Applications Rationalization Transformation and Correlated Synergy Opportunity
Source: Deloitte

CIOs and IT leadership should be driving a broad applications portfolio strategy through the implementation of an applications rationalization program. Through the applications rationalization program as part of a merger or a divestiture, IT leadership should drive the "Four Cs" within the applications portfolio in alignment with the overall transaction integration approach with greater synergy opportunity within each level of transformation seen in Exhibit 12.2.

Applications rationalization enables the integration or divestiture by supporting the operating model of the new business, and reduces operating costs of the IT environment by rationalizing the combined business applications portfolio and delivering functionality that meets requirements of the new business model.

OVERVIEW OF AN APPLICATIONS RATIONALIZATION PROGRAM

The applications rationalization program typically supports three main objectives:

1. Standardization
2. Cost reduction
3. Simplification

An applications rationalization program will typically result in substantial cost savings while improving support for the lines of business (LOBs). These savings can be significant, especially during a disruptive M&A event. Additional benefits include a simplified infrastructure and an availability of resources, allowing organizations to focus on what really matters. Applications rationalization does not just help meet technical requirements and alignment with strategy; it is also a business and financial analysis mechanism that supports improving investment for better efficiencies and resource effectiveness within the organization.

A typical applications rationalization program consists of:

- Selecting your applications based on business need and prioritizing related actions (choosing what you will do and what you won't do, and how it is done).
- Effectively managing the value of both existing and proposed applications.
- Monitoring changing priorities and application value, continually reviewing and adjusting as necessary.

Exhibit 12.3 outlines the approach to transition from the current state to the target state.

The rest of this chapter addresses each of these topics and contains some of the best practices for applications rationalization in an M&A deal.

ACHIEVING COST SYNERGIES THROUGH APPLICATIONS RATIONALIZATION

Out of the three main objectives of an applications rationalization program (standardization, cost reduction, and simplification), the most critical is reducing the applications portfolio run rate and achieving cost synergies. The standardization and simplification of applications rationalization can

An applications portfolio strategy enables standardization, optimization, and simplification and reduces operating expenses of the IT environment.

Current State

- Inflexible, redundant applications and point solutions that are unreliable and error-prone
- Complex, heterogeneous applications and database infrastructure
- Inconsistent tools and processes that are not aligned with LOBs
- Unleveraged hardware footprint, and low adoption of shared infrastructure

Target State

- Best-in-class applications and services that support the LOBs, running across *n* channels
- Bundles of applications with similar functionality
- Increased flexibility from new functionalities and external service providers
- Enterprise service bus, fewer application infrastructure choices, simplicity, lower cost
- Economies of scale from virtualized platform

Rationalization & Simplification

- Close
- Consolidate
- Compress
- Change

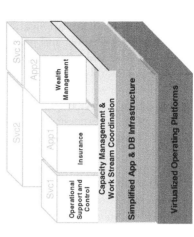

EXHIBIT 12.3 Approach to Transitioning from Current State to Target State

Source: Deloitte

179

also contribute to cost reduction. Standardizing and enabling business functions through the use of similar technologies, scalable applications, and support landscape lays the foundations for an improved applications landscape, leading to the achievement of cost synergies while helping determine that business-unit-required capabilities enable the rationalized applications landscape.

Standardization, cost optimization, simplification, and synergy realization require rationalizing applications and consolidating technical infrastructure to one set of tools and processes. Doing so can lead to a significant reduction of labor and software costs. While this may sound simple, it can obviously be incredibly difficult to execute. Rationalization projects require close coordination with other cost-reduction efforts to amplify savings without compromising service quality. Applications rationalization, when done properly, can be a cornerstone of cost synergy realization through savings from other IT aspects, such as:

- Data center and server consolidation.
- Data storage optimization.
- Technical support function optimization.
- Extensible applications architecture.
- A standardized software development lifecycle.
- IT support head count reduction.

By implementing a broad applications rationalization program, two main objectives can be met around achieving cost synergies:

1. Reduced run rate for applications:
   - Fewer applications running on a reduced infrastructure footprint supported by reduced number of resources.
2. Applications portfolio aligned with overall IT operating model:
   - The new applications footprint can support the business blueprint, which will be revised after the merger or the divestiture.

Exhibit 12.4 outlines the cost savings universe and the focus areas.

There are specific components of the applications rationalization program that will likely require attention throughout the execution of the program. The first is around budgeting and monitoring. Monitoring of budgetary spend on each applications portfolio is critical to help determine that there is a clear view of the value being created and the budget being freed up for potential reallocation. Second is to maintain the right balance between cost optimization and business imperatives, technology innovation, and IT capabilities. Future-state applications portfolios should be designed to meet the needs of the business, while improving cost and the number of resources

Planning and implementations of applications rationalization initiatives should be closely synchronized with additional IT cost-reduction initiatives.

Rationalization projects require close coordination with other cost-reductions efforts to amplify savings without compromising service quality.

Rationalization, when done properly, should enable savings from other projects, such as:

- Server rationalization
- Project rationalization
- Data storage optimization
- Improvement to hardware utilization

Applications rationalization also enables new savings opportunities such as:

- New, more efficient shared services
- Easier migration to or extension of a standard applications architecture
- A standardized, and more successful, software development lifecycle
- Optimized training for field adoption

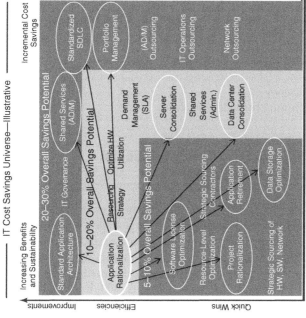

EXHIBIT 12.4 The Potential Cost Savings Universe and Focus Areas
ADM, application development and maintenance; HW, hardware; SDLC, systems development lifecycle; SW software.
Source: Deloitte

and applications to be maintained. The future-state blueprint after a merger or a divestiture will determine the systems needs for the revised business processes, including supporting new business capabilities. It is important to come up with an applications architecture that supports all business capability requirements while managing applications portfolio costs. Last, it is critical to make sure the applications rationalization program becomes an enterprise process versus a onetime event. It is very easy to implement the best applications program and then lose sight of the guiding principles of this program and go back to a nonoptimized, bloated applications footprint.

Applications rationalization also enables operational synergies savings opportunities in other functions through the following:

- Process standardization through the elimination of redundant technologies.
- Service efficiency.
- Reduced training for field adoption.

ACHIEVING OPERATIONAL SYNERGIES THROUGH APPLICATIONS RATIONALIZATION

As part of a merger or an acquisition, another key driver will be realizing operational synergies across the business. For instance, headcount reductions may not be possible without process simplification and rationalization; also, customers may want a single source for interacting with the combined company without having to follow multiple disjointed processes. To achieve these operational synergies, other functions will be looking to perform process standardization where IT takes on the enabler role for driving synergy benefits through elimination of redundant technologies and moving duplicate processes to a consolidated system. For example, IT support is required in the following areas:

- Financial and HR transaction processing cannot be combined and streamlined without combining the systems upon which people work every day (e.g., ERP applications and boundary applications).
- Supply chain synergies are dependent on a common view of suppliers and commodities, which requires IT integration.
- Operations optimization requires access to information across the entire distribution process.
- A unified customer view is dependent on customer systems linkage or consolidation.
- Process times may be reduced by removing disparate processes through system integration.

- Full-time employee (FTE) reductions frequently are dependent on the combination of processes and systems.

Exhibit 12.5 outlines the importance of IT integration and applications rationalization on maximizing the synergies.

IT applications rationalization can be accomplished through implementing some of the best practices early on in the transaction:

- Complete a functional blueprinting, including preparation by creating a one-sided blueprint.
- Get a consolidated view of employees, customers, products, and suppliers.
- Analyze the target IT's operating model and identify integration complexities.

Functional Blueprinting as an Accelerator for Integration and Streamlining the Applications Portfolio

Following an acquisition, it is important to review both companies' processes and related systems and identify ways to rationalize the systems and reengineer and streamline the processes. A functional blueprint is a tool that can foster the discussions to confirm people, process, policy, and applications for each function.

Exhibit 12.6 outlines the first step in completing a functional blueprint for streamlining the applications portfolio.

By capturing both companies' applications for each process, it becomes easier to define the integration strategy and visions of the best fit rationalized landscape at key milestones such as Day 1, interim, and end state. The interim milestone varies but most often is after the first or second quarter after closing, depending on how quickly the consolidation is expected to reach a meaningful state. Between Day 1 and the end state, an interim state is often required. In this state, interim system rationalization or master data consolidation projects may be necessary to feed disparate systems in order to convey a consolidated view to customers on Day 1 until a streamlined applications portfolio can complete and the end state achieved.

Serial acquirers as well as organizations expecting a transaction announcement can further accelerate integration by documenting a one-sided blueprint in preparation until a target is identified to complete the two-sided blueprint.

Exhibit 12.7 outlines the second step of blueprinting to define integration strategy and milestone visions.

Well-executed IT integration is critical to overall integration success and achieving the synergy targets.

Our analysis of prior mergers shows that if you don't get IT integration right, you can have lower-than-expected synergies and higher-than-expected costs to achieve desired results.

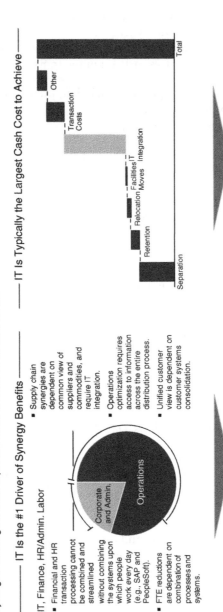

────── IT Is the #1 Driver of Synergy Benefits ──────

IT, Finance, HR/Admin. Labor

- Financial and HR transaction processing cannot be combined and streamlined without combining the systems upon which people work every day (e.g., SAP and PeopleSoft).
- FTE reductions are dependent on combination of processes and systems.

Operations

Corporate and Admin.

- Supply chain synergies are dependent on common view of suppliers and commodities, and require IT integration.
- Operations optimization requires access to information across the entire distribution process.
- Unified customer view is dependent on customer systems consolidation.

────── IT Is Typically the Largest Cash Cost to Achieve ──────

Separation | Retention | Relocation Moves | Facilities IT Integration | Transaction Costs | Other | Total

- Rapid identification and prioritization of Day 1 and Day 2 requirements is essential.
- Preclose planning can result in significant Day 1 risk mitigation and acceleration of postclose synergies.
- Business and IT must stay "attached at the hip" to realize overall committed synergies.

EXHIBIT 12.5 Importance of IT and Applications Rationalization on Maximizing the Synergies

Source: Deloitte Consulting analysis of more than 30 prior merger of equal transactions

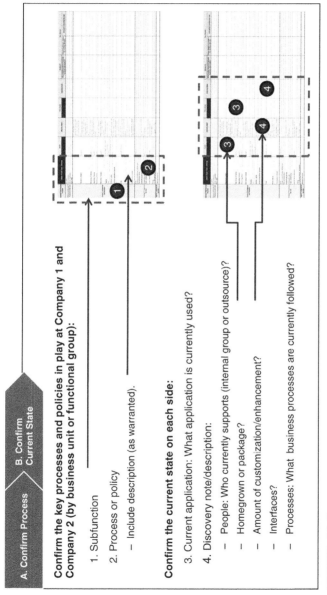

| A. Confirm Process | B. Confirm Current State |

Confirm the key processes and policies in play at Company 1 and Company 2 (by business unit or functional group):

1. Subfunction
2. Process or policy
   – Include description (as warranted).

Confirm the current state on each side:

3. Current application: What application is currently used?
4. Discovery note/description:
   – People: Who currently supports (internal group or outsource)?
   – Homegrown or package?
   – Amount of customization/enhancement?
   – Interfaces?
   – Processes: What business processes are currently followed?

EXHIBIT 12.6 Blueprint Step 1: Validate Current Business Processes, Policies, and Applications

Source: Deloitte

| A. Define Process | B. Determine Current State | C. Define Day 1 Integration | D. Define Interim Integration | E. Define End-State Integration |

5. Define the integration strategy at the process level:

- Adopt and go (adopt existing process from one as standard for both).
- Transform (new solution, hybrid of two, or upgrade).
- Eliminate (get rid of the process policy, or application).

6. Define the Day 1, interim and end state visions:

- Describe the Day 1 state (in terms of specific process, policy, or application adoption).
- Confirm interim solution for consolidated data until integration.
- Define the end state in terms of a future solution hypothesis for each process noting a compelling case or reason that an alternate solution would be a better strategic fit from a long-term perspective.

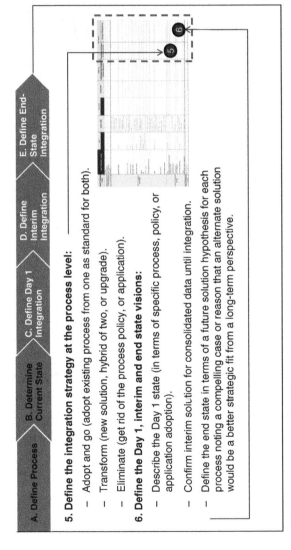

EXHIBIT 12.7 Blueprint Step 2: Define Integration Strategy and Vision

Source: Deloitte

Confirming the solution fit can facilitate the planning process by presenting compelling alternate considerations or factors that could sway the solution adoption decision. For example, if a reverse integration to the acquired company solution is a better strategic fit for employees, customers, and synergies, a shift to the new solution may be required rather than assimilating the acquisition to the existing process.

Once complete, the blueprint is then used as the Day 1 must-have requirements that IT will need to enable as well as prioritized immediate needs and projects to begin to rationalize as quickly as possible in alignment with the business integration goals. It also becomes the initial roadmap for applications rationalization to a streamlined portfolio.

Consolidating Financials, Employees, Customers, Products, and Suppliers through Information Management and Applications Rationalization

One of the Day 1 requirements will undoubtedly be consolidated financials for external reporting. This is just one of the potential operational synergies that may be required to meet the expectations of the deal. Many companies look to acquisitions to bring in new product lines or to enlarge or cross-sell products across customer bases, which all require a consolidation of master data and changes to the systems to leverage the new data set.

One of the approaches used to address this area is data relationship model (DRM)–based financial master data management, which involves:

- Managing financial master data attributes supporting Day 1 integrated financial reporting.
- Standardizing a consolidated enterprise view of chart of accounts, cost centers, and legal entities.
- Enabling consistent definitions of financial and reporting structures across general ledger systems, financial consolidation, planning and budgeting systems.

Data warehousing and information management solutions, such as Business Process Execution Language (BPEL) or Webmethods middleware, can be leveraged to support the consolidation of supplier and customer data and across acquired data stores and assist with the following:

- Standardizing the consolidated enterprise data model.
- Managing the master data attributes of supplier data.
- Supporting the management of the consolidated vendor base and achieving procurement synergy.

- Viewing consolidated customers, including loyalty programs, credit, and supports-targeted cross-marketing.

Data extraction and transformation tools for loading to a consolidated system will also be important for immediate consolidation of HR employee data, as well as archiving and moving master data as rationalization of assets commences.

Key information management and master data management tools that have been described can be leveraged to accelerate an interim architecture that supports operational synergies and Day 1 mandates. The key point is that the business will be looking to realize these synergies, and, without an approach for consolidating and handling master data, these synergies will take longer to realize or may not be efficiently accomplished.

TECHNOLOGY AND COST IMPACT IN A DIVESTITURE EVENT

A divestiture event poses particular challenges and opportunities for applications management. The organization and infrastructure will be going through a significant change that disrupts the status quo. It is important to recognize that regardless of the side of the transaction you are on, the divesting party or the divested party, significant planning and adjustments will need to occur. To help illustrate the considerations related to divestitures, we use a fictional example throughout this section. Company Mega, an international pharmaceutical manufacturer, is divesting one of its manufacturing divisions, called Company Mini.

This section focuses on the direct implications of applications and technology rationalization that technology leaders in both organizations would need to be mindful of within business functions, especially those with technology-enabled processes, external interfaces, and adjustments to resources. The technology functions should be fully aligned with the ongoing business strategy for their respective organizations, and ideally, help develop a vision for both organizations.

For Company Mega, the divesting organization, analysis and planning should be performed to address the following questions:

Does the transaction impact the ability or means to deliver business-critical functions?

Planning for the divestiture event should include analysis of technologies utilized from a technical perspective (i.e., users, interfaces, equipment) and a process perspective (e.g., order to cash, procure to pay). This review of technologies should provide a clear picture of what is required to make sure that Company Mega does not experience any significant disruption to business. A real-life example of this was a client who was divesting a smaller division, but that smaller group managed and maintained the learning management system (LMS) for the larger company. The ability to track the training of the sales force was crucial, and if the up-front business process and technology review did not occur, the divesting organization could have experienced significant exposure from losing a critical business-enabling system. Conversely, the divestiture activity could remove a requirement that would allow the divesting organization to right size to eliminate a no longer needed enabling technology.

Does the transaction create new requirements, possibly due to a transition services agreement (TSA) that requires new or modified technology operations to be met?

A divestiture can include a TSA that arranges for the divesting organization to provide support and services to the organization being divested. This could impact the approach and timing for rationalization of the applications and technology architecture. In the case of the sample divestiture, the deal could include a requirement that Company Mega would provide ongoing payroll processing for six months after close of the deal and Company Mega would also host and maintain the existing sales force automation tool for a year. Company Mega in preparing for this TSA requirement would need to develop requirements, approach, and cost estimates for this activity. It should not be assumed that the status quo would suffice. In a real-world example, a divested organization requested a TSA for its customer relationship management (CRM) application, but due to the competitive and regulatory landscape, planning needed to include dedicated servers, security and controls, instances of the software (license agreement), and addressing proprietary sales force and client information. By addressing this during divestiture planning, the organizations can properly plan for technology requirements so technology and application investments are rationalized and any negotiations with third parties can be done without undue time pressures.

Does the transaction provide the opportunity or dictate that technology services change the way they deliver services?

As with any change, an understanding of what the new requirements are is significant. In the case of the Company Mega example, divesting Company Mini removes several requirements, including application and customer support. Company Mini had a customer database bolt-on for the e-mail system that was pushed as a standard. After evaluation with both departing and remaining staff, it was identified that the bolt-on was not critical to remaining operations and that the company would remove the bolt-on and realize a savings on licenses. The transition of Company Mini also removed a requirement of 24/7 information systems customer support, so the technology resource model could be adjusted to address the less demanding requirement of the remaining organization. Conversely, in a real-world example, a technology function of a divesting company had to increase application licenses and support staff temporarily because of TSA and deal-closing conditions. Proper planning allowed the costs associated with this to be properly estimated and included in the deal before close. The organization was then able to rationalize its applications portfolio at a later time according to a strategic plan that accounted for the requirements.

Does the transaction create a change in the technology cost model due to loss of leverage or sunk costs?

Analysis needs to be performed on the application and technology portfolio to see if the technology-related investments (i.e., hardware, software, and human resources) still meet the planned budget. Examining cost metrics ranging from information systems department spend per dollar of revenue to application license fees per user before and after the transaction can provide valuable insights. In this example, it is possible that Company Mega's information systems spend could have been decreased by divesting Company Mini, which had more demanding requirements. It may also be that by divesting Company Mini, per user costs for some applications could increase because user license count thresholds are not met. The divesting organization may also want to review any accounting implications for projects that were executed for the divested organization to make sure that the impacts are properly reflected in financial reporting.

Are there timing and prioritization considerations for addressing key activities due to the transaction?

Having knowledge of any timing requirements for activities can significantly impact planning and could have financial implications. For example, timing requirements can be aggressive, requiring a ramp-up of resources to accommodate for the timing that could be more expensive than with a less aggressive schedule. The same is true for technologies where an aggressive timeline may incur more technology-related cost, but allows meeting the timing requirements for the deal. If timing is not a driving requirement, it is recommended to explore how phasing could help in realizing efficiencies for the divestiture process and the impacts of realizing synergies.

A final note for the divesting organization is that a long-term view of the organization structure and requirements is valuable, if not essential. Going through the process of rationalizing enabling technologies and resources with a short-term view can limit the ability or efficiency of growth plans in the future. Rationalization should be aligned strategically and not be just a tactical exercise.

For Company Mini, the divested organization, analysis, and planning will need to be performed to account for the following questions:

Does the transaction impact the ability or means to deliver business-critical functions?

Much like the divesting organization, the divested organization needs to perform analysis of technologies utilized from a technical perspective (for example, users, interfaces, equipment) and a process perspective such as order to cash or procure to pay. This review of technologies will take on a different perspective based on whether the divested unit is being merged with another organization or stood up on its own. Analysis of the applications portfolio may identify duplicate or obsolete applications that can be phased out based on the situation.

If the divestiture also includes a merger, analysis and planning should include all critical parties involved. If the divested entity is being stood up on its own, TSAs may play a larger role in allowing the divested entity time to become self-sufficient. It is important to note that the review and its results should be agreed to by the individual parties involved, and frequently this is done in a coordinated manner among all parties involved. In a real-life example of a divestiture that had the divested group merging with another entity, transition efforts included identifying the to-be applications and technical architecture. Due to timing considerations, the divesting organization provided extended technology support through a TSA outsourcing agreement that made the divested entity a customer of the parent organization for a period of time. There were applications portfolio rationalization activities taking place during the TSA to allow for the divested organization to run on a lower technology cost model.

Does the transition allow for a different way of running technical operations and applications?

Many times the divestiture allows for a reset in the way organizations approach certain functions, and technology is not an exception. The applications and technology portfolio should be reexamined to determine if the costs and services provided meet goals and performance targets. In some circumstances, divested organizations have significantly reduced their scale and the previous systems have become cost prohibitive. In these circumstances, the transition planning can include conversion to a lower-cost solution or architecture. Transitions can also include so-called point solutions, which are typically low-cost work-around solutions with fixed life spans (intended to be thrown away). The point solution allows for an organization to minimize applications and technology investments during the transition period and allow the divested entity to assess at a future time the right investments. As with any system/technology decision, functional requirements should be developed and assessed to minimize any significant business disruptions. Point solutions are useful mechanisms in some cases to buy time for analysis to rationalize the applications and technical architecture.

Does the transaction create a change in the technology cost model due to loss of leverage or sunk costs?

As with the divesting entity, analysis needs to be performed on the applications and technology portfolio to see if the technology-related investments (for example, hardware, software, and human resources) still meet the planned budget. Examining cost metrics ranging from information systems department spend per dollar of revenue to application license fees per user before and after the transaction can provide valuable insights. In our example, it is possible that Company Mini's information systems spend could increase by removing the leverage of the larger organization. User costs may also go up due to smaller scale and also the acquisition of hardware and licensing on behalf of the new organization. In some cases, software vendors may accommodate the existing pricing structures, and review of related contracts and engaging vendors may help in realizing favorable financial terms.

Are there timing and prioritization considerations for addressing key activities due to the transaction?

Timing requirements are very important for any project, and it is valuable to view timing with two considerations. The first consideration is financial impacts and how the timing of the transition impacts technology costs, including resources, licenses, and hardware. The second consideration is functionality and how business processes work and mature in the new environment. Both considerations should be thought about together, as lack of focus on one could produce a bias that artificially increases costs or decreases organizational effectiveness.

A final note for the divested organization is that a clear understanding of short-term tactical goals is very important for the entire organization. Long-term vision is also very important, but there are numerous examples of successfully divested organizations where time and energy were given to reinforce short-term achievements. The level of change and disruption in a divested organization is typically much greater than that of the divesting organization. Having a managerial process in place to monitor and react to developments can minimize not only technology disruptions but also disruptions to other functions. Information systems can be a key enabler to help monitor organization development and aid in the transition if properly utilized.

EMERGING TRENDS

Emerging trends from private equities may present the future of streamlining IT assets all together as part of an acquisition or a divestiture. During the recent recession and credit crunch, private equity investors have become much more focused on limiting capital investment for acquisition integration while maintaining the minimalist ongoing operating budget to meet investor expectations. There has been a growing trend for focused acquisition of specific product lines rather than full business units so as not to take the existing overhead of back-office functions and to stand them up fresh based on the new company size. The more interesting aspect, however, is this has naturally led to outsourcing these functions as the fastest way to stand up new organizations while minimalizing capital spend and a new method for streamlining applications portfolios.

Companies and private equity firms are more frequently going into acquisitions with the stance being that no IT assets will be acquired—a "greenfield" will be created and a right-sized solution will be built from the ground up. While a minimal amount of critical legacy assets will likely still need to be procured or transferred, this still opens a huge potential opportunity. Many of the disruptive IT trends now come into play, such as moving to the cloud and SaaS solutions for fully outsourced and vendor-managed applications portfolios. (See Chapter 10 for an overview of cloud and software as a service [SaaS] computing.) Even the historically internal IT sacred ERP landscape is moving to cloud-based solutions from the same providers as before, as well as new players that will host and maintain the application or provide it as a service and make it available via the web. In the cloud or SaaS model, remaining applications and infrastructure can be outsourced and the new IT organization can focus on governance, vendor management, and meeting the needs of the business. As the cloud and SaaS models continue to mature and companies become more confident with them, we will see a change in the business to push for more business process–based outsourcing as a full service that includes any applications required for the process, thus further reducing the application landscape and the required focus from internal IT.

This approach is not for every deal, but can be very helpful where the deal is not a merger of equals or where the seller's landscape is dramatically different from the divested unit, or when deciding to operate as a stand-alone business. IT outsourcing to an SaaS can also be the fastest way to stand up critical Day 1 requirements such as the order-to-cash process and general ledger accounting for the new business. Cloud and SaaS solutions continue to have their critics, but are slowly overcoming them as the technology grows to meet the needs. Either way, they already provide solutions that can be leveraged and should be investigated to simplify applications portfolios during an acquisition or when preparing for a divestiture.

BEST PRACTICES FOR APPLICATIONS RATIONALIZATION IN AN M&A SCENARIO

The primary objective of applications rationalization is more cost-effective support of business processes through a simplified standard technology portfolio both within and across lines of business (LOBs). This should be developed by first understanding the business objectives and IT needs of each individual LOB, and then identifying and exploiting opportunities to establish shared or standardized business processes and common enabling IT capabilities across LOBs. Outlined next are the best practices to adopt as part of applications rationalization.

Establish a Program Management Office and Governance Model

Establishing a program management office (PMO) to oversee the applications rationalization efforts is a best practice to support alignment and rationalization of the applications with business objectives, capabilities, expectations, and outcomes. Securing executive-level sponsorship along with the right business-level participation and accountability is a key to achieving the goals of the applications rationalization in an M&A scenario. The PMO plays a vital role in institutionalizing that level of rigor and consistency for program planning, execution, tracking, and reporting. The PMO will allow for managing all the cross-functional dependencies, enterprise-level security, external influencing factors, and key risks associated with applications rationalization. Establishing the right technical and business governance model is critical for sustaining the application landscape following rationalization to review new applications that get introduced to the landscape for strategic alignment, lowering technology support costs and redundancy. Implementing a strongly enforced governance model with both business and IT participation can limit some of the pitfalls associated with redundant applications being introduced and thereby impacting the IT operational costs dramatically. (See Chapters 4 and 23 for additional insights on governance.)

Create an M&A Playbook

Serial acquirers often compile integration and divestiture wisdom in a playbook. Such compilations of wisdom often delineate the step-by-step processes required for post-merger IT integration, and describe specific approaches that CIOs and their teams can embrace to achieve their goals in both the planning and the execution stages. The playbook generally provides details for consistent approaches to estimating, analyzing, and planning to determine the transitional and end-state applications and technical architecture.

Assess the Application Landscape

Review the target's applications portfolio, associated business processes, dependencies, licenses, vendor contracts, and support costs, and create an inventory of the application landscape. Using standardized templates to collect the data will save a lot of rework later on. Mapping systems to applications and processes will provide a viewport into the impact of any disposition changes or decisions that are made along the way. This will enable the acquirer to assess the portfolio and identify the appropriate end state to be achieved as part of integration.

Establish Shared Accountability with the Business

Make rationalization of systems a performance metric for executives in charge of each function; by doing so, the business will have a shared accountability for hitting reduction in applications used by each function or business unit. This works well in IT organizations that do not have a good charge-back model for applications portfolio spend by application. In the case where a charge-back model exists, this will naturally happen, as the cost-saving synergies will be borne by the application costs in the business unit budgets.

Define Your End-State Portfolio

M&A deal leaders often expect IT to achieve the majority of desired synergy goals by eliminating redundancies in systems and staffing. The applications rationalization efforts that CIOs pursue to meet these goals are challenging, but are made more so if carried out haphazardly.

Carefully assess the IT capabilities of the target company with your acquisition goals in mind. Identify the applications that will allow you to achieve the IT synergy goals, while keeping the business processes in mind that need to be aligned to maintain continuity. Having a process-centric view would allow you to identify application overlaps and functionality that applications offer to determine the target portfolio. Do not hesitate to move away from custom home-grown applications and toward standardized platforms that align with the overall IT strategy. Defining a scoring model to identify which applications need to be retained based on functionality, supportability, and costs is critical to finalizing the end state.

Develop a Road Map and Blueprint

Based on the analysis and the scoring model, develop a sequenced road map with interim objectives and target dates, taking into account all the dependencies, including influencing factors like tax strategy, plant strategy, and market integration. Identify early adopters and low-hanging targets that can help realize the synergies with immediate effect. There may be business-as-usual project dependencies that can influence the timing of the rationalization of certain applications (primarily, regulatory needs like submissions, timing of quarterly close, year-end, etc.). It is important to develop this sequenced road map and get it reviewed by both IT and business stakeholders ahead of time prior to execution.

Identifying cross-functional dependencies is equally important to establish and pinpoint the timing of the disposition of the applications that fall in the "Four Cs" category.

Execute and Track Synergies

Working with the leadership team and business stakeholders, define the necessary program metrics that need to be tracked, including the synergies that are realized as part of the applications rationalization. Identify and agree on the tracking approach and reporting mechanisms for the program. Application retirements may lead to contract terminations, support consolidation, and asset reduction. Having clear-cut planned monthly or quarterly targets for synergy realization, and tracking it against the actual dispositions on a periodic basis, will help with identifying any leading or lagging indicators that contribute to the program execution.

Consolidate Functionality Wherever Possible to Enterprise Resource Planning Landscape

In most companies, the ERP system is the core platform that supports the bulk of enterprise operations. Thus, a post-merger integration plan should focus first and foremost on integrating the target's ERP system. (Based on our experience, approximately 80 percent of integration costs will be incurred with this aspect of the integration.) Other applications can be on a parallel track taking into account the necessary upstream and downstream dependencies as needed.

Protecting Intellectual Property and Exposure

In many scenarios, business, legal, and regulatory compliance may require data to be archived prior to retiring the legacy applications following rationalization. Most companies try to integrate key processes and thereby systems to realize synergies rapidly and often focus on active data migration to target systems, leaving legacy records behind in source systems. Careful consideration should be paid to what is considered active versus historical data, which is usually determined by LOBs as part of the integration planning. Active data are data that would need to be referred to on a regular basis, and historical data are considered purely referential in nature to support future audits or for litigation support. Working closely with the records management and legal groups to identify the retention requirements usually pays huge dividends in managing corporate risk and exposure.

The Proper Perspective

Invariably, there will be obstacles on the path back to pre-acquisition efficiency levels. In some M&A events, synergy goals change like the weather. In others, delayed decision making by the business side can derail integration initiatives that are well under way. It is important to remember that many of these challenges can be mitigated with careful planning and close monitoring as the integration unfolds.

WRAPPING IT UP

An M&A transaction is a disruptive event that can be leveraged to streamline the applications portfolio. When done properly, applications rationalization as part of an M&A transaction can be a driver of cost-synergy realization for savings from other IT aspects, including data center and head count rationalization. Furthermore, other business functions will be looking to perform process standardization where IT takes on the enabler role for achieving synergy benefits through elimination of redundant processes and technologies for a consolidated system. In the case of a divestiture, proper applications portfolio strategy planning can account for increased costs being able to transfer in the deal and avoidance of stranded costs left with the seller after the divestiture. Thus no matter whether the transaction is an acquisition, a merger, or even a divestiture, applications rationalization can help achieve synergies while standardizing, reducing costs, and simplifying the applications portfolio.

- **Accelerate identification of projects.** Establish and initiate rapid assessment and validation of rationalization opportunities; prioritize, plan, and launch into projects.
- **Establish strong sponsorship, leadership, and governance.** Confirm visible "top of the house" sponsorship with leadership accountability, and implement a transparent governance process.
- **Goal setting, accountability, and incentives.** Establish cost-reduction targets by region, by LOB, by year, and so on to drive focus to the program. Consider trade-off incentives to increase participation.
- **Lockstepping with the business.** The process of rationalizing applications and licenses should be driven with strong business persuasion and support to help realize the expected savings. This requires working closely on sequencing of retirements and process redesign.
- **Accelerate the move to services.** Design functionality into reusable and extensible services to extend savings beyond those possible under business-unit-focused efforts.
- **Introduce greater level of new project governance.** Protect from creep-back of IT spend by changing the way that new projects and products are introduced, approved, and staffed.
- **Manage project sequencing to increase impact.** Aggressively pursue the largest savings first; follow an iterative approach that captures savings in waves and takes into account what is achievable given dependencies.

Third-Party Contracts in M&A

Identifying and Managing Common Implications

Christine McKay
Joseph Joy
Ramkumar Jayaraman
Ninad Deshmukh

Your suppliers, information technology (IT) and non-IT alike, control the fate of your deal far more than you may expect. They may even have the power to stop it.

Whether infrastructure or application, your IT suppliers own some or all of what you bought from them. You simply have a license to use it, and many licenses deny users the rights needed to support a deal such as assignment or transition services rights. Non-IT suppliers, especially those providing outsourced services such as contract manufacturing, property management, and the like, may also restrict your rights during a transaction.

Though we often understand how critical these suppliers are to maintaining business continuity, few buyers or sellers have fully considered their potential impacts on operations and cost. Suppliers, on the other hand, understand their power during these times. Therefore, they will seek to leverage the importance of business continuity in various ways. They may threaten to discontinue service on Day 1. They may attempt to charge exorbitant fees for granting assignment or transition rights or to assess punitive termination penalties. For IT, they may require both the buyer and the seller to upgrade to newer versions or buy additional licenses or products. Products previously taken off maintenance may need to have it reinstated, and some IT suppliers may use the deal as an opportunity to initiate an audit and / or seek to renegotiate the entire contract.

Given suppliers' power during a transaction, strategic and financial buyers and sellers alike must adopt new philosophies for mitigating risk and capturing value.

CHALLENGES INHERENT IN DIFFERENT TYPES OF M&A TRANSACTIONS

For the purpose of understanding the challenges posed by the different types of M&A transactions, we broadly classify transactions as mergers and divestitures.

During a merger, companies come together to form a bigger company. This provides a few advantages to the buyer. For example, the buyer may have higher buying power with the supplier (although it depends on the size of the supplier) and may be able to negotiate a higher discount. However, it can lead to overlap and fragmentation in the supplier base. This can also increase operational cost by potentially increasing invoice processing costs, supplier management costs, and the like.

Divestitures, in contrast, present the opportunity for the seller to reduce its supplier base and reduce its third-party spending. However, it can also generate stranded costs that remain after the transaction is complete for the seller. It depends on whether the contract can be terminated ahead of the contract date, whether the contract is assignable, and whether the transition services agreements (TSAs) may be provided to another party. It may also cause increases in product or service costs due to decreased volumes, expand the need for TSAs, and prompt suppliers to seek termination penalties. (See Chapters 14 and 16 for detailed discussion of TSAs.)

Knowing these issues in advance helps both parties in the transaction address them effectively and improve their understanding of the synergies that each can get out of the transaction. Establishing an efficient strategy for addressing third-party contracts during a transaction has three primary challenges: identification, analysis, and disposition.

TYPICAL REALITIES

Unlike other work streams in the transaction, both companies have a common objective and responsibility. Both want to reduce postclose supplier costs or at least keep them constant. The seller also wants to minimize transaction-related costs associated with completing the deal and securing supplier support for Day 1. However, sellers often feel they have limited, if any, opportunities to leverage the pending transaction to improve their

IT cost profile through their suppliers. Instead, they brace themselves for inevitable cost increases due to reduced buying power. They expect cost improvements solely through volume reductions. Additionally, sellers frequently fail to plan for many pre-Day 1 costs imposed by their suppliers. For example, contracts may prevent assignment or limit the ability to provide TSAs. Sellers need to secure these rights and obtain suppliers' support for a smooth Day 1 transition. Regardless of contract provisions, IT suppliers may withhold support unless the seller makes a penalty payment. At times, these penalties can be significant. This is true for both software and hardware. Costs can further increase if the seller previously made operational decisions that need to be reversed, such as discontinue maintenance on certain products. Many contracts allow the supplier to impose penalties for reinstating maintenance, which can further erode benefits from volume reductions. The supplier may also prevent the assignment or transfer of products that are not under maintenance that can increase stranded costs.

Conversely, buyers often believe they are entitled to better pricing and implement a "dialing for dollars" approach. In this approach, procurement calls most if not all of its supplier base to ask for bigger discounts. When suppliers capitulate, companies may achieve savings of roughly 5 to 10 percent, depending on the supplier and the product or service category. This approach can completely backfire with IT for a number of reasons. Some suppliers are so large that few buyers are likely to catapult themselves to a new discount level. Certain IT purchases are more volume driven than others, such as telecommunications and hardware. Even when a buyer moves into a new discount level, most suppliers will require new purchases under an existing contract. Prior to Day 1 and where the seller has a single enterprise license or when a supplier refuses to allow assignment in part or in whole, the buyer may need to negotiate for the purchase of its own license(s). Having a common supplier providing common products or services generally simplifies the process and enables the buyer to roll new volumes under its existing contracts at its existing pricing. This improves the buyer's negotiation leverage because it eliminates the pressure created by the Day 1 close date and gives the buyer time to develop a more comprehensive negotiation strategy with better information. When the buyer decides to use similar products or services purchased through its existing supplier relationships, the buyer may benefit from its existing agreements. However, because the Day 1 date drives activity, suppliers hold significant leverage in this situation. Suppliers know this and often use it to gain additional revenue and/or renegotiate the existing contract to their long-term benefit. Additionally, the buyer has imperfect information about the seller's volumes and usage prior to Day 1, which creates another disadvantage. The sales and purchasing agreement typically defines the level of support the buyer will receive from the seller in regard to third-party supplier agreements. Where the seller has limited obligations, buyers can incur higher costs caused again by imperfect information but also when buyers allow the supplier to drive timing. Buyers frequently underestimate both pre- and post-Day 1 costs, which offset potential synergies significantly.

Suppliers, as previously mentioned, hold more leverage than either the seller or the buyer, especially prior to Day 1. The supplier will extend this leverage by taking advantage of the organizational uncertainty caused by the transaction. They frequently talk to their business contacts, suggesting that they may withhold Day 1 support. Suppliers may threaten to discontinue service that can impact business-as-usual operations. They may raise noncompliance issues, prevent contract termination, disallow contract assignment without significant penalties, or do a myriad of other things. As soon as a key supplier starts using any of these tactics, the business sometimes starts to panic. In turn, it pushes the procurement function to resolve the situation quickly, issue the purchase order (PO), and be done with it. Given timing pressures and the need for expediency, this generally means the supplier captures much if not all the value.

As shareholders are scrutinizing transactions more carefully, their expectations for real, recurring savings have grown. In the quest to exceed promised savings targets, some companies are throwing away the old script. Instead, they are using the transaction as an opportunity to restructure some of their most critical supplier relationships and realize dramatically better results without impacting Day 1.

As a result of the growing scrutiny from all stakeholders, both buyers and sellers try to gather as much relevant information as possible before the transaction. Buyers and sellers initially attempt to understand how their contracts landscape would look as a result of the transaction. Primarily, both parties in the transaction try to understand two main areas:

1. **Transaction costs.** Transaction costs are directly related to enabling the transaction. Buyers and sellers each incur transaction costs. These can be unplanned costs incurred to execute the transaction, such as buying new hardware or additional licenses, engaging advisers, or hiring temporary resources, and so on. Understanding these costs prior to closing will be necessary for the seller to do its financial close and can be required for regulatory filings. Combining all of these expenses can skew the cost of the transaction beyond the sticker price. This can lead to a case of buyer or seller remorse, or both! The good news is that these costs can be managed.

2. **Risks.** The scope of contracts going with the transaction (i.e., transferring from the seller to the buyer) can create various risks. For example, is the target dependent on any a small number of major suppliers for its operations? Will there be a fragmentation of the supplier base? Are there potential conflicts between suppliers in the new baseline? Does a major supplier have the market power to make the transaction costly or unmanageable? Will the loss of certain suppliers create operational risk for the company following the transaction?

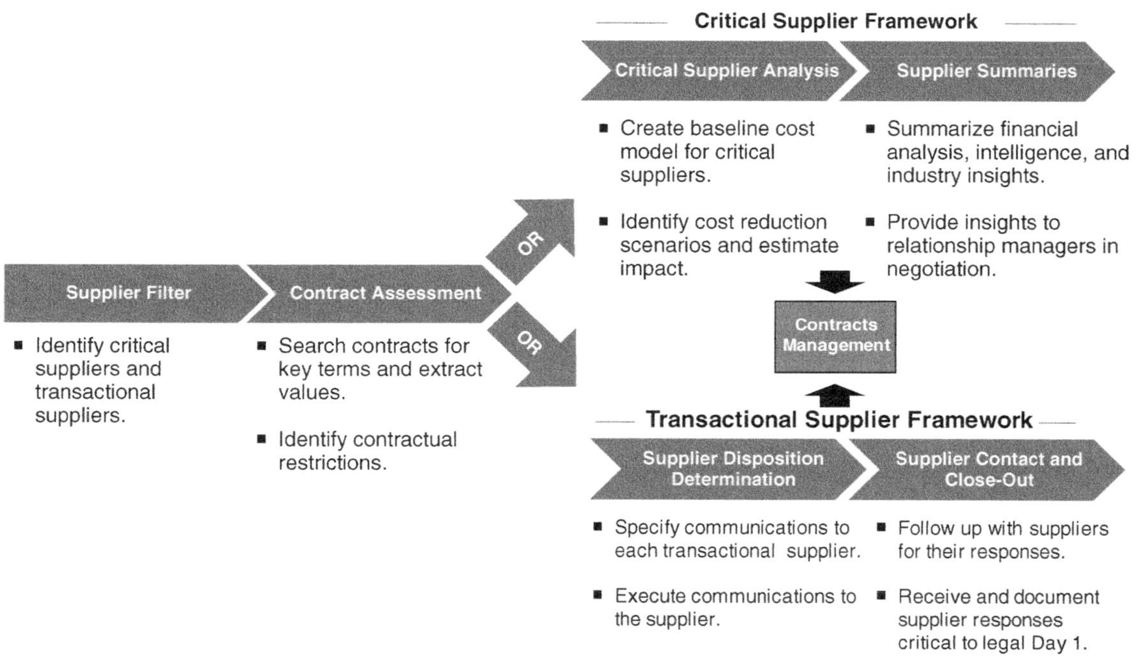

Critical Supplier Framework

Critical Supplier Analysis
- Create baseline cost model for critical suppliers.
- Identify cost reduction scenarios and estimate impact.

Supplier Summaries
- Summarize financial analysis, intelligence, and industry insights.
- Provide insights to relationship managers in negotiation.

Contracts Management

Transactional Supplier Framework

Supplier Disposition Determination
- Specify communications to each transactional supplier.
- Execute communications to the supplier.

Supplier Contact and Close-Out
- Follow up with suppliers for their responses.
- Receive and document supplier responses critical to legal Day 1.

OR

OR

Supplier Filter
- Identify critical suppliers and transactional suppliers.

Contract Assessment
- Search contracts for key terms and extract values.
- Identify contractual restrictions.

EXHIBIT 13.1 Contract Management Approach

Answering these questions for both buyer and seller is complicated by a limited timeframe to gather and act on the relevant information. Moreover, the buyer expects the seller to provide most of this information before the transaction in order for the buyer to decide what course of action it should take. This increases the onus on the seller to have a good handle to answer a lot of these questions for the buyer as well as for itself.

Consider Exhibit 13.1 as we review contract management in the rest of the chapter.

PRIMARY CHALLENGES

During M&A transactions, these tactical realities lead to two primary challenges:

1. Managing risks
2. Managing costs

Risk Management

There are a variety of risks that crop up in the process of managing contracts. Some of them are discussed in the following subsections.

Contract Ownership Typically, one would expect the contracts to be owned by the central procurement organization, but contracts are often owned by the procurement division as well as by each business function that needs third-party products or services. This means companies have shadow contracts and multiple contract owners popping up across the organization. This dissipates the ownership of contracts across the organization, making identification, decision making, and execution difficult.

Format and Identification As the number of contract owners proliferates, the format in which each owner within a certain organization creates contracts also continues to proliferate; that is, contracts are created by various entities within a company. For example, there are a number of contracting officers within an organization who may be creating and storing contracts in their hard drives or as hard copies. Consequently, the scope of contracts involved in a transaction is spread across hard copies, soft copies in hard drives or other storage media of contract owners, and in one or more contract management solutions. It is often difficult to simply locate and identify various contracts, which, in turn, makes analyzing more complicated.

Volume   In addition to the contracts being in various formats and languages, the volume of contracts can be daunting. Some companies have thousands of contracts, and each client may have two to three master services agreements (MSAs) and multiple amendments for each MSA. The volume of the contracts multiplies as a result. Identifying all the MSAs and amendments for each supplier can be daunting, to say the least.

Contract Details   This is specific to a small number of suppliers, which are typically technology giants providing multiple products and services to their clients. Oftentimes, these products and services are part of the same contract, and many times they are spread across various years of contract modifications. Contracts' data are not typically available in a format needed to check if they impact the transaction. This is often the easier part of the process once the contracts are located and the information is available in a format that can be analyzed. However, often key contract information has to be extracted again for M&A analysis. All of these complexities mean the locating and processing of contracts becomes a sleuthing operation.

Contracts Extraction   Even if contracts are issued through the procurement division, many of the records may not contain all the information needed to be analyzed for M&A purposes. Relevant contract data have to be extracted in order to meet the transaction needs and the buyer's requirements. Nevertheless, a company that has a good handle on its contracts landscape is further ahead of the curve than one that starts cataloging this after the transaction is announced.

Disposition   The logistical challenges do not end there. Once contracts are analyzed, the suppliers need to be contacted. The type of communication required is based on the outcome of the analysis. Communication may be as simple as sending a notification or as complex as requiring an amendment to the existing agreement. This involves getting in touch with the suppliers and helping ensure the contracts are in compliance with their policies.

Overall, there are multiple challenges in each stage of managing contracts for M&A. Companies that have ample transaction lead times are better able to address these challenges as they approach Day 1.

Cost Management

In order to preserve deal value, it is important for both buyer and seller to manage costs associated with the separation of contracts in a divestiture and the transfer of contracts in a full sale. Even though such costs may not be altogether eliminated, it is possible to contain such costs by giving attention to them early in the post-announcement phase.

As mentioned earlier, third-party supplier costs associated with M&A can be classified into the following four categories:

1. **Transaction costs.** Onetime costs associated with separation of shared functions or assets that are required to support the operations of the divested business in a disposal.
   Example: Supplier fee for transfer of software and hardware, right to process data for the buyer until the buyer can make alternative arrangements, purchasing new software licenses where transfer is not allowed.
2. **Operational costs.** Delineating transaction costs from operational and stranded is also important. Costs associated with reversing operational decisions made prior to close in order to facilitate transfer of assets to buyer or that change the as-is business operations. Operating costs can be those related to reversing a previous operating decision or to changing the as-is business operations. Operational costs can become dis-synergies.
   Example: Cost increases due to volume reductions, reversing past operating decisions (e.g., reinstating software maintenance), upgrading an existing and functioning software tool beyond its normal capabilities.
3. **Stranded costs.** Costs associated with retained assets or functions that are not required to support the remaining operations after disposal.
   Example: Costs of unused portions of third-party products or services due to contractual obligations like annual maintenance that may not be prorated.
4. **Dis-synergies.** Increases in unit costs for the seller due to reduction in overall volumes.
   Example: Due to a reduction of licenses after close, the contract may automatically trigger a reduction in discount level for the licenses, resulting in increased unit costs compared to prior to close.

TACKLING CHALLENGES

Risks and costs can be significantly reduced by proactively planning for them in advance of Day 1. The following sections describe in detail important aspects of managing costs and risks.

Risk Management

In order to help manage contract risks, executing the following four steps is highly recommended:

1. Identify business intent requirements early.
2. Know your suppliers and contracts.

3. Where possible, automate.
4. Control communication with suppliers.

Identify Business Intent Requirements Early   Business intent is how the business functions of the seller wish to hand over a product or service used by the sold entity and provided by a third-party supplier under a contract to the buyer. The objective of identifying business intent is threefold:

1. Provide continuity of business operations on Day 1.
2. Request rights from suppliers as appropriate to help ensure contractual compliance on Day 1.
3. Minimize cost impact associated with third-party products and services due to the transaction.

Once the business intent is captured, typically the seller's procurement function works with suppliers to secure the rights needed on Day 1.

Descriptions of some of the most common forms of business intent are shown in Exhibit 13.2.

Business intent is meant to drive procurement activities. The constraints documented in supplier agreements should not be the deciding factor.

The challenge is to drive business to provide comprehensive and accurate business intent in advance of Day 1 in order to drive the rest of contracts management process. This can be hindered by a few factors:

- Often the business is unaware of all the suppliers that support its processes. Large suppliers typically have large contracts that provide products to multiple parts of the business. These cannot be ignored due to their business criticality and complexity. Smaller suppliers with specific uses may be forgotten during the process, which can create issues further into the process.
- This situation can be further complicated when the business does not distinguish the supplier from the reseller. For example, many products from big technology companies (suppliers) may be procured from licensed resellers. In such situations, the seller company has to identify each reseller for the products used across its target divisions.
- Other typical challenges include the compressed timeframes, resource availability, and managing scale or scope of the process. Oftentimes, the timeline to Day 1 is very compressed, with business and procurement resources focused on their full-time jobs. Depending on the scale of contracts, the process of gathering business intent is often short-circuited and may miss a number of crucial suppliers.

EXHIBIT 13.2 Common Forms of Business Intent

Business Intent	Description
Assign in full	Transfer all units (quantities, licenses, etc.) of a product or service to the buyer. This is applicable when the product or service will not be used any further by the seller.
Assign in part	Transfer only certain number of units (quantities, licenses, etc.) of a product or service from the existing pool to the buyer. This is applicable when the product or service is supposed to be used by the buyer as well as by the seller after the transaction. In such cases, seller copies the existing agreement for the buyer but it includes only those units of products or services that are specific to the divested entity.
Buyer stand-up	Buyer needs a particular product or service currently used by the divested entity but either intends to use a similar product or service that it already has or creates a new contract with the divested entity's existing supplier. In such cases, the seller needs to provide the buyer with information on the number of units currently used.
No action needed	Buyer does not need a particular product or service, and no action needs to be taken by the seller.
Terminate	Buyer does not need a particular product or service and the seller intends to terminate the contract for that product or service since it will not be used anymore by the seller.
Transition services agreement (TSA)	Short-term contract between seller and buyer where the seller may continue to host IT applications/infrastructure and business processes on behalf of the buyer and provide services to the buyer for a predefined duration and fee after Day 1. Whenever there is a TSA, the business intent at the end of the TSA should be documented.
Reverse TSA	Short-term contract between seller and buyer where the seller may continue to receive services or access to IT applications and business processes hosted by the buyer for a predefined duration and fee after Day 1 in case the seller is assigning the product or service to the buyer.

■ Some contracts may not be assigned to the buyer. If this is critical to the seller's operations, the buyer must allow sufficient time for contract negotiations since it will be responsible for securing its own contracts that cannot be assigned.

Some of these challenges may be mitigated by identifying the suppliers and contracts very early in the process and refining the master list regularly prior to Day 1.

Know Your Suppliers and Contracts This is often the bottleneck in the process. As explained in the challenges section, companies with a contract management system may still not have all contracts loaded into it. Each company is different and needs a unique way to identify contracts. It is imperative to be creative in identifying contracts and suppliers depending on the type of client in question. For example, accounts payable data may be used to identify suppliers and the responsible party; top-down and bottom-up identification processes may be used to capture all the contracts. Some companies lend themselves to electronic means of contract discovery, depending on the type of IT network, policies, and so on that exist in the organization.

In most cases, it is useful to create a **prioritization** mechanism to help identify high-priority suppliers and disposition accordingly. The 80/20 rule works pretty well in most cases (that is, 80 percent of supplier spend is represented by 20 percent of the suppliers). This implies that 80 percent of the suppliers represent a small spend for most companies. But this increases the complexity of addressing third-party spend. In order to address the supplier base appropriately, the supplier base may be segmented into high-, medium-, and low-priority suppliers. This segmentation can be based on not only the supplier spend but also the size of the supplier and other factors. Once the segmentation is complete, address each segment using a different strategy.

Information gaps are bound to exist in almost all organizations. For example, not all MSAs or amendments may be available or found after a data gathering effort. These situations have to be dealt with on a case-by-case basis with the help of the program governance structure. Identifying the different types of challenges and remediation approaches in advance helps lead to quick and timely execution.

Having a high-level contract collection or **volume goal** gives the procurement team and the business team a goal to work toward. These goals set by executives may be used as a call to action to identify the contracts.

Staying ahead of the need and managing the volume requires a dedicated and organized procurement team. This team should be accountable for working with the business to identify and collect contracts. They need to have a reasonable degree of authority in order to motivate the business to provide the appropriate information.

Where Possible, Automate   Automated options are available to identify and extract data from contracts. This is a great option for accelerating the process of gathering contracts and extracting contract data. Yet, this option is often stymied by the IT policies and approvals needed to install and utilize such software in company networks before Day 1. Moreover, the software needs time to run and manual intervention to make it work well. But if this installation approval process is sped up, it can make the process much faster to identify a baseline. The major components of automation are:

- **E-discovery.** This consists of software that traverses the IT network to identify contracts. The speed by which contracts are discovered depends on various factors such as the file naming convention and optical character recognition (OCR) capability. Once the contracts are discovered, they need to be pulled into a central database or file location to be processed.
- **Data extraction.** Once the contracts are consolidated, the data need to be extracted. The technology for this is well established, such as OCR. The quality of OCR output, however, depends on the input—that is, whether the document is in machine-readable format, how much handwritten information is on the document, and so on.
- **Text mining.** This involves using the data extracted to build the database of terms and conditions needed for analysis. Although there are software tools available for this purpose, they have very low accuracy as of the time of this publication.
- **Output tracking.** Once the text is mined, it needs to be exported in a format that can be analyzed. There are number of tools in the marketplace that perform this effectively.

Essentially, automating the process of contract review is a good option if it is feasible, but some technology components are still catching up to the business needs at this time. The alternative is to partially automate and use manual options where needed. This can end up slowing down the process and introducing inaccuracies but may be the best option if contract data is not readily available for analysis.

Control Communication with Suppliers During M&A transactions, the sales and purchase agreement that defines the terms of the transaction should state the seller's obligations regarding information sharing and communication with the buyer for activities related to suppliers. Suppliers often have specific contractual language that dictates communication requirements for M&A activity. Communicating with nonstrategic suppliers too early in the process can create panic among suppliers, who then inundate the seller with questions concerning the transaction and its impact on their contracts. Communicating late could create issues in executing contractual amendments or terminations. Moreover, getting conflicting information about the transaction and status of a contract can be very detrimental to the seller, which is managing this process. Hence, communications with suppliers have to be managed carefully in order to mitigate these outcomes.

Communication leading practices strongly recommend the following components be included:

- **Set up standardized communication channels across business units, functions, and geographies.** In order to mitigate conflicting messages to suppliers and other stakeholders, it is important to set up one or more central points of contact (PoCs) for supplier communications. In smaller organizations it may be enough to have a single PoC for all suppliers and stakeholder communications, whereas larger organizations may need multiple PoCs. Such PoCs may be assigned for major suppliers or groups of suppliers or categories such as IT, business services, professional services, and so on. The zone of responsibility in such cases has to be clearly defined so that there is no overlap between the PoCs. Moreover, it is important for the PoCs to coordinate among themselves to help provide consistent communications across the overall supplier base.
- **Plan communications and follow-ups with each supplier.** Detailed plans and checklists should be created to execute and track the communications with each supplier. Communication processes and documentation may prove helpful to both the seller and the buyer should a supplier file a lawsuit in the future that is related to the transaction. Procurement needs to work with each stakeholder to define these plans and execute them as appropriate. These plans have to roll up to overall program management to identify and mitigate risks and issues. It is not enough just to send communications to the suppliers, but the suppliers should also acknowledge receipt of these communications. Moreover, supplier responses should be documented in order to decide and act on contract dispositions and business impact.
- **Stay in the details.** Given the complicated nature of contracts, it is important to stay in the details of each activity in order to avoid surprises. For example, communications to suppliers should detail each consideration such as assignability, early termination, and so forth so that the buyer is not blindsided by details that could result in costly affairs.

Leading Practices Leading practices for IT risk management in a merger, acquisition, or divestiture scenario from a contracts perspective are in the list that follows. These are based on the successes and pitfalls while dealing with IT suppliers in transactions across industries:

- Prioritize critical suppliers from more transactional ones.
- Have a clear supplier communication strategy.
- Silence means acceptance.

- Ask for and expect everything.
- Ask for it once.

Cost Management

In spite of the threat or burden of higher cost such as those in IT, cost-reduction/synergy opportunities exist, especially during a period of acquisitions or divestitures. Yet, companies often choose to forgo these opportunities and stick with the same old script that they have been using with their suppliers. To rewrite the script and elevate the supplier discussions to a more strategic level, buyers and sellers alike need to incorporate five key principles.

1. Believe
2. Engage
3. Focus
4. Control
5. Communicate

Believe   It is important to believe that anything is achievable. The very nature of M&A and divestitures means that both companies are focusing on growth. The seller intends to grow by focusing limited resources on fewer things. Buyers look to increase market share, expand into new geographies, and so forth. Suppliers can benefit by gaining access to a new customer, positioning themselves as the favorite in a supplier rationalization effort, introducing new products or services, and more. They love the potential for growth, but they loathe the ambiguity inherent in any M&A or divestiture transaction. They have short-term worries such as losing business to a competitor or forfeiting sales to another representative within their own company. These concerns can be both immediate and forward-looking. In spite of their hope for future growth, it is the uncertainty that can drive many to overreact. They are often the suppliers who threaten and beat their proverbial breasts. The reality is that few of them want to lose business. They are not incentivized to break your business by causing immediate disruption. As a result, anything is possible.

Engage   Engaging strategic suppliers early in the transaction process is important. As we know, IT enables business operations, and it will do so during the transition as well. In some cases, these systems are seen as strategic to the business and creating competitive advantage. These often are heavily customized, have a unique name, and are assumed to be owned by the company. However, this may not be the case at all. Once the transaction team (i.e., corporate development) has engaged a buyer, it is critical that the procurement team become involved. This can prevent the transaction team from selling something that the company doesn't actually own, such as highly customized software applications. Just as IT enables business operations, procurement enables IT. Understanding the nature of the transaction and buyer/seller obligations regarding third-party suppliers allows IT procurement the chance to plan more effectively and execute more quickly.

Focus More effective and faster execution requires a much more focused approach. While "dialing for dollars" can generate a certain amount of savings, applying it to all suppliers would be unwise. Certain suppliers should qualify for more special treatment. To determine who these suppliers are, evaluation criteria should be developed and then applied to your supplier base. Potential criteria may include:

- Business criticality
- Spend
- Renewal dates
- Time remaining until renewal
- Structural lead time issues
- Complexity of agreement
- Specifics of relationship
- Supplier risk
- Resource capacity
- Data availability

Don't expect this to result in a list of hundreds of companies. Rarely are there more than 50 suppliers on the list even for very large, multinational companies. Some suppliers will be obvious whereas others will surprise you. With the list in hand, you can now determine your priorities and identify resource requirements. More importantly, the list allows you to develop a plan and start to execute against it.

Control Now, you need to take control of the process. Almost immediately after a transaction's announcement, suppliers can come out of the woodwork. IT suppliers in particular start pounding on the doors. Sales representatives call their direct contacts, their contacts' bosses, the janitor, or anyone else who may talk to them. They'll tell everyone what you have to do, why you are risking noncompliance, and why you have to act immediately or they'll discontinue services. They'll play the seller and the buyer against each other, telling the seller one thing and the buyer the exact opposite. They do this because it's successful. In other words, the suppliers take control of the process and set the tone for discussions.

As all good negotiators know, controlling to process improves the probability of success. To do that, buyers and sellers need to take a different approach to their process:

- **Set and control the timeline.** Suppliers hate uncertainty. Commit to reaching a resolution by a certain date. Give them a high-level work plan so they can communicate to their executives.
- **Know thyself.** Data level the playing field and provide unemotional support whether talking to your own stakeholders or to the supplier. Oftentimes, companies use data ineffectively or, worse, not at all. During a transaction, IT needs things now. That reality drives the IT team's behavior. They often don't care about cost. They just want it *done*. They can become so focused on the Day 1 date that they lose sight of the larger business objectives. Push them early to think about their overall business intent: What will happen on Day 1? If appropriate, what will happen when TSAs are exited? IT procurement professionals need to consider the impact of these things on the broader supplier relationship and leverage it in their negotiations.
- **Analyze your suppliers.** Like the individuals who work in them, companies tend to focus entirely on their own needs. People are prone to negotiating based on what "feels right." Such faith-based negotiations can prolong the negotiation process. Data-driven negotiation helps reduce supplier uncertainty. Data can show you what is important to the supplier. Whether the buyer or the seller, combining your internal analysis with a detailed understanding of the supplier will help you unlock value in your existing contracts and position you for a more attractive relationship later. When suppliers stress urgency, buyers and sellers each need to focus on the future relationship. Few suppliers are willing to abandon your business.

Communicate Understanding future supplier relationships requires procurement to work in partnership with both IT and the business or functions. This can be challenging given the tenuous relationship between procurement and IT within many companies. At times, their objectives are misaligned. During a transaction, IT appropriately focuses on work plan execution. While supporting Day 1 remains a significant part of the procurement team's role during a transaction, they concurrently are tasked with reducing costs. To make this work, procurement needs to better understand the changing nature of the demands on IT and work to keep suppliers flexible enough to respond to those changes. Information technology, on the other hand, needs to acknowledge that the supplier also has a voice in the process.

When procurement successfully takes control of the negotiation and the communication as previously discussed, the risk of operational disruption is minimized. When supplier uncertainty decreases, economic risk decreases as well. This makes it easier for the procurement team to achieve their objectives.

Leading Practices   What follow are five leading practices for IT cost management in a merger, acquisition, or divestiture scenario from a contracts perspective. These are based on the successes and pitfalls while dealing with suppliers in transactions across industries.

1. Focus on critical suppliers who can drive value.
2. Understand the impact of contracting philosophies.
3. Analyze suppliers' motivations and expectations.
4. Challenge business intent.
5. Sufficient today means it is sufficient tomorrow.

PROGRAM MANAGEMENT

A company may have thousands of suppliers impacted by the transaction. Each supplier may have multiple master services agreements (MSAs) and amendments. Moreover, the format of contracts may vary across each of these suppliers. The scale of managing the contracts during an M&A transaction could be a daunting task for most large companies. An essential element to help manage this complexity is to set up a program management office (PMO) to address the risks and issues and follow the process. Some of the major elements of managing the process are discussed next.

Defining Roles and Responsibilities

The PMO is generally not responsible for executing all contracts management processes. For example, the PMO may be responsible for gathering the business intent, but the business and functions are responsible for providing the information and IT is responsible for automating the contract extraction and tracking. But these roles and responsibilities should be understood across the organization. Here are typical stakeholders and roles:

- Steering committee:
  - Provides guidance from an overall transaction perspective.
  - Reviews overall project status and helps provide timely action on escalated issues.

- PMO:
  - Manages contracts integration or separation process.
  - Establishes plan and deadlines, and coordinates with stakeholders as appropriate.
  - Communicates with internal and external stakeholders.
  - Establishes deliverables and templates, and monitors process.
- Procurement:
  - Identifies all known suppliers and contracts.
  - Gathers business intent from business and functional owners.
  - Communicates and negotiates with suppliers.
- Business and functional owners:
  - Identify suppliers and contracts that originated in the business or function.
  - Agree on business intent for supplier contracts.
- IT
  - Assists procurement, business/functions, and PMO-run reports as requested.
  - Assists in contract data extraction as requested.
- Legal:
  - Provides or approves supplier communication templates.

Note: Oftentimes, there are additional stakeholders, and responsibilities vary by company. These roles and responsibilities have to be updated to address the requirements of the transaction and the company.

Defining Plan, Milestones, and Expected Outputs

Another common source of confusion is the process itself. The PMO is responsible for defining the plan in concert with appropriate stakeholders. This includes not only defining major milestones, output expected, and responsible parties, but also obtaining concurrence from the responsible parties and holding them accountable for the process. This is generally not a trivial task since the stakeholders and the PMO may end up being bogged down by their day-to-day responsibilities in addition to new job responsibilities that come with the transaction.

Defining major milestones and expected output provides clarity into what is feasible and the issues and risks that can result from not following the process. Hence the PMO's role is critical to sustain this process.

Any contracts management plan includes two critical milestones: **Day 1 Ready** and **Day 1 Complete**. Day 1 Ready refers to the milestone when all rights gathering and preceding tasks are complete, whereas Day 1 Complete refers to the date when the transaction is completed. The PMO should establish this distinction and work toward these dates.

Managing Execution

Last, but not the least, the PMO has to manage the execution of the plan. Some of the things to be kept in mind are the following.

Facilitate Early Inclusion The PMO has to make sure all the stakeholders are identified and included early in the process. In one transaction, the legal department was not involved early enough. When legal was finally brought into the project, it identified additional issues in assigning contracts that were not apparent to the other functions. The transaction could not be closed without addressing these issues. This led to delays in approving vendor communications and required both the transaction team and procurement to make adjustments that had some impact on Day 1.

Set Expectations and Priorities The PMO is at the intersection of internal and external entities and reports to the steering committee. This makes it imperative for the PMO to set expectations with each of these entities. When the expectations are in conflict with each other, the PMO should consider bringing the parties together (if appropriate) to resolve such conflicts.

WRAPPING IT UP

While it is easy to focus on the aspects of M&A transactions that drive growth and revenue, few companies proactively manage third-party supplier risks, especially those related to IT. These unmitigated risks can have costly effects on businesses due to lost operational efficiencies and noncompliance. The cost of these risks can be immediate and punitive and could negate synergies. However, suppliers who threaten either business continuity or excessive fees are also opening the door to renegotiation. That means suppliers can also be the source of significant value for both the buyer and seller. By having clear and focused renegotiation strategies, companies can realize significant value more quickly.

When engaging in an M&A transaction, the seller and buyer each should understand their current IT contracts landscape. Carefully plan your postclose landscape. Involve chief information officers (CIOs) and chief procurement officers (CPOs) early in the deal process to avoid undermining the deal value due to third-party contracts. Be prepared with knowledgeable resources, clear communication strategies, and a deep understanding of business intent and of your suppliers' intent. Leverage the transaction environment for your advantage. Your suppliers may have the ability to control the fate of your deal far more than you may expect, but only if you allow them to do so.

CASE STUDIES

The following case studies illustrate the need for effective contracts management in a divestiture and merger setting.

Divestiture at a Multinational Bank

Issue One of the world's largest multinational banking and financial services companies (parent), with over $100 billion in revenue and 250,000 employees, was preparing to divest one of its business units (target) in the United States for strategic reasons and sell it to a regional competitor (buyer). The parent had significant acquisition experience but had limited divestiture experience. The parent and the target had a dispersed regionally based contract management organization without a standard IT system to track all contracts impacted by the transaction. The parent was already facing various litigations from its suppliers for contract breaches and wanted to avoid any further issues that could impede the separation.

Risks The parent did not have a clear understanding of the overall supplier base impacted by the transaction, as well as the suppliers and contracts that it needed in order to help ensure business continuity after Day 1. Due to a limited timeframe and resource availability, the company faced a number of risks such as a delay in Day 1, brand impact, and the following supplier-related risks:

- Possibility of supplier litigation.
- Loss of buyer confidence in target's ability to function independently.
- Impact to the brand of parent and target.
- Business continuity at the parent and target.
- Stranded costs at the parent.
- Increased operational costs at target and buyer.
- Delay in Day 1.

Actions   The company partnered with an external consulting firm to streamline and accelerate the contracts separation process. At a high level, the process followed for contracts separation included:

- Set up governance structure and meeting cadence, and identify complete list of stakeholders. Established a common approach and standardized deliverables across the two companies.
- Set up standardized channels across business units, functions, and geographies.
- Identified scope of suppliers and contracts involved in transaction, and further isolated global and local contracts.
- Identified business intent and short-listed critical suppliers and contracts.
- Automated the process of extracting and analyzing contracts.
- Identified stranded costs, cost reduction, and negotiation strategies.
- Created a mechanism to identify and escalate risks to Day 1 early, and created risk mitigation plans.
- Estimated and tracked savings efficiently, and helped provide consistent definitions of financial impacts.

Results

- Secured rights for 100 percent of suppliers.
- Identified cost-avoidance opportunities amounting to approximately 15 percent of contracts budget over multiple years.
- Minimized one-time costs to approximately 1 percent of typical budgets.
- Achieved hassle-free Day 1 from procurement team.

Merger between Two Energy Companies

Issue   Two large energy companies (Company 1 and Company 2) with similar revenues merged to form a $30 billion integrated energy company to realize integration efficiencies and gain protection against potential foreign buyouts. One of the objectives of the deal was to realize annual cost savings of more than $1 billion. The two companies had different ERP systems, providing the same functions for the most part, which contributed a majority of their IT expenditures. The merger provided an opportunity to assess the future of these ERP systems in the integrated company and determine the potential for cost savings. The leadership of Company 1 had reason to believe that both companies were paying more than what was required for these ERP systems.

Risks The ERP systems were critical to the business operations of both companies. The two companies could not afford the risk, at least initially, to rationalize them into a single system. Besides, the contracts for the two systems were very complex in terms of pricing and terms and conditions, especially in a merger situation. However, it was crucial that the costs associated with the two systems be reduced to make the transaction a success. It was even more crucial to ensure business continuity after Day 1. The newly merged company faced the following risks with the suppliers of these two ERP systems:

- Noncompliance of contracts after Day 1.
- Loss of business continuity for the merged companies.
- Higher costs resulting from supplier negotiation due to limited time-frame.
- Delay in Day 1.
- Loss of market confidence if the companies could not present a plan to reduce costs.

Actions Company 1 partnered with an external consulting firm to evaluate the contracts of the two ERP systems.

The effort involved the following phases:

- Data preparation:
  - Collect and review contracts
  - Determine contract value drivers
  - Validate against long-term ERP plan:
    - Platform/database
    - Applications
    - Business unit requirements
  - Establish current-state usage baseline
  - Establish negotiation baseline
  - Conduct vendor research
- Planning:
  - Define parameters:
    - Functional components
    - Road map
    - Terms and conditions
    - Metrics
  - Establish timeline:
    - Initial proposal review
    - Revised proposal response
    - Agreement in principle
    - Finalized agreement

- Conduct scenario analysis:
  - ◦ Develop and validate
  - ◦ Impact and pricing analysis
- Establish negotiation team:
  - ◦ Define accountabilities and authorization levels
- Negotiation:
  - Engage counterparties
  - Recommend licensing scenario
  - Establish mutual agreement in principle
  - Harmonize terms and conditions

Results

- Negotiated the total spend on one vendor for the next six years down to $9.5 million from the initial proposal of $12 million.
- Reduction achieved by both reduction in volumes and reduction in unit costs.
- Volume reductions:
  - Performed detailed usage analysis for engineering products and gathered future-state requirements for all relevant internal stakeholders. Reduced licenses for the biggest business unit by almost 50 percent to provide for a 95 percent service level.
  - Provided flexibility in contract to add licenses at original cost (no penalty for incremental licenses).
  - Achieved volume reductions that contributed $2.5 milion of the total $4 million savings from the baseline.
- Cost reductions:
  - Pricing negotiation was focused on license cost, incremental license cost, and escalations.
  - License cost was reduced by 15 percent from the initial proposal.
  - Yearly escalation rate was reduced from 3 percent to 1.5 percent.
  - Pricing reductions contributed $1.5 million of the total $4 million savings from the baseline.

LESSONS LEARNED

Here are some lessons learned from past transactions that should be applicable to most contracts management scenarios in an M&A setting:

Capture Business Intent for Third-Party IT Products Early

Business intent is how the business functions of the seller wish to hand over a product or service used by the sold entity and provided by a third-party supplier under a contract to the buyer. The objective of identifying business intent is threefold:

1. Ensure continuity of business operations on Day 1.
2. Request rights from suppliers as appropriate to ensure contractual compliance on Day 1.
3. Minimize cost impact associated with third-party products and services due to the transaction.

Do's and Don'ts

- To ensure the best interests of the business function, don't let contract provisions drive business intent. New rights can generally be negotiated with sufficient notice.
- If a provision is silent in the contract, a notification to the supplier might be sufficient in most cases.

Why Is It Important?

- Suppliers need lead time of up to six months to grant required contractual rights.
- Not providing enough lead time may lead to a situation where contractual compliance may be compromised on Day 1.
- Supplier may have leverage to extract a higher fee if it realizes that the transaction won't go through without its consent.

Know Your Suppliers and Contracts Well

Document all the third-party suppliers and related contracts impacted by a transaction. Documentation should include the contract provisions associated with Day 1 requirements.

Dos and Don'ts

- Start the documentation process as early as possible in the transaction cycle.
- Automate the documentation process as much as possible.

Why Is It Important?

- There are precedents where supplier contract noncompliance has resulted in penalties to the tune of millions for the seller.

Control Communication with Suppliers

Restrict business functions' communications with the suppliers to business as usual. Allow only certain individuals or a specific function to talk to the suppliers regarding the impacts from the transaction.

Dos and Don'ts

- Set up guiding principles for supplier communication early in the transaction cycle for business functions, procurement, and deal teams.
- The buyer should not speak to a supplier directly without involving the seller.

Why Is It Important?

- Certain information may allow the supplier get better leverage to extract fees and higher pricing from both buyer and seller.

CHAPTER 14

M&A IT Architecture and Infrastructure

Developing and Delivering Transition Services Agreements

Olivier May
Kevin Charles

In the M&A world, the following situation is a familiar one: a diversified corporation decides to exit a line of business. The rationale is generally sound; the business unit did not quite fit into the long-term strategy of the enterprise or was simply not meeting performance expectations. Typically, the buyer for this business unit falls into one of two categories: a financial buyer such as a private equity group, or a strategic buyer such as a corporation that seeks to buy a compatible line of business (it is important to note that different types of buyers typically have different operational requirements of the carved-out business during the transition period). In a divestiture situation, the close of the financial transaction, whether it's a carve-out, spin-off, or other, generally marks the beginning of a buyer-seller operational relationship. To this extent, the seller or parent company often finds itself in the business of providing services to the divested entity or "child." Typically these new activities are known as transition services and are governed by what is referred to as a transition services agreement (TSA). (In some cases the child will also be required to provide limited services back to its former parent. Services that are provided from the child to the parent are referred to as reverse transition services.) How you manage and structure these legal agreements can have a measurable impact on your ability to operate the carve-out or spin-off for both the buyer and the seller, as well as significant implications for the way you approach negotiations during an M&A transaction, and could impact the timing of critical milestones in the transaction.

Succinctly, TSAs are arrangements whereby the divested company pays the parent company (and vice versa) a fee to continue to provide services, such as production, back-office, and shared service operations for a specified period of time after the transaction closes. The result is an interim state linking the parent and the divested company together until the two companies can operate independently.

Being a service provider is not typically in either organization's DNA; therefore, the provision of transition services is often difficult to manage and can distract from normal business. Therefore, the presence of TSAs should be seen as a necessary evil, and they should be used only for the most critical of business functions to help ensure business continuity and minimize negative impacts on customers. The use of reverse transition services adds further complexity to the postclose relationship and should be carefully structured. Transition services may be a high-cost option for both parties, often resulting in subpar service for the receiver and continual distractions for the provider.

Based on our experience with multiple transactions of various sizes, leading companies that excel in managing transitional services do five things effectively:

1. **Plan early and resource appropriately.** Create detailed and aggressive TSA development plans that accommodate all phases of the transition early on, and identify and appoint experienced cross-functional teams.
2. **Foster deal team and business collaboration to document appropriately.** Focus on aligning the legal agreement with actual service requirements, and identify service requirements at the appropriate level of detail.
3. **Price services conservatively.** Implement approaches to effectively price transition services.
4. **Establish governance approach.** Align on governance of TSA prior to close. This includes service readiness, invoicing, change management, performance management, and issue management.
5. **Plan exits and remove stranded costs.** Plan for the exit of transition services and the removal of stranded costs (i.e., costs that were associated with the divested business that should no longer be incurred) after the transition period ends.

The remainder of this chapter explores each of these in more detail.

PLAN EARLY AND RESOURCE APPROPRIATELY

Plan Early

Transition services are usually required when executing a transition and provide some confirmation to both parties that there will be minimal disruption to customers or clients during the transition period. In some instances, TSAs are an operational requirement, and in other instances an insurance policy and a show of good faith. Regardless of the reason for having a TSA, one thing is clear: transactions that take a pragmatic approach to completing a deal begin planning for transition services early in the process. Their perspective tends to be that if they start early they can develop a solid TSA and inform transition plans, and by so doing eliminate (or reduce) the likelihood of the last-minute stress on the transaction and functional teams. Planning for TSAs early in the process, even if only as a contingency, can benefit a transaction in several ways over the long run:

- Helps to create a sense of control during what can be a chaotic time.
- Uses the plan for transition services to influence the plan for Day 1, the transition period, and the eventual end state.
- Can be used to influence the employee selection and conveyance process.
- Helps to limit scope creep and facilitate a smooth transaction execution from deal close to full separation.

To reap the benefits of planning early, both buyer and seller should focus early on developing a divestiture road map that includes TSAs. This road map should lay out all of the major separation activities and key interdependencies, including legal and regulatory hurdles, operational and functional separation activities, cost reduction efforts, internal/external communications, and TSA development requirements.

Once the overall road map is developed, a blueprinting exercise should be used to design the three critical phases of the transaction (Day 1, transition, and end state). Buyers need to clearly understand which aspects of the shared service organization will be included in the purchase of the company, which aspects will need to be accommodated either by the seller for some period of time or by the purchaser's existing infrastructure, and the timing to transition the required services. For financial buyers, such as private equity firms, this point is particularly important. Often, the receiving company does not have the ability to provide basic shared services, resulting in the need to create these capabilities. Therefore, the interim TSA period must accommodate a standing up of critical business functions, which can be costly if conducted within tight timeframes. At a minimum, TSA planning should address services in scope, cost, duration of agreements, activity owners, issue resolution processes, as well as service extension and termination clauses.

Prepared sellers can be well served not only by planning early but also by developing entire TSA programs ahead of time. This typically includes a suggested menu of services, complete with costs, service levels, governance process, and exit approaches that can be quickly socialized with potential buyers. In our experience, the investment in time to do this greatly accelerates the TSA development process, reduces stress, and creates a sense of confidence in the potential buyer that the business and its customers or clients will not be negatively impacted during the transition process. This sentiment goes a long way in easing the challenges of negotiating a purchase agreement.

In arriving at a purchase agreement in a recent multibillion-dollar transaction, the notion of transition services and general terms was discussed. Although it was agreed that transition services would be necessary to conduct business immediately following deal close and during the transition period, the immediate foci of early integration planning were strategic end-state decisions. The result was a basket of transition services that were identified and negotiated in a fairly short period of time, which placed additional planning pressure on functional teams. The hasty negotiations also resulted in the need for an update process after close. Focusing on TSAs early would have allowed functional teams time to get a more detailed understanding of the operational capabilities and requirements of the divested unit relative to the acquiring company's existing capabilities. This, in turn, would have led to a more judicious use of TSAs only where absolutely needed.

Resource Appropriately

Transition Services Agreements require dedicated and knowledgeable personnel to plan, scope, and manage their development and execution. It is a best practice to create two complementary teams to manage the TSA. The parent company representatives are designated as the "carve out and hand off" (COHO) team. These should be people who are knowledgeable (or very knowledgeable) of the operations and have enough influence to operate efficiently from a cross-functional perspective. Complementing this on the purchasing side is the "receive and operate" (RO) team. The RO team needs to have a full command of integration processes and the interim requirements that will enable them. The COHO/RO structure provides for clear roles, escalation pathways, and designated process owners to minimize business disruption for both companies. In addition, the teams should include experienced negotiators with a line of sight into all integration issues.

On a recently completed deal, the TSA team was extremely knowledgeable about the business operations and was able to ask the right questions to avoid hidden pitfalls. To leverage the cross-functional negotiations required for several other supporting agreements, the TSA teams drove for and initiated regular cross-functional negotiation strategy sessions. By doing this, the TSA team was able to avoid making requests or concessions that were not aligned with the overall deal priorities. The team was able to communicate internally to avoid negotiating locally operational solutions.

Planning and Resourcing Best Practices

- **Plan early.** Whether you end up with a TSA or not, the planning will inform transition planning, minimize impact on teams, and signal the level of experience and commitment to a smooth transition.
- **Use your experts.** Engage functional experts with broad cross-functional experience to help define service requirements and solve transition issues.
- **Stick to the plan.** Establish a road map for TSA development, and stick to it. Chances are the impact of TSA development will not be felt as acutely if managed over a protracted period.

FOSTER DEAL TEAM AND BUSINESS COLLABORATION TO DOCUMENT APPROPRIATELY

Align Agreement and Schedules

TSAs generally consist of two parts. First, the actual legal or cover agreement that provides the terms, conditions of service, term, limitations, and indemnifications that will be in force during the term of the TSA, along with the typical legal disclosures in terms of recitals, arbitration, confidentiality, jurisdiction, warranties, and the like. Second, there are usually schedules or exhibits attached to the legal agreement that detail the actual services, costs, duration, service levels, and, in some cases, exceptions to the services that will be provided.

The trick to developing workable TSAs is to make sure alignment exists between the schedules and the legal agreement throughout the process so that both documents support each other and are practical to implement. The legal agreement should be developed by the legal/deal team with open and consistent input from the business. Likewise, the schedules or exhibits should be developed by the business with consistent input from compliance and legal/deal teams. In this way, both parties can inform each other of required or desired solutions, positions, or limitations within the context of the larger deal and considering operational implications.

The importance of this transparency is difficult to overstate. For example, in one transaction, the legal agreement contemplated a dual employee structure where certain employees would be shared during the transition period in a literal sense. Each of these employees would become a part-time employee of each company, complete with two offices, two phone numbers, two e-mail accounts, two paychecks, two bosses, and two tax forms. As you can imagine, the transition period was difficult and saw very high attrition within this employee group. Had the right operational resource been involved in the negotiations, this resource would have been able to inform the outside counsel that this structure would not work within the context of the targeted employee group.

Document at the Right Level of Detail

The documentation requirements of TSAs vary depending on which side you are on. On the sell side of a transaction, there is an inherent advantage to developing very specific service schedules as a means of limiting the number of services that will need to be offered. After all, the seller's primary concern is usually to exit the business and hence limit TSAs as much as possible. On the buy side of the deal, however, the motivations tend to be a little different. Buy-side transaction teams are most concerned about stability during the transition period, and as such tend to want the most flexibility in the transition services.

In practice, both parties should seek to document the services at the appropriate level of detail (that is, the level of detail where any employee can read the service descriptions and understand what is required). As the deal is executed, there is typically substantial employee turnover, particularly on the seller's side. Having undocumented or vaguely documented agreements can place both the service provider and the service receiver at risk of issue escalation and service interruption. At best, time is wasted in trying to reclarify the agreement; at worst, working relationships can be damaged. Somewhere in between the best and the worst, valuable management attention is redirected from more critical issues. Although it is not always practical to do so, schedules and exhibits to the TSA should be developed and documented by local functional owners to support the centrally negotiated master TSAs. This creates a sense of ownership, level-sets expectations, and fosters working relationships that typically prove to be easier to manage during the transition period.

Collaboration and Documentation Best Practices

- **One TSA.** Direct the deal team and the business teams to develop one agreement where schedules and legal agreement support each other and can be practically implemented.
- **Details—not too much, not too little.** Documenting services at the right level of detail will foster confidence and enable communications while limiting the administrative and interpretative burden.
- **Develop locally; support globally.** At the end of the day, the service providers are the ones who have to live with the agreement. It makes practical sense that they should have a big role in defining the services (with guidance on documentation) they will have to deliver.
- **Share schedule broadly.** Socialize schedules with all stakeholders (business, risk, legal, compliance, finance) throughout the process and seek their input. Waiting for surprise comments at the end of the development cycle will just cause heartburn.

PRICE SERVICES CONSERVATIVELY

The Pricing Challenge

Pricing is one of the most important elements of a TSA and can be quite a challenging task to complete. The reason for this is that the web of internal allocations, transfer pricing, and hidden service components can make it difficult for businesspeople to understand the true cost of providing services. For example, a TSA designed to help close the books typically considers the cost of the employees' time based on salaries, but further examination reveals that the true cost of the service may very well include a portion of benefits, the cost of licenses for the systems that the employees may need to access, the cost of any vendors that play a role in the process, and the cost of employees from other departments that support the service, including IT. As you can see, determining the price of a transition service can quickly become very complex.

In addition to the challenge of decomposing the true costs of services, there is also the issue of projecting the cost of the service forward into the transition period. Most companies simply look at the previous year's costs, but this does not capture the escalation in unit cost due to inflation and changes in economies of scale.

Most sellers are not in the business of divesting services and typically lack the systems, tools, M&A experience, and skills to accurately analyze service costs. In such situations, sellers should attempt to identify some benchmarks that can serve as a gauge for identifying standard costs for their particular industry and size. These benchmarks can be obtained by performing a quick survey of outsourcing services and the current market rate for these services. Benchmarks from previous transactions can also be used to provide a sanity check; however, care must be taken not to rely too heavily on past transactions, as each is distinct.

To simplify the process, buyer and seller should approach the agreement with a clear understanding of the price and cost drivers. Clearly defining the cost components and assumptions used to calculate the price can accelerate and simplify the pricing process. For example, both parties may agree ahead of time which cost elements will be considered in TSA pricing, such as full-time employee (FTE) allocations, office space, ancillary services, location, server utilization, and network bandwidth.

Understanding the cost drivers will also help both entities develop exit strategies, and inform provisions in the legal agreement. For example, activities that are likely to decrease over time (e.g., desktop support migration) might require step-down events where costs go down as the buyer becomes less dependent on the seller's services. Other activities that are more likely to remain constant (e.g., mainframe hosting) might be defined at a fixed cost until the last remaining user or resource is removed. These latter services are candidates for accelerated exit if the cost and disruption risks are high.

Pricing (price escalations in particular) can also be used as a lever by both parties to drive to independence. Take the case of a buyer that received TSA services from the seller at a lower cost than it could get in the market, due to economies of scale. In an effort to push the organization to independence, the buyer quickly agreed to significant price escalations after a short period. In this way, sellers provided an incentive for the service receivers to accelerate exit where they would likely look for opportunities to continue receiving cheaper services.

Pricing Approaches

Costs for providing services should be determined prior to finalizing the TSA schedules. In calculating the costs for transition services, several methods can be leveraged to determine the true service costs.

Exhibit 14.1 outlines a best practice approach for determining TSA pricing.

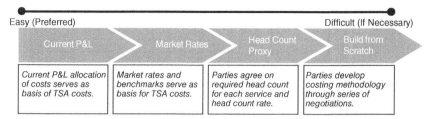

Current P&L allocation of costs serves as basis of TSA costs.	Market rates and benchmarks serve as basis for TSA costs.	Parties agree on required head count for each service and head count rate.	Parties develop costing methodology through series of negotiations.

EXHIBIT 14.1 Approach for Determining TSA Pricing

For each shared service:

- Start by using an existing financial statement–based cost figure (if not available, use the next least difficult metric).
- Service providers (often corporate functions) can assist if costs are difficult to quantify.
- TSAs will often incorporate multiple costing methods across schedules.
- Lines of business or functions should, where possible, prepare initial cost projections to facilitate negotiations with providers.

Once the cost has been determined, corporate can employ the following techniques to price each service:

- **Cost plus.** Provided services should be priced at cost plus 10 percent (or other percentage) for all services; however, this percentage can vary and include market inflation.
- **Cost escalation.** Services that go beyond negotiated durations will incur a penalty that can increase over time.
- **Migration costs.** Costs associated with migrating services from the provider to the recipient should be the responsibility of the divesting unit/buyer.
- **Minimum fee.** A minimum fee will be in all TSAs to protect against investments lost due to a Day 1 + 1 cancellation of services.

One-Time Costs and Typical Exclusions

The general principle of transition services is typically "provide the services in the same manner that you did prior to the transaction." Some transaction teams assume that this means business as usual. However, the change in ownership places an additional burden on services providers in terms of limiting access to systems, and implementing connections with an entity that is now running on different networks and is encumbered by antitrust guidelines. These differences typically impact three categories of costs that can be substantial:

1. Setup costs:
   - Project (labor) to set up environment, infrastructure, and resources to provide TSA services.
   - Additional software or hardware costs.
   - Shipping and any other costs.
2. Exit/wind-down costs:
   - Project (labor) to break down environment, infrastructure, and resources to provide TSA services.
   - Removal of software or hardware costs.
3. Pass-through costs:
   - Typically third-party costs that are volume-based.
   - Impact of economies of scale that may increase costs.
   - Cost of assignment and penalties for early exit or extensions.

Transaction teams may also choose to negotiate the treatment of one-time costs related to transition services.

Costs not typically included in the TSA schedule:

- Costs incurred before closing date that were mutually agreed to by both parties through a work order request (with underlying statement of work) or similar agreed method.
- Costs incurred due to material growth in service requirements. Note: Reduction in service requirements will not be credited to the buyer unless the buyer terminates service.
- Any infrastructure project setup costs related to segregation of the infrastructure environment.
- Asset purchase or lease buyout costs (software and hardware).
- Costs associated with any third-party contracts, including licenses, that the seller agrees to purchase directly from the vendor on the closing date.
- Costs incurred by the seller related to assisting the buyer in responding to regulatory requirements, legal proceedings brought by a third party, or systems changes (e.g., report requests or changes in functionality).

Pricing Best Practices

- **Keep it simple.** Pricing is complicated. Develop and agree on simplifying strategies that will get you close enough.
- **Align with services.** Pricing strategy should be clearly aligned with the nature of services being provided, and account for the fact that

some new services may be introduced and a stepwise or bundled exit may need to occur. Try to bundle services that have natural linkages versus offering a detailed menu of services (e.g., e-mail services should be priced per user and include all elements from licensing to server and infrastructure components).

■ **Look forward.** The costs of services will change over time. Build in mechanisms to escalate pricing due to increased costs, for additional services, and as an incentive to drive early exits.

ESTABLISH A PRACTICAL GOVERNANCE APPROACH

Governance Structure

The real work begins when the deal closes and the TSAs go into effect. As the services are being delivered, it is important to continually track and manage the services performed under the TSAs. A TSA management structure should be developed to help manage the postclose delivery of services. The governance structure also helps to manage and maintain the relationship between the buyer and the seller. Sellers will inevitably focus on cleaning up the business of the remaining company (RemainCo), and will then quickly shift their attention to remaining business activities. Buyers are focused on integrating the new business and may rely heavily on the services supported by the TSAs. These differences in focus emphasize the importance of developing a governance structure before the TSAs are rolled out to help ensure services are being executed as planned.

Both parties will mutually develop a governance structure, management process, and dispute resolution channels. The development of governance structures can improve the likelihood of achieving the desired outcome through the mutual understanding of the key roles and responsibilities within each group across companies. Issues should be resolved at the service level whenever possible, and escalated to the leadership team if necessary. Regular reviews with functional or area leadership may be required to provide the information necessary to determine whether issues require escalation. Before exiting TSAs, in-depth reviews should be performed to determine whether the buyer is properly positioned and capable of assuming responsibility for the services provided by the seller once the TSA expires.

Key roles and responsibilities for the governance team include:

■ Define services to be provided by both the buyer and the seller.
■ Establish the scope, standard of performance, and service-level agreements (SLAs) (i.e., commitments to provide services at defined levels).

- Determine compensation for services and payment terms.
- Identify legal representations, warranties, and indemnifications.
- Identify the primary points of contact for all aforementioned activities.
- Establish clear change control and approval processes for changes to SLAs and the TSA.
- Define TSA exit and plan.

Exhibit 14.2 presents an example of a TSA governance structure and a brief description of the roles and responsibilities of each group.

Within the process group, the following key functions will support the day-to-day management of the TSAs. Key roles and responsibilities are shown in Exhibit 14.3.

Issue Escalation

Issues pertaining to transition services should be resolved at the work stream level between both parties. To the extent necessary, however, an escalation process can be established to address TSA issues not resolved at the service level. An overview of this process is shown in Exhibit 14.4.

Service Readiness

Legal Day 1 of any merger, acquisition, or divestiture is a period of great change for an organization. Any drastic organizational change that disrupts day-to-day operations brings with it considerable risk. It comes as no surprise that careful planning and fastidious testing of standing operations and processes must occur in order to mitigate this risk and help ensure operations run smoothly before, during, and after a cut-over. In the presence of a TSA, this testing and certification of readiness takes on even greater importance. Following a cut-over, two organizations that previously worked together as one will be counterparties under the TSA. Business units and functional areas will provide services to each other in a way similar to a vendor and service recipient relationship. There will be SLAs to meet and invoices to be paid. Therefore, testing and service readiness certification assume an even more significant role.

Operating under the new agreement, functional leaders will have to adjust the way their groups operated prior to cut-over. It may also be the case that they are required to provide new, additional services in order to stand up the new organization for complete separation. To initiate these services, a program must be followed to identify, implement, and test the required changes to operational processes.

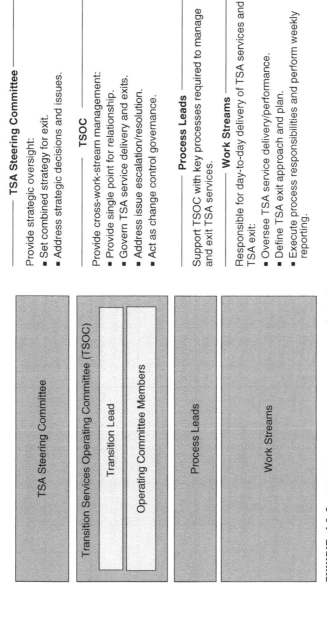

TSA Steering Committee

Provide strategic oversight:
- Set combined strategy for exit.
- Address strategic decisions and issues.

TSOC

Provide cross-work-stream management:
- Provide single point for relationship.
- Govern TSA service delivery and exits.
- Address issue escalation/resolution.
- Act as change control governance.

Process Leads

Support TSOC with key processes required to manage and exit TSA services.

Work Streams

Responsible for day-to-day delivery of TSA services and TSA exit:
- Oversee TSA service delivery/performance.
- Define TSA exit approach and plan.
- Execute process responsibilities and perform weekly reporting.

TSA Steering Committee

Transition Services Operating Committee (TSOC)

Transition Lead

Operating Committee Members

Process Leads

Work Streams

EXHIBIT 14.2 TSA Governance Structure Schedule

TSOC Processes	Description
Program Management	▪ Provide overall coordination of TSOC activities. ▪ Consolidate executive-level reporting. ▪ Support TSOC transition lead.
Program Management Support	▪ Assist in TSOC execution and provide tactical support to transition leads and work streams.
Performance Management	▪ Aggregate and validate TSA performance (against SLAs).
Exit Planning	▪ Develop exit planning prioritization criteria and review projects. ▪ Develop overall exit plan and road map.
Change Control and Work Authorization	▪ Manage TSA changes—scope changes, early exits, extensions, new services, and work authorizations (SOWs). ▪ Align changes with other processes—invoicing, exit planning, performance management, invoicing.
Invoice Management	▪ Create, review, approve, and pay TSA invoices. ▪ Perform forecasting and planning. ▪ Address invoice queries.
Compliance	▪ Provide support for audit reviews. ▪ Monitor service provider compliance to internal supplier management and external compliance requirements.
Contracts Transition	▪ Develop weekly governance reporting to TSOC on vendor management. ▪ Provide oversight and coordination of contract transfers and dependencies with TSA exits.

EXHIBIT 14.3 TSA Roles and Responsibilities

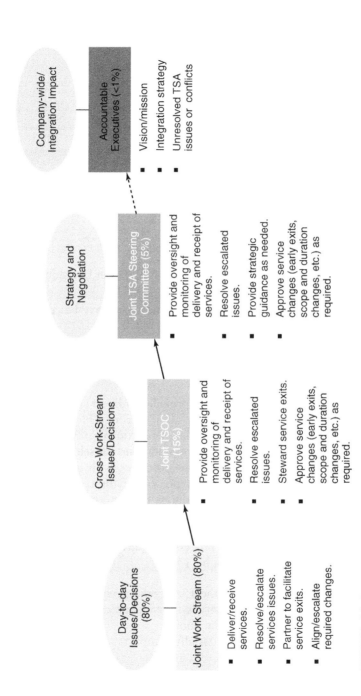

EXHIBIT 14.4 Issues Escalation Process

Company-wide/
Integration Impact

**Accountable
Executives (<1%)**

- Vision/mission
- Integration strategy
- Unresolved TSA
  issues or conflicts

Strategy and
Negotiation

**Joint TSA Steering
Committee (5%)**

- Provide oversight and
  monitoring of
  delivery and receipt of
  services.
- Resolve escalated
  issues.
- Provide strategic
  guidance as needed.
- Approve service
  changes (early exits,
  scope and duration
  changes, etc.) as
  required.

Cross-Work-Stream
Issues/Decisions

**Joint TSOC
(15%)**

- Provide oversight and
  monitoring of
  delivery and receipt of
  services.
- Resolve escalated
  issues.
- Steward service exits.
- Approve service
  changes (early exits,
  scope and duration
  changes, etc.) as
  required.

Day-to-day
Issues/Decisions
(80%)

Joint Work Stream (80%)

- Deliver/receive
  services.
- Resolve/escalate
  services issues.
- Partner to facilitate
  service exits.
- Align/escalate
  required changes.

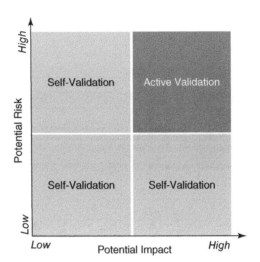

EXHIBIT 14.5 Active Validation versus Self-Validation Decision Matrix

There are two types of readiness validation that may be conducted to key processes are operational Day 1:

1. Self-validation
2. Active validation

In self-validation, functional leads provide readiness sign-off. This type of validation is sufficient for proof of readiness from a functional point of view. Processes that are contained within a functional group and have no or minimum cross-functional impact are candidates for self-validation.

Multifunctional processes, or those processes with significant cross-functional impact, require the second type of validation, active validation. Active validation calls for proof of readiness from a cross-functional point of view. Process owners sign off on service readiness in active validation. Active validation should be conducted for all high-impact, high-risk, cross-functional processes. Examples of processes requiring active validation may include the following (and see Exhibit 14.5):

- Critical systems as defined in the TSA legal agreement.
- Key processes, including materials in/materials out, cash in/cash out, taking an order, and closing the books.
- Transactions that can materially impact buyer/seller financial statements.

- Transactions/flows with fraud exposure risk.
- Processes feeding or supporting key management decisions.
- Newly created processes or transactions built to accommodate transitional activity.

Self-Validation Functional leads conducting self-validation perform the following steps:

- Functional teams are provided with a self-validation checklist.
- Self-validation templates help functions through various aspects of functional readiness.
- Functional leads declare their function "Day 1 Ready," "Day 1 Ready Conditionally," or "Not Ready."
- Teams identify key risks, potential pitfalls, and appropriate mitigation strategies.
- Functional leads sign off on validation.

Active Validation Process leads conducting active validation perform the following steps:

- Validate processes identified as high impact/high risk in working sessions.
- Develop validation scenarios and probing questions to test readiness of the critical processes.
- Validate readiness through global working sessions.
- Identify potential failure points and develop contingency plans to address the possibility of Day 1 failures.
- Have process owners sign off on validation.

Service Readiness Testing Reporting To make sure there is program-wide knowledge sharing, the Day 1 readiness team will provide ongoing readiness reports as follows:

- Day 1 readiness team issues report based on consolidated findings from self-validations and active validations.
- Report is used to communicate overall readiness to Day 1 program leads.
- Report to refine Day 1 resource model.
- Program-wide view of readiness, including Day 1 readiness risks, potential failure points, and contingency plans.

Invoicing

Invoicing and payment terms are described and agreed to within the TSA legal agreements, along with the general construct under which the TSA services are to be delivered. Generally, charges for transition services are invoiced monthly in arrears, with payment due within 30 days of receipt of applicable invoices. Service recipients will receive a single invoice for all TSA charges. This invoice can be itemized or bundled as agreed. There are pros and cons to each approach, but the decision is usually driven by corporate culture, the controls environment, and the level of trust that is engendered throughout the negotiation process.

Itemized invoices should align to the TSA schedule of services and detail each service-specific cost (e.g., labor, setup cost, or stranded cost) as a separate line item. In less complex agreements, charges may simply align with the TSA schedule of services and not detail the specific type of cost. In both cases, TSA coordinators, both buyer and seller, should be tracking costs on a service-by-service basis in collaboration with functional leaders in order to help ensure that invoicing properly coincides with service termination and subsequent cost reduction, and to provide a cost-avoidance incentive for accelerated exits.

A hybrid approach of bundling related services and treating them as a single group for invoicing and exits can simplify the process. When this is done, these services tend to be exited as a group, and any early exits do not qualify for cost relief.

The invoicing process can be one of the more challenging aspects of TSA governance. Business units that previously worked together on a daily basis will now be interacting as vendors and service recipients. It is therefore often the case, particularly in the months immediately following cut-over, that the business units providing services under a TSA operate in a business-as-usual mode, failing to accurately track costs. Furthermore, initial forecasts may prove to be inaccurate as needs rapidly change in the post-transition environment. Some services will need to be extended past their initial duration, while others will be found to be unnecessary. Any such change will impact the TSA invoicing.

In order to manage the proper tracking of costs, preparation and validation of invoices, and collection of payments, the TSA governance body should develop and maintain effective processes that include the necessary controls and reporting requirements. For complex deals with detailed transition services agreements, it is a best practice for a small operational team to manage invoicing activities, collaborating with the larger TSA governing body and staying abreast of approved schedule changes and approaching service terminations. (See Exhibit 14.6.)

	Provider	Recipient
Invoice Preparation	• Aggregate services provided under TSA by functional area throughout month. • Apply appropriate mark up and taxes. • Deliver invoice within 30 days of month end.	• Track services received under TSA by functional area throughout month. • Prepare aggregated invoice forecast for use in validation process.
Invoice Validation	• Answer questions raised by functional lead counterpart during initial validation process.	• Compare invoice forecast based on tracked services received to actual invoice. • Follow outlined process to resolve discrepancies.
Resolve or Escalate Disputes	• Settle disputes at the service level. • If dispute cannot be resolved, escalate to appropriate authority. • Utilize standardized process for dispute resolution and escalation.	

EXHIBIT 14.6   Invoice Process Roles and Responsibilities

Invoicing Process   Assuming there are both forward and reverse services being provided under the TSA, both buyer and seller will have to perform two invoicing-related processes at month's end:

1. Invoice preparation
2. Invoice validation

Invoice Preparation   In order to prepare the month's invoice for delivery to the service recipient, the service provider performs the following steps:

- Monthly recurring, pass-through, and one-time charges are aggregated and validated by each functional lead.
- Invoice is computed, markups and taxes are applied, and invoice summary by TSA work stream is generated.
- Invoice is delivered to service recipient within 30 days of end of month (or sooner), and accounts receivable (A/R) balance is updated.
- Service recipient receives invoice, performs validation process, and pays invoice within 30 days of receipt (or sooner).

Invoice Validation In order to validate a received invoice for correctness, the service recipient performs the following steps:

- Service recipient receives invoice within 30 days of end of month in which services were performed.
- Invoice is reviewed by TSA coordinator; functional-specific reports are distributed to functional leads.
- Functional leads verify that invoiced actuals are in line with services received, and approve charges.
- Service recipient delivers payment within 30 days of receipt of invoice.

Issue/Dispute Resolution In certain cases, an invoicing discrepancy might arise as a result of the invoice validation process. The issue resolution process resolves these discrepancies:

- If a functional lead finds a discrepancy under 10 percent within the functional invoice, the dispute should be settled between respective functional leads with the assistance of finance teams.
- If a functional lead finds a discrepancy over 10 percent within the functional invoice, a dispute is created.
- The TSA governing body reviews the dispute and determines action.
- If a correction is required, a credit will be issued in the following month's invoice.

Performance Management

As part of the TSA, the service provider will be held to and measured against SLAs. It is important to precisely define in the TSA what service levels are expected. Often, the seller has not been measuring performance for the services in question. In these cases, it is critical for both parties to agree on the performance metrics and, once agreed, to document them in the TSA.

The service provider will report performance on SLAs on a predetermined basis, typically monthly, and provide supporting material when available. The performance management team (a process lead as part of the transition services operating committee [TSOC]) will be responsible for aggregating and synthesizing the results and providing them to the seller. The primary objectives are to:

- Track and report service quality against TSA SLAs.
- Resolve service quality issues that arise.
- Proactively respond to emerging service quality trends.

Focus Area	Description
TSA Service Owners	• Develop SLAs reporting (for TSA services). • Provide performance measures and supporting documentation. • Notify performance manager of any new SLAs that will be shared.
Performance Manager	• Aggregate metrics in a reportable format and distribute to seller. • Maintain standards for performance reporting. • Monitor TSA and SLA performances. • Capture escalations from TSA service owners on any SLA or performance targets.

EXHIBIT 14.7 TSA Roles and Responsibilities

Roles and Responsibilities Performance tracking of TSAs will be supported by the TSA service owners, who have intimate knowledge of the TSA services and expected performance metrics, and will be managed by a performance manager. (See Exhibit 14.7.)

Performance Management Process When it comes to reporting performance on SLAs, a simpler process is generally easier to manage and document. A process can be designed to aggregate all SLAs from TSA owners and roll them up into an overall performance measure. There is an opportunity to automate this process by creating a database or template that is used consistently by TSA service owners. (See Exhibit 14.8.)

Governance Best Practices

- **Align on roles and responsibilities.** During the TSA negotiation process, agree on how the TSA will be managed, what roles will be required, and what is needed to effectively manage the TSA.
- **Match governance with corporate culture and controls.** Little good ever comes from developing a cottage industry around managing TSAs, except in an instance where the corporate culture will not accept anything else. If both companies are cost-conscious and tend to scrutinize invoices down to the last five minutes of billable time, you would be well advised to build a governance process to support this type of review.
- **Empower the team, but manage your risk.** Pushing decision rights down to the levels where the work is being done is more than good

Performance Management Step	Key Tasks	Deliverables
Validate SLA reporting requirements.	▪ Review existing performance levels. ▪ Establish SLAs for each TSA service. ▪ Define reporting requirements necessary to support SLA management. ▪ Define reporting requirements necessary to support non-SLA day-to-day performance management.	▪ TSA schedule SLAs ▪ Operational plans ▪ Vendor scorecards
Perform monthly SLA reporting.	▪ SLA data is collected for each TSA and sent to performance manager. ▪ Performance manager aggregates all SLA results and reports on total SLA performance each period.	▪ Vendor scorecards ▪ Monthly performance dashboards
Report results and issues to leadership.	▪ Determine if service delivery adheres to performance metrics. ▪ Create and distribute performance reports. ▪ Provide ad hoc operational reports to meet business and customer needs. ▪ Review performance summaries. ▪ Aggregate performance results for each period and provide to leadership.	▪ Performance reports

EXHIBIT 14.8 Performance Management Processes

management theory; it minimizes the management burden. As you do this, however, maintain oversight so the right decisions are being made.

▪ **Get ready—TSAs require change.** As much as we hear "business as usual" in a TSA environment, it is anything but. Most TSAs require some small changes that are easily overlooked, especially when there are cross-functional dependencies. A light but effective testing and readiness program will help you start off on the right foot.

▪ **Invoice simply.** Invoicing should match the costing process, but finding ways to simplify the process of collecting and validating invoices will save a lot of organizational angst.

- **Bundles are your friend.** Detail-oriented managers generally have a hard time accepting that bundling service levels, costs, and invoices will reduce or limit the burden of managing TSAs. It does, as long as there is agreement up front and the understanding that this is just a temporary solution, not a long-term vendor relationship. The fact of the matter is that everyone's time is better spent if people are less focused on managing TSAs and more focused on completing the transition.

PLAN EXITS AND REMOVE STRANDED COSTS

TSA Exit Planning

Planning TSA exits is one of the most critical steps in the TSA development process. TSA migration and exit plans should be created as part of the TSA development process and should be crafted with the end in mind (e.g., articulate how to exit TSAs while drafting the TSA schedules). The blueprinting process will help identify a preliminary and end-state vision, leading to the development of more detailed Day 1 separation plans and an intended exit strategy for TSAs.

Why should you start planning exits so early? As soon as the deal closes, the quality of TSA services will gradually worsen for two primary reasons. First, the seller is selling the business for a reason: it no longer wants to be in that business. The seller's focus after the deal closes will be on rightsizing the remaining business and making money with a new or modified business model. Second, as the seller gets its house in order, there will be continued personnel changes and attritions. Buyers need to be aware of this and anticipate having to exit TSAs quickly for their own sakes. Again, this is not intended to be a long-term arrangement.

A critical component of successful exit plans is making sure that there is an understanding of the dependencies within and across services. For instance, security access and control services are typically among the last services to be exited (even if they are operationally ready to transition this activity to the buyer), since controlling access to the environment is critical to facilitating service levels on services such as network routing and server hosting.

In addition to the sequencing of exits, consideration should also be given to the appropriate bundling or phasing of exits to reduce or limit the impact on the organization. As it turns out, many services tend to be dependent on some critical activity before they can be exited. It could be a data center move that triggers the end of several exits at once. Given the impact on the organization to prepare for exits, a phased plan to spread out the exits should be considered and developed. This may mean that some services stay in force a little longer than required, but this may be necessary, as trying to do too much at one time may result in a critical step being dropped. It is also advisable to lay out the sequence of TSA exits on a road map and layer in other business-as-usual activities that will also absorb management and staff attention, such as month-end and quarter-end closes or regulatory filings. In general, TSA exits should be spliced into the road map to help ensure there is enough capacity to meet business needs and exit needs without creating a huge demand spike or introducing risk that things might fall through the cracks.

A typical exit planning process is outlined in Exhibit 14.9.

TSAs should be managed like projects, as parts of the overall separation plan. Both parties should understand and agree to this approach. The exit checklist for each TSA will typically include the following:

- Dependencies on other TSA services or major technology.
- TSA required exit steps (applies to each TSA):
  - All vendors and contracts associated with the TSA to be terminated.
  - People movement has occurred.
  - Provisioning or deprovisioning of key employees.
  - Data cleansing of any buyer/seller shared tools or systems.
  - IT application and infrastructure testing.
  - Knowledge transfer.

Last, there is typically the "chicken or the egg" discussion. Which do you plan for: TSA exits or the underlying projects that enable TSA exit,

Exit Process Step	Key Tasks	Deliverables
Define exit approach	• Assess options to exit service. • Identify dependencies. • Establish preliminary exit timeline. • Document exit approach.	• TSA exit approach • TSA exit tracking
Define exit plans	• Agree to solution design(s) and assumptions. • Develop TSA exit road map, which includes all dependencies and critical steps to terminate the TSA, including regular business functions.	• TSA exit plans • TSA exit road map • Prioritization
Execute exit plans	• Ramp up resources. • Manage dependencies. • Track execution. • Track completion of exit checklist.	• Resource requests • TSA exit tracking • Readiness checklist
Terminate service	• Submit termination notice. • Perform data extracts. • Review and execute data deletion plan. • Track exits against exit road map.	• Termination notices • Data deletion • Exit dashboard

EXHIBIT 14.9   Exit Planning Process Steps

or both? Each organization tends to handle this decision differently. What follow are some considerations that will help define the unit of measure for progress tracking.

Addressing Stranded Costs

When a company divests itself of a sizable business unit, it is frequently left with a disproportionately large cost structure relative to its new size. Many times companies neglect to consider these stranded costs and simply assume that the cost structure will be brought back in line automatically or transitioned with the sale. For each company undergoing a divestiture, a review of stranded costs should be part of the overall program. Stranded costs associated with TSAs should be a part of this larger effort. (See Exhibit 14.10.)

The following are areas of consideration when identifying stranded costs after the exit of a TSA:

- Onshore FTE costs
- Offshore FTE costs
- Fixed costs
- Vendor costs
- IT-specific costs
- Operations-specific costs

Divestiture	Postdivestiture
■ Scope the transaction to determine the costs that will be eliminated from the seller and passed on to the buyer with the divested business. ■ Note that the divestiture offering will continue to change from preannouncement to Day 1 as the transaction terms are negotiated with the buyer.	■ Quantify stranded costs or the costs remaining after the divestiture that should be removed to achieve the target-state vision. ■ Evaluate the overall cost structure and identify cost reduction opportunities due to the decrease in relative size/volume following the divestiture.

EXHIBIT 14.10 Stranded Costs Overview

Identifying and eliminating stranded costs are essential to capturing the value of a transaction. The following articulates the components necessary to identify stranded costs effectively.

The good news for TSAs is that costs are fairly well defined (see pricing section), so as the TSA exits, there should be a fairly good picture of what cost elements need to be removed. For volume-based services, this is relatively simple. The volume should fall to zero. For services that are employee-based, there need to be reallocation conversations. Where will the percentage of employee time that was previously used to support a TSA be absorbed, and what does that extra time do to the overall resourcing picture?

Based on the head start TSAs have in the stranded costs races, it is often an effective place to launch an enterprise-wide initiative to identify and remove stranded costs. The downside of this is that invariably functions will absorb employees' post-TSA free time with other initiatives. Documenting how employees are being redeployed (and in some cases having a business case to justify the redeployment) will help avoid the slow creep in organizational size that is so often seen after a transaction.

It is worth noting that stranded costs planning should begin soon after Day 1 to capitalize on the momentum created by the transaction. If there is too much of a gap before stranded costs discussions begin, the organization tends to see those costs as yet another round of change that is not necessarily associated with a transaction.

TSA Exit and Stranded Costs Best Practices

- **Begin with the end in mind.** Begin planning the TSA exit approach while identifying the service needs.
- **Manage dependencies.** When exiting services, leverage a cross-functional process to double-check for dependencies before you turn a service off. Hitting the light switch in the kitchen should not trigger the garage door.
- **Stagger your exits.** Map and manage the volume and complexity of TSA exits against all other organizational initiatives.
- **Strike while the iron is hot.** Implement disciplined stranded costs identification and reduction programs soon after close.

WRAPPING IT UP

TSAs often become an afterthought in the development of the mergers, acquisitions, and divestitures strategy. Leaving these details to be sorted out in the period of time between the signing of the asset purchase agreement and the close of the transaction often leads to inefficiency and cost in trying to close the deal. It has been our experience that engaging cross-functional TSA teams with deep operational knowledge and experience to identify and document TSA requirements and service terms early in the M&A lifecycle facilitates a more efficient use of resources and a shorter time to independence for the carved-out company.

If you take nothing else from this chapter, keep this in mind: TSAs are necessary, but temporary, arrangements to facilitate a transition. With declining performance levels and burdensome interactions, a simple approach should be considered, which can facilitate your ability to focus on completing the transition.

Many times organizations will draw a parallel between the TSA and an outsourcing contract. True, both require specialized skills and an eye for the future, but the mind-sets are very different. When either party approaches TSAs as a typical vendor relationship, the transition period will likely be difficult. TSA services providers are not traditional providers of services, and treating them as such can create false expectations, overly burdensome demands, and painful distractions.

The most critical success factor is to *begin the task of creating TSAs as early as possible*, keeping them simple, having a clear understanding of the desired objectives, and leveraging the proper functional experts from each area in scope.

CHAPTER 15

Day 1 Implications for IT Functions

Sejal Gala
Sandeep Dasharath

Day 1 is a significant event in the M&A lifecycle, because it represents the official change in ownership, with the buyer organization assuming control of the target organization. The Day 1 scope will vary based on whether the transaction is a partial or whole acquisition and also based on the buyer or seller perspective. However, a constant across most transactions is that information technology (IT) is a major part of Day 1.

Most business or functional changes have underlying implications for IT. As a result, IT should make sure it is engaged early in the planning process across the major functional areas. Furthermore, plans should be aligned to help confirm that changes are not conflicting and there is sufficient IT capacity to execute all required IT work.

As documented in Exhibit 15.1, in our experience, there are six core areas that have critical IT dependencies on Day 1.

TOP DAY 1 PRIORITIES FOR IT

On Day 1, a multitude of things must happen almost simultaneously. The following are some of the key action items and considerations.

Finance Separation

Most transactions require financial separation as a basic legal and regulatory requirement. The level of scrutiny of the financial separation increases if public entities are involved on either side, and will typically require independent verification. Financial processes for major corporations are

EXHIBIT 15.1 Areas with Critical IT Dependencies

Core Area	Typical Functional Requirements	IT Implications
1. Finance Separation	Stand-up of new process as part of buyer or stand-alone. General ledger and balance sheet separation. Cleansing of the remaining company's system and data.	Potential mobilization to stand up new system. Enterprise resource planning (ERP) financial module or core system separation. Relinking supporting systems to new core financial process. Data extracts required for conversion to new process. Interim post-Day 1 access requirements.
2. HR Separation	Stand-up of new process as part of buyer or stand-alone. Cut-over of payroll and benefit systems. Employee transition to new HR processes. Potential severance of employees on Day 1. Rebadging of employees to new company.	Potential mobilization to stand up new system. ERP HR module or core system separation. Relinking supporting systems to new core HR process. Data extracts required for conversion to new process. Change from employee to contractor application access.
3. Rebranding	Notification of transaction and legal ownership change. Broader marketing and sales rollout of rebranding changes.	Basic web and customer-facing changes to text. Broader support of company branding changes.
4. Network Connectivity	Access to the buyer applications. Secure access to seller systems provided through transition services agreement (TSA).	Develop a Day 1 (and often pre-Day 1) secure method to access buyer network. Extensive firewalling effort to provide secure network access to seller network.
5. TSA and Data Segregation	Functional TSAs (for example, finance, operations) have back-end IT TSA requirements. Internal and risk guidelines require segregation of data to restrict access. Execution of segregation requirements before the close date and potential reporting to regulators.	IT should create a full inventory of IT infrastructure and applications that will be required to support other TSA services. IT solutions developed to segregate data and prioritized for feasibility. Extensive implementation of segregation projects.
6. E-Mail and Communication	Access to buyer e-mail system at close. Continued access to legacy e-mail system for historic mail. Transition of historic data from legacy to buyer e-mail system.	Determine/develop a secure method to access buyer e-mail at close. Modifications of access to legacy e-mail to address security requirements. Support of e-mail and data migration program.

usually supported by stand-alone financial systems or a module that is part of a broader ERP platform, and database management services. The IT department should start planning early with finance to prepare for Day 1 requirements, especially if a stand-alone finance system needs to be stood up.

- **Stand-up of new applications and processes as part of buyer or in a stand-alone mode.** A critical determinant of the type of required IT support is based on the overall configuration of the transaction and whether the divesting or spun-off unit is going to be integrated into the buyer's system. While all cases require IT effort, stand-up of a new system or clone of an existing system usually requires the longest lead time. It is critical for IT to thoroughly evaluate the requirements of the new system. If the spun-off unit is much smaller than the parent, a more basic financial system may be required, and simply cloning the parent's financial system would not effectively fit the long-term needs of the new unit. Finance systems have multiple IT dependencies and back-end connections that should be strategically separated without impacting other crucial systems. In the case of migration to the buyer system, IT should be prepared to provide data extracts in a timely fashion and have standby support for ad hoc data requests.
- **General ledger and balance sheet separation.** In most cases, the divested or spun-off unit financials should be separated from the parent financials and integrated into buyer financials or be stand-alone. In the case of public companies, an external auditor will need to assess the separated financials. At a functional level, finance needs to slice and dice the general ledger and balance sheet and derive what the carved-out financials will include, and also redefine the parent financials minus the carved-out component. IT implications of this process mainly relate to databases, creation of new data views, and reconfiguration of databases to support new financial needs.
- **Cleansing of the remaining company's system and data.** The seller should be able to separate financials of the sold entity so that they are no longer reported in the seller's systems. However, there rarely is a clean break on Day 1. On Day 1, the seller frequently needs to allow the divested or spun-off unit to continue accessing its financial data for a few months, to complete ongoing financial entries such as order to cash, manufacturing, and services. While the new unit is accessing the seller's financial systems, it becomes tricky to eliminate the revenues generated by NewCo from the seller's books and consolidation systems. In addition, the seller may need the new unit to continue to provide data to support the next quarter close. These services to be provided by the new unit should be documented in a reverse TSA. The presence of a firewall typically complicates this access; hence post-Day 1

financial system requirements should be carefully assessed. Sometimes, an interim manual process can suffice and not compromise the security of the firewall. The finance department often isn't fully aware of all the access implications of post-Day 1 processing requirements; therefore, it is important for IT to present the options and implications to enable an informed decision to be made.

Separation of Employees/Human Resources

Similar to financial separation, human resources (HR) process separation is another basic legal and regulatory requirement. The majority of employees typically are rebadged from the parent into a buyer or stand-alone organization. The presence of international employees increases the complexity of the separation process. Human resources processes for major corporations are usually supported by stand-alone HR systems or a module that is a part of a broader enterprise resource planning (ERP) platform; however, HR separation is becomes more intricate because of the presence of back-end systems (for example, payroll payment) and also front-end interfaces (for example, time and entry and intranet access to benefits) that are typically interlinked in a complex web of HR applications and data links that need to be carefully separated. Furthermore, IT's engagement in the HR separation process will need tight coordination with a change management and communication plan. On Day 1, users will note even seemingly minor changes in personal details, web interfaces, and customer support. If the process is not planned properly, employees may experience confusion and distress on Day 1.

- **Setup of new applications and related processes.** Similar to finance, a critical determinant of the type of required IT support is based on the overall configuration of the transaction and whether the divesting or spun-off unit is going to be integrated into a buyer. Requirements should be carefully reviewed to make sure the new HR system meets the long-term needs of the new unit. HR systems have multiple IT dependencies and back-end connections that must be strategically separated without impacting other crucial systems. In the case of migration to the buyer system, IT should be prepared to provide data extracts in a timely fashion and have standby support for ad hoc data requests. Due to the confidential nature of employee information, especially personally identifiable information (PII), tight controls should be established in the data transfer process.
- **Cut-over of payroll and benefit systems.** Typically in transactions, a separate payroll and benefit system should be set up as a new stand-alone process or migrated to the buyer's functionality. Stand-up of

a new HR system before close typically requires extensive IT work. Careful attention should be paid to web links to external providers such as payroll firms. Often the issues faced on Day 1 relate less to the core system, but instead to links and dependencies with ancillary systems. Due to the high employee sensitivity surrounding this close requirement, enough planning and governance capacity should be dedicated from functions and IT to enable an issue-free Day 1.

■ **Employee transition to new HR processes.** The transition process relies on a strong change and communication management plan. IT's involvement in the change plan will involve enabling clear, effective, and timely online communications. Sophisticated IT departments that have evolved from being more than a service utility to being a business enabler can support the development of change management plans with a point of view on how electronic and online channels can support the overall change strategy related to the transaction.

Rebranding

The rebranding strategy for each transaction varies based on the level of product, customer, and marketing change required to meet future growth goals. At its simplest, there is limited rebranding. At the more complex end of the spectrum, entities eliminate legacy brands and choose to operate under a new brand. In our experience, it is increasingly typical for the "Customer Day 1," when brand changes have been finalized, to be set at a different and later date than close or Legal Day 1. This approach has helped companies reduce the level of risk associated with customer experience during the close phase.

Notification of Transaction and Legal Ownership Change Even in simple transactions, the core externally facing websites and portals need notifications posted to meet legal notification requirements. The technology has to be ready in most transactions with web-related resources to execute quick hypertext markup language (HTML) changes to web pages and potentially update forwarding on legacy URLs and domain names.

Broader Marketing and Sales Rollout of Rebranding Changes Whether customer Day 1 coincides with legal Day 1 or is set a certain time period after close, IT may be requested to make substantial and broader-ranging name changes across external and internal applications. It is important for IT to inventory early all the potential areas of IT impact due to branding changes. It is not uncommon, when faced with information regarding the extent of impact related to a brand change, for marketing to decide to limit or adjust its expectations on the required level of change. It is important for marketing and IT to work closely together and make an informed decision.

Network Connectivity

Network connectivity needs from the business have two major themes related to Day 1, both with significant IT implications:

1. The need to access the buyer network on Day 1 to connect to applications required to operate in the new entity (for example, HR applications, time and expense, and e-mail).
2. The need is for secure access to the seller network for transition services agreement (TSA) services that could not be separated by Day 1.

In both these cases, based on the long lead times to order equipment and perform testing, the IT organization should start early to identify requirements, develop a solution, gain security approval, and set up the necessary infrastructure. In our experience, the IT organization's activities should start as early as preannouncement to plan potential network implications of potential deals.

Establish Connectivity to Buyer   There are a number of functions that require connectivity to the buyer promptly on Day 1, including human resources, critical business applications, and finance. This connectivity requirement may be complicated by two factors:

1. The functions sometimes need access even before Day 1 in order to perform testing.
2. Cross-company network connectivity is heavily scrutinized by internal information security and risk teams, and this issue is further exacerbated if the companies involved are competitors.

It is important for IT to educate the functions on the implications of pre- and post-Day 1 connectivity needs and collect early potential requirements. Further, IT and information security teams from both buyer and seller entities should work closely to develop a solution that meets their respective companies' security and risk guidelines. In our experience, this process requires negotiation between both parties, and it is often wise to include a program manager or similar business-centric individual who can help both IT departments effectively surface their positions and concerns and work toward a mutually acceptable solution.

Provide Secure Access to TSA Services One of the most significant initiatives the IT department on the seller side will undertake is establishment of a secure, firewalled approach for the divested unit to continue to access the seller network. In addition to the infrastructure challenges associated with this work, there are high interaction requirements with the business to itemize all the applications that may need to be accessed after Day 1, document and implement associated firewall rules (IP address and protocol), and line up testers from these functions to test the access before Day 1. It's not uncommon for multinational companies with extensive access requirements in multiple locations to spend four to six months setting up and testing the firewall infrastructure through a systematic country-by-country approach. Due to the highly business-centric dimension to firewalling efforts, IT departments should consider pairing up their networking experts with functional or business-centric analysts who can drive the collection of functional requirements, support development of test plans, and coordinate extensive weekend testing requirements.

Transition Services Agreement and Data Segregation

Similar to the large-scale firewalling efforts described in the previous focus area, other major pieces of work for seller IT departments are driven by the need for divested units to continue to securely access TSA services after close. Because of the growth of shared services and consolidated back-end (especially IT) functions at major corporations, it is not uncommon to enter into multiyear TSAs in order to provide the divested unit sufficient time to separate from the parent the shared applications and infrastructure. What that means for IT departments is they should structure effective TSA IT schedules (that is, detailed service and pricing lists supporting TSA) and develop IT solutions to support often extensive data segregation needs related to continued provision of services after close.

Functional TSAs Have Back-End IT TSA Requirements Often the provision of other functional TSA services (e.g., finance, operations) has implications for IT in terms of the scope of IT TSAs that need to be provided. Also, it is not atypical for functions to allow associated IT infrastructure and applications to remain with the buyer. In this case, while no functional TSA services may exist, IT TSA services may be required. Furthermore, there is a core set of TSAs, often related to infrastructure services, that need to be provided if the divested unit cannot set up its own infrastructure in time for close. This type of TSA often includes network, data center services, e-mail, active directory, desktop and help desk support, and cross-functional applications.

In most circumstances, IT drives to reduce the level of IT TSA services that need to be provided. This is because operating as an effective outsourcer to another entity carries financial, security, and operational risks that should be mitigated wherever possible. Some approaches to reduce the level of required IT TSA services include:

- Reviewing options to provide functionality through means other than direct access to applications (for example, through provision of data extracts).
- Having the divesting unit start early to set up its stand-alone infrastructure.

Internal and Risk Guidelines Require Segregation of Data to Restrict Access

The provision of the functional TSA services to a divested business unit imposes operational and security risks to the parent organization's systems. However, implementation of standard segregation and security restrictions can help protect the integrity of the restricted data.

In the earlier section, we discussed how divested units are provided secured access to the seller's network and systems through network and firewall restrictions. Though this provides the first layer of security to the seller, there may be stricter risk guidelines for individual functional and business groups that call for segregation at data level to limit risk to the seller's private business data.

Data may be segregated at different levels:

- Application-level data segregation:
  - Logical separation of data by access restrictions.
  - Physical separation of data by setting up a clone of seller system on new seller- or buyer-managed environment.
- User-level data segregation:
  - Divested business units are provided with new restricted accounts that have limited privileges and permissions.
  - User accounts are restricted to access only permitted data within seller's system.
  - Tight regulations and risk review prior to allowing administrative access.
  - Clear IT TSAs are defined to provide restricted access for a stipulated duration.
- Infrastructure-level segregation:
  - Logical separation of network drives and storage.
  - Specific regulations for network data access protocols such as file transfer protocol (FTP) and secure shell (SSH).

• Separation of active directory (AD) forests and organization units (OUs) to segregate user data on exchange and e-mail systems.

Execution of Segregation Requirements before Close and Potential Reporting to Regulators Segregation of data requires IT to plan and make sure access is only to the permitted part of private data. For IT, this means clear identification of sensitive data during the pre-Day 1 planning phases. Segregation methods are then finalized depending on factors such as feasibility of implementation, duration of TSA access, and cost of segregation. Data segregation measures are then implemented and validated on Day 1 to help facilitate restriction of data. During the Day 1 separation process, IT works in conjunction with respective functional and application owners to confirm that segregation measures are successfully implemented.

Before Day 1 close, it is IT's responsibility to establish a clear plan to execute identified segregation requirements in order to guard the integrity and safety of the seller's restricted data. Through the course of TSA duration, security measures are continually checked to monitor any threat to data. Furthermore, data segregation measures implemented by IT are important toward the fulfillment of internal and external audit processes as well. Many financial organizations undergo mandated regulatory and compliance audits on a periodic basis. Data segregation methods implemented by IT assist in meeting the security requirements set by these processes. Also, banking and federal organizations submit finalized data segregation plans to regulators who monitor the plans during separation of entities in order to protect the safety of private business and customer data.

E-Mail and Communication

Similar to financial separation, separation of e-mail and communications systems is very critical to the business objectives of the transaction. On Day 1, separate e-mail accounts are the first signs of separation to the outside world. Moving divested unit employees from the seller to the buyer e-mail system requires answering a complex set of considerations such as TSA requirements, duration between Day 1 and Day 2, size of the organization, nature of target e-mail system, and security guidelines at both seller and buyer organization.

Since e-mail separation is one of the first steps toward rebranding and communication to the outside world, it is very crucial to make this exercise seamless and free of disruptions to the end user. Apart from separation of e-mail, careful planning is required by the seller and the buyer for the migration of other communication media such as fixed-line telephone systems and mobile devices.

E-mail and communication are common areas that contribute to the effectiveness and outcome of a transaction. IT spends significant effort for planning the separation of e-mail, primarily because of the large number of dependencies that e-mail has with infrastructure and application systems.

▪ **Continued access to the legacy e-mail system for historic mail and transition of historic data from the legacy system to the buyer e-mail system.** Through the course of TSA duration, the divested business unit requests access to the seller's legacy e-mail system until the final migration of all mailboxes to the buyer's e-mail environment. IT TSAs defined specifically for e-mail dictate the terms and guidelines for such access to the legacy e-mail system.

Allowing access to the legacy e-mail system poses a security risk to the legacy e-mail and active directory environment. However, IT mitigates these risks by meticulously planning the segregation of network and data as seen in the preceding sections.

Some of the influencing considerations that impact the access to legacy e-mail systems are:

- TSA duration and cost of continuing to access legacy e-mail systems. From a security standpoint, it is in the interest of the seller to cut off access to legacy e-mail systems at the earliest time. Similarly, the buyer has the incentive to cut off access to legacy e-mail systems in order to avoid TSA penalties and to earn credit for early TSA termination.

- Security and regulatory guidelines around how much historic e-mail can be accessed, for how long, and what level of access can be provided. In certain cases, read-only access is provided versus actual transfer of historic data.

- Information management and risk governance enforces security policies that are implemented by IT to protect the integrity of legacy e-mail system data.

▪ **Steps for IT to prepare for Day 1.** Across the six focus areas listed, IT needs a methodology to assess requirements, perform rapid problem solving, planning, and execution as a joint process with the key functional teams:

- Blueprinting and problem solving
- Risk review and periodization
- Integration Day 1 planning
- Day 1 readiness checklist
- Command center and cut-over list

WRAPPING IT UP

Day 1 is a significant event in the M&A lifecycle, because it represents the official change in ownership when the buyer organization assumes control of the target/acquired organization. Many business or functional changes have underlying implications for IT. As a result, IT should make sure it is engaged early in the planning process across the major functional areas. Furthermore, plans should be aligned to make sure changes are not conflicting and there is sufficient IT capacity to execute all required IT work.

Based on the breadth and depth of IT involvement, IT should proactively drive engagement across functions. Also, it is critical for IT to manage the risks associated with close activities, and make sure it facilitates an issue-free Day 1.

CHAPTER 16

Transition Services Agreement (TSA)—Untangling the Web

Simon Singh
Nikhil Uppal
Jennie Miller

Divestitures are usually tricky to pull off, particularly when the affected people, processes, and systems are deeply integrated within the seller's business, or when services and infrastructure are shared across multiple business units. Identifying and carving out the pieces in a divestiture can be a complex and time-consuming process; however, with experience and careful planning, an effective outcome for both parties can be achieved. During the planning process, participants from the affected business units on both sides must think through the transition period from close of transaction (Day 1) to complete separation of the businesses (Day 2) to determine the strategy for each business process, associated applications, and underlying infrastructure.

Adding to the integration challenge is the time constraint that is associated with most mergers and acquisitions (M&A) deals. Statistically, small carve-outs can close as quickly as 30 days after announcement, and even larger deals (in excess of $1 billion) average only 115 days to close.[1] In many cases, this does not give the buyer enough time to respond, particularly when there are antitrust concerns or confidential information that cannot be shared until after the deal closes.

These complex challenges can be effectively addressed by using a transition services agreement (TSA) in which the seller agrees to provide specific services on behalf of the buyer to maintain business continuity while the buyer prepares to receive and operate the new business. A TSA can accelerate the negotiation process and financial close by allowing the deal to move forward without waiting for the buyer to assume responsibility for all critical support services. (See Exhibit 16.1.)

TSAs come in many shapes and sizes but commonly fall into two types: forward and reverse. The forward TSA, the most frequently type applied

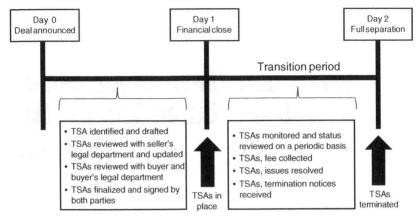

EXHIBIT 16.1   Transition Services Agreement (TSA)

Copyright © 2012 Deloitte Development LLC

in a carve-out, is used when the seller has agreed to provide services on the buyer's behalf for a defined period of time. The reverse TSA is used when the buyer provides specific services on behalf of the seller for a defined period of time. In most cases the reverse TSA is used for services that are being handed over to the buyer at deal close, but those services are tied to a critical aspect of the seller's remaining business and cannot be operational without the transitioned service until an alternative support service is put in place.

Additional complexity is introduced in the carve-out when there is a combination of forward and reverse TSAs between the buyer and seller. This can create a complex relationship between buyer and seller that requires appropriate management in the form of a parallel governance structure on both the buyer's and the seller's sides of the deal, covering key service delivery processes such as service performance levels and billing.

Within the TSA exists another level of classification: business TSAs and information technology (IT) TSAs. Business TSAs provide business function–specific services such as customer care to clients or building security services. Information technology (IT) TSAs provide, as the name suggests, IT services such as hosting and maintenance of the data center or applications used by specific functions of the business.

Understanding the interdependencies between the envisioned business TSA and the underlying architecture that supports it is critical to proper delivery and billing of the business TSA. A large portion of the underlying architecture supporting a business TSA consists of IT services. Therefore, in order to have an effective business TSA, it is imperative to understand the IT services that support the business TSA and map those IT TSAs to the business TSA. This mapping will ultimately facilitate proper exit planning and help ensure a smooth transition as services are exited. It also protects the business against terminating any services that are not ready to be exited that could negatively impact business operations and customers.

Based on our experience, the majority of TSAs are forward in nature, with a small percentage in the reverse direction. Likewise, IT TSAs are much more common than business TSAs and will likely command over half of the total number of TSAs in place.

Transition services agreements are most often used in carve-outs where the buyer lacks the necessary IT capabilities or capacity to support the business on its own. For instance, many private equity (PE) firms rely on TSAs until they can identify and engage an IT outsourcing vendor to take over key IT operations and other service delivery components.

KEY CONSIDERATIONS FOR DRAFTING AN EFFECTIVE TSA

Drafting an effective TSA is a complex, time-consuming task and should not be underestimated. TSAs are unique in that they require input from key stakeholders across the enterprise to capture very specific operational and systematic details that take time to implement, especially if third-party vendors are involved from a support standpoint. Exhibit 16.2 illustrates the time- and cost-saving benefits realized when investing in a well-structured TSA.

Although well-drafted TSAs require substantial time, they can provide some real benefits, such as reduction in the transaction costs for both the buyer and the seller. Some practical and time-tested tips to help both buyers and sellers avoid the common pitfalls when drafting a TSA include the following:

- **Partner with the business.** IT is a business enabler. Every business TSA should be evaluated and paired with the corresponding IT TSA. Stand-alone TSAs should be avoided unless there are no reasonable alternatives. For example, individual TSAs may be required for distinct and separate services and for different geographic regions that are providing or receiving services.
- **Understand your costs.** This is one of the most important elements of a TSA. To avoid disagreements down the road, both parties must go into the agreement with a crystal-clear understanding of costs and

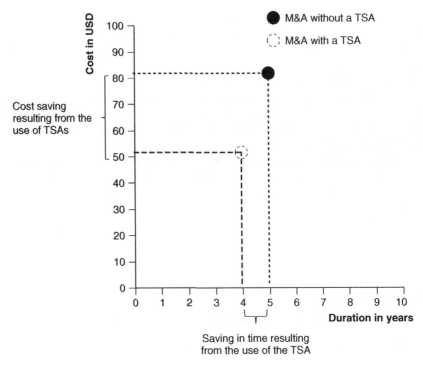

EXHIBIT 16.2 Time- and Cost-Saving Benefits of a Well-Structured TSA
Copyright © 2012 Deloitte Development LLC

cost drivers. Clearly define the cost components and assumptions that will be used to calculate costs. Identify both fixed and variable cost elements, as well as the factors that will drive cost, such as head count, office space, location, server utilization, and network bandwidth.

Understanding the cost drivers will help both buyer and seller develop a fair plan to migrate off the TSA. For example, activities that are likely to ramp down over time, such as desktop support migration, might include step-down events where costs decrease as the buyer becomes less dependent on the seller's services. In contrast, activities that are more likely to remain consistent across the business over time, such as mainframe hosting, should be defined as a fixed cost until the last remaining user or resource is removed from that service.

Note that identifying the costs and cost drivers for transition services can be challenging, particularly since most sellers are not in the business of selling services and may lack the systems, tools, experience, knowledge, and skills to accurately analyze service costs.

In such situations, sellers should attempt to identify some benchmarks that can serve as a gauge for identifying standard costs for their particular industry and size. These benchmarks can be obtained by performing a survey of outsourcing services and the current market rate for these services.

■ **Define the charge-back rules.** The TSA must clearly define what services the seller can charge for and how the charges will be made, unless these issues were already covered in the purchase agreement. Defining clear charge-back rules in the TSA allows the tactical teams to focus on delivering services without unnecessary debate. Prior to Day 1, both buyer and seller should agree on the scope of services to be covered under a TSA. For example, near the end of the TSA the buyer may be expecting the seller to provide migration services, such as extracting data, cloning systems, and sharing knowledge and best practices with the new service provider and/or buyer. Defining the charge-back rules for such activities before the deal closes can help both buyer and seller determine an effective migration plan, and leaves the buyer with some bargaining power with the seller.

■ **Connect the dots.** A master services agreement (MSA) can provide an overall structure for all of the TSAs, explain the hierarchies of various documents, and contain lists of the services to be provided. It can also define the billing terms and conditions and describe the overarching principles for terminating the TSA. Last but not least, an MSA can help avoid contradictory language by providing a central location for legal terms and conditions so they can be defined and referenced in supporting agreements and exhibits.

■ **Put it in writing.** Once the services that will require TSAs have been determined, it is time to "put pen to paper." Agreements for every function should follow a standard format and template that has been approved by the legal department. Keep in mind that this is the most time-consuming aspect of finalizing TSAs, as both buyer and seller contribute to the editing of the content and both legal departments must approve the verbiage. Designate the manager or executive responsible for delivering the transition services as one of the primary authors of the TSA. This approach helps produce a better, more realistic agreement and helps avoid confusion and finger-pointing at a later point. Also, it is important to get input from subject matter specialists in each area where services will be provided (for example, telecom, networks, and help desk) as early as possible.

■ **Writing should be consistent, clear, and concise.** Try to be specific and exact, rather than open-ended and general. Detailed service descriptions enable more accurate cost estimates and can provide a clearer understanding of what is or is not covered by the agreement. Breaking the high-level hosting service into more discrete services, such as platform (for example, Wintel and mainframe), job scheduling, backup, and server monitoring, could allow a step-down in TSAs, thereby reducing costs and accelerating the transition. The specifics of the step-down arrangements should be detailed in the TSA, as in some cases there are no cost advantages to terminating certain services early if the agreement is structured as an all-or-nothing arrangement.

Splitting larger services into discrete elements requires an understanding of performance dependencies across different services. Generally speaking, the buyer and seller need to agree about when certain performance levels can switch to a "best effort" basis as a result of changes in other services. For example, if the buyer has taken over responsibility for application monitoring, the seller will not be able to guarantee application uptime.

STRUCTURING THE TSA

When structured the right way, a TSA can save time and help ensure that the separation is smooth. Failure to carefully structure the TSA can inhibit or delay the divesture and increase the overall separation cost. Therefore, it is imperative that a structured approach be taken. The four phases to structuring the TSA are:

1. Solution design
2. Requirement gathering
3. Service definition
4. Service documentation

Setting foundational guiding principles up front can allow for easier identification, more amicable negotiation, and quicker enablement of TSAs. TSAs should be viewed as the option of last resort and not as a way for the buyer to avoid the responsibility of addressing existing holes in the business. An important distinction established in the beginning should be: "What you get today is what you will get tomorrow, no more but perhaps a little less." From an M&A perspective, the buyer will oftentimes seek a position for increased service levels, enhanced scope, or service optimization. In situations like this the seller should hold firm that TSAs will be delivered as they have been pre-Day 1. The first (not so obvious) corollary is if a service is not functioning or operating as required or is partially broken pre-Day 1, it will remain as such post-Day 1. Second, TSAs for services that are not delivered pre-Day 1 should not be developed. This situation is not always possible and will vary depending on the realities on the ground; however, post-Day 1 TSAs should be avoided. The seller is not set up to act as a service delivery organization and as such has limited ability to deliver services to an external third party that it is not used to delivering prior to the transaction.

MANAGING TSAS

If structured correctly, managing TSAs should quickly become a business-as-usual process. Setting the correct tone at the commencement of the TSA period is critical to a successful TSA delivery.

- **Get to work.** Signing the TSAs is just the end of the beginning. The real work starts when the deal closes and the TSAs go into effect. As the services are being delivered, it is important to continually track and manage the services that are being performed. It is also critical to keep track of the migration activities and related step-down in services. The relationship between buyer and seller will inevitably change once the deal has closed, regardless of how well they might have worked together leading up to Day 1. Sellers will focus on cleaning up the bits and pieces that the divestiture left behind, and then quickly shift their attention to their retained businesses and other priorities. Buyers may find themselves wrestling with unanticipated service costs and struggling to capture the intended, proposed, contracted, and expected integration synergies as quickly as possible.
- **Identify relationship managers.** To keep things moving forward, each company should identify and assign a service coordinator to manage its part of the overall relationship. These people are similar to the vendor managers who currently exist in many organizations. They do not need to delve deeply into the details of day-to-day operations; rather, they need a holistic view of the services being provided and an understanding of the overall requirements. Their job is to monitor the services being delivered against the TSA and keep the separation activities on track.
- **Resource management.** Retention of key transition resources is another important issue. Sellers will generally want to get on with their business by shifting people to new assignments as quickly as possible. To maintain acceptable staffing and performance during the transition, buyers must specify in the TSA exactly which key resources and groups will be retained to execute the required services.
- **Be realistic about performance levels.** Avoid the common trap of demanding (or promising) better service than existed prior to the

transition. In most cases the historical service levels were sufficient to support the business and struck a reasonable balance between service cost and true business needs. Buyer and seller should focus their attention on completing the transition as quickly as possible, rather than get distracted trying to maintain high-than-necessary service levels. That said, it is important to precisely define in the TSA what service levels are expected. Simply stating that "existing service levels will be maintained" is generally not sufficient. Often, the seller has not been measuring performance for the services in question. In these cases, it is critical for both parties to agree on the performance metrics and, once agreed, to document them in the TSA.

Execution of a TSA revolves around service volume. Typically, broad language stating the service is to be delivered in the same manner as before the spin-off is used to cover this point. However, our experience in helping clients with post-Day 1 TSA management shows that this broad and generic language often results in misaligned expectations on what can be considered in scope from a volume perspective. It is for this reason that we recommend clients document both the volume metric and level by individual service where possible to surface any potential misalignment pre-Day 1.

Furthermore, after the carve-out has been dissolved, the buyer receiving services may decide to acquire another entity. If this happens, what are the seller's obligations? A new acquisition may result in wholesale changes to service scope and volume. It is again for this reason that we suggest tying each service to a volume metric and volume level such that the service provider (seller) is not unduly burdened by the buyer's repeated M&A.

Finally, complex TSAs such as services shared by IT, finance, or human resources rely on a bevy of third parties to assist in the delivery of the service in question. It should be stipulated that third-party relationships required by the buyer to receive a service should be the responsibility of the buyer. In turn, the liability associated with nonperformance of third-party services is not borne by the seller. This division of liability is not always feasible, but should be considered as a going-in position to any negotiation.

- **Establish an exit protocol.** A formal exit protocol is the final step in the effective use of a TSA. Both parties should understand and agree on the process required to terminate the service provider relationship (for example, requiring the buyer to provide a 30-day notice to terminate e-mail services). In turn, the seller should acknowledge the termination, clarify any termination fees, and bill appropriately. Additionally, the seller should complete any knowledge transfer that was agreed to in the initial planning, close out the accounting, and take care of any cleanup activities, such as deleting, archiving, or inactivating the resources receiving the service. Regardless of whether one is seeking support or negotiating to limit its scope, there are some key points to consider that have a direct impact on the structure of the TSA and the effectiveness of its execution after the carve-out has been finalized and the split has occurred.

GOVERNANCE OF TSA SERVICES THROUGH A PARALLEL STRUCTURE

In order to manage the TSA services most effectively for the duration, it is imperative that a governance structure be designed to address the needs of the multiyear service relationship between buyer and seller, with complex day-to-day management requirements and significant project work to exit the TSA services. From the relationship perspective, there will most certainly be multiple TSA services (both forward and reverse) that will span across several business functions, meaning that there will need to be a balance of management of the people, processes, and technology across the two parties. Inherent in the management of people, processes, and technology are the complex day-to-day requirements, including the ongoing relationship to govern delivery of services, daily monitoring of customer-sensitive services, constant change control for service changes and exits, and monthly billing and service-level agreement (SLA) reporting and validation. A governance structure to establish and operationalize these process-monitoring requirements is vital to the health and success of the deal. Last, and most important to both the buyer and the seller, is the project work to achieve exit from TSA services. There is significant work associated with this, including TSA exit solution design to terminate the services, scope and statement of work (SOW) creation to engage buyer/seller support, project governance and tracking to exit the TSA, and the data disposition once a service has been exited. As a legal document, each TSA details a specific service to be provided at a specific cost, for a specific duration; it requires careful management just like any other service a business would provide to a customer. Note: In many cases, a governing body for the life of the TSA is written in the MSA.

Similar to the challenges associated with structuring the TSA, establishing the governance structure takes time due to the coordination effort needed to staff and train resources. To be optimally effective, the governance structure should be in place prior to Day 1 with a focus on driving post-Day 1 governance and exit from the transition services. It is advantageous for preparation to take place while the TSAs are being finalized in order for

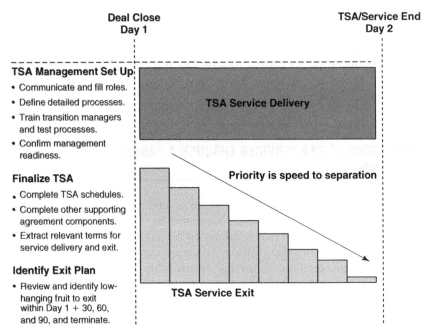

EXHIBIT 16.3   Governance Structure Aids in Speed to Separation
Copyright © 2012 Deloitte Development LLC

all governance processes and process leads to be operational on Day 1. (See Exhibit 16.3.)

The benefits of designing a transition services governance structure include:

- Helping ensure the quality delivery of transition services and adherence to terms of the transition services agreement (TSA).
- Driving speed to separation from TSA dependencies as a priority for both buyer and seller.
- Minimizing disruptions to operations as transition services are ramped down.

The most important element of the governance structure is that it is truly a parallel approach to governance. It is important to ensure equivalent roles on both the buyer and seller sides as well as having resources assigned to those roles that are involved from start to finish of the structure's rollout. The benefit of a parallel structure is that it helps to drive consistent decision making and information flow between the buyer and seller. (See Exhibit 16.4.)

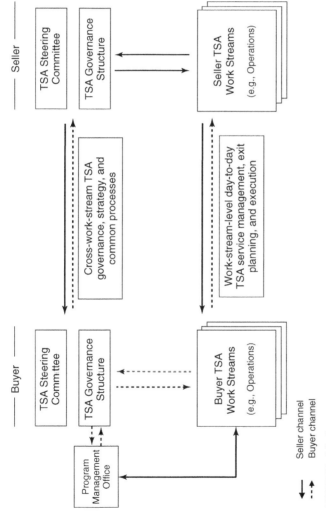

EXHIBIT 16.4 Governance Structure Interaction Model
Copyright © 2012 Deloitte Development LLC

When standing up a governance structure, it is important that ground rules be set, including clearly defined objectives and guiding principles that are agreed to between the buyer and seller specifically:

- Focus is the TSA. Integration and business as usual are managed outside the governance structure.
- Assign primary responsibility for management of day-to-day TSA service delivery to the teams.
- Provide thin, but strong, central governance (i.e., keep the TSA team lean, but with the power to make decisions quickly).

These objectives and guiding principles will help to drive accountability across the TSA program and help ensure there is a solid framework with defined roles, specific management, and decision-making authority.

This parallel structure also applies to the business processes that will help to operate the buyer/seller relationship for the duration of service delivery and exit. In previous carve-outs where there were multiple forward and reverse TSAs in play, the most successful clients had 10 discrete processes in place to carry out TSA service delivery and service exit. Each process should have a dedicated process lead and delegate to manage the tasks and requirements on both the buyer and seller sides of the deal. It is also important to maintain this parallel structure across the processes so that there is a balance of powers and representation for the business when issues in service delivery arise.

- **Relationship management.** Govern TSA service relationship through central points of accountability that manage, review, and communicate major decisions and issues:
  - Manage relationship across service delivery teams.
  - Set overall strategy and priorities.
  - Manage weekly governance.
  - Address work stream TSA issue escalations and implement mitigation plan.
- **Performance management.** Oversee service delivery to make sure the quality services are delivered to agreed levels, including helping ensure service SLA tracking, service issue resolution, and service changes:
  - Develop consolidated monthly TSA SLA report.
  - Provide service requests to change, add, or remove TSA SLAs.
  - Understand any issues with TSA service-specific performance and support remediation.
  - Monitor progress of service improvement plans.

- **Exit planning and execution.** Drive systematic ramp-down of dependency on transition services through development of TSA exit plans that outline service provider and recipient responsibilities:
  - Establish TSA exit priorities across service delivery teams.
  - Make sure consistent processes are in place to define exit plans.
  - Track exit plan lock dates through weekly governance process meetings, and raise any concerns.
  - Track TSA exit milestones through weekly governance process meetings, and raise any concerns.
  - Validate and track all termination requests.
  - Submit service termination requests to other party.
  - Coordinate with invoicing to remove billing.
  - Negotiate service terminations.
- **Change management.** Provide advisory support regarding TSA terms and conditions, and address ambiguities and control changes to TSA terms through systematic process:
  - Execute TSA changes through change process.
  - Interface with corporate development and legal as necessary.
  - Approve or reject TSA changes.
  - Statement of work (SOW) management—engage TSA service provider to support TSA exit migration efforts through formal process of presenting scope and developing and signing off on the SOW:
    - Establish consistent process for SOW request.
    - Make sure there are consistent terms and conditions in SOWs.
    - Address cross-work-stream SOW issues.
- **Invoice management.** Control monthly service billing and associated validation and execution of funds transfer:
  - Perform centralized monthly invoicing.
  - Validate or create forward and reverse TSA invoices.
  - Remove terminated service billings.
- **Financial management.** Oversee TSA services budget and manage positive or negative impacts to business during service delivery and as services are exited:
  - Maintain overall TSA-related budget.
  - Work with the exit planning and execution process to oversee services' exit strategy and approach.
- **Risk/compliance management.** Monitor service provider compliance to internal supplier management and external compliance requirements:
  - Define overall compliance requirements.
  - Monitor cross-work-stream compliance requirements and/or collect work stream reports.

- Monitor closure of compliance gaps.
- Provide coordination support for audits.
- **Contract transfers.** Manage compliance to contractual requirements and perform necessary contract transfers and negotiations in support of TSA exits:
  - Maintain list of contract dependencies.
  - Maintain contractual compliance.
  - Execute transfers and negotiations.
  - Support license transfers.

RATIONALE FOR ACCELERATED EXIT OF A TSA

Thus far in this chapter we have talked about how TSAs can help reduce stranded costs for the seller and acquisition/integration costs for the buyer. TSAs also provide additional benefits with respect to the objectives of the carve-out, including:

- Faster and smoother close
- Better end-state solutions
- Clean separation

Remember, it is important for both the buyer and seller to understand that TSAs are truly meant to be interim solutions and it is in the interest of both parties to exit from them as soon as is reasonably possible. From the seller's standpoint, a TSA can be a nuisance and a hindrance for the following reasons:

- The main reason a seller is divesting the business is to focus on another part of the seller's operations, so when the seller has to continue to deliver services after the deal closes, the seller feels as though it is still managing that divested business unit rather than being rid of it altogether.
- In many cases, the seller's core business does not to provide services to another business; thus delivery of services may be a foreign or new concept that adds undue pressure and expectations on the seller's organization.

From the buyer's standpoint, achieving a swift exit from TSA services is important for the following reasons:

- In most cases, the cost of services provided to the buyer by the seller via a TSA is substantially higher than what the buyer would have to pay if the services were run in-house or sourced from an external vendor. The substantially higher costs often lead to the buyer missing out on the potential synergies that could have been achieved had unnecessary TSAs been forgone.

- The buyer, by default, inherits any and all existing inefficiencies or flaws that were part of the seller's processes or systems, thereby reducing the potential operational synergies that could have been achieved if the buyer ran these services in-house or sourced them from an external vendor.
- The buyer needs to remember that the service delivery and exit relationship between the buyer and seller is not the typical merchant/customer relationship due to the seller's tendency to deprioritize delivery of these services, thereby impacting the overall quality of the services.

The aforementioned considerations provide ample reasoning for the buyer and seller to avoid putting unnecessary TSAs in place or extending a TSA beyond what is reasonably required to reduce the impact on the business and customers of the carved-out unit.

KEY CONSIDERATIONS FOR TSA EXIT

A TSA is a double-edged sword, because of the multitude of different incentives driving the buyer and the seller. The sellers want to keep the number of TSAs as low as possible and the duration of services as short as possible. Many are divesting the business so they can fund or focus on another part of their remaining business. As a result, from their perspective TSAs can become a nuisance and a distraction from achieving this objective. Therefore, it is advantageous to keep the number of TSAs as low as possible. Sellers may insist on a set of provisions designed to limit their liability in the event of situations in which the seller is grossly negligent in its delivery of the service or is accused of willful misconduct. The buyers, in contrast, tend to use TSAs as a way to address missed Day 1 requirements or to defer difficult integration decisions.

Based on the aforementioned dilemma, it is imperative for the TSA exit to be well planned. The following are the key considerations to contemplate when planning to exit and then actually exiting the service on Day 2.

TSA exit considerations from the seller's point of view include:

- **Reduction of stranded costs.** With the division or the business unit sold, various IT assets such as licenses and applications may not be required by the parent. The most effective way for the seller to recover these costs is to transfer such assets to the buyer and ask the buyer to pay the seller for them. The seller can convince the buyer to take these assets as a part of the divested unit because this would help ensure the least disruption to the business.

- **Data migration considerations.** In most cases the unit being carved out and sold is to a competitor, and hence the seller would want to minimize the data migration, making sure that the proprietary data is not shared with the buyer. This also helps ensure that the burden of the data transformation (extract, transform, and load [ETL]) is not on the seller.
- **Training and consulting considerations.** The seller will as soon as possible deploy the resized (after the divesture) employee base to other business units within the seller firm. This helps the seller realize cost-saving and operational efficiencies. With this intent, the seller wants to make sure the number of trainings and/or the consulting hours are capped. Most sellers charge a significant premium to incentivize the buyer to own the exit activities.

TSA exit considerations from the buyer's point of view include:

- **Maintain as much of the existing IT infrastructure as possible.** The buyer generally pushes the seller to provide as part of the carve-out as much of the existing IT infrastructure as possible. Private equity firms, in particular, look at getting as much support as possible because this reduces the effort and cost associated with setting up the independent unit. In some cases (generally seen in cases of a strategic buy), the buyer might negotiate with the seller that the existing IT infrastructure is not needed and the seller will keep the IT infrastructure and reduce the overall cost of the deal. This situation can arise because the buyer already has the IT required to establish the business and wants to use the time between Day 1 and Day 2 to help migrate all IT applications and data to the new environment.
- **Training on existing processes and applications.** The buyer is keen on getting trained by the seller's staff on the key processes and applications of the newly integrated business unit. The challenge to this request is that the seller wants to deploy the held-back remaining employees elsewhere within the organization, and under such a bandwidth constraint the seller finds it difficult to provide training to the buyer.
- **Data migration and disposition.** The buyer would like to make sure that before the TSA is exited, the functions have all (and most likely more than) the data that is required to run the business. The buyer

would also generally like the seller to get rid of the data completely that as shared with the buyer. In this situation two complexities arise: (1) the fact that the seller, in most instances, would have sold the business out to a competitor and hence is apprehensive about providing data, and (2) existing laws and regulations might mandate that the seller preserve a portion of the data even after the divesture.

WRAPPING IT UP

The complex challenges associated with a divesture can be effectively addressed by employing a TSA. A TSA provides the buyer with a window in which to stand up needed services and operations to accept the newly carved-out business unit into its overall portfolio with a minimal impact to normal business operations.

In order for TSAs to be effective, it is imperative they are well structured and clearly identify the scope of each service in documentation. This helps ensure that the buyer and seller know what they are signing themselves up for, and can help them to maintain an amicable relationship between the buyer and the seller.

Though the TSA is an effective way to provide the buyer setup time, it is highly important for both the seller and the buyer to recognize that TSAs are meant to be a temporary situation and that a well-crafted exit strategy for each of the TSAs is required. Failure in planning for the TSA exits can prolong the divesture and ultimately increase the overall cost of the deal for both the buyer and the seller.

Note

1. "A Way to Design and Manage TSAs to Achieve a Fast and Clean Separation," Deloitte Consulting LLP, 2008.

CHAPTER 17

IT Risk, Security, and Controls in M&A

Identifying and Managing Common Considerations

David Caruso
Kelly Moynihan
John Clark
Jamie Fox
Joseph Joy
Scott Kaufman

UNDERSTANDING THE IT RISK, SECURITY, AND CONTROLS CURRENT STATE

Mergers and acquisitions (M&A) and related transactions present a vast array of tangible and intangible benefits to the stakeholders of the entities involved. Yet, these benefits can be greatly diminished through the misunderstanding and mismanagement of common IT risk, security, and control considerations. While no two M&A transactions are the same and no blueprint can be used to minimize security and IT issues totally, there are consistent actions that can help reduce the risks to organizations while also helping to improve operating effectiveness.

The first step in combating and managing common M&A IT risk considerations is to obtain a thorough understanding of the parent and target organizations' IT environments. Information such as asset inventories, employee rosters, and infrastructure diagrams can provide a snapshot of the environment for which controls must be applied. However, there will be limited insight initially into how the companies operate. Regardless of the M&A transaction size, budget, or potential cost savings, one of the key responsibilities of a chief information officer (CIO), chief information security officer (CISO), chief privacy officer (CPO), chief compliance officer (CCO), chief risk officer (CRO), and office of general counsel (OGC) (collectively, the leadership) should be to gain an understanding of the current state of IT operations and determine how current-state IT risks could potentially impact M&A objectives and goals.

Understanding the M&A Activity

While it is likely a CIO, CISO, or other leader will generally understand the type or types of potential risks of an M&A transaction, IT security and control risks and issues can present themselves differently depending on the nature of the M&A activity. Additionally, the size of the transaction does not have a direct correlation to the impact of IT risk and security issues. Smaller projects involving nonpublic companies can even introduce greater risk into the environment, as IT compliance requirements may not be as strictly adhered to or as well reported.

Equipped with a basic understanding of the M&A project type and the organization's current IT environment, the CIO and CISO are better prepared to assess for additional risks that may be presented by the M&A project. The following is an overview of various M&A initiatives and examples of common IT risk, security, and control issues associated with each area:

- **Synergies.** In an effort to quickly reduce costs and increase functionality, due diligence of IT risk can be overlooked after the initial planning stages. Consequently, lax documentation and adherence to procedures persists, security configuration and network architecture change management activities diminish, and access requirements become an afterthought. All of these activities can introduce new and often substantial risks via both IT and human error.[1]
- **Integrations.** Due to the introduction of new technology platforms, such as disparate critical business applications or technology infrastructure and data centers, the IT environment becomes exposed to both internal and external threats. Malicious outsiders can become aware of M&A activity through industry communications and begin targeted attacks. The already constrained employee resources can begin to rubber-stamp user access, exception, and change requests in order to meet other pressing deadlines. In a short timeframe, the organizations

must determine how to transition systems and how to protect the sensitive information stored within, while performing business-as-usual duties and preparing business continuity plans.

■ **Divestitures.** Due to the changing nature of the operating environment, and occasionally the entire business model, compliance and audit requirements are in a state of flux during divestitures. Employees are transitioning physically and electronically, leading to a noticeable impact on morale. Additionally, systems and applications may be shared in the interim stages, with segregation-of-duty requirements overlooked to complete the project's goals.

Understanding the Current IT Risk and Control Environment

The ability to achieve the M&A project goals of financial savings and increased competitive advantage frequently resides within the less glamorous data centers and development areas of information technology. While CIOs and CISOs argue for the importance of IT focus during M&A activities, the risks and associated controls that drive these initiatives are often overlooked (or forgotten).

A broad IT risk management program directs organizations to the appropriate areas for managing threats and security issues. The program assists in the reviews of IT systems, applications, and operations for a range of IT-focused areas. The most common IT risk management areas are:

■ Architecture
■ Asset management
■ Business continuity management
■ Change management
■ Contracting and outsourcing
■ Information security
■ IT financial control
■ IT human resources (HR)
■ Operations records management
■ Physical and environmental problem management
■ Privacy and data protection
■ Project management
■ Technology licensing

A broad and effective IT risk management program is typically comprised of three areas: IT risk governance, assessment, and response.

Risk governance involves the creation of an IT risk management framework to be applied across all companies involved in the M&A transaction.

The framework includes prioritization of IT-related risks and controls that an organization may utilize for self-assessments, based on the noted likelihood and impact of these risks. These risks and controls should additionally be aligned to the common IT risk management areas noted earlier to help ensure that assessments encompass the entire IT environment, and should be based on common industry standards, such as the following: COBIT 5.0, International Organization for Standardization (ISO) 27002, Generally Accepted Privacy Principles (GAPP), and other regulatory, legal, and business-specific requirements.

In order to properly assess the current state of the organizations involved in the M&A project, it is necessary to understand how these risks and controls are designed and are operating through **risk assessments**. As such, IT risk and control evaluations should be performed by the appropriately identified parties across the organizations. These assessments will allow technology management to better understand areas where controls are operating well, and thus issues are minimized, and areas requiring more oversight throughout the M&A transaction (i.e., IT risk areas where a number of issues are noted).

Another component of the IT risks and controls assessment is to identify the risk profile of the known risks. Risk scores are determined through assessing the severity and frequency of a risk that has not been mitigated by any controls. Due to the abbreviated timeframes of most M&A activities, performance of risk assessments and remediation of identified issues must also be prioritized to focus on the highest-risk controls. Comprehensive evaluations focusing on all controls and all areas of the organization will be more feasible following completion of the transaction.

Examples of issues noted during self-assessments that can have a substantial impact on M&A transactions include:[2]

- Noncompliance with new regulatory, legal, and statutory regulations and requirements.
- Prolonged security incidents and business interruption due to lack of integration of incident response and business continuity plans.
- Increased technical vulnerabilities around the transition and storage of sensitive information.
- Lack of appropriate control coverage for technology changes.
- Decreased access and change management control reliance due to expedited requirements.

Following the completion of the assessments, the **risk response or remediation** phase is initiated. Risk response involves the creation of action plans to remediate identified issues and the tracking of these items to completion. If self-assessments occur at the onset of the M&A activities, which is the most beneficial approach, the risk response phase allows projects to be managed with identified gaps and remediation efforts incorporated into planning activities. If the risk assessments occur during the M&A activities, or near completion, increased efforts and resources will be required to work toward compliance and operating effectiveness during already constrained periods.

Importance of IT Risk and Control Assessments

Timeframes are tight, resources are stretched thin, and patience is likely low. The last activity many organizations want to adopt before or during frantic M&A initiatives is a documented IT risk and controls self-assessment. Yet, the advantages of these reviews do greatly outweigh the disadvantages.

When IT risks are not fully addressed, especially those with high risk scores, the expected value creation of an M&A transaction can be drastically undermined. Generally IT risk considerations impact M&A transaction value in the following ways:

- Increased IT cost
- Decreased technology value
- Impacted regulatory and governance oversight[3]

Through performing assessments, planning for necessary regulations can occur and financial benefits can be realized. Additionally, early assessments can potentially help alleviate resource burdens that present themselves at the end of M&A transactions in a last-ditch effort to close gaps that were identified too late.

Overall, understanding the IT risks and controls environment will save the M&A transaction time, money, and resource fatigue and will prepare for legal, regulatory, and industry requirements following Legal Day 1. The up-front time and effort will be rewarded.

Understanding the Regulatory Environment

As mentioned, the establishment of standardized IT risks and controls should be based on common industry practices and frameworks. Additionally, these libraries should include controls relating to the specific regulatory environment of the business so that these requirements can be appropriately assessed. Understanding these regulations will allow for planning and reporting during and after M&A activities and can potentially help minimize external findings or fines.

IT Sarbanes-Oxley (SOX) Requirements Though sometimes a contentious aspect of the law, publicly traded companies have had to contend with Section 404 of the Sarbanes-Oxley Act (SOX 404) since 2002. Under SOX 404, management and external auditors must assess and report on a company's internal control over financial reporting (ICFR), or more simply, the controls for financial processes, enterprise resource planning (ERP) systems, and applications. While the technology controls aspects of SOX 404 may not be as stringent as some industry-specific regulations, it remains one of the most pervasive regulations affecting M&A transactions.

As Section 404 of SOX is over a decade old, the requirements and costs are generally well known to public companies. However, for M&A transactions, SOX 404 requirements introduce changes to an organization's environment that must be considered. For integrations and synergies, there may be a host of new applications, systems, and infrastructures to evaluate and assess internal control over financial reporting. Additionally, these systems could be integrated from a private company, where no prior regulatory reporting requirements existed. How can these systems be incorporated and reviewed for SOX regulations within the abbreviated M&A transaction timeframe, while also preparing for annual reporting?

Similar management challenges arise during divestitures. Systems that once met SOX requirements are now being separated and sometimes shared between companies at Legal Day 1. Reporting deadlines may be adjusted, Statement on Standards for Attestation Engagements (SSAE) No. 16 or Service Organization Controls (SOC) No. 1[4] reviews may be required, and the inventory of systems may have changed. To follow in a few pages, see case study 1, which highlights the SOX 404 issues and reporting requirements experienced during a divestiture.

Since the company's management and its external auditor are required to report on the adequacy of the company's internal control on financial reporting, is there anything that can be done to expedite changes and reduce costs during M&A transactions? Yes. Simply put, a top-down, risk-based approach is required—an approach that has been recommended by both the Public Company Accounting Oversight Board (PCAOB) and the U.S. Securities and Exchange Commission (SEC)!

A top-down approach speaks to management's involvement and direction in regard to ICFR from the inception of the M&A transaction. By focusing on entity-level (as opposed to process-level) controls, effort can be minimized while compliance can be maximized. Enterprise-wide policies and procedures should be followed, roles and responsibilities should be well known, and codes of conduct must be assigned. Most importantly, however, management must institute and communicate the importance of the risk and controls self-assessment.

The risk-based approach should focus on known issues with the highest risk, such as SOX controls. A repository should be created for identifying, reporting, and tracking known technology issues. Additionally, by identifying automated controls, the company can greatly reduce human error in financial reporting controls. Control monitoring technologies can be utilized to further reduce security threats. Utilizing a top-down, risk-based approach during M&A transactions can help increase compliance quality while achieving cost savings through increased efficiency and helping minimize employee error.[5]

Non-SOX Legal and Regulatory Requirements   Regulation management would be fairly straightforward if SOX was the only requirement faced during M&A transactions. Unfortunately, SOX may only the beginning. Many industry and regulatory regulations prescribe stricter and more expansive requirements for the protection of data and the minimization of IT risk, security, and control considerations.

There is no blueprint for identifying or managing a company's legal and regulatory requirements. Regulations and standards are based on the size, structure, industry, and region of the business, among other factors. Legal and compliance departments must identify and communicate regulatory requirements, while the infrastructure, IT, and information security departments are responsible for implementing associated IT controls accordingly, especially during M&A activities.

The following are examples of non-SOX regulations and industry standards applicable across two different industries.

Financial Services
- Federal Financial Institutions Examination Council (FFIEC)—Information Security.
- Federal Reserve Board (FRB) Regulations (i.e., 12 CFR 216—Privacy of Consumer Financial Information).
- Payment Card Industry (PCI) Data Security Standards (DSS) v2.0.
- Bank for International Settlements (BIS) 35: Electronic Banking and Electronic Money Activities.

Health Care
- Health Information Technology for Economic and Clinical Health (HITECH) Act.
- Health Insurance Portability and Accountability Act (HIPAA).
- Office of the Inspector General (OIG) compliance.

Additionally, international, regional, and state laws can affect entities based on their business locations, data centers, and regional departments. While the amount of regulations may seem daunting, a great deal of overlap does typically exist and the approach for managing is the same as for SOX: top-down and risk-based.

Legal and regulatory requirements for M&A transactions must be incorporated into IT risks and controls self-assessments in order to be managed effectively. Until then, issues cannot be determined and remediation cannot occur.

Reporting and Audit Requirements   As illustrated in case study 1, reporting requirements for SOX and other regulations can be significantly impacted by M&A activities. Based on the findings of the risks and controls assessment and on information communicated from the regulatory agencies identifying reporting requirements, planning and prioritization should occur.

Knowledge of reporting requirements at the start of the M&A transaction can allow for resources and effort to be efficiently managed over the course of the project. All too often, requirements are identified late in a project and a rush must occur to meet reporting deadlines, when many other key initiatives are also occurring. Proper planning to meet reporting requirements can help save costs and reduce employee burnout. Regular contact with regulatory bodies to understand requirements and performing control assessments based on these requirements can potentially help greatly reduce headaches experienced during the heart of M&A transactions.

Case Study 1

Issue   An industrial production company operating internationally, with approximately US$12 billion in revenue and over 40,000 employees, elected to divest into three separate companies to diversify and better align to the marketplace. The client was confronted with the challenge of separating systems into three disparate entities and determining SOX reporting requirements for approximately 116 key applications on Day 1.

Risks   Due to a limited timeframe and resources, the company faced a delayed close, brand impact, and the following information security risks:

- Regulatory fines.
- Security breaches as a result of:
  - Improper provisioning of company access.
  - Failure to terminate necessary system and administrator accounts.
  - Open access to critical systems due to unapproved configurations.

Action/Controls   The company identified SOX reporting requirements and developed a phased approach for splitting and transitioning system connectivity across the three new companies on Day 1. A methodology was developed to protect application data while identifying the appropriate management personnel to certify user access to financial applications. Issues with SOX systems were identified as a result of prior audit findings and risk and controls self-assessments. Information security personnel involved business owners from IT and applications early and often. As SOX 404 reporting was required for the parent organization on Day 1, these financial applications and controls were prioritized. SOX 404 reporting for the two new companies was not required for one fiscal year except for applications that were still shared. These controls were also prioritized and reviewed by external auditors through SSAE 16 or SOC 1.

Impact　During the weeks prior to Day 1, stakeholders from each business tested the operating effectiveness of these split environments, with increased resources available to provide support. On Day 1, users from the company were able to access three separate IT environments, with no loss of connectivity to network or key applications. SOX 404 reporting requirements were well known across the organizations and deadlines were able to be met as a result of prioritization and identified issues through risk and controls self-assessments.

Understanding Common IT Risk, Security, and Control Considerations

Improper regulatory compliance and unmet reporting requirements are some considerations of M&A transactions that can be identified through performing IT risk and control assessments. However, these assessments can also highlight a myriad of other common IT risk, security, and control considerations that arise during M&A activities, as discussed next.

Access Risks　While most companies perform thorough due diligence prior to any M&A activity, there still exists the risk that accompanies acquiring a new workforce and new technology. Improper user-level access provisioning during an M&A transaction may expose the involved parties to numerous risks, including those noted next. Please note that the following section introduces only some illustrative examples of the risks applicable to access management. Additional business continuity, compliance, and IT risks can arise due to poor access practices and should not be underestimated:

- **Leakage of sensitive information.**　Companies must make sure that only associates needing customer and sensitive information to perform their jobs have access to this information. Failure to adequately protect customer information could lead to lawsuits, regulatory fines, and devastating public image issues.

- **Noncompliant access controls.** Improperly provided access may lead to brand damage and diminished public image due to the potential loss of sensitive information. Both transacting parties should be fully aware of all compliance requirements throughout the integration.
- **Loss of competitive advantage.** Inappropriate access to proprietary information such as business models, proprietary tools, and best practices has the potential to critically diminish a company's position in the marketplace. While business professionalism would dictate this information not be used if accidentally obtained, proper measures should be taken to help ensure that proprietary information is secure and not accessible by associates who are not being acquired.

Case study 2 highlights access issues experience during an M&A transaction.

Case Study 2

Issue   The company is a credit card services company operating in the United States, Canada, and the United Kingdom with approximately US$14 billion in revenues and over 30,000 employees. To enhance its long-term capital generation and position itself for future growth, the organization acquired the domestic credit card unit of a global banking and financial products and services company. The client was confronted with the challenge of providing 5,500 users from the purchased credit card entity with access to approximately 75 applications by Day 1.

Action   The company developed a technical solution for providing application connectivity across company networks on Day 1. In parallel, a methodology was developed to identify the key applications and the users that needed access to those applications. As credit card companies tend to have large amounts of sensitive customer data such as credit scores, mailing addresses, and Social Security numbers, an indirect access method using a virtual desktop infrastructure (VDI) solution was selected to allow transitioning associates' access to legacy systems and data.

Impact   On Day 1, users from the acquired company were able to access applications on the purchasing entity's network seamlessly. During the initial weeks subsequent to Day 1, increased resources were available to provide access support and triage access requests to prevent business disruption.

Information Protection Risks As noted, lax access control practices can threaten sensitive information during M&A transactions. Additional common information-protection issues identified through self-assessments include:

- **External threats.** Using industry-communicated M&A project information, malicious outside organizations can begin targeting the affected enterprise's infrastructure in order to intercept the company's sensitive information, as technology changes are likely occurring.
- **Change management risk.** Information can be made susceptible to loss or manipulation if current activities are not well known and communicated. Any changes made to systems that contain shared information and data should be communicated and approved, so that information protection controls are in place.
- **Human error.** Unfortunately, simple human error can also allow unwanted risks into the M&A operating environment. From opening a phishing e-mail to leaving an unencrypted laptop unlocked, sensitive company information can too easily be communicated to unwanted parties.

The IT security and control risks present in M&A transactions are plentiful. Thankfully, there are also many practices that can minimize their effects.

PRACTICES FOR MANAGING IT RISK, SECURITY, AND CONTROL CONSIDERATIONS

The knowledge of the current state and associated IT security and control risks can prepare CIOs and CISOs for M&A transactions. However, managing identified issues can be a challenge itself, especially when resources and time are already at a premium. The following sections detail leading practices for curtailing and minimizing the effects of IT risk, security, and control considerations.

Managing User Access

As noted previously, one of the largest security challenges facing organizations is the improper provisioning and management of user access. With M&A transactions, these risks are heightened due to the constant changes occurring in systems, applications, and employee staffing. However, if the drivers behind an access management program are understood and consistent provisioning and certification practices are implemented, these risks may not cause adverse effects.

Drivers for Access Management When approaching the seemingly daunting task of access management, it is important to first prioritize access requirements. Access prioritization techniques should ask why and how access to various systems and applications needs to be provided to specific individuals.

There are four general considerations regarding providing end-user access: data protection, compliance, long-term business functionality, and temporary business continuity. Outlined next are explanations of each access driver as it relates to M&A IT.

1. **Data protection** should be the first consideration in providing user-level access. Improper access introduces the company's sensitive data to increased internal and external risk. Due to the nature of M&A transactions, external parties may target systems through improper access points to obtain critical information and in turn disrupt critical business operations. Internally, improper access can lead to mistakes in transferring data that eventually end up in the wrong hands.

2. **Compliance** with known legal and regulatory access regulations should be the next consideration in providing user-level access. Associates may be accidentally provided access to systems with personally identifiable information or proprietary information belonging to either company, increasing the company's risk to regulatory fines.

3. **Long-term business functionality** refers to the provisioning of access to applications, systems, or databases that will exist in the end-state organization and are required by the various lines of business for all associates to be able to work effectively. Examples of systems critical to long-term business functionality may include major business applications, such as ERP procure to pay, plan to manufacture, or order to cash. Access to requested applications should be prioritized by the criticality of the line of business and, in parallel, tailored according to the level of data necessary depending on one's job function (that is, the need to know).

4. **Temporary business continuity** refers to the provisioning of access to applications, systems, or databases that will be necessary to maintain business continuity while the integration is occurring, but may no longer be necessary in the end state. For example, during a divestiture, divested employees may still need access to old e-mails; thus it may be necessary to set up a read-only instance of the divesting company's e-mail system. While moving toward an end-state solution should be the top priority for CIOs and CISOs, it is also critical to make sure the temporary solutions to maintaining business continuity minimize negative associate and customer impact.

Methods of Providing Access   User access provisioning is a key activity in M&A transactions. Application, network, and service access must be provided to business and technology users who need it. Access must be removed for those users who should no longer have access. This requires an understanding of the specific systems and applications that are impacted by the M&A activity, the requirements related to access and data segregation, and consideration of potential security risks. Access can be segregated in a number of ways, such as creating a separate instance of an application or logically segregating access within an application through access controls, and sometimes may require coding changes to the application itself. It's important to consider cases where commingled data exists (i.e., where systems contain sensitive information involving more than one transaction party and that data must be logically separated). Some environments, such as file shares, data warehouse applications, and document management systems, may involve particular challenges. In those systems, it can be difficult to identify and separate access to required data for individual users or groups of users. End-user computing applications must be considered as well.

The process begins with an identification of the applications, infrastructure, and systems impacted by the M&A transaction. Once they are identified, an approach must be developed to support the access provisioning requirements of each individual system. Specific plans should be developed for each system involving business and IT users, as well as the access provisioners that add, remove, and change access to each of the systems under consideration. The list of individuals moving from one organization to another and the timing of their move is used to drive the access changes that are made. These lists typically are being changed up until Legal Day 1 cutover, and the currency of that information is critical to a smooth cut-over.

If a parent company is acquiring a business unit of another entity, it is likely that not all systems will be transitioned by Legal Day 1 and interim access will be necessary. One option considered by some organizations in these cases is the use of a virtual desktop infrastructure (VDI) solution. The virtual desktop provides access to needed systems without requiring full access to the selling organization's network or reimaging of workstations and laptops for the acquiring organization. It can help reduce risks associated with improper network and systems access. However, it's important to note that this option does not eliminate the need to perform the provisioning activities outlined previously.

A final point to consider is the technology risk-related processes and infrastructure that are currently in place. Identity management systems, directory architectures, firewalls, authentication systems, access certification processes and tools, vendor risk management, security operations centers, and a host of other areas, including governance, risk management, and compliance (GRC) processes and tools, may be affected. It is sometimes not realized how many systems these processes and tools may touch, nor the intricate relationships between them and the systems they interface with. Taking stock of this infrastructure, understanding how it is impacted, and planning for migration is a critical step in enabling the transition.

Importance of Access Certifications While timeframes for M&A transactions vary greatly, at two stages in all M&A projects the access risks can be reduced through performing access certification activities: the outset and soon after Legal Day 1. Access certifications are a means by which you can verify who has access to what systems and have that access reviewed and certified by the business owners responsible for those systems. Privileged users (i.e., super users or administrators), who are often in IT, may present a particularly high risk. There are multiple approaches to access certification: complete access certifications, delta access certifications, and triggered access certifications. The decision for which access certification should be undertaken is dependent upon the stage of the M&A transaction. The costs and benefits of each approach are:

- **Complete access certification** involves performing a complete semi-annual review of each employee's access to a comprehensive set of applications and systems. However, these reviews are often time-consuming and labor-intensive, and have the tendency to rubber-stamp access. While it is the ideal access certification to perform at the start of M&A activities in order to start with a blank slate, full-access certifications may not be possible throughout M&A activities, as access is constantly changing.
- **Delta access certification** includes reviewing only new access provisioned from the last review performed. While these reviews can allow improper access to slip through the cracks if it was missed during an earlier review, delta certifications also take less time and resources. While not the ideal solution for every access certification, the delta reviews can be efficiently used during the M&A transactions to prioritize reviews for high-risk applications.
- **Triggered access certification** includes access certifications outside of the semiannual or quarterly cycle. While applications may be shared for a period after Legal Day 1, upon their final separation an access review should take place. Additionally, changes in the highest-risk applications may also necessitate event-based access certifications outside of the normal cycle.

Access is not stagnant, and this is especially true during M&A transactions. Depending on the length of the M&A activities, one or all of the types of access certifications could (and should) occur. If access certifications and proper access provisioning techniques are not used effectively, the IT security and control risks related to access could quickly become costly realities.

Managing Changes

Updates to access are just one change that will occur during an M&A transaction. Other changes that will need to be requested and reviewed are hardware and software updates, network reconfigurations, location transfers, documentation revisions, and application adjustments, to name a few. However, it is not the *type* of change that is requested, but the manner in which the request is managed that can have the largest effect on M&A transaction risk.

System Change Management Process M&A organizations can minimize their risk through evaluating all changes requested throughout the transaction. An important point to note is that these changes do not affect simply the requesting company, but all of the organizations involved. The common challenges experienced as a part of system change management are:

- Balance of speed versus process is often lost, especially in M&A transactions.
- The change reviewers are sometimes not well prepared or suited for their role and are therefore inefficient.

The first necessity of an effective, risk-minimizing change management program is to document and communicate the change management process at the outset of M&A activities. As a result of this communication, a change review group or senior employee must be identified to perform the reviews. A change approval board may be the ideal solution to meet an organization's change management needs; however, this may not be the most feasible solution during M&A transactions. In some companies, change management activities may be undertaken by the security department with input from other key stakeholders.

The next step in the change management process is to make sure that the activities of both the reviewer and the requestor are well understood. If possible, consulting with the right mix of stakeholders from across the organization when reviewing requests can allow for broad reviews with technical, security, legal, and economic analysis to occur. Within M&A activities, however, the change reviewer must also avoid analysis paralysis. Due to shortened timeframes, decisions on a request must be made as quickly as possible.

Especially at the outset of M&A transactions, the decisions and actions of the change reviewer(s) will have lasting impacts across the organization. If change requests with minimal supporting details are approved, then future requests will also contain minimal details. Additionally, if review decisions are not communicated in an expedited timeframe, the risk of changes occurring without requests and approvals can greatly increase. In order to help prevent the reviewer(s) from simply rubber-stamping the changes that come across their desks, accountability must be incorporated into their work, possibly through performance bonuses. Regardless of the reviewer or review group in place, changes must be evaluated according to a documented process.

Exception Management Process   Similar to change requests, exceptions to controls and access requirements in place will likely be required. Typically, these exceptions are due to the shortened timeframe of M&A transactions. For example, a developer may need access to the production environment to move application changes or a password may not be set to control guidelines so that the infrastructure updates can be configured appropriately.

While exceptions are generally smaller in scale than the changes requested, the same review and approval process applies. However, there should be one additional component: tracking. Typically, exceptions are necessary for only an abbreviated time during the M&A activity and can eventually be closed out.

As exception requests are generally more frequent and higher in volume than detailed change requests, exception requests do not need to be reviewed by an entire committee. Typically within M&A transactions, exceptions will be reviewed by one or two senior members of the security organization (or the applicable custodians of the information and data being requested) who have a broad understanding of the risk and control environment. Exceptions (and change requests) should be stored in a central location, with appropriate approvals, and tracked as necessary.

Importance of Prioritization   Numerous change and exception requests will arise throughout the course of an M&A transaction. During the beginning and end stages of M&A activities, these requests will become especially overwhelming. So how can changes and exceptions be managed efficiently and effectively while also minimizing the risk to all organizations involved? A good method is prioritization.

Armed with the knowledge of the risk and control environment and associated issues, change and exception requests arising as a result of M&A activities can be prioritized based on their risk impact. Prioritization for change and exception requests should begin by focusing on projects with achievable goals and the most risk impact. Changes with smaller impact should be postponed for review until downtime in the project or denied approval and resubmitted after the M&A transaction completion. This prioritization should also be made clear to the employees of the organization so that unnecessary requests are not made and reviewed.

Prioritization does not only apply to changes and exceptions. The same logic should be applied throughout all initiatives during an M&A transaction. After approval for the low-hanging fruit, or high-impact projects with minimal resource requirements, planning should begin for high-impact projects that will take longer to implement.

Managing Data

Access and change management procedures can minimize a great deal of the IT risk, security, and control considerations present during M&A transactions. However, additional steps can also be taken to further protect the sensitive information owned and managed by the organizations. The following section introduces example practices for protecting data, which is one of the highest-risk areas present throughout M&A transactions. While the initiatives described may not provide prescriptive performance steps due to various means of implementation, the effects of not conducting appropriate data-protection measures cannot be underestimated. A lack of sufficient attention to data protection can have significant consequences for organizations involved in M&A activities, including compliance issues, competitive risks, and theft of confidential information.

Data Protection Initiatives While there is no perfect solution for protecting sensitive information, three activities can be implemented during M&A initiatives to help minimize the threat of information loss.

1. **Implementing data protection plans.** By CIOs and CISOs requiring application, system, and infrastructure owners to document their plans for data protection at the outset of M&A activities, accountability is created for the protection of sensitive information. Data protection plans should detail necessary steps for data movement, data separation, data cleansing, and the handling of any data that may be impacted by transition services agreements (TSAs). These techniques are implemented in conjunction with access provisioning changes described earlier. Additionally, the instructions communicated should identify data classification policies and incorporate the steps necessary to meet compliance obligations, including applicable global and local regulations, and take into consideration variances in data classification policies between companies. Data should be considered throughout their lifecycle—collection, storage, usage, transfer, and destruction. New third-party service providers may require changes to vendor risk management programs. Data loss prevention and forensic analysis tools can sometimes be used to help identify where sensitive data is stored, transferred, or used.
2. **Conducting technical security reviews and scans.** During IT risk and control assessments, responders will have assessed their current architecture and infrastructure data-protection mechanisms. In theory, these reviews were based on tangible evidence and not simply opinions noted by the assessors. However, if time allows during an M&A transaction, technical security reviews and scans can be conducted to further identify technical issues in systems and infrastructure, such as broken firewalls

and open access. These reviews should be performed after changes are completed across various systems to remediate any issues prior to legal Day 1.

3. **Monitoring.** One proactive step CIOs and CISOs can take is to consider implementing additional monitoring. Mergers and acquisitions can be times of uncertainty and stress for employees. In addition to moving to a new organization, turnover often occurs. Some individuals may be tempted to take data or information with them. It is a time of significant change, which may open up inadvertent risks or technical vulnerabilities that are not detected. Not all risks can be prevented (i.e., through access controls, firewalls, etc.). Companies should consider elevating the level of network and systems logging in place, as well as the correlation and analysis of those logs. Many companies consider implementing additional logging at the workstation level to detect inappropriate activity. To combat external threats, external intelligence information can be combined with internal log information to help determine whether external attacks are successfully occurring.

Managing the Human Factor

When managing IT risk, security, and control considerations in M&A activities, the majority of the focus is placed on IT: infrastructure, automated controls, change management, data protection, access provisioning, and more. As technology often drives M&A activities, it becomes all too easy to forget that the organization's management and employees have the greatest impact on the effectiveness of M&A transactions and associated risk.

Participation of Key Stakeholders and Organizational Design A common major pitfall during M&A activities is the failure to address critical people issues. While risk assessments and change reviews are highly recommended, without commitment across the organization to perform these activities, there is no way in which the M&A transaction can succeed. (See Chapter 20 for an in-depth discussion of the people aspects of M&A transactions.)

Additionally, regardless of the type of M&A transaction, employees of each organization are faced with an uncertain future. *Will the deal succeed? Will I still have my role at the end of this endeavor?* With all of these precarious situations present for a member of an M&A team, it should be no surprise that responsibilities can be forgotten, due dates can slip, and new risks can be introduced into the environment.

With an uncertain job future looming, key employees may also search for new jobs and leave the organization. With their loss come an exodus of knowledge and an introduction of new challenges. New access needs to be provided, but should it be the same as the employee replaced? Will this loss impact the project timeframes and necessitate a change or exception request that can have lasting effects on the business?

Another risk present during divestitures and integrations arises when new employees enter an organization. We've previously discussed access-related risks occurring during this situation. However, what if the newly acquired organization simply has different policies related to mobile devices or social media? In the grand scheme of an M&A transaction, these policy discrepancies seem unimportant. However, allowing the policy to continue can introduce a host of new risks into the environment, but discontinuing its use can impact the new employees' morale.

CIOs and CISOs should work closely with the HR department to identify initiatives for employee retention and also keep the lines of communication open with staff. Feedback mechanisms and monetary incentives can prevent employee burnout and minimize these risks during M&A transactions.

While partnering with HR, it is also critical that a clear organizational structure for the resulting organizations is well defined. Once that is established, if employees are transferring from information technology into information security roles, they should receive training and education. If a new company is being formed due to a divestiture, the information security function needs to have an information security leader who has the necessary line of sight into IT, internal audit, compliance, and other lines of business.

Goals, Timelines, and Expectations   With M&A transactions, it is vital that Legal Day 1 activities are completed and managed as smoothly as possible with little or no financial and operational impact to the business. Thus, it is critical to develop a work plan that meets the Legal Day 1 requirements for managing IT risk, security, and control considerations while also managing expectations to achieve key milestones.

These goals, timelines, and expectations should be communicated using the top-down approach discussed previously. Through management clearly voicing their intentions, disconnect among employees and associated implications will be minimized.

WRAPPING IT UP

Managing IT risk, security, and controls properly in an M&A transaction can be a detailed and arduous process. However, giving it the attention it deserves from the beginning can prevent many of the common M&A pitfalls on Legal Day 1 and beyond. While it is easy to focus on the aspects of M&A transactions that drive growth and revenue, unmitigated technology risks can have costly effects on businesses from both a compliance and a competitive standpoint and can counteract identified synergies. Competitors could end up with easy access to competitive information or confidential customer data.

When engaging in an M&A transaction, careful planning, understanding your security posture, and implementing security and controls are critical. CIOs and CISOs should begin to think early and think often about what information and systems will be critical to transitioning associates and should manage risk accordingly. Unapproved changes to systems or human error could ultimately result in the loss of customers and business partners. Avoiding the numerous problems associated with a security breach or compliance penalty requires an IT risk management program and supporting activities, many of which have been outlined here.

While CIOs and CISOs might be hesitant to devote resources and time to IT risk, security, and controls at the outset of an M&A deal, doing so may greatly improve the likelihood of a successful transaction.

Notes

1. "Wired for Winning?" Deloitte, 2008.
2. Ibid.
3. Ibid.
4. Statement on Standards for Attestation Engagements (SSAE) No. 16, Reporting on Controls at a Service Organization, was finalized by the Auditing Standards Board of the American Institute of Certified Public Accountants (AICPA) in January 2010. SSAE 16 effectively replaces SAS 70 as the authoritative guidance for reporting on service organizations. SSAE 16 was formally issued in April 2010 with an effective date of June 15, 2011. SSAE 16 was drafted with the intention and purpose of updating the U.S. service organization reporting standard so that it mirrors and complies with the new international service organization reporting standard, ISAE 3402 (Deloitte Technical Library).
5. "Our Sarbanes-Oxley Approach," Deloitte, 2010.

The People Aspects of Mergers, Acquisitions, and Divestitures

CHAPTER 18

The Role of the CIO in Mergers, Acquisitions, and Divestitures

Irwin Goverman

THE DOUBLE-DUTY ROLE

The CIO takes on two separate roles during significant M&A activity. While the rest of the C-suite is concentrating on combining organizations and building a future strategy for their own business functions, the CIOs, Janus-like, must face both inward to their own function and at the same time outward to accommodate all the changes their own customers demand. In most organizations, the setup of IT inside its parent organization helps it execute as if it were a company within a company (see Exhibit 18.1). If the size of the parent company is significant, the IT organization's own internal considerations and functions for combining strategy and planning, human resources (HR), real estate, finance, procurement and customer relations, and the like represent a merger within a merger of its own. The CIO will need to duplicate the approach to, and execution of, the overall organization's M&A activities, often with a shortened timeframe so that IT is ready when Day 1 lands.

While attending to what amounts to a significant and multifaceted merger of their own, CIOs generally need to lead and direct the role of IT to accommodate the often-changing and ill-defined requirements coming from the organization's overall M&A plans and actions. The CIO's position, role, and influence will vary from organization to organization, depending on the specific industry, the volume and velocity of the current IT spend, and whether IT provides services that are visible to the company's external customers. Exhibit 18.2 represents a simple model for the role of the CIO within the organization, looking at the relative volume of IT services and their integration and collaboration with the other functions as a surrogate for IT being intrinsic and important to the overall business.

The degree of difficulty, complexity, and effort involved with the CIO's outward-facing role will vary according to where the CIO stands in this

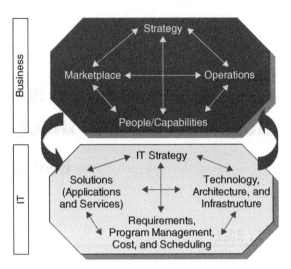

EXHIBIT 18.1   Company-within-a-Company Model

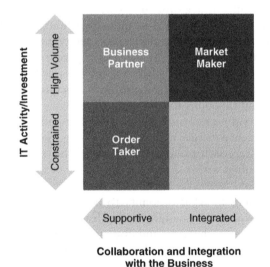

EXHIBIT 18.2   CIO Organizational Role Model

model. The "order taker" (low volume, low integration/collaboration) will most likely have a simpler role, waiting until the merged direction and requirements of the external customers become clear and then responding. The "market maker" (higher volume of activity, integration, and collaboration), however, will have a tougher role—simultaneously juggling internal

IT merger, ongoing investments in flight, and the new requirements, business models, and priorities of the combining organizations.

As if simultaneously juggling the inside and outside roles (and figuring out what they are exactly) were not enough, another complication arises from the fact that the two combining entities often have different models for, and expectations of, IT and the CIOs themselves. Even within the same industry, one organization may relegate IT and the CIO to a minor supporting role whereas the other invests heavily and places them in the center of innovation, product, service, cost, or other component of the core strategy. Figuring out all of this, making new allies within the C-suite, and merging the substantial business that IT itself represents, all the while keeping the lights on and the doors open, can create a complicated role for the CIO.

THE INTERNAL ROLE

Building on the theme that IT represents a substantial business within the business, it is helpful to dive into the details of what a modern department must deal with as it both combines and accommodates the changes imposed by the M&A activities. Exhibit 18.3 is a high-level extract from the Information Technology Infrastructure Library (ITIL), which is a set of practices for IT services management (ITSM) that focuses on aligning IT services with the needs of business. It describes the procedures, tasks, and checklists that allow the organization to establish a baseline from which it can plan, implement, and measure the core functions performed by most IT departments and both led and managed by the CIO.

Looking first at IT's core strategic and administrative functions, there are a number of considerations for combining them effectively, as shown in Exhibit 18.4.

In addition to the foundational and administrative functions, consideration needs to be made for the core operational components that deliver value directly to internal and, depending on the overall business model, external customers of IT. See Exhibit 18.5 for a summary of the operational components and how they can be approached.

The common thread to the CIO's role in all of the foundational, administrative, and operational functions in the IT model is leading and managing the process of mutual assessment (what exists in each organization coming together), reconciling and rationalizing differences (hopefully with achievement of synergies and consolidations) and clearly communicating new directions, approaches and changes.

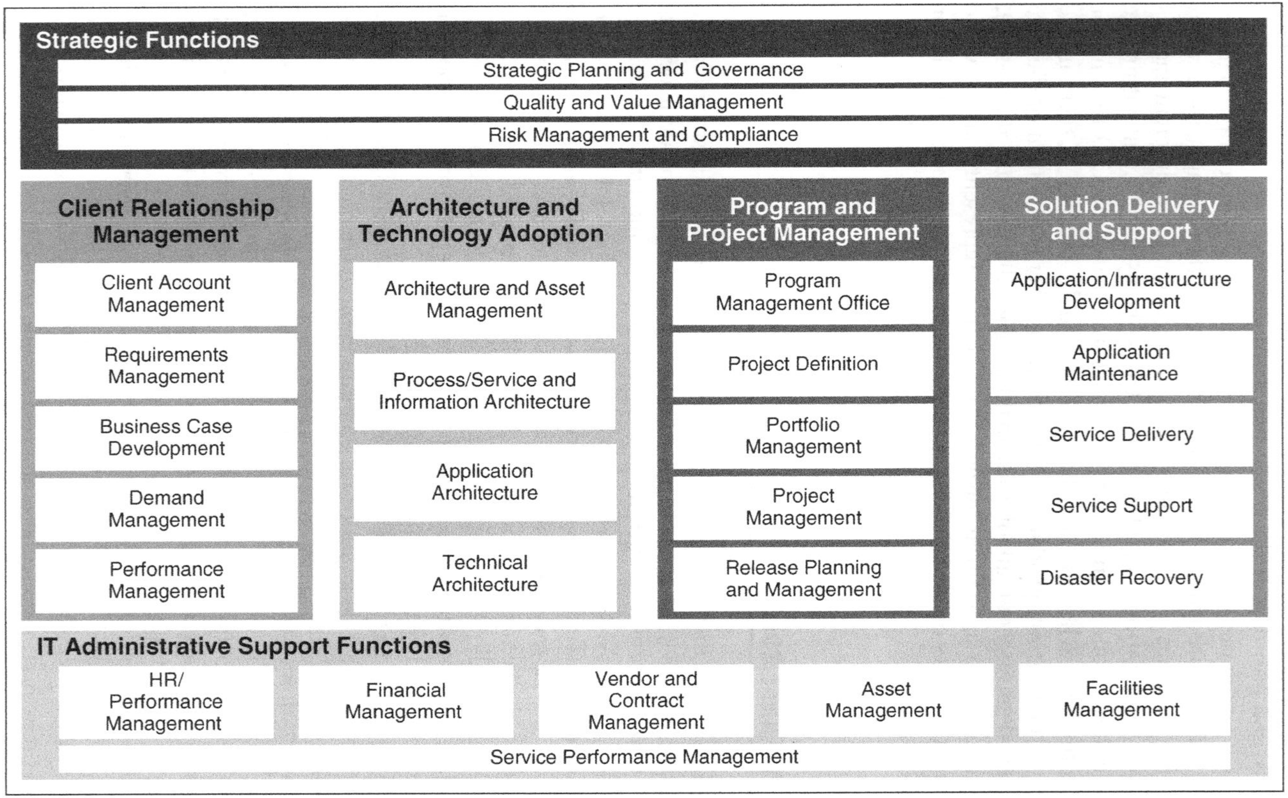

Strategic Functions

Strategic Planning and Governance

Quality and Value Management

Risk Management and Compliance

Client Relationship Management

- Client Account Management
- Requirements Management
- Business Case Development
- Demand Management
- Performance Management

Architecture and Technology Adoption

- Architecture and Asset Management
- Process/Service and Information Architecture
- Application Architecture
- Technical Architecture

Program and Project Management

- Program Management Office
- Project Definition
- Portfolio Management
- Project Management
- Release Planning and Management

Solution Delivery and Support

- Application/Infrastructure Development
- Application Maintenance
- Service Delivery
- Service Support
- Disaster Recovery

IT Administrative Support Functions

- HR/Performance Management
- Financial Management
- Vendor and Contract Management
- Asset Management
- Facilities Management

Service Performance Management

EXHIBIT 18.3 ITIL IT Functional Model
Copyright © 2012 Deloitte Development LLC

EXHIBIT 18.4 Combining Functional and Administrative Functions

Administrative/ Foundational Area	Definition and Scope	Approach
Strategic Planning	Long-range planning, technology adoption, architecture, high-level resource allocation	Compare and rationalize combining organization's objectives, priorities, constraints, and investments. Reconcile differences in expected role of CIO and IT.
Quality and Value Management	Standards and methodologies, status and progress reporting	Merge and communicate approaches, dashboards, and key performance indicators.
Risk Management and Compliance	Externally imposed regulatory requirements, value- and risk-based business protection and recovery	Accommodate newly introduced requirements (e.g., FDA, HIPAA, and PII). Reevaluate need for business interruption and recovery protection.
HR and Performance Management	Hire-to-retire and career path for IT personnel	Reconcile roles, ratings, levels, and compensation. Harmonize to overall organization's definitions and expectations.
Financial Management	Internal IT budgeting, forecasting, management, and reporting; external charge-backs and controls	Accommodate changes in overall finance approaches. Account for changes in asset life and use.
Vendor and Contract Management	Vendor identification, stratification, management, and performance reporting	Consolidate preferred vendor list; renegotiate based on changes in direction, volume, and priorities.
Asset Management	Core IT asset licensing, leasing, and maintenance contracting	Consolidate and potentially renegotiate, especially for revenue and seat-based licenses.
Facilities Management	Management of physical assets, including data centers, hardware, and real estate	Consolidate and rationalize. Potential investigation of alternative sources (e.g., cloud- and offshore-based).

More important, the internal change should be accomplished without upsetting the apple cart. Three main areas usually pose a challenge to the CIO and need special attention:

1. **Quickly and fairly assessing what you have.** When the merging organizations are of significantly different size and maturity or represent very different business models (such as geographic reach), the capabilities, expectations, skill mix, and bench strength may be out of balance in the

EXHIBIT 18.5 Combining Operational Functions

Operational Area	Definition and Scope	Approach
IT Client Relationship Management	Defines how IT faces off to the organization and has a direct impact on the CIO role model	Fully understand and react to the respective historical role of IT in each organization, and synthesize a combined (and potentially new) set of organization structures, roles, and responsibilities; strictness of governance and demand management; and expectations for value reporting and benefits demonstration.
Architecture and Technology Adoption Management	Approaches and attitude from conservative to assertive regarding new technologies, strictness of standards, and investment in workforce tools, services, and productivity	Assess existing investments, levels of service satisfaction, impact on cost, risk, and benefit. Develop options and communicate back through strategy and governance to develop future approaches.
Program and Project Management	Internal IT PMO and role of IT in partnering with the business for programs and projects that involve technology	Understand IT's role and responsibilities in both combining organizations. Clearly articulate roles, responsibilities, and expectations for both IT- and non-IT-focused projects.
Solution Delivery and Support	Design, development, deployment, and support for IT applications, functions, and services	Understand new joint expectations for the service catalog. Communicate clearly around what is in and what is out of the rationalized environment. Develop or revise service-level agreements.

respective IT organizations. Assuming the CIO comes from one of the two parent organizations, he or she will be more familiar and comfortable with the predecessor set of processes, people, and standards. It can be important (especially in supporting the other objectives described later) to figure out what is there, what is working, and what is not, and use these as the basis for the additional IT M&A activities. One useful tool is an IT-focused set of capability maturity models (CMMs), which can be used to describe both the as-is and targeted to-be capability levels for key functions performed by an organization. (See an example of CMM in Exhibit 18.6.) These can be used both to show the current state for each IT organization and, through consensus, to build realistic targets for the future combined state.

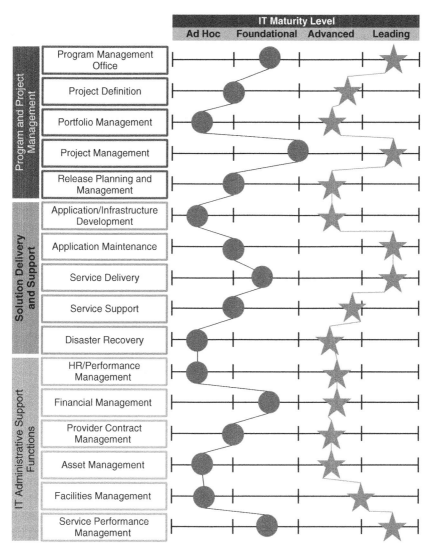

EXHIBIT 18.6　Sample Capability Maturity Model
Copyright © 2012 Deloitte Development LLC

2. **Leading the team and maintaining morale.** Most merger activity is accompanied by uncertainty and fear about change, about the future and about expectations around roles, responsibilities, and performance. Technology people can be the least bonded to the organization,

especially when good economic times and/or concentrated business geography (e.g., Silicon Valley) offers alternatives. Therefore, it is essential to attend to them. Frequent, honest, and personalized communication is important, as is maintaining an even hand in dealing with both old and new staff in the consolidation. If the consolidation is likely to cause staff reductions or geographic displacement is known to be on the horizon, special measures such as so-called stay pay may be needed to augment normal communication, counseling, and leadership.

3. **Maintaining service levels and performance.** Especially when IT functions and services are core to the business or exposed to external customers (e.g., web stores, reservation systems), it is essential to plan for and maintain service levels. CIOs are familiar with the normal dip in service levels (which hopefully is very temporary!) that can accompany major system deployments. The effect of impending change on people (see points 1 and 2), infrastructure, systems, performance measures, and the like is even greater. The role of the CIO is to see over the horizon and to identify, plan for, communicate about, and, where possible, mitigate the impact. Mitigation and maintenance of established service levels can be difficult, especially where there are transitional services agreements (TSAs) involving parties that will be uninvolved in the future, which is frequently the case, and new business models and supporting IT functions.

4. **Creating a new organization.** Given the common variations in IT organizational structure, it is unlikely that both organizations will have a consistent model. The inconsistencies in roles, responsibilities, number of levels, span of control, and, most importantly, how to face off to the user communities and stakeholders usually require significant effort to reconcile and frequently need the assistance of the company's HR professional function. Additional constraints may be imposed by union contracts, protected class identifications, and, in a global combination, workers' council rules. In all cases, and despite all the external tugging, the task of the CIO is to accommodate the components within a merged IT organizational structure that accommodates all the needed services, functions, applications, and service-level agreements/requirements. A standard organizational model, as depicted in Exhibit 18.7, would be extended to serve additional business units, geographies, and differentiated regulatory environments. Once the model is set, a significant amount of work will be required to establish job descriptions, transition plans, compensation, performance structures, and career paths.

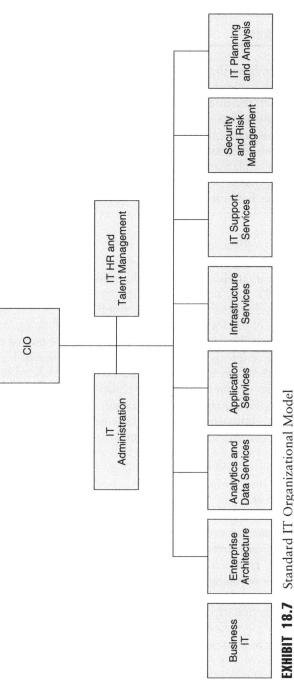

EXHIBIT 18.7 Standard IT Organizational Model

THE EXTERNAL ROLE

As the CIO attends to the priorities within the department and the construction of a new, combined IT function, he or she must also participate in the overall merger and integration activities and face off to the business as it combines. This presents special challenges for IT, because it needs to lead with new thoughts and opportunities and to participate in the combining of the other functions (e.g., marketing, supply chain, HR, finance) both to add detail to the Day 1 plan and subsequent plans, and to identify constraints around what is possible for IT to support. The role is a balance between assisting the other functions to achieve their own merger plan and synergy goals and realistically expressing the limitations on applications, IT services, and capacity.

Some of the considerations are:

- **Having a seat at the table from due diligence through Day 1 and execution.** IT may not be considered to be at the center of merged operations and expected benefits. As a result, the CIO (or designee) is not always a part of the due diligence, estimation, and planning. As discussed in Chapter 5, if the CIO is not involved from the beginning all the way through, the result may be unrealistically high expected benefits from IT consolidation, or, more harmfully, unrealistic expectations of how quickly IT can respond to support the plan for finance, manufacturing, supply chain, HR, marketing, and so forth.
- **Establishing relationships early with the new executive team.** One of the CIO's most important roles is making the market for current IT functions, services, and systems, as well as describing and promoting the art of the possible where technology could contribute to the top and bottom lines. Informal working relationships with the rest of the C-suite and other key stakeholders are important in creating two-way communication and, ultimately, the credibility and contribution of IT. Making the market is the iterative process of the CIO using the formal and informal relationships to bring new "art of the possible" ideas to the table, getting reactions to them through active listening, and establishing a mutually agreed-upon set of plans and actions.
- **Reestablishing and extending the IT governance process.** In most cases, IT functions from both organizations will be full to capacity with ongoing operations and a long list of investment and development projects. The M&A transaction will not only combine the two long lists; it will also create its own long list of integration activities, including application rationalization, infrastructure consolidation, and changes to everything from master data to reporting. The CIO's role is to protect both IT and the overall organization from harm by creating

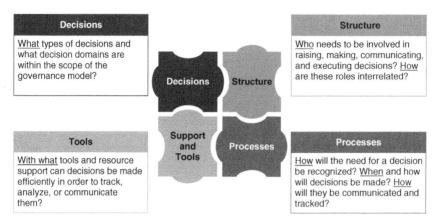

EXHIBIT 18.8 The Four Pillars of IT Governance
Copyright © 2012 Deloitte Development LLC

(or re-creating) the four pillars of formal IT governance and demand management processes, as depicted in Exhibit 18.8.

These four components help ensure that an analytical and realistic approach is taken to identifying both opportunities and constraints around what can and can't be done. A potential scope and set of processes to support the pillars and the key activities are depicted in Exhibit 18.9. As the diagram depicts, taking all the inputs from the IT governance process and translating these through demand, portfolio, and project/program management is complex, as is settling on the right indicators and results reporting for demonstrating the value of IT. Even when these processes are well defined, it is often the case that in the two combining organizations the processes will be different and there will be differing levels of patience for the detail, collaboration, and discipline required for good and realistic demand management.

▪ **Taking into account new mega requirements.** A significant M&A event may involve requirements that are totally new to the IT organization and the CIO. While it is true that many of the CIO's and the IT department's skills and processes are generic and usable across multiple business models, there may be additional requirements imposed by significant changes in:
  ● Geographic coverage—requiring multilanguage support, new supply chain and distribution models, different tax and currency accommodation, and so on.
  ● Regulatory requirements—imposing different needs and detailed skills around quality and safety regulations, protection of personally identifiable information (PII), and government reporting.

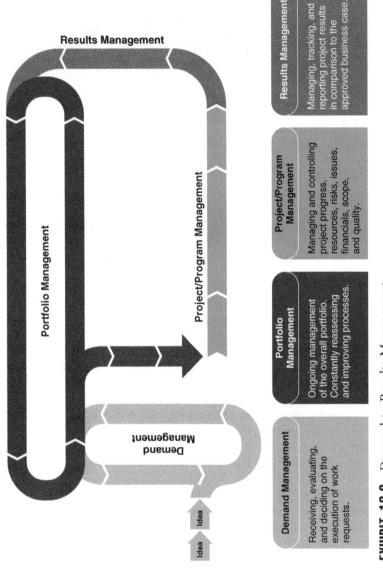

EXHIBIT 18.9 Demand-to-Results Management

Copyright © 2012 Deloitte Development LLC

Results Management

Managing, tracking, and reporting project results in comparison to the approved business case.

Project/Program Management

Managing and controlling project progress, resources, risks, issues, financials, scope, and quality.

Portfolio Management

Ongoing management of the overall portfolio. Constantly reassessing and improving processes.

Demand Management

Receiving, evaluating, and deciding on the execution of work requests.

- Unionization—creating the need for differences in HR and payroll, as well as changes in IT's own handling of the hire-to-retire process.
- Outsourcing/insourcing—identifying new business processes, interfaces, and standards for communicating with and managing manufacturing, marketing, distribution, and other external business partners.

An example of the perfect storm involving all these changes occurred recently when a pharmaceutical company acquired a medical device and diagnostic company. The acquiring IT department needed to build a process and skill set rapidly to deal with a global supply chain; outsourced manufacturing partners; Food and Drug Administration (FDA), Health Insurance Portability and Accountability Act (HIPAA), and other government reporting requirements; product complaints; and workers' council standards. The CIO had to get his own training on the new needs and immediately both manage unfamiliar IT capabilities from the device company and create new processes where they did not exist.

■ **Creating a new vision going forward.** The rapidity and scale of the overall M&A process may not create the desired environment for the creation of a new combined IT strategic plan. Typically, the activities, objectives, priorities, and demand for new capabilities will be translated into tactical, rather than strategic, plans and actions by the CIO and the IT organization. Even then, it is a little like changing the tires while driving the bus at 100 miles per hour and doing so over an unfamiliar road with a load of passengers shouting out different directions.

At some point, the dust will settle and the furious tactical activity will need to be supported by a revised strategic vision that takes into account the legacy investments, organizations, standards, architectures, systems, processes, and so on, and creates a combined vision and strategy. The objective will be to increase IT's value to the business and reduce cost, risk, and time to deployment and support for the key IT functions, services, and systems. The new strategic planning activities can also be an opportunity for candid dialogue with the executive team, key stakeholders, and the IT staff over the role, capabilities, and capacity that IT needs to provide in the future.

SOME LESSONS LEARNED

Involvement in many recent, large-scale M&A transactions has created a long list of lessons learned—some of them learned painfully! While each transaction is different because of varying as-is states, priorities, and to-be visions, some common themes have emerged. Among the most significant:

■ **Mergers of equals can be the most difficult.** It may not be intuitive that combinations involving equally sized and positioned departments would be that difficult, since you are combining two, probably well-established IT organizations. The downside is that because both organizations have similarly sized sets of people, processes, infrastructure, and systems, the process of adjudicating and selecting which platforms to adopt becomes difficult. It often comes down to which CIO ascends to take overall responsibility for the tactical M&A planning and execution and which set of equal stakeholders will occupy the C-suite going forward. The tactical stalemate also creates a more urgent need for the revised vision and strategy described earlier, as delays in getting to a solid future state can create rework and dead ends arising from the tactical and interim activities.

■ **Customer-facing efforts and services may need to trump internal work.** As discussed earlier, interruptions in services and operations are never a good thing. Disruptions and slow performance in the IT applications and services facing customers, however, can be catastrophic, both for the overall organization and especially for the CIO. While two organizations are merging operations and brands, customers are often already nervous and customer loyalty can be low. Careful risk assessment, planning, monitoring, and quick reaction are essential during this critical timeframe. Taking the pulse of the stakeholders with customer responsibilities (e.g., sales and marketing personnel) can also be key.

■ **Take advantage of new technologies and approaches.** The M&A tactical actions, bridge processes, and systems and the new strategic plan and vision all provide the CIO with the chance to reexamine and evaluate some of the newer technologies and approaches to providing services, applications, infrastructure, and support. Software, storage, infrastructure as a service, and so on can provide the temporary horsepower needed as well as the opportunity to achieve benefits by substituting on-demand resources for fixed costs. They can also lessen the lead time for IT to meet new demands for applications and services in support of changed business models.

■ **Resist the urge to rip and replace.** Historically, where the two organizations had different legacy ERP or other major systems, one of the CIO's first actions would be to force one organization onto the other's platform almost immediately. Though it is tempting in order to consolidate operations, support, and licensing cost and reduce the long-term total cost of ownership, the unintended consequences include additional disruption and risk. Also, it creates the potential for a write-off of an existing platform as well as the need for substantial effort, delay, and cost to get back to the status quo (albeit on one single platform). Newer approaches, involving focused investments in middleware technology, master data management, and consolidated reporting tools, can successfully avoid the need for an ERP platform consolidation for years—allowing for a more considered strategy and accommodation of the natural software package lifecycles and licensing periods.

Some companies recently have been very successful in more immediately supporting business-based goals, avoiding service-level dips, and deferring major capital expenditures through these approaches. More important, the major system replacements, consolidations, and upgrades can be done with reduced risk and disruption once the overall organization's and IT's objectives, priorities, and constraints are better known.

■ **Pay attention to workforce services.** The policies, infrastructure, and services connected to the organization's smartphones, tablets, desktops and laptops, instant messaging, social media, calendar, e-mail, cloud-based accessible data, and tele- and videoconferencing seem like they would be less important than the real applications provide by IT. In real-world experience, however, the focus, angst, and anger that arise when a merged entity's people's access to what they have been accustomed to is no longer provided can put morale and employee satisfaction with IT into a tailspin. In one case, the CEO of a company in an M&A transaction joked that the sole reason for accepting the acquisition offer was the opportunity it afforded to move from an antiquated e-mail and calendar system. Similarly, the CIO who ends a "bring your own device" policy or access to any cherished smartphone or laptop brand risks his or her reputation.

As importantly, unified communications, remote access to data, and all of the workforce services provide an additional opportunity to add value and increase return on investment (ROI), provided the CEO can (and is allowed to) balance all the requirements of access, cost, usability, risk, and opportunity (see Exhibit 18.10).

EXHIBIT 18.10 The Challenge of Workforce Services

WRAPPING IT UP

The role of the CIO during and after the M&A transaction is complex and difficult. The CIO would have a difficult challenge in merging his or her own house alone with its substantial investments, long lead times, and the difficulty of IT governance and demand management. Accomplishing that while being sensitive and responsive to the significant and changing demands of the business surrounding IT, the executives, the stakeholders, and the external customers is even more difficult. The CIO has the obligation to interact with the other C-suite executives and communicate about what is realistically achievable for IT merger and cost savings *and* in support of all the plans being created by the other business functions. The CIO's involvement throughout the deal is absolutely critical and may in fact prove to be "the long pole in the tent" toward achieving the organization's overall goals. The role of the CIO is to bring executive presence, technical excellence, and operational quality in execution throughout and well beyond the merger or acquisition.

CHAPTER 19

The Role of CFO

Rich Rorem
Trevear Thomas
Nnamdi Lowrie
Heith Rothman
Venkat Swaminathan
Chelsea Gorr
Jenny Xu
Mia Velasquez

The chief financial officer (CFO) plays multiple critical roles in a company's M&A transaction. CFOs have responsibility for the large number of M&A activities that directly impact the finance organization, finance support services, and many cross-functional deal activities. In addition, they often have a broader overall role in the deal transaction planning and execution. The CFO is one of the key decision makers and influencers in the overall deal structuring, due diligence, and negotiations. Often, the CFO is one of the first executives brought into a transaction and has ultimate responsibility for the financial success of the transaction. In large M&A transactions, the process from due diligence to full integration can take many months and consume the organization in integration activities geared to creating the newly combined entity. This makes the CFO role extremely challenging, as CFOs must balance transactional activities in addition to their normal corporate, operational, and functional responsibilities.

Given the CFOs' varied roles, it is important that they have significant interaction with other functional areas to help ensure the deal's success. Exhibit 19.1 depicts the key CFO roles and activities and potential areas where there is cross-functional collaboration across the M&A lifecycle.

The IT organization is one of the key functional areas where careful cooperation with the finance organization is needed to deliver on common deal objectives. Many major finance activities that occur immediately before

EXHIBIT 19.1 Typical Acquisition Lifecycle and Cross-Functional CFO Roles

M&A Strategy	Target Screening	Due Diligence	Transaction Execution	Integration	Divestiture
Key Activities and Objectives:					
• Verify business strategy. • Define growth objectives. • Compare growth vehicles. • Agree on objectives and process. • Enable M&A strategy.	• Define screening objectives. • Identify screening criteria. • Screen candidates and review results. • Profile candidates and select target. • Initiate contact with targets.	• Conduct commercial due diligence. • Conduct operational (IT, HR, outsourcing, etc.) due diligence. • Determine valuation.	• Define deal structure. • Complete due diligence. • Perform synergy analysis. • Confirm valuation. • Negotiate deal closing and proxy filing.	• Establish PMO. • Plan and manage Day 1 activities. • Plan and manage post-merger integration activities. • Capture synergy.	• Establish PMO. • Plan and manage Day 1. • Plan and manage TSAs. • Plan and manage end-state divestiture activities. • Capture synergy.
Potential Cross-Functional Roles of the CFO and Finance Organization:					
• Establish a risk-based approach to M&A strategy. • Manage the external communication to the street.	• Set financial parameters for target screening. • Screen candidates based on financial metrics.	• Lead the commercial/financial due diligence process. • Develop top-down synergy targets. • Confirm metrics used for valuation.	• Confirm all the financial aspects of the deal: due diligence, valuation, synergy analysis. • Support deal negotiation and proxy filing. • Get involved with approving TSAs.	• Manage Day 1 and post-merger planning and execution for finance. • Measure achievement of synergy targets. • Manage Wall Street communications.	• Manage Day 1 and postdivestiture planning and execution for finance. • Measure achievement of synergy targets. • Manage Wall Street communications.

Source: Bruce Brown, Heith Rothman, Himanshu Gandhi, Adhiraj Dwivedi, David Tate, and Ian Bronson, "M&A Mission Impossible Is Possible: How CFOs Manage Multiple Demands While Getting the Deal Done," 2009, Deloitte Consulting LLP.

and after the transaction close are enabled by the IT organization. Additionally, in most transactions, a very significant portion of the corporate synergy value derives from the IT function. Without close cooperation and joint planning, it can be very easy for both organizations to make incorrect assumptions that can have significant impacts on milestone timing, cause significant delays in synergy attainment, or even erode anticipated deal benefits. An example of this is when an organization makes assumptions about how quickly it will be able to migrate from multiple enterprise systems to one central enterprise resource planning (ERP) system. The finance organization quantifies all of the projected synergies that could be generated from having only one ERP system. These projections are included in the synergy deal model and communicated to Wall Street as the projected synergies associated with a transaction. The challenge arises when no one validates those assumptions with the IT organization. There have been many cases where those assumptions have proven overly optimistic and the true timeline is two to three times as long. This can result in the organization missing its synergy targets or being forced to look for savings in other areas to make up for the smaller than expected savings. There may be significant consequences to the company's stock price, corporate reputation, and executive leadership if it misses deal synergy expectations.

Leading CFOs are expected to deliver in four key roles: strategist, catalyst, operator, and steward. To succeed in these roles, the CFO must create and maintain a finance function that exceeds stakeholder expectations, achieves desired performance levels, and drives value throughout the organization.[1] These "four faces" are extremely important in the day-to-day management of the finance organization and across the M&A deal lifecycle. See Exhibit 19.2 for the "Four Faces of the CFO Framework."

1. **Strategist.** Provide financial leadership in determining strategic business direction and aligning financial strategies.
2. **Catalyst.** Stimulate behaviors across the organization to achieve strategic and financial objectives.
3. **Operator.** Balance capabilities, costs, and service levels to fulfill the finance organization's responsibilities.
4. **Steward.** Protect and preserve the assets of the organization.

This chapter further describes the four faces in the context of an M&A transaction and the key linkage between the CFO and CIO organizations in driving the transaction to a close while preserving deal value.

EXHIBIT 19.2 Four Faces of the CFO Framework
Source: "Four Faces of the CFO Framework" is a critical framework based on Deloitte's research and discussions with CFOs and other C-suite officers

STRATEGIST FACE

One of the key roles a CFO plays in the organization is that of a strategist. (See Exhibit 19.3.)

In his or her role as a strategist, the CFO is responsible for providing financial leadership in determining the strategic business direction for the company and aligning the business and finance strategy to profitably grow the business. Financial goals include near-term profitability and adherence to the operating budget for the business, shaping the long-range business plan, managing capital investments, and making sure all major initiatives exceed the cost of capital and generate sustainable economic value for the shareholders. In the strategist role, the CFO has three key objectives:

1. Making strategic decisions.
2. Leveraging financial perspective to improve risk awareness.
3. Integrating performance management.

In this context, often the CFO is involved in early-stage discussions as the company is contemplating a transaction, whether it is a merger, an acquisition, divestiture of a noncore business, or internal restructuring in response to a changing market and competitive environment. The CFO has a particular perspective not only in shaping the decision whether to

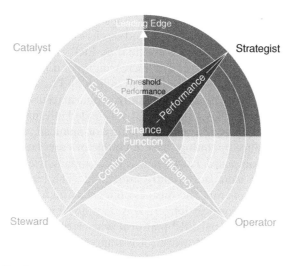

EXHIBIT 19.3 Strategist Face

proceed with the acquisition or restructuring initiative but also in defining the criteria by which such a decision will be made.

In the context of mergers, acquisitions, and restructurings, all of these initiatives typically begin with the strategic vision that the CEO, along with the CFO, the CIO, and other senior leadership team members, outlines for the company in terms of the core purpose and strategy for the organization. In many cases, the overall business strategy for the organization has an aspect of inorganic growth (i.e., growth via acquisitions) or restructuring (i.e., selling of noncore businesses or cost reduction with a focus on improving bottom-line performance). To realize the latter, the CFO, in close coordination with the rest of the C-suite, has to articulate the financial and operational impact of an M&A or restructuring strategy. CFOs play an important role in determining what markets or capabilities present the most attractive opportunities for acquisitions. Alternatively, in the case of restructuring initiatives, they have to recognize the changed market, regulatory, and competitive landscape in which their business operates and define the role and size of the business that would lead to sustainable and profitable growth.

Once the M&A or restructuring strategy has been identified, it is important that CFOs work hand in hand with CIOs and COOs to make sure the technology strategy and operational strategy are aligned with the overall business and M&A strategy. No one can predict the future, but the CFO has a responsibility to plan for it. Both technology and operational initiatives can have a huge impact on strategic flexibility. Some examples include technology architecture choices, consolidation of manufacturing or distribution networks, establishing shared services infrastructure, offshoring or near-shoring of resources, or consolidating ERP platforms. These initiatives, while saving current costs and increasing operational efficiency, may also result in increasing the cost of a transaction and time required to integrate or divest assets. In a recent case study, a pharmaceutical company had implemented a global ERP platform that was hailed internally for its ability to standardize processes, improve the quality of financial and management reporting, and reduce operating costs. A couple of years later, however, the platform integration posed a challenge as the company tried to sell noncore business lines that were now tightly integrated. The integrated platform meant the cost to separate the business lines was higher and the time to complete the transaction was longer. This does not imply the original decision to implement a global ERP platform was erroneous. (In many cases, this is the right decision.) However, it is important to recognize that such decisions should be made while carefully considering long-range plans for the various business lines.

Once the M&A strategy has been finalized, the CFO's focus shifts to identifying attractive acquisition targets that would help to execute the M&A strategy or to looking for potential buyers for noncore business lines. Both of these activities are time-consuming and demand considerable attention. While it is inevitable that investment banks and other advisers would be involved in the process, maintaining objectivity and focus on core M&A strategy is of paramount importance. It is tempting to be distracted with new ideas that are pitched by the banks that may or may not fulfill the objectives of the core M&A strategy. Maintaining discipline and staying the course while taking into account the signals of the marketplace are what makes the CFO's task art as much as science.

Finally, once a potential target or buyer has been identified, the CFO's role morphs into the leader who has the stakeholders' interest squarely in mind throughout the due diligence process. The CFO's role is to facilitate the buy-side or sell-side due diligence process and to identify significant risks that could impact the deal or impact the company after closing. Sell-side due diligence, while increasing costs up front, has a clear benefit in accelerating the overall process and increasing the value of the transaction. Buy-side due diligence has many facets, and the focus and emphasis differ based on the nature of the transaction but typically include the following areas:

- **Commercial diligence** where the target's current and future revenue stream is vetted by understanding the economics of the marketplace, competitors, and the customer base.
- **Operational diligence** where the target's core operations, including manufacturing operations, distribution and logistics, research and

development (R&D), marketing, corporate support functions, and external vendors, are analyzed.

- **Financial and tax diligence** where audited financials are analyzed and supporting work papers investigated to help ensure the reported financial statements reflect the true performance of the business.
- **Legal diligence** where the target's pending litigation, liabilities, and major contracts are analyzed to make sure the financial impact of legal liabilities and future obligations to third parties is fully reflected in the deal models.
- **Technology diligence** where the underlying technology applications and infrastructure for both front-office and back-office functions are evaluated to make sure they meet the needs of the business and that no major investment will be required after close. (See Chapter 5 for a detailed overview of the IT due diligence process.)

Technology diligence is especially important, as it is often the area where there is exposure to integration or divestiture costs and transition timing. In fact, underestimating the complexities and impact of the technology components of M&A can result in a delay in the timing of the deal close. It also requires close coordination between the CIO and the CFO as they jointly assess the financial impact and the degree of difficulty in integrating technology applications and infrastructure. In addition, it is an area where the organization may expect increased synergies, especially if there are opportunities to integrate back-office systems and infrastructure. This is an area where the CFO's role to improve the risk awareness of the organization is key. Whether it is evaluating that adequate disaster recovery processes and business continuity plans are in place or that systems for financial reporting regulatory compliance are meeting the needs of the business and regulators, the CFO is one of the final decision makers.

For the due diligence process to achieve the desired outcome, the CFO and other members of the C-suite have to be closely involved. They need to be active participants in the management meetings with potential bidders or buyers to present the business performance and future prospects both positively and accurately. Throughout the process, they may receive guidance and counsel from multiple external advisers with subject matter expertise in each of the areas outlined earlier. However, the final decision to proceed with the transaction rests squarely with the CFO and the rest of the C-suite, heightening the stakes at this stage of the process. In many cases, these decisions are among the most important decisions they may ever make in their business careers. This is especially true if it is a merger of equals or an acquisition that is larger than their current revenues, where they may be betting the future of the company on the success of the transaction. This is the time when the CFO needs to wear the capital and risk management hat to support the effective execution of the M&A strategy of the company. The CFO needs to draw the line clearly if there is a possibility of the company paying too much for the target or assuming unmanageable risk in the desire to close the deal.

Once the organization has made the collective decision to proceed with the transaction, the responsibility of the CFO as a strategist shifts to maintaining a strong link between deal strategy and deal execution. The CFO's leadership is critical to helping ensure that the strategic, financial, and operational assumptions developed during the due diligence phase are incorporated in the execution of the transaction. In our experience, this is an area where a gap exists in most organizations. In some cases, the execution is transitioned to an entirely new team, often consisting of midlevel managers who do not have the perspective or the benefit of the rationale for the decisions made during the due diligence phase. In the extreme case, they are handed a high-level presentation that lacks much of the detail needed to execute the transaction with little or no involvement from the C-suite other than to attend steering committee meetings. While there is no silver bullet for making sure there is continuity, a few simple steps can provide greater connectivity between the two phases:

- The C-suite stays engaged in achieving the objectives of the transaction after the close of the deal.
- A senior executive who was part of the due diligence team is assigned responsibility for the execution of the transaction.
- Key executives for each of the functional areas are included in the due diligence process and assigned accountability for delivering the financial and operational targets identified during the due diligence phase.
- Progress of the transaction is monitored frequently, and proactive steps are taken to address the impact of changed marked conditions or new facts about that target that invalidate due diligence assumptions.

While preparing for a transaction, in addition to maintaining business-as-usual operations, the CFO may have to create a new organization with a new or different set of short- and long-term goals that affect people, processes, and systems. This implies that the work for the organization in the near term increases, and choosing the right person for the right role is crucial. Many times, outside contractors or consulting firms may be involved to absorb the short-term workload and provide guidance based on their experience of prior transactions. The added challenge for the CFO includes maintaining morale of the organization and culture through the transition.

Ultimately, value for an acquirer is usually dependent on five key results: transaction strategy and management, revenue growth, operating expense savings, asset efficiency, and reduction in cost of capital. Achieving all or most of these results requires the right strategy and high levels of effective management of both day-to-day responsibilities and the transaction process itself. Deal execution in and of itself may not be conceptually difficult, but it requires a strong focus on operations, the right cadence, and the ability to avoid being overwhelmed by the size of the effort.

CATALYST FACE

As a catalyst, the CFO is responsible for stimulating behaviors across the organization to achieve strategic and financial objectives. (See Exhibit 19.4.)

The CFO's main objective is to gain business alignment to effectively identify, evaluate, and execute strategies. The CFO is involved in setting the strategic and financial goals and has responsibility for monitoring and reporting on the attainment of these financial goals. This is particularly important in M&A-related activity, as it is likely to have a large impact on the organization's financial and strategic goals.

The primary focus area is the development, tracking, and reporting of the M&A synergy targets. The CFO is responsible for setting the financial goals against which the success or failure of the transaction will be measured. Typically, when a deal is publicly announced, there is a stated goal of the projected amount of revenue and cost synergies that are expected as a result of the transaction. Financial analysts take these projections into account as they assess the potential benefits of the transaction and incorporate the benefits into their financial models. There can be a direct impact on the stock price if the deal is perceived to be a poor strategic fit or if the financial

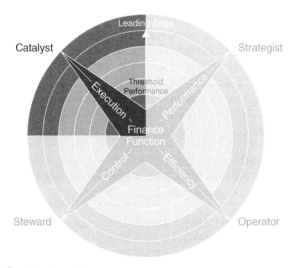

EXHIBIT 19.4 Catalyst Face

projections seem unreasonable or are not provided. (See Chapter 7 for a detailed discussion of synergies.)

The CFO is generally involved in setting synergy targets, which are a direct output of the financial and operational due diligence process. Given the limited timeframe and small number of people involved in the process, the initial synergy analysis tends to be a top-down analysis. There should be initial synergy targets established for each corporate and functional area. The IT function tends to be a significant portion of the overall synergies and can influence how quickly many of the other functional synergy benefits can be achieved. It is extremely important that someone in the IT organization is part of the initial due diligence process and helps to validate the reasonableness and the timing associated with synergies. To be conservative, organizations may deliberately set an internal synergy target that is 20 to 30 percent higher than what is publicly announced and internally hold their teams accountable to achieve the higher number. That way, the CFO is reporting "good news" to Wall Street when the company exceeds the estimated synergy targets.

Once the deal is announced, there should be a more thorough exercise during the integration planning process to conduct a bottom-up analysis to tie the overall high-level functional synergies targets with individual projects and the cost to achieve them. To be able to identify and track synergies as specific projects with owners, cost to achieve and timing make up an important component of the planning process. This is also a valuable tool to hold synergy project owners accountable to attain the synergies. It is critical that cross-functional dependencies are identified and agreed to during this process. Otherwise, functional teams might make incorrect assumptions about the ability and speed with which another function might be able to support their synergy projects. The IT organization is a key enabler for a number of functions to achieve their synergy targets, particularly finance. For example, the finance organization may be considering a head-count reduction based on the assumption that financial systems will be consolidated. The IT organization may have a much longer road map for financial systems consolidation that would impact the finance synergy project. If the two organizations plan together, they can jointly make a decision on whether the head-count synergy project needs to be modified or extended or whether the IT organization can prioritize the systems consolidation earlier.

In order to effectively track and report on synergies, there are four major challenges CFOs should address:[2]

1. Isolating performance improvements.
2. Factoring costs to achieve.
3. Aligning incentives with target attainment.
4. Developing reliable tracking systems.

Isolating Performance Improvements

Accurately isolating performance metrics during an M&A transaction can be challenging, as two businesses likely have different ways to account for costs and to track performance improvement. Examples of this can be how firms recognize revenue or what costs are included in cost of goods sold.

Establishing a baseline across the two companies involved in an acquisition so there is a true comparison where future performance can be measured is a means to overcome this challenge. This baseline can be benchmarked against the rest of the industry and should be developed before synergy targets are provided to functional teams. As discussed earlier, care should be taken to understand and isolate cross-functional dependencies and synergies.

Factoring Costs to Achieve

It can be very difficult to accurately estimate the true integration costs required to capture the synergies. Often, there are legal or regulatory restrictions that prevent the sharing of information prior to close that would allow for a better estimation of costs.

Establishing clean teams and clean rooms is one way that companies deal with the legal restrictions on the sharing of competitively sensitive data prior to close. Clean teams are typically made up of dedicated team members from both companies or external advisers, and are required to hold all information in close confidence. Hence, the team can receive competitively sensitive information from both companies, perform analysis, and create recommendations before traditional employees are legally permitted to do so. This usually impacts the most critical areas of the deal success. The commercial function is an example of an area where clean teams are often used due to the highly sensitive nature of the information and criticality of addressing commercial issues before deal close. One of the reasons companies rely heavily on external advisers to work in clean teams is to avoid the legal complexities in the case of employees should the transaction fall through for some reason.

Aligning Incentives with Target Attainment

Sometimes the team that established the synergy targets is different from the team that is responsible for implementing them. In many cases, this causes programmatic failure in aligning the proper incentives so that everyone has a vested interest in synergy attainment. Furthermore, many times synergy target and operating budgets are kept separate; there is no linkage between them, making it impossible to hold executives accountable for deal performance.

At the beginning of the transaction, management should establish an incentive and accountability program for everyone involved in the setting and attainment of synergy targets. Specific incentives should be clearly mapped to the attainment of actual synergies, reflect the reasonableness of the initial synergy plans, and be linked to operating budgets.

Developing Reliable Tracking Systems

The ability to achieve and report on synergy attainment is only as good as the tracking systems that are put in place. It is often difficult to use existing financial systems to account for the short-term synergy initiatives, as they tend to get mixed into the ongoing business.

One strategy that is often employed is an off-line tracking mechanism that can augment existing financial systems. This off-line mechanism can provide a real-time view of the progress of the synergy cost attainment by creating integration-specific cost centers where all integration activity is captured.

OPERATOR FACE

During the first four phases of the M&A cycle, the CFO, as operator, should continue to monitor the impact of the potential acquisition on ongoing finance operations while streamlining information requests. (See Exhibit 19.5.)

However, it is during the fifth and final phase of the M&A lifecycle when the CFO's operator role is especially critical.

Implementation of an M&A integration or divestiture almost always creates a significant period of disruption and change to both the acquirer and the target. In this period of change, the CFO as operator must balance the finance organization's key priorities:

- **Immediate**—continuing to deliver the finance organization's operational responsibilities without a reduction in service levels or an increase in risk.
- **Medium term**—helping ensure the strategy, financial, and operational assumptions of the transaction are realized.

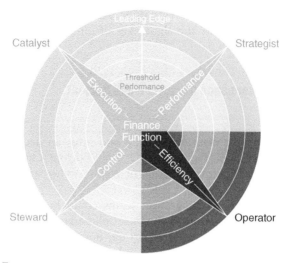

EXHIBIT 19.5 Operator Face

■ **Long term**—developing a finance operating model that can deliver the new company's (NewCo's) long-term vision while retaining current service levels.

M&A integration or divestiture can create the specific opportunity for the transformation of finance operations, as employees are expecting change and, particularly if it's a merger of equals, there may be the funding to allow it. After all, if changes are being made, the organization may as well get it right the first time.

Yet, at the same time, core processes must continue without interruption: customers must be invoiced, cash collected, vendors paid, planning and budgeting completed, management reporting delivered, and tax returns filed. In addition, transaction success requires that necessary synergy targets are met. The burden to implement and track cross-functionally often sits with the finance organization. Thus, M&A implementation can equally result in declining service levels, burnt-out midlevel management, and misaligned projects within the finance function and cross-functionally. Similar to the CIO, the CFO must keep the lights on throughout the integration, as both have critical and interlinked roles in facilitating business-as-usual operations.

As a strong operator, the CFO will engage the finance organization to make the most of this period of change instead of spending their time managing crises and putting out fires. In order to effectively deliver the immediate, medium-term, and long-term priorities, the CFO must demonstrate the ability to leverage system capabilities, implement a strong program management structure, and apply problem-solving skills. The following guiding principles will help the CFO navigate the challenges of integration and leverage the opportunity for change.

Define a Clear Governance Structure and Recruit the Right Team

To manage competing priorities during and after an acquisition and to address integration challenges, the CFO should define a governance structure that clearly delineates the scope of responsibility and appoint work stream leaders.

For example, finance integration teams could be divided into seven clear work streams: tax, treasury, financial planning and analysis (FP&A), close consolidation and external reporting, internal and external compliance, financial transaction processes, and operating model design. As the two businesses were most likely structured differently, it is also important to define the scope of each of the work streams. Creating a clear governance structure that assigns clear ownership and responsibilities reduces the chances of priorities slipping between the gaps, and creates a clear path for decision making within the finance organization. Further, by creating a reasonable division of labor among finance staff members, the CFO is more likely to maintain enthusiasm and acceptance of change.

The governance model should identify interdependencies both within the finance organization and cross-functionally. Of particular importance is making sure that finance system leadership has a seat at the table within this governance structure. Before finalizing the finance governance structure, the CFO should consult with the CIO and appoint appropriate IT leads and counterparts for the finance team leads. Setting regular checkpoints between the appointed leads, including the CIO's team, facilitates consistent alignment of priorities and effective communication of decisions, and monitors the impact of integration projects on business-as-usual operations.

Over time, the internal team will gain experience and M&A-relevant skills, which can lead to increased speed, flexibility, and commitment to the deal process. The development of the team's capabilities and knowledge transfer for future deals can be accelerated by fully documenting key tasks during an M&A transaction.

Adopt a Phased Approach

With so many potential objectives, the CFO should stress to the team that phased implementation is acceptable. The CFO should set realistic goals for the finance organization and communicate them clearly, both to the finance work stream leads and to the CIO. Working with the work stream and IT leadership, the CFO can define a set of projects to be executed over time to meet these objectives. (See Exhibit 19.6 for commonly followed phases.)

Prioritization of goals and the resulting projects reduces the potential to overload key leaders in the organization, and balances the priorities of sound business-as-usual operations and longer-term achievement of finance transformation.

As seen in this example, alignment with the CIO's vision for each of these phases is critical to success, and the CIO should be instrumental in helping set priorities.

Once provided with clearly prioritized objectives and a list of projects such as that set out above, the finance leadership team can work to define a road map to achieve these goals without interrupting business continuity.

Actively Manage the Message and Structure

While the CFO can provide strategic direction, implementing a clear governance structure and a phased approach is going to fall on nonexecutive management. Managers will already be struggling to deliver other special projects alongside their day-to-day finance transactional responsibilities. On top of this, integration creates significant uncertainty regarding the employees' future position in the organization. Publicly announced synergy targets without an understanding of internal integration strategy will create a climate of discontent and will distract from the overall positive growth story generated by the transaction.

The CFO should develop a communications plan and, within the proposed governance structure, create pathways to allow management to receive timely, informative answers to their questions. The communications plan could be initiated by a CFO road show to introduce the governance structure and finance objectives to finance employees. By incorporating key members of the acquired business unit into the transition plans, the CFO will also facilitate more efficient communication. Further, these key members will help assimilate their coworkers into the new organization and overcome cultural hurdles.

Finally, a clear cross-functional communication path can help ensure that the demands on management are prioritized and streamlined. This is particularly relevant in global M&A transactions, where local finance leadership tends to be overloaded with data requests and support roles in critical cross-functional integration projects. In these situations, a streamlined communication path between the CFO and the CIO and their respective integration leadership teams can help streamline these requests and

EXHIBIT 19.6   Example of a Phased Approach with Illustrative Priorities and Projects

	Phase 1 Priorities and Projects	Phase 2 Priorities and Projects	Phase 3 Priorities and Projects
Treasury	Coordinate with HR, A/P, and A/R on bank accounts requirements. Plan and execute foreign exchange hedges for significant exposures associated with acquisition.	Define unified risk management philosophy and tolerances in policy. Define banking strategy and preferred partners. Refine cash mobilization and pooling. Undertake technology gap analysis to assess short-term and long-term debt, cash management, and hedging requirements.	Unified banking platform. Consistency in hedging practice and statistical approaches to assessing hedge effectiveness. Implementation of unified treasury system.
Tax	Complete preclose tax opportunities and identify postclose tax-planning integration activities. Manage acquired asset-related tax costs.	Foreign credit tax planning. Other tax synergy projects. Legal entity consolidation.	Integrated tax function utilizing same processes. Transfer pricing policy harmonization.
Financial Planning and Analysis (FP&A)	Define a small set of high-level performance metrics for the unified business. Automate a small subset of critical reports that are directly related to the company's key performance indicators.	Unify top-down and bottom-up budgeting and planning process. Define a detailed data architecture with clear path as to how underlying data will be sourced from ERP systems, data warehouses, and reporting systems.	More detailed performance metrics at the functional level. Implemented system for automated reporting, eliminating manual processing.
Close Consolidation and External Reporting	Develop manual process for consolidation and report of acquired entity financials. Align close calendars. Map chart of accounts. Finalize public segment definition.	Accounting policy harmonization. Single systemic process for close and consolidation.	Implemented single automated consolidation system.

EXHIBIT 19.6 (*Continued*)

	Phase 1 Priorities and Projects	Phase 2 Priorities and Projects	Phase 3 Priorities and Projects
Internal and External Compliance	Put aligned signing authority matrix in place. Determine changes to external and internal audit and SOX existing audit processes, if needed.	Harmonization of audit processes and policy harmonization. Harmonization of disclosure committee practices and procedures. Alignment of SOX controls and quarter-end sign-off.	Fully integrated risk assessment process, audit plan, and one common internal audit process leveraging best practices.
Financial Transaction Processes	Develop and implement business-as-usual processes for combined customers.	Standardize procure-to-pay and order-to-cash processes under different ERP systems.	All finance processes processed on single ERP with common interface for customers, vendors, and employees
Operating Model Design	Determine team for merged organization.	Create global and regional finance organization design and transition plan. Finance shared services vision and opportunity assessment. Rationalize finance organization.	Implemented shared services vision and centers of excellence that can scale appropriately to meet organization growth requirements. Transparent and credible performance evaluation system.

appropriately allocate work, helping to alleviate some of this added pressure on local finance directors.

Maintain the Momentum

Following the rush to reach Day 1, it is not unusual that the organization loses track of both medium-term synergy and operational targets and fails to act on the opportunity for long-term transformation. The CFO, as an effective operator, must also maintain the momentum as the combined organization moves forward.

The CFO must track and openly report overall measurement realization of synergy targets and progress toward merger goals. To effectively track these targets and goals, the CFO must work closely with the CIO to make sure there is a data management process in place that allows the CFO to easily pull and report key metrics. Further, to reinforce the importance of performance and accountability, the CFO should also set key performance indicators and link synergy realization and performance improvement achievements to individual compensation and incentive programs.

Having effectively stimulated change and set the right strategy, acquisition success will also depend on the CFO being an effective operator. The CFO must turn the operational integration challenges into an opportunity for improving the effectiveness of the finance organization and delivering on the integration goals without sacrificing efficiency and service level. Evaluating alternatives and timing for the implementation of an effective and efficient operating model is central to realizing long-term synergies and enhanced service levels.

A sophisticated system solution is critical to all elements of the finance organization and will feature heavily in the finance organization's integration plans. The CFO must work hand in hand with the CIO in defining an aligned governance structure and in setting and communicating phased integration priorities.

STEWARD FACE

The fourth and final role a CFO plays in the organization is that of a steward. (See Exhibit 19.7.)

In this role, the CFO is responsible for protecting and preserving the critical assets of the organization and accurately reporting on financial position and operations to internal and external stakeholders. In a typical M&A transaction lifecycle, the steward role increases as the deal progresses through transaction execution, and peaks in integration or divestiture phase. In a short time period, CFOs and other finance executives have to make important decisions in order to:

- Enforce organization compliance with financial reporting and control requirements at deal close and through the ongoing integration.
- Manage business complexity while minimizing risk as the business executes on its strategies and integration or divestiture initiatives.
- Facilitate adequate assessment and mitigation of risk, as well as compliance with applicable regulatory or other legal requirements as a newly combined organization.

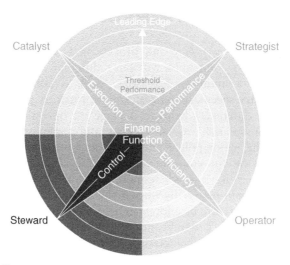

Catalyst • Strategist • Steward • Operator • Leading Edge • Threshold Performance • Execution • Performance • Control • Efficiency • Finance Function

EXHIBIT 19.7 Steward Face

Making sure there are adequate risk assessment and control requires collaboration between CFO and CIO organizations early in the deal lifecycle. In most deals, the acquirer and the target operate under a number of different legacy ERP or other systems. Oftentimes, specialized systems and tools exist in functional silos or business units. The CIO organization will be an invaluable partner to reduce the risk of misreported financial and operational results of the newly combined company.

One of the most challenging tasks of a steward role is the first financial close after Day 1. CFOs are under pressure to get it done fast while providing sufficient controls to maintain an adequate level of information quality, accuracy, and data integrity. Deep IT systems knowledge and accounting expertise are equally instrumental in achieving this objective. From our experience, a joint IT and finance controllership task force is one of the best practices that can lead to a first financial close that achieves the expected value. Closing the books is just part of the equation. The CFO's organization must efficiently close the books, while providing the necessary financial reporting to provide visibility into financial and operational metrics required to manage the business. The cross-functional collaboration helps balance the short-term and long-term goals of a steward. CFOs will have to attack three key areas:[3]

1. Harmonizing accounting policy and process
2. Integrating financial data
3. Enabling the consolidation

Harmonizing Accounting Policy and Process

Harmonizing accounting policy and process is a necessary step during integration. The two companies will have different accounting policies and processes for a number of reasons, such as company IT system constraints, industry-specific practices, and so forth. A phased approach to harmonize the differences helps to manage the operational complexity while minimizing the risk exposure. First and foremost, the acquirers should identify the major policy differences and prioritize the ones with significant impact on the consolidated financials. For instance, the two companies may have different policies in revenue recognition and inventory valuation, which could materially impact the consolidated financials. The differences should therefore be addressed before the first financial close.

On the other hand, a significant process difference could have little impact to the consolidated financials; however, it may impact operations efficiency, system complexity, or data integrity. Such differences are best assessed in conjunction with the CIO organization, and be considered to determine the go-forward solution in the integration phase. For example, a target in the processed material industry kept the same standard cost for 10 years, while using a specialized tool to report production variances. Although it was different from the acquirer's accounting policy of updating standard cost annually, the consolidated financials were not impacted when the production variances were consolidated to the same cost of goods sold (COGS). The difference was addressed in a systematic way during the ERP rollout.

Integrating Financial Data

The integration of all financial data typically requires a careful mapping of the chart of accounts (COA) from both companies and financial data structures. Some of the difference in data definitions could be attributed to accounting policy variations; thus, it requires policy harmonization. Most of the COA differences involve diligent reconciliation of data definitions at the detailed account level. For example, there is often a disparity in the types of expenses that are classified as COGS versus sales, general, and administrative (SG&A) expenses.

The COA and financial data structure mapping is a relatively simple and less expensive solution to initial financial data integration. However, this can become a roadblock if the only people who actually know what the numbers mean or what the underlying policies and processes are have left the company or been let go as a result of merger. Getting early knowledge of who those critical resources are and having a plan to retain them will be necessary to help keep the risk of misreporting under control. To some people's surprise, in addition to the finance organization, these critical resources often reside in the IT organization as well.

Enabling the Consolidation

There are multiple approaches to consolidating two companies' financial data. In most cases, acquirers choose to support the first-month close differently than their approach to long-term financial consolidation. However, the short-term solution could help achieve longer-term benefits. When choosing a tool to tackle the first close, it's important to consider the company's long-term strategy, because that may affect what you do in the short term. For example, if your company plans to continue growing through multiple acquisitions, you might want to invest in a specialized consolidation tool that is designed to make consolidation of different system platforms easier. However, it may make sense to start the ERP integration as soon as possible if the announced synergy targets were built on a single ERP assumption in the long run. In this case, the existing ERP, along with some manual solutions, is used for consolidation in the short term before moving as fast as possible to an integrated ERP as the long-term solution.

As an important part of the company's overall IT system solution, the CFO needs to closely engage the CIO's organization throughout the journey in evaluating the first-month close plan during the transaction execution phase. This assessment and planning journey will be critical to finalize the company's long-term financial reporting solution and ERP structure and then lead to an achievable synergy target during the bottom-up synergy analysis. Having adequate reporting accessible in an automated platform is a common challenge during an M&A transaction. If not done correctly, companies frequently fly blind until they can invest in the technology solutions required to meet stakeholder reporting requirements. Further, the aligned CFO and CIO approach to the overall IT integration strategy is a key step forward to delivering the large portion of the synergy target, while fulfilling the steward role of maintaining compliance and minimizing risk.

WRAPPING IT UP

Our experience suggests that to effectively perform the "four faces" of the CFO role during an M&A or restructuring process, an increasing level of cross-functional collaboration, especially with the CIO organization, is called for to get the transaction done while preserving deal value.

While the CFO's role requires performing each role of the four faces throughout the M&A lifecycle, there is a significant emphasis on the roles as a strategist and a catalyst during the M&A strategy, target screening, and due diligence phases. As a strategist and a catalyst, it is important that CFOs work hand in hand with CIOs and COOs to make sure the technology and operations strategy is aligned with the overall business and M&A strategy. Technology initiatives, in particular, can have a huge impact on strategic flexibility, as technology architecture choices or consolidating ERP platforms influence the target screening criteria and ultimately the deal value. Therefore, technology diligence is especially important since it is often the area where there is a high amount of exposure to integration or divestiture costs and transition timing. It requires close coordination between the CIO and the CFO as they jointly assess the financial impact and the degree of difficulty in integrating technology applications and infrastructure.

IT is an area where the organization may expect increased synergies, especially if there are opportunities to integrate back-office systems and infrastructures. It is extremely important to make sure IT executives are part of the initial due diligence process and help to validate the reasonableness and the timing associated with the synergies. Consequently, CFOs will generally receive more acceptance and cooperation when it's time to build bottom-up synergy programs and execute the integration initiatives with broader cross-functional collaboration.

The CFO role as an operator and a steward increases as the M&A transaction progresses toward transaction execution and integration or divestiture phases. As an operator and a steward, CFOs should help ensure that the strategy, financial, and operational assumptions of the transaction are realized while limiting, controlling, and monitoring risk and facilitating compliance. To manage competing priorities during and after an acquisition and to address integration challenges, a governance structure is one of the best practices to promote collaboration among the midlevel managers of both the CFO and CIO organizations. Of particular importance is making sure financial systems representatives have a seat at the table within this governance structure. (See Chapters 4 and 23 for a discussion of IT governance during the integration process.)

With the right governance in place, a CFO will be able to perform as the master operator to set and communicate phased integration priorities. This approach reduces the potential to overload key leaders in the organization and lessens the risk of transaction and finance transformation priorities significantly impacting business-as-usual operations. Month-end closing is a key function where the right governance structure will play an important role in the transaction's success. The different accounting policies and processes, in addition to the segregated and often incompatible financial data structures, make the first-month close one of the most challenging tasks. CFOs are under pressure to get it done fast while providing sufficient controls to maintain an adequate level of information quality, accuracy, and data integrity. A joint IT and finance planning task force is one of the best practices to enable a first financial close that achieves the expected value, because the cross-functional collaboration helps balance the short-term and long-term goals of a CFO in safeguarding the financial assets and facilitating compliance.

Ultimately, acquirer value is usually dependent on five key results: transaction strategy and management, revenue growth, operating expense savings, asset efficiency, and reduction in cost of capital. Doing these well requires the right strategy and high levels of effective management of both day-to-day responsibilities and the transaction process itself. Deal execution in and of itself may not be conceptually difficult, but it requires a strong focus on cross-functional collaboration and operations, the right cadence, as well as the balanced effect to control and manage risk.

Successful M&A transactions increasingly rely on the ability to screen the right target; however, more importantly, the ability to effectively integrate the two businesses with the right synergy target is critical to success. For example, in the case of a single ERP system synergy target, the acquirer could avoid having severe impacts on milestone timing, keep from encountering significant delays in synergy attainment, and reduce the possibility of eroding anticipated deal benefits.

With the importance of information access on the rise, the need for stronger collaboration between CFOs and CIOs is critical throughout the M&A lifecycle. Our experience has demonstrated that the lack of IT input to define the M&A strategy and due diligence has a domino effect on the integration phase and ultimately may not deliver the synergy target. Engaging the CIO organization during the early stages is crucial to the M&A deal's success. Companies are catching on that a stronger union is needed as corporate executive structures shift, with more CIOs reporting to CFOs.[4] Start the conversation and invite your CIO to lunch today!

Notes

1. "Four Faces of the CFO Framework" is a critical framework based on Deloitte's research and discussions with CFOs and other C-suite officers.
2. Jim Kissel, Kevin Charles, and Ollie McCoy, "Synergy Hunt: Meeting the Challenge of Tracking and Reporting Synergies," Deloitte LLP.
3. Trevear Thomas, Miles Ewing, Patricia Kloch, and Mayci Cheng, "Financial Consolidation After a Merger: Choosing the Right Approach for the Job," "Deloitte Consulting LLP."
4. "CFO Signals Survey," U.S. CFO Program, 1Q2011, Deloitte LLP.

CHAPTER 20

Managing the People Side of IT M&A

Tammie Potvin
Don Miller
Suseela Kadiyala
Michael Proppe
Sarah Hindley
Laurel Vickers

During a merger or acquisition, attending to IT professionals is one of your highest priorities. There will be a lot to think about: managing anxiety, keeping people motivated and productive during the transition period, and retaining key talent. As a leader, you'll need to be quick and decisive to stay ahead of things. Our experience indicates that, for planning purposes, it is critical to focus on the following four priorities:

1. **The M&A announcement and mitigating the rumor mill**—building and executing a strategic, meaningful communication plan.
2. **The future-state IT organization**—defining a new IT organization and operating model that align with the new company's objectives and strategic direction.
3. **IT skill sets**—taking a clear look at the skills and talent you have, as well as what you will need for longer-term success. What talent decisions will you make to realize M&A objectives and synergy targets in the IT department?
4. **Effective workforce transition**—creating lasting change by helping IT professionals understand and adapt to the integrated company's direction and associated new ways of working.

This chapter describes these four priorities and provides some considerations and guidance on each. It's not easy helping people through the aftermath of a merger or an acquisition, and your leadership will be tested. Having and executing specific, detailed plans for employee communication, organizational design, talent management, and workforce transition can help smooth the road ahead.

KEY PRIORITY: COMMUNICATING FOR IMPACT

As soon as the transaction is announced, IT professionals from both organizations will become hungry for information. Questions will surface immediately:

- What does this mean for me?
- Will I have a job? Will it change significantly? Will I have to learn a new system (and will I be able to keep up)? Will I have a new boss?
- Will I like working for this new company? Who are they, anyway? What's their culture like?
- Will my compensation and benefits change?

In the absence of a clear channel for communications where people receive regular updates from their leaders, the rumor mill will kick into full gear. IT professionals will search the web, blogs, Twitter, and many other networks to learn what they can about the other organization. As a leader, you can help control rumors and the panic they create by planning for and delivering targeted, open, and honest communications. Spending time with employees to address their fears and concerns is your first priority during a merger (even if that means telling them you don't have all the answers yet, but are working on them). You'll need to have a plan to clearly communicate what you know about the systems and architecture of the acquiring organization and that the decisions about those systems and the architecture will be carefully thought through before and *if* any changes are made.

The overall merger integration schedule will, in part, dictate your IT communications timeline; you will have to align your plans with the enterprise-level road map and key merger milestones. Additionally, the enterprise-level integration team may provide some general communication guidelines, templates, coaching, and content that will be useful in building your IT communication plan and delivering effective messages. If the team doesn't provide you with a communication planning template, consider using a simple spreadsheet (see Exhibit 20.1), organized around specific

Communication Activity	Target Delivery Date	Content Key Messages	IT Leadership	IT Integration Leads	IT Integration Teams	Infrastructure	E-Business	Technology Teams	Architecture	Business Services	Help Desk	Analytics	Channel	Sender	Comments Feedback
							Audience								
Day 1 Announcement Preview		Day 1 messages Managing change Acquiring company details	X	X									Face-to-face meeting	CIO	Update town hall deck based on feedback.
Day 1 Announcement		Deal details, including: * Rationale * Benefits * Integration team structure /charter * What to expect * Acquiring company details	X	X	X	X	X	X	X	X	X	X	Town hall	CIO	
FAQs		Answers to common merger questions	X	X	X	X	X	X	X	X	X	X	IT intranet	IT integration leads	
Acronym List		Cheat sheet with IT acronyms from acquired and acquiring companies	X	X	X	X	X	X	X	X	X	X	E-mail	IT supervisors	

EXHIBIT 20.1 Sample Communication Plan

Source: Deloitte Mergers & Acquisitions Communications Methodology, 2013

merger phases (preannouncement, Day 0, preclose, and Day 1), and including columns for:

- Target audience
- Key message
- Content owner/developer/reviewer
- Available source documents
- Sender
- Vehicle
- Target delivery date
- Assessment/feedback

Having a specific plan for what will be communicated and when can help you and your IT leadership team proactively mitigate rumors, minimize speculation, build trust, and possibly even minimize attrition.

MERGER STAGES

Preannouncement

Due to confidentiality constraints, you will likely be limited on communications prior to the deal being announced. For the IT department, your efforts at this stage should focus on building the detailed communication plan (described previously) so that you are ready for announcement.

Extensive planning and preparation will enable a smooth announcement and transition communication and limit rumors. As you complete an initial draft of your IT communication plan, think about all IT groups, their different communication needs, the best channels for reaching them, and ways to align your messages with overall integration goals. So how do you get started?

- Make a list of all IT groups (e.g., infrastructure team, help desk, and business intelligence). Who will require special attention, such as those who may be supporting outdated systems? Document anticipated communication needs.
- Identify who will own the IT communication plan. A dedicated person who is well networked and has his or her ear to the ground will be invaluable for helping to make sure that communications are targeted and relevant. Managing the communication plan may be a pretty big job—you may have to dedicate this person full-time through the transition period.

- Include feedback channels in your plan. How will you periodically take the pulse of employees to learn their reactions and concerns and find out if your communications are effective?
- Validate that your IT communication plan aligns with the enterprise-level integration communication strategy and plan. And clarify with the legal department what can be communicated during each phase of the transaction.

Day 0

Day 0, also known as announcement day, is the beginning of the journey for all employees. Providing your IT team with transparent, honest information will set the stage for all future integration communications. Prepare IT leaders and make sure they are visible immediately after the announcement. Provide leaders with guidelines on ways to work with their teams in the days following the announcement. For example, arm them with an elevator speech about the merger, answers to anticipated employee questions, and common talking points about what the IT leadership team is doing to plan and manage the integration.

Promptly deliver the message that a clear integration plan will be developed. If possible, identify and announce IT integration leads and share their charter. Other common Day 0 messages include:

- Communications to IT customers (both internal and external) and vendors. Talking points may be, for example: "IT customers will continue to be supported by their current technical support team, using existing systems and practices and under the terms of their current maintenance agreements. Any changes in the existing approach will be clearly communicated well in advance of the change."
- Background information on the acquiring company, including culture, history, business/industry sector, strategy, and so forth.
- Repetition of enterprise-level integration team messages to reinforce support for the merger, typically delivered at IT subgroup meetings.

Beware of a common Day 0 pitfall: big announcement, followed by radio silence.

Preclose

During the preclose phase, the IT team will be keen for more information. Don't lose announcement momentum. Continue to communicate what is known, and communicate when the unknowns may become known. The IT team will be scanning every message for clues as to their group's future and implications for them personally. Be aware of what you are (and are not) saying with each e-mail, meeting, and presentation, and make sure you are aligned with the enterprise-level communication plan to help ensure that other announcements do not inadvertently cause alarm within the IT team.

Communicate with candor. Employees will be skeptical, and the key to earning their trust and respect is being as up front and honest as possible, which includes admitting "I don't know" at times. Most likely the IT staff's concerns boil down to five key questions every person asks once a deal is publicly announced:

1. Will I have a job? Will my IT skills be needed in the combined organization?
2. Will my pay and benefits change?
3. Whom will I report to?
4. Will my title and status change?
5. Do I need to relocate?

The time between announcement and Day 1 can be difficult to navigate, depending on the specific situation with which you are faced. Exhibit 20.2 provides some general guidance to help address some of the difficult questions or communication challenges that may surface during this merger phase.

Beware of a common preclose pitfall: making premature promises (for example, in answer to the five previous questions) based on one's genuine desire to address people's concerns and reassure them.

Answers are not known, but there is a need to reassure workforce	Answers are leaked to the media and/or employees	Answers are known, but legal restraints prohibit communication to workforce
• Describe the integration planning process designed to answer open questions. • Promote increased leadership visibility; prepare the IT leadership team, and ask them to spend time with their direct reports. • Capture the appropriate tone; don't make promises you can't keep, but be generally positive and upbeat about the deal.	• Ensure a SWAT team is in place. • Implement a contingency communication plan. • Work closely with the enterprise-level integration team to make sure the approach and messaging are aligned.	• Clearly communicate deadlines for when more information will be available. • Keep staff focused on their day-to-day work; reinforce the importance of staying on task while merger integration continues.

EXHIBIT 20.2 Communication Challenges
Source: Deloitte Mergers & Acquisitions Communications Playbook, 2013

Day 1

Day 1 sets the tone for the rest of the integration, so send the right message starting *today*. Remember to honor the past while welcoming the future. Most of the communications on Day 1 will be managed at the enterprise level; however, you should conduct a short IT town hall and celebration (with all senior leaders participating—no exceptions). IT leaders should also plan to walk the floors and spend time with their direct reports, answering any questions they might have.

Post-Day 1

During this time, new IT plans and the operating model will be rolled out, people will be moved into new roles and take on new responsibilities, decisions will be made regarding the termination of certain applications, and some IT professionals may even be transitioned out of the organization. Current projects may be canceled, while new projects and programs are approved.

With a lot of integration activity coming to a head at the same time, you'll need to make sure your communication plan is broad and detailed, leaders have their communication assignments, and you reserve some time in your schedule for unanticipated communication needs (e.g., putting out any fires that may start up). Engage human resources (HR) to help managers and supervisors with transition communication, secure feedback on your communication efforts (are people getting what they need and are you having the intended effect?), and reinforce your expectations around the new IT operating model. Repeat key messages about your vision for the combined IT organization, stay positive, and publicly praise examples of behaviors that support your vision. This is a critical time for the integration, so make sure your IT leadership team is using "us" and "we" as opposed to "them" when referring to the other company's IT resources.

EFFECTIVE M&A COMMUNICATION

The overall goals of the IT communication plan should be to:

- Educate employees on the new company's vision, direction, and goals.
- Educate employees on the combined IT organization's strategic direction, organization structure, operating model, and application architecture.

- Build confidence in IT leadership's vision and plan for the future.
- Answer individuals' questions about where they fit and how they will be impacted.
- Dispel rumors.
- Help accelerate performance by providing practical information on what to do when across all merger phases.
- Build one IT team culture.

Internal IT department communication is frequently given less attention than it deserves during a merger. This can be the result of leaders feeling the need to focus more on decisions around systems and architecture integration rather than on the IT team itself. Sometimes it's that leaders just aren't as comfortable dealing with people issues. But during a merger, these are some of the most urgent and pressing needs.

A clear, strategic communications plan is a relatively straightforward way to support your IT team by providing them with the information they will desperately crave. Even without all the answers, the plan will help IT leaders provide consistent messages that will bring confidence and reassurance.

Don't underestimate the power of communications to retain your IT team members, keep them focused on running the business, and get them excited about the future. This is a great time to show strength in your combined IT leadership team and provide excellent team and customer service by simply communicating clearly and often.

The most important rules of thumb are: know what you can and can't say at certain points in the merger integration process (don't make promises you can't keep), and say *something*—let employees know that you know that they have personal concerns and that you working to address them.

KEY PRIORITY: DEFINING THE FUTURE-STATE IT ORGANIZATION

If your first priority is communicating directly and openly with your IT employees immediately after the merger is announced, your second priority will be to begin to define what the new IT organization will look like and how it will operate (this is, after all, what most employees will be interested in anyway—the new structure and where they fit in it).

Whereas the task of communicating with employees is relatively straightforward (be honest, be visible, and tell them what you know when you know it), the task of integrating information technology processes, resources, and structures can be a bit more complicated. First, acquiring companies often look to gain significant synergies from support organization or back-office functional consolidation, so there will likely be specific expectations to meet with your design. Second, things become even more complex if the acquired company's model is significantly different from your own (e.g., more geographically dispersed, highly decentralized—it might even be difficult *finding* all of the IT resources in some decentralized structures). Third, designing an organization entails detailed assessment and reflection, creating multiple design alternatives to test/vet/validate, discussing and making tough decisions, and transition planning—all of which takes time. And you don't want to rush the design process, since an ill-conceived IT organization can present a variety of problems for the future-state organization, including:

- Unreliable or inadequate IT systems and data management.
- Duplication of IT resources and efforts.
- Inefficiency and high cost of IT capabilities and investments.
- Poor IT service delivery and responsiveness.
- High turnover among IT staff.
- Poor alignment with the strategic priorities of the business.
- Lack of clear IT roles, responsibilities, and accountabilities.

STEPS IN M&A ORGANIZATION DESIGN

Executives are often stymied over where and how to begin a restructuring effort. And while there is no simple formula for building a future-state IT organization in a post-merger environment, it may be helpful to think of the task as having several distinct steps. (See Exhibit 20.3.)

Your HR department may have a similar organizational design methodology and associated templates to use. They may be able to provide you with some guidance and assistance as you progress through these design steps. Additionally, consider working with a trusted group of senior IT advisers (depending on confidentiality requirements and where you are in the merger cycle). They can be beneficial in terms of testing some of your design choices and proposed structure. Although, keep in mind that they may have their own agendas as far as design is concerned; therefore, consider all input and counsel carefully, and leverage the guiding principles you established at the beginning of the redesign effort to finalize decisions.

	Organization Design Step	Description
Step 1	Conduct a current state organization assessment.	• Review due diligence collected on the acquired company. • For both organizations, assess the drivers of IT performance, including things such as spans of control, number of staff in certain positions, clarity of job descriptions, talent/talent gaps, and so on.
Step 2	Define design principles and guidelines.	• Establish decision guidelines such as using the new company's business strategy to drive IT design, willingness to challenge the status quo, and criteria you will use to assess your final IT organizational design.
	Review and Validate	
Step 3	Create the high-level operating model.	• Define all major processes and subprocesses to be performed by IT. • Group processes and subprocesses. • Draw top layers on the organization chart to reflect grouped processes and subprocesses.
Step 4	Create the more detailed organization design.	• Draw the next several layers on the organization chart. • Evaluate workload requirements and associated resource requirements. • Define positions and associated competencies (selection criteria) for future IT leaders and employees. • Work with HR to conduct job grading and banding. • Define proposed governance and cross-functional touch points.
	Review and Validate	
Step 5	Define employee slates and select employees.	• Work with HR to identify all IT employees to be considered for future-state positions. • Work with HR and IT leaders to select employees based on future-state position and skill requirements.

EXHIBIT 20.3 Organization Design—Key Steps
Source: Deloitte Mergers & Acquisition Organization Design & Selection Methodology, 2013

Making Design Decisions

Several enterprise-level decisions will have an impact on your IT design:

- **Level of overall company integration.** What decisions have been made around target level of integration? Will the companies continue as essentially stand-alone operations, or is a high degree of consolidation expected? For instance, if the decision is to adopt and go for the first several months post-merger and then move to a consolidated organization downstream, you may have a little more time to make design decisions. If the new company is looking to consolidate rapidly to achieve specific synergies, you will have to work closely with the enterprise-level integration team to make sure these targets figure into your IT organizational planning.
- **New company's operating model.** As the new company's operating model is defined, you will need to assess resource and skill requirements quickly to support expanded geographies and new markets, increased product and service offerings, streamlined processes, and technologies required to serve external customers. In what ways will IT be required to help the business realize its specific merger-related goals?

To determine an effective IT organization structure and operating model, you should consider everything from the operating model of the new company to the speed and timing of the integration and the new skills needed to support the integrated company's specific processes. Understanding and confirming the enterprise-level integration approach early on in the deal transaction will allow you to shape decisions around structure as well as the IT talent agenda, what skills you need where, and the associated career development and learning requirements to transition smoothly into postclose operations.

IT Design Considerations

As you progress through organizational and operational design steps, there are two major decisions about the IT organization you'll have to make:

1. Centralized or decentralized?
2. In-house or outsourced?

Remember: There is no single right answer to these questions and, in fact, you may end up with a hybrid model. There are pros and cons to each alternative, so carefully consider your objectives and what will work most effectively in the new company as you make your decisions.

Centralized or Decentralized? This question has traditionally been the sole focus of most IT organization redesign efforts. While it is an important concern, it should not be your only one, as this will create a one-dimensional view of structure, minimize your options and creative thinking, and possibly limit your ability to achieve synergy targets.

Centralized IT organizations have all resources owned by the IT organization and are typically grouped by processes, services, or applications. Centralized IT organizations drive process standardization and provide economies of scale, but they must also be ready to prioritize and manage multiple, concurrent business unit requests (which can end up causing friction with and complaints from the business), as well as provide resources with the right level of knowledge to partner effectively with the business.

Decentralized IT organizations are those in which all IT resources are owned by the business. This structure gives the business functionally dedicated resources and drives improved understanding of the business among IT professionals. Potential risks to mitigate within a decentralized organization include multiple IT strategies, plans, and activities as well as increased costs due to duplicate IT resources across the business functions.

A hybrid IT organization blends some IT functions into the business (e.g., application development) while other IT resources are managed centrally (e.g., IT architecture). This structure provides improved speed and responsiveness in IT service delivery. The speed of service delivery is offset by reduced economies and a potential overlap in responsibilities and resources.

In-House or Outsourced? In outsourced organizations, specific IT resources and capabilities are managed by IT, but owned by external service providers. A smaller number of strategic IT resources are owned by the company itself. This structure can leverage economies of scale and allow IT to focus on its core, strategic capabilities. While potentially cost-effective, this structure requires the ability to manage multiple service providers as well as mitigate cultural challenges when directing global resources.

A hot topic with CIOs given the popularity of offshore outsourcing as a leading practice over the past decade, the in-house versus offshore question continues to spark lively debate within IT circles. From due diligence, you should have a comprehensive picture of the acquiree's current vendor contracts and service agreements. This, coupled with the detailed synergy goals of the M&A deal, should inform your decision about whether to keep certain IT processes in-house or to outsource resources. In one technology company merger, the success of the acquired company's largely outsourced IT organization helped influence decisions about the IT organization strategy of the combined company. Leadership decided to keep only core IT capabilities in-house and maintain a significant allocation of outsourced IT service delivery to manage costs.

It's important to reiterate that there is no single right answer to these questions. How you answer them will depend on your new company's strategy, its synergy targets, and what you want to accomplish with the IT function along with the changes you want to make. You may even find yourself defining a desired IT organization and operational hybrid design that takes several years to implement—so you may go through several interim or temporary structures to get to the preferred end state.

Rising to the Challenge

Successful IT organization design, specifically within the context of M&A, requires objectivity and a desire to align structure to strategy, clear guiding principles to drive the effort, input from the enterprise-level integration team, and the support of an experienced HR department. As you embark on your redesign effort, remember these four truths about M&A organization design:

Truth 1: The structure you initially define will likely change over time. Things will evolve. Some governance models may not work the way you intended. Assess how things are working, and be willing to make some tweaks to your initial design.

Truth 2: In the design process, it can take weeks to finalize each layer of the organization. There are few shortcuts to organization design, as you will want to involve leaders in making decisions about their own areas. If the organization is global, it can take even longer to drive design decisions to employees outside the United States (taking into consideration country-specific labor laws). Plan announcements and set expectations accordingly.

Truth 3: Senior leaders leave, especially during a merger. Avoid designing the organization around a specific person, and if you do, have a backup plan that you can mobilize quickly.

Truth 4: The design of the organization is the most tangible and immediate indicator of how the new business will run. Make conscious choices and trade-offs, and know what you are signaling with each decision and announcement. When and how an announcement is made, and by or to whom, can matter as much as what is being announced.

KEY PRIORITY: ASSESSING AND SELECTING IT TALENT

Once you have designed the IT organization and operating model for the new company, it's time to select the right staff to fill roles. And while you and your IT leadership team will have certain people in mind for certain roles, it's still wise to invest the time to do a careful assessment of the IT talent you've acquired in the target organization, as well as a review of people in the acquiring company with whom you may not be as familiar. This will inform your decisions and help ensure you have the necessary talent in the right roles to drive an effective integration and long-term operation.

As you consider skills required to support the new operating model, consider the level of IT maturity in both organizations and what the objectives of each function were prior to the deal. For instance, you may be dealing with one IT organization that is focused on running an efficient cost center to support the enterprise, while the other is more of a strategic adviser and collaborator with the business. Exhibit 20.4 outlines critical IT job families, roles, and emerging trends to consider as you begin making talent decisions.

A note about transition services agreements (TSAs): TSAs define skills, capabilities, systems, and infrastructure required for specific time periods. Special attention should be paid to identifying and securing resources for the length of all TSAs, including any requisite skill needs and gaps. The goal is to be prepared to exit TSAs in a timely fashion. The due diligence team will have captured the high-level scope and scale of applications and tools that require TSAs. Preparing for Day 1, your focus will be on identifying competencies and proficiencies required to maintain applications and tools, which, in turn, will aid in planning for hiring requirements, training plans, retention planning, and knowledge transfer activities. (See Chapters 14 and 16 for additional information on TSAs.)

Job Family	IT Role	IT Trend	Requisite Competencies
Technology Management	• Strategy manager • Technology development manager • Process improvement manager	• Focus on process improvement • The push to be strategic	• Strategic thinking/thought leadership • Business insight
Customer Relationship Management	• Relationship manager	• Collaboration between IT and the business	• Business acumen • Business process knowledge • Consultative planning • Negotiation
Project Management	• Program/portfolio manager • Project manager	• Collaboration between IT and the business	• Business insight • Consultative planning • Continuous improvement
Architect	• Enterprise architect • Business architect • R&D/innovation architect	• Move to service-oriented architectures • The push to be strategic	• Business agile architecture • Business process knowledge • Strategic thinking/thought leadership

EXHIBIT 20.4 Common IT Job Families
Source: Deloitte IT Organization Design Methodology, 2013

Conduct a Broad and Detailed Talent Assessment

Conducting a talent assessment will help you understand current-state capabilities, how they line up against the new operating model, and if any gaps exist in the newly combined IT departments. A detailed talent assessment will help answer these specific questions:

- Where am I today and where do I need to be to support the new company's operating model?
- Do I have any immediate resource shortages?
- Where do I have gaps in specific technical or nontechnical skills?
- Are there opportunities for sharing skills or pooling resources?
- What strategic business adviser skills do I have? Is this more or less than I need?
- What is our current-state ability to perform work that directly aligns with the business's and IT's strategic objectives?

An objective talent assessment will not only help you assign the right people to the right roles, but also provide you with a clear understanding of specific gaps between current IT skills and those that will be required in the new organization. Then, you can make informed decisions about whether gaps can be closed with learning and development programs or if you need to hire externally.

There are three major steps in conducting an assessment (see Exhibit 20.5).

As you consider what core skills to assess, be sure to include both nontechnical skills like project management, vendor management, and relationship management as well as traditional technical skills, such as architecture, systems integration, and operations. This will help you identify candidates for stretch roles and complex programs, determine a potential leadership pool, and begin to think about possible development and succession strategies for key areas within IT.

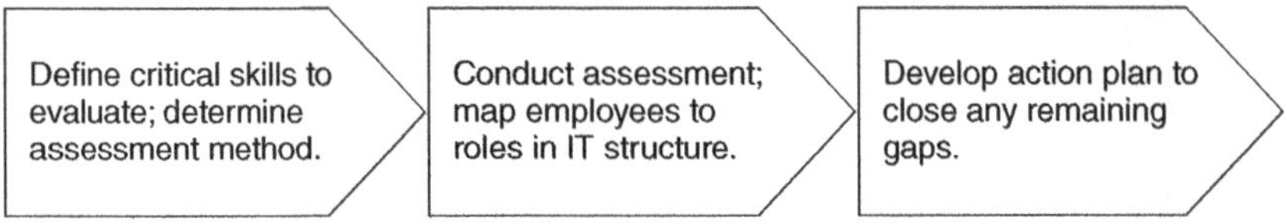

Define critical skills to evaluate; determine assessment method.	Conduct assessment; map employees to roles in IT structure.	Develop action plan to close any remaining gaps.

EXHIBIT 20.5 Skills Assessment Approaches
Source: Deloitte IT Organization Design Methodology, 2013

Assessment Method	Pros	Cons
Self-Rating	• Creates a sense of empowerment. • Inspires greater trust in the process and ownership of the results.	• Allows potential for biased self-promoting responses. • Validity may be limited by the employee's level of self-awareness.
Manager Rating of Subordinate	• Manager has insight into subordinate's skills and work experience. • Provides greater sense of validity as a result of using a more experienced rater.	• Potential for personally biased responses (halo effect, recency, leniency, or harshness). • Manager may not have *full* insight into subordinate's skills and experience (e.g., matrix reporting lines).
Self-Rating and Manager Rating of Subordinate	• Balances empowerment with objectivity. • The ability to identify and explore discrepant ratings can result in a greater sense of understanding and collaboration. • Both parties have greater trust in the process and ownership of the results.	• The process of analyzing and synthesizing dual ratings is more complex than other methods. • Discrepant ratings may be a source of conflict.

EXHIBIT 20.6 Talent Assessment Methods
Source: Deloitte IT Organization Design Methodology, 2013

In terms of planning and conducting the assessment, a variety of methods may be used (see Exhibit 20.6 for examples). If you decide to conduct a self-rating assessment, include clear definitions of the skills and competencies you choose to assess, to help ensure that employees from both organizations use a consistent standard in their self-evaluations.

Whatever method you chose, remember, a talent assessment can cause heightened feelings of anxiety among employees. They know they are being evaluated for roles in the combined IT organization. How you message the assessment is critical. Clearly communicate the reasons for the assessment and how it will be used to define the future IT organization.

Select and Slot IT Professionals

One of the final steps in defining the organization structure and operating model is working with HR to identify the employee slate (see step 5 in Exhibit 20.3)—basically, the list of employees who should be considered for specific jobs and roles in the new structure. Once you have conducted a detailed employee assessment, you will have the data you need to begin selecting and slotting people into positions.

If possible, engage your leadership team in selecting staff for their areas. It will be important for them to have a say in the staffing of their teams, as they possess some of the best functional knowledge and understanding of current gaps and existing talent to support the future state. However, make sure they objectively review staff assessments and available due diligence information, challenge their thinking, make sure they are considering both the short- and long-term needs of the organization, and question them if you think favoritism is being shown. Engage HR for guidance in the selection and slotting process. Not only can HR professionals reinforce good selection principles and practices, but they can also provide legal guidelines and answer questions about other HR matters.

Plan and Execute Retention Strategies

The importance of talent retention cannot be underestimated during an M&A transaction. For IT, retention efforts should focus on critical workforce segments to accommodate the requirements of TSAs, critical enterprise programs, and knowledge transition.

In general, a transformation like this—an M&A—can have a significant impact on employee morale and commitment to the organization. Until announcements are made about new roles and positions, trepidation and uncertainty can cause a mass workforce exit if not managed proactively with tailored communications and strategic talent retention planning. (See Exhibit 20.7.)

1 Identify and Categorize Critical Talent	2 Assess Departure Risk	3 Select and Implement Retention Tools	4 Manage Employee Retention
• Who has important, high-priority skills? • Who has highly marketable skills (high demand and low supply)? • Who would be difficult to replace?	• What market trends are impacting critical workforce segments? • Will we be asking people to relocate? • Will competitors and headhunters be contacting our people?	• What do IT employees care about? • What formal employee retention program can we put in place? • Will we need a formal outplacement program?	• Who will I assign to manage employee retention programs? • How can I stay personally engaged with employees to assist with retention? • How will we measure success of employee retention programs?

EXHIBIT 20.7 Steps in Employee Retention
Source: Deloitte Workforce Retention Methodology, 2013

Again, HR can be a valuable ally in these activities. HR may have planning tools you can leverage for things like assessing turnover risk, and may be able to provide you with support and coaching based on their experience with talent retention strategies.

KEY PRIORITY: MANAGING CHANGE

You have:

- Defined the new company's preferred IT organization structure.
- Identified the IT and managerial skills you will need.
- Determined who within the two organizations will fill certain positions.

You're now ready to begin transitioning people into their new roles. For some, this may mean promotions or career acceleration, but for others, lateral moves or even job loss. You'll have to deal with everything from fear of the unknown to people lobbying for certain technology solutions and jockeying for positions, to anger and resentment, to people feeling disenfranchised and the accompanying loss of productivity.

A skill you will need in order to handle all of this is change management. People will be flustered. No matter how much you communicate, it probably won't be enough. You'll have to have thick skin. You'll need to be a good listener and counselor. It may feel like managing the merger is a full-time job. But there are some fairly straightforward steps you can take to lead people through change.

START WITH YOUR LEADERSHIP TEAM

You will have to get other senior IT leaders aligned around the new company's vision, and help them understand new priorities and possibilities associated with the merger. They will need a fast education on things like the acquiring company's history, background, and structure; products and services; and IT infrastructure and architecture; and the combined company's vision, strategy, integration plans, and operating model.

Starting with your senior team is the right thing to do, as it's important to get this group on board so they can help cascade change to the rest of IT. Starting with senior leaders means first making sure they know where they fit in the new company. Address their concerns over job security. Then, introduce them to their counterparts in the acquiring company (as far as possible within confidentiality constraints). Open lines of communication and get them talking to one another. This will help build relationships and unite the IT leadership team.

One tactic to consider is to conduct an IT leadership summit or working session so that you can get everyone on the same page about:

* The new company's direction and strategy.
* Your vision for the combined IT organization.
* Enterprise-level integration team structure, charter, plans, activities, and timeline (who's who and who's doing what).
* Steps you plan to take in the near term to transition the IT organization.

Getting your senior IT staff together like this can reap many benefits, including soliciting their input on IT vision, operating model, and integration plans (making them feel like part of the solution); building trust and accountability among the leadership team; establishing ground rules for working together during the transition period and beyond; and reaching consensus on change management activities needed for the rest of the IT organization. Coming out of this summit, each leader should meet with his or her direct reports, providing them with the details about what was discussed, next steps, and things they can expect (for example, a regular cadence of communication and merger updates from IT leadership). This sends a positive message to IT employees that the leadership team is working together and is carefully planning to address their concerns.

Follow this larger summit meeting with one-on-one conversations with individual leaders (for example, enterprise program management lead, architecture and strategy lead, infrastructure services lead) where you work together to define integration details for their respective areas. You will likely be asked by the enterprise-level integration team to provide a specific work plan for IT, so there may be parameters (tools, deadlines, status reporting protocol) within which you will need to work. Make sure that you've identified these and shared them with leaders responsible for detailed IT integration planning so that they have all of the appropriate information and coaching they need to do it right the first time (to avoid rework, which will cause frustration with the merger and you). Once initial plans are drafted, get the larger leadership team back together to review, integrate, and validate those plans. Importantly, this will be another opportunity to discuss the people and organizational implications of integration activities (for example, if plans are to sunset certain home-grown systems, what does that mean for IT staff reassignment and/or expectations management with system end users?).

Finally, in terms of dealing with the senior IT leadership team, don't be concerned if you don't have all the answers. That's why you have the team—to help define the broad set of activities needed to fully integrate the IT organization. Make them part of the solution, giving them responsibility and accountability for M&A success (consider defining specific merger-related goals in their performance and development plans if possible). Leaders should set an example for the rest of IT, so don't be shy in asking for their active support.

Speaking of leaders, consider the next layer down—midlevel managers and supervisors—to be some of your most important assets in accomplishing a smooth integration. Since employees take their cues from their immediate supervisors, it's important to get this group on board and up to speed. They should be briefed on topics such as:

- Who the acquiring (or acquired) company is—company background and profile, including vision/mission, products, markets, locations, size, and so on.
- Business case for the merger or acquisition—the "why" behind the deal.
- What will happen in the interim period between announcement and Day 1 and in the first six months of the new company's operations.
- The steps you plan on taking to integrate the IT functions—for example, rationalization of the IT organization structure, reviewing due diligence information, and so forth.
- Your expectations of them in terms of managing day-to-day operations as well as supporting merger-related activities (especially important to them will be knowing who from their teams may be needed for the integration team).
- If/how they will be expected to interact with counterparts from the acquiring company.
- Their role in maintaining employee productivity. What's expected of them to keep people focused on work and to minimize the rumor mill.

Creating manager transition guides or briefing packets—delivered to managers and supervisors in face-to-face sessions—is an effective way to help ensure they understand what's expected of them, what will be happening when, and where to go to get more information should they need it. You should attend these face-to-face sessions to provide your take on the merger and to acknowledge that the transition won't necessarily be easy, but that you have confidence in supervisors' abilities to make the merger a success. After the sessions, consider conducting a brief survey to find out how they were perceived, if they were helpful, and what other information should be covered.

In general, provide a lot of communication directed specifically to the middle-layer IT managers. Give them information and specific materials they can use to keep their employees informed. Provide FAQs and answers for anticipated employee questions. Most important, this group will be able to provide you with insight into employee perceptions and whether your messages and change management activities are effective and having their intended impact. Ask supervisors regularly how their employees are handling the transition. Use this information to make real-time adjustments to your change management plans.

TRANSITION EMPLOYEES

The biggest merger-related task will be preparing employees for new roles and new ways of working.

First, be prepared to have an all-IT town hall at announcement. Again, you should be present to provide any deal details and answer questions. This doesn't necessarily have to be a long session, and at least some of the content will likely be a repetition from an initial companywide town hall organized and delivered by the enterprise-level integration team. However, this first IT meeting will be important in setting the tone for open communication throughout the transition—it demonstrates that IT leaders understand their people's need for information and are committed to doing what it takes to meet that need.

Once decisions have been made about who will fill what roles in the new IT organizational structure, have managers and supervisors meet with their employees one-on-one to communicate personal news and impact. For these meetings, enlist the help of HR. Likely some transition guidelines will have been provided by HR to all functional leaders. If not, ask for them, as there may be labor laws, special merger-related early retirement offers, succession and retention strategies, and the like that they will know about (and you may not unless you ask). HR should be a great ally in employee/workforce transition, as they've most likely done this before—for example, managing through a restructuring and/or layoffs. HR professionals can address the common questions about if or how people's pay might be affected, if health care provider(s) and contributions will change, if employees will be eligible for any new benefits (for example, educational reimbursement), and the paid time-off policies of the new company. Also, they will know what defined programs are in place to help any displaced IT employees with their transition out of the company, such as whether there will be resume-writing support or access to services provided by search and placement firms.

You will also have to plan for specific onboarding, orientation, and training sessions for employees. For example:

- Acquiring company's new employee orientation.
- Day 1 celebrations—these may be planned at the enterprise level, but you should consider if there are special events or things you want to do within IT. This is a great activity to assign to an employee committee with representatives from both the acquired and acquiring companies.
- Mandatory standard training required by the acquiring company (for example, safety, ethics, sexual harassment training).
- Employee readiness sessions that introduce employees to any new processes, policies, procedures, IT team members, and so on.
- New skills development (for example, ERP configuration training) for staff who will be serving in new roles or new areas.

Work with the enterprise-level integration team to determine timing of IT staff training, plan your work and schedules appropriately, and make sure managers, supervisors, and their employees know about training requirements as far in advance as possible.

One final note about employee transitions: One of the hardest things for IT staff is when a special project they have been working on gets canceled. For example, if the acquired company has just started an ERP upgrade, but the acquiring company is running the latest version of a different package, chances are the upgrade project will be terminated rather abruptly. This leaves people on the project without a home, without something to work on. Be as proactive as you can in reviewing any in-progress projects. Which ones will be canceled or temporarily suspended? How many people are working on them? Can they be reassigned? What will you do with those employees, and how will you announce this to them and to other project stakeholders? The important thing is to be prepared to leverage your resources appropriately, communicate openly with them, and keep everyone as productive as possible.

CONSIDER CULTURAL IMPLICATIONS

Finally, when addressing the people side of M&A, there's the question of cultural integration.

- How different are the two companies' cultures? How different are the IT groups? Will they clash?
- Should the two cultures be melded or blended in some way? How does one go about integrating two different cultures?
- If the companies span multiple geographies, will you be dealing with different country cultures as well (for example, offshore technical support teams)?

These are tricky questions, because they force you to answer the larger question, "What is culture, anyway?" *Organizational culture* is defined by Wikipedia (at the time of this book's publication) as:

> *the collective behavior of humans who are part of an organization and the meanings that the people attach to their actions. Culture includes the organization values, visions, norms, working language, systems, symbols, beliefs, and habits. It is also the pattern of such collective behaviors and assumptions that are taught to new organizational members as a way of perceiving, and even thinking and feeling. Organizational culture affects the way people and groups interact with each other, with clients, and with stakeholders.*

As the definition indicates, culture incorporates a lot of things that are rather intangible—hard to pin down or observe directly, such as working norms, and the way people perceive or interpret things. In trying to understand another company's IT culture, you would have to look at things like the mission statement (if there is one), how IT staff interact with one another (for example, how managers communicate with their staffs—formally versus informally? relying on command and control? meetings versus e-mails?), and how new employees are brought on board (for example, assigned a personal mentor and put through a series of prescribed training courses versus given an employee handbook and put to work). So, understanding another's culture isn't necessarily an easy thing. First, to observe cultural indicators personally might take some time since you'd be looking for patterns of behavior. And second, would your observations tell the whole story anyway?

There may be some cultural insights about the acquired company available to you from the due diligence team, although generally the same attention is not given to collecting culture-related due diligence information as is given to financial, market, and technology infrastructure data collection during target screening. That said, ask for whatever culture data exists, and leverage it. There are also culture assessment surveys that an integration consultant could help you conduct. A culture survey may even be planned by the enterprise-level integration team for the entire organization. Culture surveys can help you get to know the other company and pinpoint where there may be challenges as people from the two IT departments begin to interact with one another. As such, they can be a valuable tool in getting to know the other company and targeting integration efforts.

Most important, though, you should consider if there are opportunities to make some long-desired changes (for example, creating a stronger culture of accountability). What would you really like to change about the current IT culture or the way your team currently works or operates? Pick one or two things to focus on, such as service level agreements, working relationships with the business, turning IT into more of a business partner, or instilling more of a service mentality among IT staff.

Focus on these things and really reinforce them. Define your cultural objectives in terms of desired behaviors at all levels. Then, build these into your communications (talk about them every chance you get), your change management plans (ask leaders to reinforce these with their direct reports), and performance management plans for IT staff (set specific, tangible goals at the individual level). Reward and recognize people who exhibit the behaviors you are looking for. In this way you will reinforce the kind of IT culture you want.

Bottom line: Culture does matter. Even though it's somewhat intangible, almost everyone agrees that it's powerful. While you can't change it overnight, a merger can present an opportunity to make some desired changes.

ASSESS INTEGRATION PROGRESS

Monitor how you are doing in terms of integrating your IT department, leaders, and employees. If the enterprise-level integration team doesn't conduct a comprehensive employee readiness survey to measure perceptions and determine integration gaps, conduct one for your IT department. Secure quantitative feedback on change management efforts, the readiness and productivity of your people, and their understanding of new processes, procedures, and priorities. If available, examine objective productivity and performance indicators as well (e.g., percentage of IT projects on plan and on budget, or unplanned turnover). Also, don't overlook qualitative indicators of how things are progressing. Ask for feedback from midlevel managers and supervisors, talk with people from various geographic locations, and take the pulse of IT staff working on the integration. This kind of anecdotal evidence is a good supplement to quantitative data. Focus your assessment on what the enterprise-level integration team is asking for in terms of integration metrics, so that you can report progress appropriately.

Applying an objective, analytical approach will give you insights into your efforts and allow you to make adjustments to create a more precise change management solution. For example, you can identify pockets of resistance and focus your attention and efforts there. Engage your leadership team, as appropriate, to help address specific integration gaps in their areas. This will help solidify any newly appointed leaders in their roles, providing an opportunity for them to build credibility and relationships with their new direct reports.

WRAPPING IT UP

The people side of a merger can be the toughest, because you are dealing with human emotions, and most people just don't like change. Employees are especially wary given the economic downturn of the past several years. They've seen others lose their jobs, and they do not want to be one of the statistics. Your leadership mettle will be tested. And what may have gotten you to the top IT leadership spot (your IT experience and expertise) may not be your most important skill in the wake of an acquisition announcement. Rather, your empathy, ability to make quick decisions, and communication and change management skills will be important now. IT managers and staff will be looking to you to "make things okay." Following these final guidelines might make your job as their leader a little easier:

- Communicate your excitement about what the target company's IT team is bringing to the table. Express your enthusiasm over working with them. Recognize the different capabilities they may have that the acquiring company does not.
- Don't forget about the IT professionals in the acquiring company. While your natural tendency will be to focus on the acquired company's IT employees, remember that the acquiring company's IT professionals will have questions, too. Everyone in a merger wants to know if and how it will impact him or her.
- Begin to define the IT operating model early in the M&A process. Once the operating model for the combined company is defined, identify what changes might be needed by IT to support the future state. Starting early will help in defining your talent agenda—organization design, critical roles, retention plans—and engaging your leadership team for support.
- Leverage any talent due diligence data and information available to you. We've said that sometimes careful people-related due diligence may be lacking (more emphasis is given to financial, market, and technology infrastructure data). If you have minimal due diligence information

on your IT staff, this may be one of the things you get your senior leadership team working on right away, so that you can make informed decisions about the short-term and long-term capabilities or gaps you may have.

- Don't sugarcoat things; be straightforward with people. Tell the IT organization what you know, when you know it. Dragging things out will cause rumors to start and will damage productivity.
- Be accessible, visible, and communicative. Do a lot of walking around. Visit different IT locations (geographies). This will pay great dividends, as it will ease people's fears and build their confidence. Strong leadership will help them to stay focused on their jobs.

Finally, the merger will mean a lot of work for you. You'll have to juggle multiple priorities, including:

- Continuing day-to-day operations.
- Supporting IT integration activities (and this may require a lot of IT staff).
- Managing the transition of the IT organization—making decisions about structure, roles and responsibilities, specific technologies, service-level agreements, budgets, outsourcing contracts, training and skill development, and so forth.

Ask for help if you need it. Fully leverage your HR professionals' expertise. Not only can they help with specific HR-related questions around employee transition, benefits, pay, and the like, but they should also be able to provide you with some coaching on effectively managing change.

CHAPTER 21

Planning for Business Process Changes Impacting Information Technology

Blair Kin

The impact on people working in organizations that merge is a well-documented topic and often a clear indicator for the success or failure of the future combined organization. In this chapter, we do not focus on the affected employee group as a whole, but specifically on how information technology (IT) changes impact people throughout the organization and the importance of planning each step of the technical integration of the two organizations while keeping in mind the resource skill sets needed to implement the change successfully.

Personnel changes at all levels have an impact on the IT landscape. Systems need to be converted and converged into future-state business processes that will support the organization's ongoing needs. Leadership changes at the top will create new priorities and business requirements that will need to be addressed by the IT systems. Changes in the organization's IT support, shared service centers, or operations will also impact how these changes are implemented and adopted. The success of these changes can have a lasting impact on the new organization's ability to achieve the predefined benefits of the merger.

PRE-DAY 1 PLANNING

The leadership team faces a number of critical early decisions that will set the future direction of the combined organization's IT systems. It may seem obvious, but one of the first major decisions is determining who the leadership team will be going forward. Having a clear understanding of who the decision makers are for the various IT systems adds focus to the integration team's efforts. All of these experienced leaders will bring with them expectations of the types of information they will require for making strategic business decisions. Many will have strong preferences on systems that they are familiar with, have a history with, and have an understanding of specific systems' capabilities. Both reporting packages and performance indicators for the organization have the potential of being impacted by the requirements of the new leadership team. As the leadership team sets the future direction of the organization, they will require information or data to make decisions. These information needs create requirements that the IT systems need to support. Leadership preferences play a major role in selecting IT systems. As an example, a major real estate organization selected its human resources (HR) system based entirely on one executive's past experience with a system that did not fit with the larger application suite, and this created costly integration issues for the organization. The system was a leading application for supporting HR functionality; however, with more careful consideration, the organization would have realized that system did not fully meet the organization's requirements.

External market pressure to deliver many of the strategic integration benefits as early as possible weighs heavily on the leadership team. Typical benefits involve market synergies, staff consolidations, moving to shared service models, improved product mix, ability to improve service to an expanded customer base, as well as multiple other areas specific to the merging companies. All of these areas directly link back to IT systems. Leadership will need to set the direction of what the future IT landscape will look like and provide a road map for the organization to follow. This is a critical next step and can be challenging in the midst of clearing other legal or regulatory requirements of the merger.

A clear understanding of the high-level business requirements and priorities for the organization is required to support the decision process. Each member of the leadership team will bring his or her past experiences and future expectations into the decision process. There are areas that are more closely linked to one member of the leadership team than others, and that leader should have added input into the final decision. For example, the CEO is responsible for the overall future direction of the new organization and needs to provide a vision for where the organization is headed, what markets will be key to the company's success, products and services, and overall strategic vision for the organization. The CFO needs to meet the internal and external reporting requirements that align with the organization's vision. The COO needs to have the tools to execute in the markets identified, and the CIO needs to have the IT infrastructure and system capabilities to deliver against all of these requirements. Establishing clear business area owners across the organization's IT landscape and creating an integration team to build the IT road map provide the necessary organizational structure to collect requirements, set priorities, and make decisions quickly for the organization.

The ability to set a clear direction for your core IT systems will provide the next layer of management with the direction they need for planning and addressing potential gaps in functionality as well as infrastructure. Without this road map, decisions will likely be delayed and efforts to consolidate the two organizations can be negatively impacted. This is a time when the best possible decisions need to be made in a timely manner. That is not to say every decision will be perfect, but not making these difficult decisions has the potential to have lasting negative impacts on the integration efforts.

Once the leadership team has set a clear direction, scope and timing of the integration need to be considered. These integrations involve all aspects of people, process, and technology. Setting a clear scope and timing of what areas need addressing immediately is critical. Depending on the match of the two organizations, you may be able to take on more changes in the beginning than other organizations could do. The very nature of merging two organizations creates a rare opportunity to implement the change. People understand that continuing to operate as usual will not realize the benefits of the merger, and processes will need to change to accommodate the integration. This is also a time when there is specific budget set aside to address the technology component of the merger. Having a clear road map, scope, and timing can enable organizations to implement change that would otherwise be much more difficult to achieve.

Regardless of the organization, a critical first step requirement is to close the books at the end of the first month of operations accurately and in a timely fashion. This is a critical first step that the markets will be watching closely to gain a better understanding of how well the two organizations will merge together. All other changes to IT systems will need to be balanced against this critical requirement.

There are options on how to accomplish this initial close most effectively, and these options need to be balanced against the benefits and synergies identified for the merger. An understanding of what functions can be quickly converted and consolidated onto one system is crucial, as well as what other functions will require a longer-term transition. It is important to remember that many times these changes are taking place in an environment where staff is being consolidated across the two organizations, leaving potential knowledge gaps.

Selecting the future financial system is the first priority, linking back to the critical first requirement of closing the books. Making this decision enables the organization to start looking at how to integrate other critical business support systems with the financial system most effectively. Identifying where your financial information will be consolidated and reported from establishes integration requirements for all other systems. It is not uncommon for divisions of the company to remain on their old financial systems, consolidating and reporting numbers to the main financial system for external reporting. The leadership team's ability to clearly make and communicate this decision is the first step in establishing the road map. In addition to selecting the future financial system, other systems such as the human resources system to pay employees or operations systems for managing the order to cash process or collection of revenue also need to be determined as part of laying out the road map.

The road map created as part of the pre-Day 1 planning sets the direction and timing for how the two organizations will merge their IT systems. These priorities set in the road map should be aligned to the benefits identified with the merger. The more detailed set of system requirements will continue to be further defined as the integration team continues their efforts. This road map should provide the integration team with an understanding of the resource needs to accomplish the integration. Having the right team in place can be a major challenge with all the competing priorities resulting from the merger.

DAY 1 INTEGRATION IMPERATIVES

The merging companies' balance sheets and income statements need to be combined, and the process of integrating the subsystems that feed financial information into the ledger needs to be the first to take place. Adjustments to the ledger structure based on the addition of new legal entities also need to take place. Many industries have complicated legal entity structures and may require the addition of new reporting ledgers feeding the U.S. generally accepted accounting principles (GAAP) ledger. This new structure is what the subsystems need to feed in order to facilitate proper reporting. Having the right team in place that understands the capabilities of the subsystems to properly feed the ledger is needed to implement this first system change to reflect the new legal entity structure.

Regardless of the timing and scope of integrating each of the subsystems, there will need to be changes based on rebranding of the newly merged company. Changing the name of the company and the logo needs to be addressed at the system level for all systems that generate information to external parties. Even if one organization is completely absorbed by the other, if the absorbed organization has systems that remain in use, then changes will need to be made for communications from the system to external organizations. The IT staff will need to have a full understanding of what functions will remain in use so the proper changes can be made.

This effort is time-consuming for the IT staff that is already engaged in changes to other complicated post-merger integrations.

The road map with corresponding scope and timeline will set the direction for what systems will be merged on Day 1. New system operating business units will need to be established, linking to the new legal entity reporting structure. Common areas of integration are discussed next.

General Ledger for Reporting

In order to have a consolidated view of both internal and external reporting, several changes need to take place. The additional legal entities have to be established, creating potential new ledger structures, and the existing chart of accounts for each organization will need to be rationalized and consolidated. This exercise may require adding additional granularity to the chart of accounts or rolling up certain areas of the chart to gain consistency across entities for future comparative reporting. These decisions are foundational in nature and impact the changes across the combined entities' subsystems reporting into the ledger. The next step is to actually perform the conversion of point and time chart of account balances and historical ledger data. Beginning balances are a clear requirement for conversion. Decisions need to be made as to the value of the historical information and the associated effort of the conversion. As organizations extend past two years of converted historical data, the value of that data starts to degrade and the ability of the conversion team to properly reflect changes to accounts, business units, and adjustments over time becomes more complicated. Many companies fall into the practice of leveraging their general ledger as a data warehouse, bringing in data that could be analyzed by leveraging other reporting tools. Converting this historical information adds complexity to the general ledger that may not be required, creating delays in the financial reporting process. It is important to keep in mind that the value of different components of this historical information may have more value than others and can be maintained outside the general ledger.

Human Resource Employee Compensation and Benefits

Many organizations have a difficult time addressing the conversion of employee compensation and benefits as part of their Day 1 conversion and, as a result, are left with a large resource-intensive effort to consolidate employees and the associated benefits programs onto one platform. Organizations with union considerations may face additional challenges negotiating new contracts to standardize benefits and policies to facilitate this consolidation. Leveraging the change resulting from the merger may provide an opportunity to address this challenging area to avoid managing multiple human resource systems working with multiple benefits providers. Historical tracking of specific employee data may be required to interface with benefits providers for proper administering of benefits to employees. Regardless of your organization's capabilities to address the challenges of this conversion on Day 1, new account mapping to the general ledger will be required for proper reporting. This integration requires cross-functional resources from finance, human resources, and IT to enable the proper mapping to the general ledger. Changes to employee compensation and benefits as a result of the merger and associated system changes need to be clearly communicated to employees. Small changes in payroll calculations can create variances in total compensation that impact employee confidence at a time when employees are already experiencing extensive change.

Sales Enablement and Revenue Recognition

Sales and revenue recognition is an area where consolidation can be limited by the type of sales or products the two merging organizations provide to their customers. The closer the product offerings of the two organizations, the more opportunity there is for consolidation of these systems. Consolidation requires merging open accounts receivable for the active customer base as well as the setup information for the customer master. This area can require custom billing formats or may involve complexities arising from custom contracts provided to certain customers for pricing or other sales programs. Expansion into new markets, especially internationally, may create additional regulatory reporting requirements that need to be addressed, requiring specialty skill sets in the organization. The historical information in these systems typically supports strategic forecasting and planning activities requiring additional attention for retention. Strategic planning and forecasting groups rely on this information for building trends in support of long-range analysis.

Procurement and Payment Processing

Consolidating procurement and accounts payable functionality on Day 1 can provide big benefits in other areas such as cash management, and can reduce complexity in working with multiple banks and the integration and cost associated with these complexities. Most modern procure-to-pay systems have a great deal of flexibility, addressing the requirements for a broad range of purchases, including services, assets, as well as the full range of commodities. This area also is commonly supported by a shared services center. As part of the merger, this may be an area of targeted head count reduction, requiring this conversion to happen as close to Day 1 as possible to gain the associated benefits. Consolidating vendors into the vendor master and centralizing your vendors into one system are relatively straightforward activities. Adjusting the banking integration to match the centralized payment process may create a few specific requirements for certain industries, but also tends to be a relatively straightforward activity. Open purchase orders in the eliminated system can be run down over time, reducing overall effort for this consolidation.

Additional Financial System Functions

We have focused on reporting, human resources, sales, and the procurement cycle. These are areas that are common to almost all organizations. Additional IT system areas will vary for different industries, but a few common ones are fixed assets, project costing, treasury, manufacturing, and inventory, as well as forecasting and planning functions. Depending on the organization, some of these areas may require conversion and consolidation as close to Day 1 as possible. Understanding the scope of the effort is important in order to estimate the level of resource assistance you need from both your business users and your IT staff.

One thing is clear—organizations need to balance their Day 1 activities against available resources and technical skill sets to accomplish these activities within the timeframe allotted. Taking advantage of this window of opportunity early enables the organization to adopt and adjust to new business processes sooner, as well as make adjustments to head count in alignment with the overall business case benefits of the merger. The more you complete early on, the sooner these benefits can be realized for the organization. Typically, organizations have between 60 and 120 days to plan and execute this change. Taking on too much change or poorly handling the Day 1 conversion can lead to errors that can be very time-consuming to correct. If errors start to build, either from errors in performing the conversion or errors resulting from end users working in new systems, the effort to recover can be further complicated by the loss of institutional knowledge resulting from potential staff reductions.

Once the organization has determined what functions will be integrated on Day 1, it needs a clear project plan to document the activities and assign tasks to resources across the IT staff and functional user group. There are multiple areas that need to be accounted for to implement the plan. The technical components are driven by the IT group; functional users need to be dedicated to each area of the plan to clarify business requirements and perform validations as systems are integrated and data are converted, and end users of the systems need to be ready to perform their jobs leveraging the new system. Having a project plan that details each of these resource requirements will enable the organization to compare skill sets of the team against the tasks. There may be gaps in skill sets that need to be addressed. Poorly implementing this change can create downstream impacts that can be time-consuming to recover from and can impact the accuracy of reporting information.

LONG-TERM INTEGRATION REQUIREMENTS

Adjusting to the longer-term business process changes and systems integration can take years to accomplish fully. The benefit of consolidating business processes and the supporting technology provides consistency across the organization and improved transparency, enabling better decision making for the organization. Reporting errors or variances that are not discovered until late in the close process during the validation of consolidated numbers requires going back into the subsystems or regions for explanation. To the extent corrections need to be made in the subsystem, these transactions will have to be posted to the ledger, requiring previously completed steps in the close process to be redone. This adds not only time to the close process, but also uncertainty. Being able to track and address variances midmonth enables the organization to respond quickly and make adjustments. This avoids month-end surprises to which the organization needs to respond while working within a tight timeframe. Standardizing the business process and systems helps avoid this organizational risk.

Standardizing business processes across the organization enables it to consolidate systems as well as move toward a more cost-effective shared services organizational model. Additional benefits are realized through the consistency of reporting, enabling comparative analysis. The IT infrastructure savings can also be significant and provide improved overall IT support for end users of the systems.

Business Case

Having completed the road map early on with a high-level scope and timeline for the integration as well as addressing the Day 1 critical integrations, it is time to build a clear business case to support and detail out the remainder of the integration effort. The business case enables the organization to maintain its priorities and make trade-offs with a larger view of the organization's strategic plan and vision for the future. Part of the business case is identifying benefits with a clear return on investment to the organization. Having the organization's leadership team stabilized and the direct reports to leadership in place is important for setting a clear direction within the business case. Once these are set, major changes will defeat the intended purpose of the business case to provide focus to the integration team's effort. In addition to identifying the benefits for the organization, the business case needs to also include how to track the benefits, because without a process to measure benefits the organization can lose focus on achieving the stated benefits.

Business Requirements

Detailed business requirements for each area of the integration provide the integration team with the guidelines to keep the team focused on what the organization really wants to achieve. Having thousands of requirements should not be the goal. Instead, stay focused on the core or high-level requirements that will help define design and act more as guiding principles that the integration team can refer back to and work the design within these guiding principles. This gives the team flexibility in arriving at solutions for the design that most effectively accomplish the integration objectives. As any long-term project works its way through the typical phases of a project, it is common for people to think that requirements are changing. This should not be the case. Your business requirements or objectives should remain the same and tie back into your business case and benefits. What does frequently happen is that as a company moves through the phases of a project, new types of requirements are added to provide additional detail. For example, as you work through the detailed design you may add specific design requirements for how the actual integration of a sales entry screen should look to facilitate ease of use for the organization's end users. These detailed requirements are important for how the business process is automated within a system, but should not be confused with defining the business requirements for the organization. They are lower-level design requirements that help direct your teams for the building and implementation of the new business process.

Design

With a clear plan and set of objectives laid out for the integration team and buy-in from the organization as a whole, the team is ready to start the process of design for each remaining integration area. The design phase solves how the business process will change and function going forward. Gaps in the solution are addressed, and alternatives are worked to arrive at an improved business process that meets the business requirements previously defined.

From an operations point of view, this is the time to look at the business processes the organization was not able to address as part of the Day 1 conversion and integration. These are areas that may go to the core of your business capabilities—for example, how you manufacture products or improve the services you are able to provide your customers. These are applications that support the generation of revenue for your organization. These systems tend to be complex in nature and many times specialized for an industry. They can be important to sales enablement and generate data for strategic planning and forecasting.

It is important to understand where you are heading as an organization to build the most effective or required business process in these areas. Having the right team in place from both an IT and a business standpoint that can work within the requirements and build to the future is important for the success of the new systems. If continued acquisition is a strategy for future growth of your organization, building with an eye on the future is important. Having a repeatable and scalable business process becomes more important than delivering specialized functionality with more detailed data capture. These are trade-offs the organization needs to make when looking toward the future. There is a cost to data, and that cost needs to be balanced against ease of use of the application.

If growth through acquisition is part of the long-term plan, sticking with industry standard applications provides the opportunity to merge with other organizations that are already running on the same IT platform. This provides synergies in merging with one of those organizations. Technology staff members have similar skill sets, and that common understanding of the software reduces the learning curve for complex conversions and integrations. In addition, your user community is accustomed to working in what is in most cases a very similar business process. All of these aspects provide advantages over merging different and custom business applications. This is clearly an area where taking a long-term view and understanding future requirements such as working in an international environment become critical to the long-term return on investment needs to be considered.

Addressing these challenges may involve changing or adding additional applications to meet the organization's needs. Selecting new systems can be a complicated and challenging process. Determining what system or systems most effectively meet the organization's needs requires understanding your own requirements first.

There are many choices out in the marketplace for systems to meet organizational business requirements. Balancing the choice between leading-edge systems that may have new functionality against more established systems is not easy. Understanding what software vendors will be investing in and how they will be growing their systems' functionality can be complicated. In addition to the ability of the system to meet your organization's requirements, you need to consider the effort to bring your internal support functions up to speed on the new system, as well as the availability of skilled resources out in the marketplace that can help implement the system. All of these considerations may lead to the need to conduct a system selection process. Understanding how the system meets the organization's needs as well as understanding your total cost of ownership over the next 5 to 10 years is the goal of the system selection process. It is important to keep in mind that a system that does not deliver a clear upgrade path for your organization to follow will most likely not support the organization's needs in 5 to 10 years. Without an upgrade path, the system will not keep up with advancements in hardware, infrastructure, and business process functionality. This will impact the system's ability to meet the needs of your changing business requirements over time and will lead to the need to replace the system. All of these components should be considered as part of your total cost of ownership analysis. Understanding the market for services in support of your selected software is also an important consideration. It should be expected that there will be areas that will require external assistance in implementing the new software.

Your back-office systems are designed to manage the assets, liabilities, expenses, and revenues of the organization. In addition to this core function, these systems also provide the financial indicators to manage according to the financial objectives of the organization and perform the reporting functionality to support external reporting. External reporting can drive complex regulatory requirements for international, local, and statutory reporting. Your chart of accounts and overall code block design need to meet the reporting requirements of the organization. Hitting the right level for your account structure is the first step. The leading practice is to target a lean or thin account design. This limits the number of overall accounts to streamline rolled-up reporting across the organization.

Leveraging subaccounts and alternate accounts can help reduce the top level of accounts to help meet this objective. Subaccounts can be used in specific markets where more detailed accounting is required, but the overall results need to be summarized into a higher-level account. Alternate accounts can be leveraged to meet international reporting requirements where the account for reporting purposes in that market needs to meet a specific naming requirement. This enables the organization to tie the alternate account to the main account and use the alternate account only to meet these specific reporting requirements.

Once the account structure is in place, the next major component of the code block is the department. The leading practice is to have the department represent a function. Many organizations have multiple meanings rolled into their department structure. Two common components embedded into the department ID are location and business unit or legal entity. Extracting these attributes into separate components or chart fields within the code block enables more flexible reporting of your financial data across the organization's functions. Account and department ID, along with legal entity, is the core of the code block. Additional chart fields or segments such as product, location, book code, affiliate, and project ID are just some of the additional chart fields that organizations may leverage to satisfy additional requirements to facilitate their internal and external reporting.

Designing the correct code block structure for your organization is required for both upstream and downstream business process design. The subsystems need to feed the general ledger. This financial data needs to map to the correct accounting coding in the general ledger. Once this financial data is aggregated for the accounting period, the month-end close process can start. Core components of the close involve allocations to allocate revenues and expenses across the organization. In an international setting, currency translations and revaluations are used to facilitate reporting of multiple currencies. These processes as well as other organization-specific transactions prepare the ledger data for consolidation and equalization. Getting this right provides benefits to the organization and speeds the close process. This shifts the role of corporate accounting from processing of complex transactions to analysis with a higher value added back to the organization. This tends to create skill set gaps within the organization. Many accountants are not prepared to move from an environment of calculating entries for month-end processing to an environment of value-added analysis that is used to drive improvements back into the organization. In the end, this reporting is intended to meet external compliance needs but also to set financial objectives that will be used to drive operational performance. Not having the right team that understands how to accomplish this type of change for the organization can be the largest impediment to realizing the business case and associated benefits for the organization.

Working these accounting requirements into your back-office accounting systems and continuing the process of consolidation and integration become more of a tactical exercise. Understanding where you can best leverage shared service models balancing the ability to support the business with economies gained through centralization are specific decisions that every organization must address. Decentralized models may enable certain functions to be absorbed within a wide range of job responsibilities. Pushing these activities out into the organization can drive responsibility for accuracy and timeliness to those areas, but can also lead to errors or gaps in understanding in completing the business process. Centralization along with the right level of service can provide enormous benefits to the organization. Typical areas that can leverage shared services include contracting, purchasing, accounts payable, accounts receivable, billing, fixed assets, human resources, benefits, payroll, and general accounting.

Closing out the design is the most challenging part of these types of integration projects. Many stakeholders feel uncomfortable making decisions to move into building things they cannot touch or feel first. Not fully understanding how the end product will impact the ability for them to effectively complete their jobs is an uncomfortable feeling. There are impacts to people as a result of these changes, and the less they understand the changes and how the change will impact them, the more uncomfortable they will be and as a result the more they will resist the change.

There is also the concern that all their needs will not be met by the new systems and that anything left out will most likely never be accomplished. This feeling can be summed up by a quote from an executive from a large health care organization: "I don't want to fall into our standard 'delay and never do' approach." These concerns are typical with every major project. One way to help the organization move forward is to conduct periodic design reviews. These sessions require effort but help move organizations out of the "but what if" mode and into an understanding of the change and its impacts on not only the organization but also themselves. An effective design review should demonstrate how the future system will automate the business process. Since these sessions happen at the completion of design, not everything will be in place, but the core business process should be defined. Showing as much of that business process and providing additional details and change impacts around functionality that will be layered into the solutions helps move projects forward out of design and into the actual build process. This process gives your stakeholders a chance to better understand what the new business process will deliver and address any concerns they have with the new process. This reduces overall risk to the project and helps the project move forward in a transparent way.

Build

Once the design for each business process is complete, the organization needs to build the actual system. This area of the project could require a wide array of skill sets depending on the approach. The organization may be implementing an entirely new system to support the design that meets the requirements for the business process or simple be merging data and process into an existing business application. This may require functional support to help ensure the business process meets the stated objectives or to validate the data being consolidated. It may also require IT support to build programs to move data or modify code as well as changes to the underlying IT infrastructure. Outside specialty skills may also be required to complete the build-out of the business process.

Not having the right skill set in place for the change can lead to issues. An example of the types of issues an organization can face involved an international company's consolidation of fixed assets. The company relied on its Asia region staff to integrate their fixed assets into the new system. The Asia staff were able to effectively complete this task and meet the complex local reporting requirements. This integration was finished quickly and provided immediate benefits to the organization. A few months into addressing other integration areas, however, it was discovered that although the Asia staff had an excellent understanding of the local reporting requirements, they had incorrectly set up the assets for U.S. GAAP reporting. This led to the organization needing to disclose a restatement to the prior quarter financials, as well as pull together a team to address the errors and clean up the system. This put a resource strain on the integration team as well as creating concerns about the accuracy of other regions' data. Much of what had been gained by moving fast without the complete set of skills involved in the integration needed to be either redone or revalidated to make sure of the accuracy of the financials.

Testing is a critical component of building the new system. Testing helps ensure that the system will operate as designed and meet the overall business requirements that have been identified. There are multiple forms of testing, and not all may be required, but it is important to have a basic understanding of typical testing cycles. The most basic test is to validate just the actual object of functionality or transaction that is changing. This is typically termed a "unit test" for unit of functionality. This term can apply to multiple types of unit tests, depending on the object. More comprehensive testing would include integration testing where the functionality is integrated into the larger business process to understand how it impacts the overall system from an end-to-end perspective. Performance is also a consideration for understanding not only how long it takes a user to interact with this functionality, but also its impact on the overall system performance. Correcting performance concerns may require changes to the actual code, database, or network. Once the applications have been tested and meet the design requirements, the system is ready to be deployed to the organization.

Deployment

The deployment of the business process requires careful consideration as to the impact it may have on the end-user community. Understanding the change impacts on end users helps ensure your user community is properly trained to transact in the new environment. Errors can stack up fast in modern IT systems. These errors can be very time-consuming and challenging to correct. Errors create a lack of confidence in the new business process across the organization, and once confidence is lost, resistance to the change grows. If your users are not able to adopt the new system and improve their performance, your benefits from the business case will not be realized. At the end of the day, the user community needs to adopt the system and improve their performance as a result of the new business process. Hitting the right level of training and support is important to achieving the desired and expected results. Implementing the new business process may also involve a complicated set of cut-over activities. Data may need to be converted and validated into the production environment. Changes to the existing systems may need to be made so that the new business process works seamlessly with the existing IT systems. These activities need to be planned and well coordinated to reduce the chances of conversion errors in the system.

Long-Term Support

Once the new business process has been implemented, it needs to be supported. There are multiple options for how organizations support their IT business applications. The benefits of all your efforts are not realized until the new business process is implemented in your production environment. Your postproduction support organization is critical to realizing the benefit. The earlier that postproduction support is addressed, the greater the probability of realizing desired, required, and expected investment value.

Postproduction support is a critical component in the deployment of any system. Logically, a project is not successfully completed until the system is stable and meets the business requirements. Though stabilization can be very subjective, key performance indicators (KPIs) and metrics help in defining stability of a system. One of the key KPIs that measure stability is end-user support request volumes generated over a period of time.

Postimplementation support approaches place emphasis on designing the right support solution and analyzing the organization's post-go-live support requirements. The activities that are a part of this effort focus on these key areas:

- **Support organization.** Assessing the organization's current support model for fit with the newly expanded organization. Based on successfully implemented support models, determine changes to the existing structure and processes.
- **Technical support infrastructure.** Assessing the organization's current technical infrastructure for support determines changes to the infrastructure based on the future support model requirements and implementation.
- **Managing ongoing operations.** Developing the appropriate procedures, processes, and tools to manage the organization's ongoing operations after integration.
- **Continuous improvement.** Establishing a process for ongoing assessment and evaluation to determine if the program or project goals were achieved and to identify additional areas for improvement.

There are multiple options on how to implement a fully functioning support organization, ranging from completely internal support to completely external support. The nature of a merger enables organizations to evaluate the benefits of each as well as a blended model maintaining some critical IT business-support activities in-house while others are externally supported by third-party vendors. Staffing and the skill set of your current IT staff play an important role in deciding where to invest additional capital.

WRAPPING IT UP

An organization's IT systems and infrastructure have become the foundation on which organizations conduct business. Without the proper IT systems and infrastructure in place, organizations lose their ability to compete in the marketplace effectively. It is hard to think of a business process that does not rely on some form of computer automation. These systems need to support the organization's business requirements. Mergers create the need to adjust the IT landscape to account for new business requirements. How effectively an organization manages the change is critical to the success of the future organization.

The leadership team of the combined organization needs to be able to address short-term tactical needs as well as longer-term strategic needs of the business. IT systems play a critical role in supporting both. The leadership team's ability to make decisions to establish a clear road map enables the organization to stay focused at a time when there are multiple competing requirements for the organization's resources.

The road map should define the following:

- Who the business owners are for each business process area.
- What the high-level business requirements or objectives of the organization are and the priorities of these requirements.
- What major systems will be used to meet these requirements.
- When each business process area will be addressed for the integration.

This road map is an investment that provides the integration team with direction to address challenging decisions and avoid the need to continually take decisions back to leadership. Acting fast is critical for meeting the time constraints involved with the merger integration. With this road map, Day 1 integration imperatives can be identified and a detailed plan to address each can be created.

The ability to create consolidated financial statements is a clear place to start and for all organizations as a top priority. Addressing legal entity structures and making the needed adjustments to the existing reporting system is a first step. Additional business process areas need to be able to feed the financial reporting system to create consolidated financial statements. Additional areas may be identified for Day 1 integration based on resources and the complexities involved with each area. The ability to address more areas early on can provide clear benefits to the organization, but taking on too much can lead to costly errors. Striking the right balance is important to the success of the integration.

Longer-term integration requirements necessitate additional organizational structure to keep the organization focused. The road map still sets the general direction, but the addition of a business case for the remaining areas to be integrated sets clear objectives and focuses the integrations on achieving a targeted return on investment. The business case helps the organization to maintain a larger view, focus its priorities, and make trade-offs where necessary.

With a clear business case in place, the organization can refine its business requirements and establish a plan that is in alignment with its objectives. This plan serves as the basis for starting the detailed design, building the designed business processes, deployment to the organization, and long-term support of those business processes.

Taking the time to build out the road map and business case helps the organization understand the challenges it faces in integrating the two entities. This understanding helps identify resources with the right mix of skill sets and the supporting technology required for the change. Many times, not having this understanding can result in organizations underestimating the challenges ahead or not taking full advantage of the opportunities.

M&A IT Project Governance, Testing, and Business Intelligence

CHAPTER 22

Integration Management Office Best Practices

David Lake
Mauro Schiavon

This chapter contains an overview of the integration management office (IMO), a key component of any successful merger or acquisition. It highlights key roles, responsibilities, and activities. In addition, it provides a high-level overview of legislation that governs M&A transactions and shows how it affects the complexity of deal management along with other variables. Last, it contains some IMO best practices that will help your organization be more effective and successful in managing merger integration efforts.

The IMO is the centralized organization responsible for developing and executing an effective integration strategy starting at the early stages of the pre-announcement phase all the way to the execution of the integration or divestiture. Some of the key activities for the IMO include the coordinating integration activities, facilitating timely decision making, and resolving issues.

ROLES AND RESPONSIBILITIES

Exhibit 22.1 is an example of a typical structure for an integration team. Some of the key roles are the steering committee, integration manager, communications manager, function leads, and cross-function leads, as follows:

- Steering committee:
  - Provide strategic guidance.
  - Establish priorities.

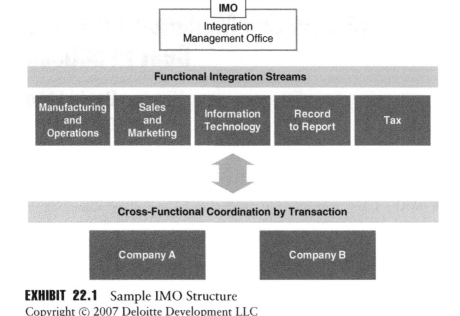

EXHIBIT 22.1   Sample IMO Structure
Copyright © 2007 Deloitte Development LLC

- Communicate the importance of the integration.
- Sign off on major decisions and communications.
■ Integration manager:
  - Responsible for defining and executing against the integration strategy. (Note that in some cases there might be a need for an integration manager from each company to facilitate effective decisions within each company.)
  - Develop a clear governance structure.
  - Proactively manage the politics, change, and communication.
  - Manage issues and risks across the project.
  - Manage weekly status reporting.
  - Log key project decision.
  - Manage the change request process.
  - Manage the project budget.
■ Communications manager:
  - Establish and execute against the communication plan.

▪ Functional integration streams (function leads):
  ● Coordinate all functional integration activities.
  ● Drive business design and integration.
  ● Focus on resolving operating issues and concerns.
▪ Cross-functional coordination by transaction (cross-functional leads):
  ● Coordinate all integration activities across functions.
  ● Resolve transaction-specific issues.

KEY ACTIVITIES

The key activities for an IMO are in the areas of governance, coordination, communication, and execution and tracking, as follows:

▪ Governance:
  ● Establish IMO program governance.
  ● Define team member roles and responsibilities.
  ● Establish meeting cadence for stakeholder engagement.
▪ Coordination:
  ● Identify and bring integration teams on board.
  ● Finalize project tools, such as issue tracking, status reporting (see Exhibit 22.2, titled Status Report Template), decision logging, and document management.
  ● Establish change management process (see Exhibit 22.3, titled Change Request Template).
  ● Develop team charters and objectives.
  ● Document, prioritize, and sequence initiatives and plans.
▪ Communication:
  ● Perform communications assessment to determine the existing communication activities, audience groups, and key messages.
  ● Develop communications plan to capture the process for developing and distributing project communications.
  ● Develop and deliver project communications.
▪ Execution and tracking:
  ● Establish and communicate a detailed project road map and detailed work plan.
  ● Prioritize IMO plans and initiatives.
  ● Provide support through detailed planning efforts with subject matter experts.
  ● Reorient teams from planning to execution.
  ● Define and monitor progress against key performance indicators (KPIs).
  ● Document and execute integration strategy.

WEEKLY STATUS REPORT

Team:
Project:
Date:
Overall Team Status Upgrade (G, Y, R):

Reason If Y or R:

Status Reporting Legend
Green = Major milestones on track
Yellow = Major milestones at risk; action plan in place
Red = Will miss milestone; significant issues

Milestones

Milestone Description	Baseline Date	Estimated Date	Actual Date	% Complete	Status (G,Y,R)

Key Accomplishments This Week (ONLY the Top 3–5)

To Do Next Week (ONLY the Top 3–5)

Open Issues/Dependencies/Escalations

Title and Description	Submitter	Owner	Escalation Level	Due Date

Important Decisions

Decision	Decision Maker	Date

EXHIBIT 22.2 Status Report Template

Title:	XXXXXX	Change Request Number:	CR #
Description of Change Request			
Date:		Requested by:	
Prepared by:		Team:	

Priority	Required Delivery Date
☐ **Critical:** Legal, compliance, or safety issue ☐ **High:** Severe revenue, productivity, or customer satisfaction issue ☐ **Medium:** Moderate business impact ☐ **Low:** All other requirements	_____ ; ☐ **Required for production hot fix** ☐ **Required for stabilization release** ☐ **Required for maverick go-live** ☐ **Candidate for wave III** ☐ **Required for other:**_____

Description of Requested Change and Quantified Business Justification:
We need:
We discovered this CR when:
Without this, the business will:
Contingency plan in case change request is rejected:

Impact to project—It is your responsibility to communicate with <u>ALL</u> team leads.						
All CRs must include design, build, test, and production support estimates.						
Teams Impacted	Impact Description	One-Time Cost—Estimate of Effort		Run Rate—Estimate of Effort		Estimated Provided By
	(timeline, milestones, etc.)	Resource # and Vendor	Duration (in hours)	Resource # and Vendor	Duration (in hours)	
Manufacturing and Operations						
Sales and Marketing						
Information Technology						
Record to Report						
Tax						

Change Request Status: To be completed by PMO			
CR		Total Cost	
Status:		Date:	
Approved by:		Title:	

Status Key
Approved Rejected On Hold Undergoing Review

EXHIBIT 22.3 Change Request Template

SAMPLE IMO TEMPLATES AND DELIVERABLES

Exhibit 22.1 offers a sample of an IMO organizational structure. There are many variations possible for this structure. However, it is critical that one be established and the roles and responsibilities related to it clearly documented and communicated.

It is essential, given the scope and pace of any merger, acquisition, or divestiture, to have weekly status reports that provide detailed information on the status of activities and milestones and are updated on risk, issues, and decisions that were made. Exhibit 22.2 is a sample template for a status report.

It is critical that all changes to the project scope, approach, budget, and timing be documented. Exhibit 22.3 is a sample template for a change request form.

MANAGING THE DEAL

There are some key factors that compound the complexity of managing an M&A deal. They follow and include IMO best practices on how to address them.

Legislation and Other Complicating Factors

The following paragraph is not intended to provide legal advice (only an attorney can do so). However, there are two pieces of legislation that are of particular interest and have a direct effect on IMO activities:

1. The Sherman Antitrust Act mandates that the companies involved in the M&A transaction must continue to compete in the marketplace. This directly impacts the ability to freely share information between the two companies before Day 1 and requires the IMO to put in place rigorous governance surrounding documentation sharing, focusing in particular on controlling competitively sensitive information.
2. The Hart-Scott-Rodino Antitrust Improvements Act (also known as the HSR Act) prohibits the two companies involved in the M&A transaction to act as a single company prior to regulatory approval. In addition, it provides specific rules that will prevent illegally jumping the gun, helping the two companies to remain in compliance.

This legislation has a deep impact on several key project activities owned by the IMO:

- Planning and implementation of postclosing activities.
- Decision-making processes and procedures.
- Documentation and information governance (each company must make decisions related to its business independently; thus careful control of sensitive information is required).

The IMO will also face other challenges that will compound the complexity of M&A program management and will require the IMO to adopt mitigation strategies to effectively manage the deal while remaining legally compliant:

- Organizations are becoming more global in nature, with operations and key stakeholders located anywhere in the world. This factor directly impacts the decision-making process and could adversely affect the overall deal timeline.
- Access to communication outlets such as social media, mobile communication (texting), and e-mail is constant, ubiquitous, and difficult to monitor. The threat of unintentional information leak has increased dramatically during the past few years alongside the growth of social networking, requiring M&A IMOs to rethink and rewrite communication protocols.
- Increased pressure to plan and execute the deal in the shortest possible time to improve and increase synergies.

The next section provides some of the best practices for how to address these factors.

IMO Best Practices

The following best practices items have been effective in numerous M&A projects and can help IMOs in their efforts to effectively manage transactions.

Adopt a Collaborative Project Management Tool The advent of business globalization has changed the fabric of the traditional domestic company, creating complex organizational structures that are spread around the world. It is not uncommon to have an M&A team that is composed of individuals who can collaborate only on a virtual basis. To bridge this gap, it is important to deploy a collaborative integrated project management tool that will enable streamlined and highly regulated project management processes and procedures.

Collaborative systems provide simultaneous access to multiple users at the same time, leveraging a centralized database that contains all aspects of the project such as plan, schedule, issues log, and task list. These systems are most commonly web-based and allow users to access and update areas they are directly responsible for (e.g., task completion update, issues update, and closure). Information is updated and visible globally in real time. These tools are highly configurable to allow selective access to only specific areas, thus greatly increasing the level of control. Automated work flow features allow for automated sequencing of decision making, as well as providing a clear audit trail with respect to that decision. Here is how a collaborative project management tool can greatly improve the planning and execution of a complex M&A deal:

- Project planning:
  - The master project plan is created and the initial baseline is set, thus providing a single source of truth.
  - Strict access control enables the IMO to control information access and extend it on an as-needed basis.
  - Tasks are assigned to specific individuals or teams. Users all over the world will be able to log in with individual credentials and be able to review the overall plan as well as review tasks and activities that they or their team are directly responsible for.
- Progress tracking and status reporting:
  - Once logged into the tool, users are typically able to update tasks online and raise issues or alert the IMO of any potential slippage.
  - These tools typically provide highly configurable dashboard and reporting capabilities, thus significantly streamlining the creation of progress status reporting.
  - Status progress and dashboards are available for consultation at the highest level of the organization, thus dramatically improving visibility to key executives and stakeholders by providing a real-time single source of truth.
- Issues and risk management:
  - Issues and risks databases provide the IMO with the ability to tightly monitor and report on issues and their prompt resolutions.
  - Assignment of issues and risks to specific individuals provides automated queuing of these tasks in one's in-box, regardless of the geographical location.

- Audit trail of issues and risks resolution is provided as well as the ability to attach any supporting documentation, decreasing the risk of noncompliance and facilitating any audit review throughout the deal planning and execution.
- Decision-making governance:
  - The ability to segregate information access and to provide automated work flow functionality to log decisions, supporting documentation, and sign-off by key stakeholders allows IMOs to balance the need for compliance with the need to document decisions and provide access to the information to relevant stakeholders, as well as support any audit review during and after the deal planning and execution.
- Documentation management:
  - Strict governance of documentation sharing is a key success factor during an M&A deal. Collaborative project management tools should be combined with the utilization of a collaborative documentation-sharing platform that provides the ability to selectively grant access to information to users or groups of users.
  - The utilization of a collaborative platform removes a significant amount of complexity in documentation management. In addition, access control and reporting features support compliance to antitrust law.

A quick search on any web search engine for project and portfolio management software will yield a list of the most reputable and widespread tools in the marketplace.

Control the Decision-Making Critical Path During the course of an IT M&A project, stakeholders will be required to make hundreds, if not thousands, of decisions that span from business process standardization and integration all the way to system customization and business-critical functionality. The difference between decision making in an IT M&A project and a normal IT project rests on the requirements imposed by the HSR Act. In every other aspect, decision making is very similar and subject to the same dynamics.

The objective of the IMO is to comply with the law while helping ensure that decisions are made efficiently and in the shortest possible amount of time. The goal is to have the right person make a decision and for that decision to stick, as most likely it will be the foundation of other decisions that will be made during the course of the project.

One of the main issues that plague large global organizations is what we call the decision-making chain reaction effect. This phenomenon occurs in large organizations when decision makers are not properly identified and project team members are required to literally hunt for the proper stakeholder or decision maker. Every time a new element of the organization is touched, a chain reaction is initiated where several other individuals need to be consulted who, in turn, need to consult with several others before filtering down a decision. In many cases, after several cycles the decision is reverted back to the steering committee, which is likely to close the issue with an executive decision or, in some cases, initiate additional cycles of review. The chain reaction effect has a profound impact on the deal timeline, as decision closure is dragged on for an extended period of time, with the potential to ultimately result in deal timeline slippage.

There are two best practices that mitigate and contain the decision-making chain reaction effect:

1. Staff the M&A project with seasoned team members on both sides of the deal, all with deep knowledge of their organization business processes, systems, and organizational structure. These individuals will accelerate the decision-making process by quickly understanding the context of a specific decision and assessing who needs to be involved or consulted in the decision-making process. There are hundreds, if not thousands, of decisions that need to be made during the course of an M&A IT project, and containing the decision cycle time by going through the process more efficiently will help avoid unnecessary time waste.

2. Religiously maintain a responsible, accountable, consulted, and informed (RACI) matrix for all the business areas relevant to the M&A project. This list will become the single source of truth and the guide utilized by the team members to go through the decision-making process in a more formal and efficient way. When published, the list will also drive more accountability at all levels of the organization, thus providing the team with the right level of support when needed.

Establish Ironclad Communication Control   As mentioned, M&A deals are subject to a lot of scrutiny from a legal compliance perspective. All of the team actions and statements are subject to review and can be utilized in a court of law if necessary. It is paramount that the IMO enforces an ironclad communication control and policy with all the project team members. In particular:

- All team members should utilize the IMO to coordinate and structure meetings that involve both companies. The same procedure should be followed also to request and obtain documentations.
- The Justice Department or any other third party with an interest in the M&A transaction will likely seek information produced during the course of the planning and execution of the deal. This makes it paramount to tightly control any type of project-related document,

which includes any written documentation such as meeting notes, e-mails, presentations, voice mails, and meeting recordings. This also includes comments or opinions posted on one's personal social network accounts directly related to the project at hand. While one might consider these sites private, the information can find its way out of what one considers the circle of trust and can be used in court in a similar way to any other written document. The IMO should educate the project team on the sensitivity of project documentation. A good rule of thumb for every team member is the *Wall Street Journal* test: Would the team member feel comfortable if something that he or she is considering writing or saying appeared on the front page of the *Journal*? If the answer is "Maybe not" or "No," then the team member should avoid voicing or writing those thoughts.

■ Enforce the utilization of the collaborative platform to store and classify all the communications and documents related to the project. This will provide an additional checkpoint for the team members as well as a comprehensive and transparent view of all communications and documentation to any interested party.

Focus on Business-Critical Elements   One of key objectives of an M&A transactions is to achieve synergies in the shortest possible time. The focus might be on revenue synergies or cost synergies or both together. Or the goal might be to add the target company to a portfolio and allow it to continue operations with minimal changes.

Based on the strategy specific to the M&A deal being executed, the IMO should focus its resources and activities on business-critical elements, deferring noncritical items to a postexecution phase. In other words, always keep an eye on the end goals and allocate resources and funds to achieve those goals with the least investment. For example, when defining the scope of business processes that require standardization, focus first on those that will allow the realization of the significant cost synergies and postpone the rest to a second phase. The same approach should be followed when looking at business process integration or a combination of both.

WRAPPING IT UP

There are a number of critical path activities required to stand up an integration management office. In our experience, the three key aspects of a successful IMO are a clearly documented and communicated integration strategy, a comprehensive and transparent communication approach, and a solid project governance model. Once the IMO is up and running, the focus will then shift to executing against the integration strategy. Since communication will be critical, it is recommended to engage project stakeholders from both parties and encourage open dialogue. In summary, taking the time to conduct proper planning to enable the integration management office to successfully execute against the integration strategy is critical to success.

CHAPTER 23

IT Program Governance during the Deal

John Uccello

Delivering on the intended benefits and synergies from the combined organization requires a significant degree of planning from an information technology (IT) perspective. Additionally, these activities must be in compliance with the conditions of the agreement and applicable federal laws on pre-merger work. The establishment of a program governance structure, as allowed by law, comprised of IT participants from both companies, can enable effective controls with specific lines of communication and responsibility to build the foundational program and help achieve the IT objectives of the deal.

The high-level activities associated with the establishment of an effective IT program during the deal are shown in Exhibit 23.1.

ESTABLISH GOVERNANCE MODEL

The first step for designing the IT planning program across the two organizations is to define what the governance model will look like. This critical step establishes the organization structure of the deal team, defines the team member roles, establishes governance processes, monitors the budget, and controls the IT organizations as they plan operations as a consolidated company.

The IT organizations of both companies will be very busy during the pre-Day 1 period, as the employees begin to understand more about each other and their business operations. Employees will be researching one another's organization through formal reports and informal channels, such as the Internet. The rumor mill will be in full force, and tight-knit groups of IT employees who have worked closely together over the years at each company will be concerned about their future in the combined organization and will be questioning what it will look like in the future.

EXHIBIT 23.1   IT Program Governance Activities

Activity	Purpose
Establish Governance Model	Define the roles and responsibilities, reporting relationships, and governing tools to control the program in a structured manner.
Establish the Program Management Office (PMO)	Establish the structure, detailed execution plans, tools and templates, and reporting cadence of the PMO. Engage team members and launch the program.
Execute the Plan	Manage the day-to-day execution of the program to plan for Day 1 as an integrated IT organization.

An effective way to bring a sense of calm, structure, and methodical purpose to dispel the confusion and rumors is to quickly develop the IT governance organization to plan the integrated company and set the controls in place. This organization will align with the overall deal organization structure, with IT governance being a key member of the broader program. The IT governance organization should be comprised of a leadership/executive team that sets direction for each of the companies (acquirer and target), as well as technology department team members from both of the companies (two in a box); the team members should all be the "A" players from both of the organizations, with decision-making authority for their locus of control.

The tasks associated with creating the IT governance organization are:

- **Conduct as-is review of existing governance structures.** If they exist, the shell structure from each company may jump-start the consolidated governance model. The various IT departments and key players may already be outlined in existing models to accelerate a common understanding to build upon as the teams come together.
- **Create the governance structure.** With the appointed IT leadership from both companies, review existing models and conduct brainstorming sessions and facilitated workshops to determine and finalize the governance controls and the program management office (PMO), including:
  - Names, roles, responsibilities, structure, accountability, and authority of the deal team.
  - Processes and timing/cadence for the governing body (e.g., frequency and timing of status meetings, escalation path and criteria, and management tools and templates).
- **Implement the structure.** This includes obtaining approval from the overall deal governing body, communicating the organization structure to all levels, and executing on the structure.

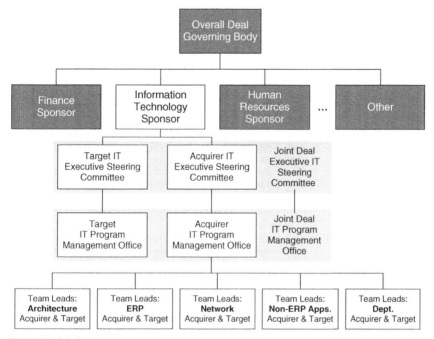

EXHIBIT 23.2 Example Program Governance Organization

An example of a program governance organization is shown in Exhibit 23.2 along with roles and responsibilities in Exhibit 23.3.

Implementing IT governance in an organization where it does not already exist can be challenging, especially during the time of a deal due to competing timelines and priorities and legal restrictions on what data and strategies can be shared. Each organization will still have obligations to its IT customers to fulfill to keep business operations going, and it will be important for the champions of implementing a governance model to communicate the value of governance, as well as the deal in general. All team members should fully understand their roles in the deal and be committed to its objectives. The objectives of the combined IT governance organization should center on maximizing the value derived from aligning IT infrastructure investments.

At this time, the governing body should develop communications materials, and hold town hall meetings and workshops to communicate the objectives of the organization, its structure, team members, roles, and responsibilities, along with requests of the population at large in tandem with the overarching integration management office's messages. It is critical that authority be provided to the team members to fulfill their roles as

EXHIBIT 23.3 Example IT Governance Roles and Responsibilities

Role	Responsibilities
Information Technology Sponsor	Owns the program for IT, secures funding, participates in progress reporting, and helps to govern the project to meet the objectives of the deal.
Target IT Executive Steering Committee	Establishes the target company's IT program strategy, including envisioning the benefits and impacts of the divestiture as they relate to IT, for the period of the deal. The committee will help to ensure that the program team meets the objectives of the strategy.
Acquirer IT Executive Steering Committee	Establishes the acquiring company's IT program strategy, including envisioning the benefits and impacts of the acquisition as they relate to IT, for the period of the deal. The committee will help to ensure that the program team meets the objectives of the strategy.
Joint Deal Executive IT Steering Committee	Consisting of members of the target IT executive steering committee and acquirer IT executive steering committee, this group participates in status report updates from the program management office, to align on the strategy as an acquirer or target company, and clears roadblocks to achieve the objectives of the deal.
Target IT Program Management Office	Develops the management plan and control tools to execute on the strategy and objectives of the target IT executive steering committee.
Acquirer IT Program Management Office	Develops the management plan and control tools to execute on the strategy and objectives of the acquirer IT executive steering committee.
Joint Deal IT Program Management Office	Consisting of members of the target IT program management office and acquirer IT program management office, this group is responsible for developing the joint management plan and control and execution tools to drive the team leads to achieve the results of the deal prior to Day 1.
Team Leads	Team leads are brought together from the acquirer and target organizations to plan the technology for their respective areas of expertise.

leaders of the deal, and that said authority is communicated openly both within and outside of the defined structure.

ESTABLISH THE PROGRAM MANAGEMENT OFFICE

After the governance model is established, the IT program management office (PMO) will establish the detailed execution plan, including all of the tools and tracking mechanisms and templates to accelerate the execution.

This includes developing the reporting metrics, establishing a status meeting cadence to meet the objectives of the deal, and launching the program. The IT PMO will document and track initial risks and mitigation; develop the detailed project execution plan; document contingency plans; develop the status report templates; identify the project documentation repository; and provide templates and tools to track issues, decisions, action items, and corrective actions. It is critical to launch the project with all team members understanding the control mechanisms put in place by the PMO, major milestone dates, and interdependencies. Thus, once the PMO is established and the plan is developed, a kickoff meeting should be held with all parties who are members of the governance model.

Direction and Control

As previously noted, acquisition projects can be some of the largest, most complex projects ever undertaken by an organization. In order to provide effective direction and control, the project organization and activities should be structured in a hierarchical manner, as defined by the governance model. Some activities in this hierarchy are performed in a top-down fashion, while others are performed in a bottom-up fashion.

- The hierarchy is used top-down to:
  - Define goals, objectives, and guiding principles.
  - Set targets and key milestones.
  - Monitor progress and drive corrective actions.
- The hierarchy is used bottom-up to:
  - Report progress.
  - Raise issues and risks.
  - Request decisions.
  - Provide a check on top-down assumptions and targets.

As project artifacts and work items are developed, the project repository should be used as the official place to store and find documentation on project decisions made and pending, issues resolved and pending, and reports made and scheduled. (Note that access to this repository may be limited based on the applicable regulations and terms of the deal.)

Status Meetings

A project status cadence should be developed in such a manner that the progress reporting flows in a meaningful way from the bottom of the structure to the top. The PMO has responsibility for establishing the cadence using the input of team members to settle on the time and duration of the meetings; however, the PMO should set the criteria for the execution of these meetings, develop the templates to be used by the teams reporting the status, and develop the list of invitees according to the schedule and meeting content. Status meeting cadence is typically weekly, but may be more or less frequent depending on the timeline of the deal, the complexities, and the number of participants. An example status meeting cadence, where information flows from the bottom up, may be represented as shown in Exhibit 23.4.

In many companies, business leaders sometimes take technology infrastructure for granted, and need to be reminded of the pervasiveness of IT infrastructure in the business. It may also be necessary to highlight the long lead times sometimes required for the technology organization to enable proposed business changes. Involvement of the IT PMO in many of the meetings (e.g., sponsor meeting, governing body meeting), while not explicitly stated, is often prescribed by companies to help the information flow and objectives to be understood by all parties.

In all the meetings, a status report typically includes:

- Accomplishments since the last report.
- Planned accomplishments not achieved.
- Progress on planned milestones.
- Issues, actions, and risks for escalation or assistance.
- Decisions for approval or informational purposes.
- Cross-program dependencies where assistance is needed.

Day	Status Meeting	Objectives	Participants
Monday	Team Lead	Team leads report status, issues, risks, actions, and plan tracking versus milestones.	PMO All team leads
Wednesday	Steering Committee	PMO prepares and reports a consolidated status of the team leads, with escalations.	Executive steering committee PMO
Friday	Sponsor	Steering committee prepares and reports status as it relates to the strategy and objectives.	Sponsor Executive steering committee
Biweekly	Governing Body	Members of combined sponsor leadership discuss progress toward objectives.	Overall governing body Sponsors

EXHIBIT 23.4 Example Status Meeting Cadence

A project scribe is recommended as a member of the PMO team, who will take meeting notes to be filed in the project repository as documentation. These notes can be referenced by team participants who were unable to attend the status meeting, and also allow the team to maintain a chronology of accomplishments, decisions, issues, risks, and escalation.

Develop the Detailed Plan

A detailed project plan will help to keep the project on track, with visible milestones, accountability, and early detection of potential deviations from plan. This can be accomplished only if the project plan has been agreed upon by the resources who will be executing the tasks, if the tasks are at a low-enough level of detail that tracking can be accomplished, if the goals and timing of the tasks are real and attainable, and, finally, if the plan is kept up-to-date.

There are many excellent books describing the process of developing a detailed project plan, whether through reuse of an existing project plan, through work breakdown structure workshops, or developed in detail by project team members from the top down or the bottom up. The development of a detailed project plan and associated tracking tools is outside the scope of this book. It is the responsibility of the IT PMO to help ensure that the project plan is at the right level of detail for the program, resources are allocated appropriately, and processes are put in place to track the plan updates on an ongoing basis. Major milestones that should be tracked by each of the team members and the IT PMO should tie back to actual activities in the plan, and the status reports should also report on the progress of the program against these milestones. This is the primary way by which early detection of any plan variances can be elevated to other members of the program.

Conduct the Kickoff

It is critical that all team members involved in the deal participate in a kickoff meeting hosted by the IT PMO in the early weeks of the program (typically week 1 or 2 after the formation of the governance organization). The objectives of the kickoff meeting are to:

- Align the project team to the strategy, goals, and objectives of the program.
- Communicate the governance structure, reporting authority, and control mechanisms for the execution of the program.
- Communicate the project milestones, status cadence, tools, and templates to be used to control the program.

- Allow the integrated project team an opportunity to begin the forming stage of teams.
- Build excitement and enthusiasm for the program.

Depending on the size of the program, the kickoff meeting could be as short as a couple of hours, or as long as a business day—all depending on the level of detail to be discussed with the subteams. For extensive programs, the use of breakout sessions may be useful as a means to allow the subteams to formulate their working relationships. During the kickoff meeting, the topics should be covered by the leadership team, with presentation materials to guide the conversation. (See Exhibit 23.5.)

EXHIBIT 23.5 Kickoff Meeting Topics

Topic	Objective	Facilitator
Mission and Vision	Share the accomplishments to date of the program; align the project team to the strategy, goals, and objectives of the program; and build excitement and enthusiasm for the program.	Overall governing board leadership, executive sponsor, executives of the organizations
Program Scope	Align the team on the overall scope of the program, describing the boundaries of what will be accomplished for all the work teams.	Program management office, project managers, team leads (contributing for their work streams)
Program Schedule	Review the overall timeline of the program, major milestones, and deliverable expectations.	Program management office, project managers
Organization Structure	Describe the program organization structure, accountability, authority, and escalation channels. Discuss roles and responsibilities.	Program management office
Program Governance	Describe the governance methodology, project tools to manage the program, status meeting cadence, and expectations of the teams for documentation and storage in the project repository.	Program management office
Breakout Workshops (depending on time and needs of the program)	Various workshops where team participants can break out to plan for and resolve particulars while the team is together.	Various

It is preferred to conduct the project kickoff in a single location where all participants are in the same room. This may not be feasible for very large project teams, and may be cost prohibitive for distributed teams, in particular, when the project team is global in nature. It is possible to conduct the kickoff with participants co-located in regions, especially if videoconferencing equipment is available, with program leadership participation in each of the major regional areas. Alternatively, senior leadership may consider a road show where multiple kickoff meetings are held in geographic regions when it is impractical to get the full team to a single location at a common time. When scheduling remote participation, the IT PMO needs to be conscientious of time zone, language, and cultural differences.

EXECUTE THE PLAN

Once the program team is in place, roles and responsibilities are defined, team members are on board, the baseline plan is developed, and the program is launched, the ongoing execution of the plan can occur. During the preclose period, there will be a significant amount of confusion and disruption to business as usual. The structure of the PMO, along with the detailed plan for guiding the project team, is a crucial stabilizing force that will bring clarity of purpose to the team members.

Executing the plan is comprised of the following key activities:

- Update the plan.
- Report progress.
- Resolve issues and escalate.

Update the Plan

Updating the plan, while seemingly a relatively innocuous activity, is one of the keys to helping ensure that the IT PMO has the information it needs to determine whether the program is on track and controlled. There are various ways in which the project plan can be kept up-to-date, from utilizing a server-based project management software, where all team members enter their percentage completion of owned tasks, to manual entry of the reported status.

One of the keys to effective governance is to make sure that the tasks in the project plan reflect the progress of the project team, that progress against milestones is accurately captured, and that deviations from the project plan are identified. The IT PMO maintains responsibility to regularly review team progress against the planned tasks. Where there are significant deviations, the IT PMO should engage with the responsible parties and team leads to understand the variance. If the tasks in question are on the critical path, techniques to accelerate or reallocate resources will need to be deployed (such as crashing or fast-tracking). Any issues that are preventing the timely completion of tasks on the critical path need to be recorded (if they are not already) and escalated according to the project governance structure that was put in place to resolve the roadblocks and issues. The PMO should address in a timely fashion any such deviations where the critical path is involved.

Report Progress

Through the regular project cadence and scheduled meetings, team members report their status up through the governance chain. Metric-based reporting is an excellent way in which progress can be gauged. The IT PMO should assist the team leads with defining which metrics are most meaningful to their work streams and which will produce a better measure of progress on a regular basis. For example, metrics that represent the scope of the disposition of existing applications may be used for a work stream that is evaluating and planning for the merging of the application landscape of the two companies. The metrics can include a count of applications for each company, categorized by business function, the number of applications reviewed, the number with rework needed, the remaining applications to be reviewed, complexity analysis for the disposition of the applications, and those that require a more detailed business case to be effectively dispositioned.

By monitoring and tracking the progress against plan tasks and milestones, and reporting progress against metrics, the program can be controlled and resources applied where they are most needed to keep the plan on track.

Resolve Issues and Escalate

On a regular basis, issues will arise within the project teams that need to be resolved or escalated. Many issues are resolved regularly within each of the project teams as part of day-to-day execution of the project plan, through meetings and discussions, and through an analysis of the issue versus the objectives of the program. However, there will be a number of issues that cannot be resolved within the work stream, as they are issues that require evaluation and decision making across the teams or will require decisions and evaluation by the PMO, executive leadership, or others outside the program (including vendors and other third-party stakeholders).

Issues should be thoroughly documented using the tools defined for the program. When issues are resolved within the project team, the resolution should be documented and the issue should then be closed. When issues are to be escalated, the team lead should identify to whom the issue should be escalated, or work with the PMO to identify appropriate parties to assist with the resolution. If there is a more immediate need to resolve an issue, the team members should not wait for the next regularly occurring status meeting to bring the issue forward.

As part of the regular status cadence reporting process, reporting of issues to be escalated should be brought forward using a bottom-up approach—from the team leads to the PMO, and on to the executive leadership team members. Resolution of the issues should occur at the lowest level possible so that roadblocks are cleared closest to the work being accomplished.

WRAPPING IT UP

The period prior to the closure of the deal frequently is a very challenging time for the companies and their employees. Oftentimes, massive disruption is feeding the rumor mill, employees are concerned for their futures, key resources may be leaving in anticipation of what the deal could bring for them personally, and there is a tremendous amount of work to be accomplished in preparation for Day 1 as a combined company.

The IT department has a monumental task: to continue to support its customers with hardware, software, network, and applications to maintain the current state, while at the same time working to meet the objectives of the deal and planning for the combined or divested technologies. The two companies need to bring their best and brightest IT resources to plan for the closing of the deal. This planning period will be critical to the transition to Day 1 activities. A well-defined and well-executed program governance can help to bring structure and stability to a chaotic period, guide the planning efforts, alert participants to activities heading off track, and bring a sense of controlled purpose to employees.

CHAPTER 24

Important Role of Data in an M&A Transaction

Lynda Gibson
Anil Tondavadi
Chris Vu

Mergers and acquisitions (M&A) can present major challenges for the acquirer and the acquired alike. The rewards can be significant, but the risks are generally high—not all M&As deliver the targeted shareholder value. While many executive careers have prospered because of successful mergers and acquisitions, many others have gone off the rails due to unsuccessful mergers.

Technology and the role of information technology (IT) have become critical—without the appropriate executed strategy, the entire M&A event can go up in flames. Ideally, IT leadership is involved up front in the strategic conversations, as an equal at the executive table. This participation can allow for the discussion of potential technological issues and solutions as part of the decision and planning processes. However, in our experience, conventional technology integration techniques may fall short of achieving desired, required, expected, or anticipated post-merger integration business targets because they rely heavily on traditional approaches that sometimes fail to take into account specific information management (IM) challenges and opportunities. In particular, these focus on:

1. **Data integration planning** to develop a future-state enterprise data architecture, including data integration and access patterns, that is based on key data domains and aligned with the tactical goals of each business function and the strategic integration objectives of the organization.
2. **Data consolidation** that involves the transformation, migration, and integration of data across comparable products, services, and systems between the two entities.

3. **Data coexistence** that involves the management and update of data for similar business functions but across disparate systems.
4. **Data quality** to determine the consistency, accuracy, and applicability of the data elements for reporting and decision making.
5. **Data readiness** that assesses the data availability and granularity, and refreshes frequency to support views for different business functions.
6. **Information rationalization** to develop a single version of "the truth" by building an information inventory that determines the leading source of information and reduces redundancy across customers, products, markets, and offerings.

Looked at holistically, there is a unifying theme among these six challenges—effective data management both during and after the merger. While some companies may acknowledge that data are critical to benefit return on investment (ROI) realization, their focus on active data management frequently is minimal and inadequate for realizing planned business benefits. Instead, their focus is on traditional M&A IT activities, such as application integration and rationalization, infrastructure planning, and business continuity, yet leaves aside data management.

With the number of mergers and acquisitions increasing and with IT's role more critical than ever, both business and IT integration project teams need to focus on data and information needs in addition to traditional system integration issues. In this chapter, we examine the premise that effective data management is critical to successful mergers and acquisitions. We look at the pitfalls associated with traditional IT M&A approaches, giving examples from real companies' experiences. We then present 10 keys to effective data management to leverage, manage, and improve the value from M&A.

CURRENT CHALLENGES AND LOST OPPORTUNITIES

Mergers may result in major challenges for IT leadership. Fragmented systems and applications come along with unhappy staff who are awaiting redundancy notices. On the information management front, data are fragmented across company and divisional boundaries. Among the chaos and unknowns, the demand for quality, consolidated, real-time, and accurate information is enormous and the pressure is intense for IT to deliver. These demands come to managers as they struggle to understand their new organization, board members who need to know the merger is going as planned, government agencies needing to make sure of regulatory compliance, and, of course, financial institutions.

The financial benefits from mergers and acquisitions result from an increase in the top line and savings in the bottom line. In both cases, consolidating data from multiple systems and making sure the resulting information is correct are critical. Yet, through interviews with various clients we have determined that in many cases, the role data play in a transaction is typically understated and data's potential to positively impact synergies is not well understood. Here are the five typical situations:

1. Few organizations manage data with the same rigor as other enterprise assets during a merger or acquisition, such as finances, products, services, and infrastructure. Though it might be difficult to place a monetary value on an organization's data assets, they should be viewed and treated as being among the most valuable enterprise assets and drivers for achieving results and the desired objectives.
2. More often than not, active data management is an afterthought in the M&A lifecycle, typically thought of during the post-merger integration phase. This late stage of the lifecycle offers very limited opportunities to define and refine the needs and priorities, hence, limiting the organization's ability to benefit from and monetize data.
3. An initial focused effort is seldom made to prioritize those specific data domains that deliver business value and to understand the dependencies between them. This situation often results in the delayed execution of integration projects and costly Band-Aid solutions that do not align with the strategic enterprise data architecture.
4. There is a lack of a standardized, repeatable approaches and best practices to data and application integration across business functions. In addition to this, some organizations do not have a clear delineation of the roles and responsibilities across different functional and technical leaders. This often leads to delayed integration projects that do not serve their intended purpose.
5. Organizations rely on highly manual processes and temporary interfaces to deliver data for business-as-usual operations and client or regulatory reporting for an extended period of time after the completion of the transaction. This is generally due to insufficient time spent in planning and tracking data integration activities.

TOP 10 WAYS TO USE INFORMATION MANAGEMENT TO IMPROVE M&A

To help facilitate effective M&A results and outcomes in the information management area, companies should consider the following critical success factors.

1. Make Sure There Is Alignment of the Enterprise Information Management Strategy with the M&A Strategy

Organizations that have a sound enterprise-wide information management strategy and are actively implementing critical aspects of their strategy are generally much better placed to take advantage of new information assets from mergers and acquisitions than those organizations that do not have a strategy or whose strategy sits on a shelf. We have found that this information management strategy is a precursor to monetizing data and obtaining value from existing information assets and is an essential part of an effective merger or acquisition. This may lead the management team to ask questions in two specific areas:

1. Does the M&A strategy align with the information management strategy?
2. Are the characteristics of the acquired company similar to or different from your company?

As depicted in Exhibit 24.1, establishing or aligning the current information management strategy early in the M&A lifecycle is crucial to achieving the desired outcome and results, as information is a key enabler in each phase of the M&A.

The M&A strategy should drive the development and execution of an information management strategy based on the business priorities and value creation or value protection. For example, if the strategic goal of a company is to grow a business unit by increasing the distribution channels through an acquisition, the enterprise IM strategy should set goals around managing and using the information generated from these additional channels.

An understanding of the acquiring organization's business characteristics, M&A goals, and IM strategy can enable the development of a strategy around the potential benefits and issues that can arise due to data integration, consolidation, and rationalization. For example, as illustrated in Exhibit 24.2, if the target company has a custom-developed customer database and the acquiring company has a fully integrated customer relationship management (CRM) system, integrating the data could prove difficult and result in significant delays in moving to a smooth, joint operation.

Alignment of IM goals with M&A goals is a key step toward achieving the required objectives. Areas of focus should include:

- IM strategy alignment through the M&A lifecycle, covering the periods prior to, during, and following M&A.
- Information consolidation versus coexistence.

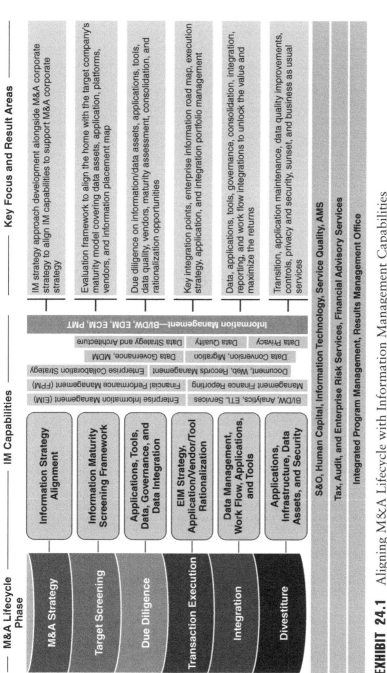

EXHIBIT 24.1 Aligning M&A Lifecycle with Information Management Capabilities

Source: Deloitte

What is the go-forward short-term market strategy with the acquired firm's:

What you should do in the short-term with the acquired firm's:

	Customers	Products	Channels	Transaction Application	Data Integration	BI Tools and Applications
Market penetration	No Change	No Change	No Change	Coexist	Coexist	Replace
	No Change	No Change	Change	Coexist	Keep	Replace
	No Change	Change	No Change	Coexist	Coexist	Replace
	No Change	Change	Change	Coexist	Replace	Replace
Market diversification	Integrate	Integrate	Integrate	Replace	Replace	Replace
	Integrate	Integrate	Keep	Replace	Coexist	Keep
	Integrate	Keep	Keep	Keep	Keep	Keep
	Integrate	Keep	Integrate	Replace	Retire	Keep

EXHIBIT 24.2 Alignment of M&A Strategy with IM Goals

Source: Deloitte

422

- External information needs (for example, financial industry, clients, regulatory agencies) versus internal information needs (for example, operations).
- Short-term goals versus long-term goals, including:
  - Data consolidation across the acquired and acquirer.
  - Identification of the system of record.
  - Separation of operational versus performance data.
  - Consolidation of reference information and data versus coexistence of reference data and information.
  - Day 1 operating model versus a long-term steady state model.

Some of the key capabilities that should be considered when establishing a long-term IM strategy include business intelligence, data warehousing, data analytics, cloud computing, mobile data management, and big data management (which is the expansion of high-velocity, complex, and diverse data). The development of these capabilities can directly impact the top line and bottom line of an organization. Business intelligence and data analytics add value to the top line by predicting future cross-sell and up-sell opportunities by analyzing previous customer interactions. Cloud computing, mobile data management, and big data management can impact the bottom line by reducing or controlling costs, or can pose data challenges if not managed effectively.

Considering the critical role that data play in the execution of merger and post-merger activities, it behooves organizations to adopt an information management framework early in the post-merger lifecycle. This can (or will likely) speed up the execution of post-merger integration activities and, more importantly, help to achieve the stated benefits of the transaction.

2. Develop a Detailed Information Management M&A Road Map

Using the IM strategy described as the basis, some organizations will develop a detailed information management M&A road map. This road map will align different stakeholders to a set of key information management initiatives within the organization and help plan and coordinate integration activities around them. It will be a key enabler for senior executives who will be required to make tactical decisions during and after the merger.

Organizations that create an IM M&A road map would typically focus on the following:

- Detailed component-level mapping of the IM road map with the M&A road map across the phases covering:
  - How the data assets will be integrated (reference, master, and transactional data).

- What should be the Day 1 organization (existing and new organizations).
- Data organization (span of control, data management, operational readiness, and reporting).
- Operations (Day 1 operating model, long-term operating model).
- Future-state road map (point of departure and point of arrival) application-data consolidation, retirement, enhancements, and goal of moving toward a single truth of data.
- Communicated across the organization:
  - Communication strategy.
  - People realignment strategy.
  - Skill calibration.
  - Operational calibration (in-source/outsource, on-site, best shore, off-shore model).
- Understandability by the business as well as IT:
  - Business-driven and IT-enabled.
  - Business ownership for change and readiness management.
  - Integration of business process with IT and data process management.
- Focus on the building of IM capabilities that can support the key objectives of the merger:
  - Use IT as an enabler and data/information as value driver.
  - Build foundational services alongside Day 1 operational readiness.
  - Create data organization and framework for continuous improvement.

As is shown in Exhibits 24.3 and 24.4, a detailed IM road map consists of two phases, pre-merger and post-merger. Depending on the size, industry, and M&A goals, an IM road map will be customized to meet the goals. The exhibits show examples of sets of phases and activities to be included in this road map.

3. Develop an Active Program Management Approach

Post-merger integrations are not for the frail and tend to pose challenges on a daily basis. The traditional program management approach is well suited to tackling the challenges faced during M&A, as it involves laying out the integration road map and providing a set of guiding principles for the individual integration projects to manage their pieces of the puzzle. An effective trend is to move away from these traditional practices and institute an active program management process that is agile in responding to the challenges and that focuses on the alignment of individual integration project objectives to enterprise program goals alongside the integration goals.

Enterprise Value Delivery for Information Management (EVD for IM) Method Roadmap

System Delivered & Operate Begins

Disciplines	Vision	Plan	Design	Build	Deliver
Information Strategy & Architecture	Verify Client Business Strategy; Assess EVD for IM Maturity; Develop Future State EVD for IM Blueprint	Assess Data Domains, Application Landscape; Define ECM Requirements, Architecture; Develop Information Models & EIM Roadmap	Develop Data Values, Architecture & Sourcing; Define Logical Data Flow & architecture; Define Archiving Approach & Unit test	Develop & Conduct IM Unit test; Develop data standards & Physical data model; Create Database Objects & develop archiving solutions	Implement Data Archiving Solution Utilities
Information Governance	Assess Information Governance	Define Information Governance Requirements	Develop Governance Charter; Design Governance Organization & Processes	Develop Information Governance Policies; Develop Information Governance Processes	Transition Information Governance Organization
Information Quality		Assess Information Quality Processes; Define Data Quality Functional Requirements	Develop Information Quality Functional Specifications; Develop Information Quality Technical Design	Build Information Quality Solution	Deliver Information Quality Solution
Reporting & Analytics		Asses & Define BI & Analytics Capabilities, Requirements, Processes	Develop BI Functional Specifications; Develop BI Technical Design	Develop Semantic Layer; Build Business Intelligence Solutions	
Master Data Management		Define Master Data Requirements	Develop Master Data Functional Specifications; Develop Master Data Technical Design	Build Master Data Solution	
Enterprise Content Management	Assess ECM Processes	Define ECM Requirements	Develop ECM Functional Specifications; Develop Enterprise Content Management Technical Design	Build Enterprise Content Delivery Solutions	
Metadata Management		Define Metadata Requirements	Develop Metadata Functional Specifications; Develop Metadata Technical Design	Build Metadata Solution	Implement Metadata Solution
Data Protection & Privacy			Identify Pri&vacy Requirement Sources; Perform Privacy Data Flow Mapping		Develop Privacy Process and Governance Gaps; Develop Privacy Roadmap
Data Integration			Develop Data Integration Approach; Develop ETL Functional & Technical Specifications	Build ETL Source & Target Connections; Build ETL Programs	Deliver ETL Solution
Performance Management		Assess Current State Processes; Define Requirements	Design Processes; Develop Consolidation Specifications; Develop Planning Specifications; Develop Reporting Specifications	Develop Processes; Build Consolidation Solution; Build Planning Solution; Build Reporting Solution	

EXHIBIT 24.3 Phase 1—Pre-Merger IM Road Map

Source: Deloitte

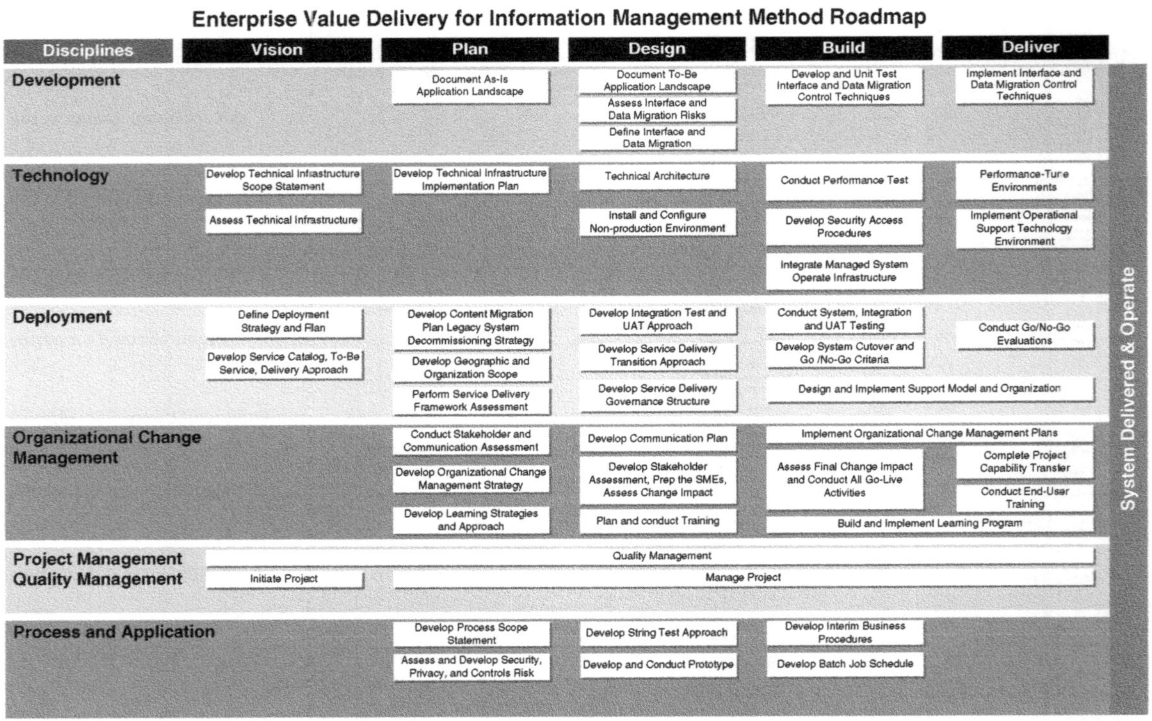

Enterprise Value Delivery for Information Management Method Roadmap

Disciplines	Vision	Plan	Design	Build	Deliver
Development		Document As-Is Application Landscape	Document To-Be Application Landscape; Assess Interface and Data Migration Risks; Define Interface and Data Migration	Develop and Unit Test Interface and Data Migration Control Techniques	Implement Interface and Data Migration Control Techniques
Technology	Develop Technical Infrastructure Scope Statement; Assess Technical Infrastructure	Develop Technical Infrastructure Implementation Plan	Technical Architecture; Install and Configure Non-production Environment	Conduct Performance Test; Develop Security Access Procedures; Integrate Managed System Operate Infrastructure	Performance-Ture Environments; Implement Operational Support Technology Environment
Deployment	Define Deployment Strategy and Plan; Develop Service Catalog, To-Be Service, Delivery Approach	Develop Content Migration Plan Legacy System Decommissioning Strategy; Develop Geographic and Organization Scope; Perform Service Delivery Framework Assessment	Develop Integration Test and UAT Approach; Develop Service Delivery Transition Approach; Develop Service Delivery Governance Structure	Conduct System, Integration and UAT Testing; Develop System Cutover and Go /No-Go Criteria; Design and Implement Support Model and Organization	Conduct Go/No-Go Evaluations
Organizational Change Management		Conduct Stakeholder and Communication Assessment; Develop Organizational Change Management Strategy; Develop Learning Strategies and Approach	Develop Communication Plan; Develop Stakeholder Assessment, Prep the SMEs, Assess Change Impact; Plan and conduct Training	Implement Organizational Change Management Plans; Assess Final Change Impact and Conduct All Go-Live Activities; Build and Implement Learning Program	Complete Project Capability Transfer; Conduct End-User Training
Project Management	Initiate Project				
Quality Management			Quality Management — Manage Project		
Process and Application		Develop Process Scope Statement; Assess and Develop Security, Privacy, and Controls Risk	Develop String Test Approach; Develop and Conduct Prototype	Develop Interim Business Procedures; Develop Batch Job Schedule	

System Delivered & Operate

EXHIBIT 24.4 Phase 2 — Post-Merger IM Road Map

Source: Deloitte

426

The attributes of an active program management approach include the following:

- **The integration program should be goal-aligned.** It should establish objectives, goals, and success factors and help make sure all projects within the program are aligned and deliver the expected benefits with the desired outcomes. It is important to invest adequate time in scoping and planning the different integration projects, their objectives, and their dependencies.
- **The integration program should be results-focused.** The program should integrate metrics, risks, and dependencies with realization of benefits across the projects. It should measure and report the health of individual projects for leadership decisions.
- **The integration program should be milestone-driven.** The program should go beyond tracking of traditional project metrics. Project outcomes should be regularly measured using key performance indicators (KPIs) against program goals and objectives with the required controls. Once projects are defined, appropriate milestones should be put in place and the project activities need to be tracked against them on an ongoing basis. Key performance indicators should be clearly defined at different timeframes to make sure the intended benefits of the M&A are being realized. The progress of post-merger activities should be tracked and reported to leadership on a periodic basis so as to identify risks at an early stage in the process and develop mitigation approaches to handle them.
- **The integration program should be collaborative.** The program should provide a framework for discrete project teams to work in an integrated and collaborative manner, fostering adoption by stakeholders at all levels impacted by the program.

Effective data management practices are integral to making active program management a reality, and will result in the provision of lagging, leading, and predictive information to senior executives to make key tactical and strategic decisions. The following are the seven standard steps associated with setting up an active program management office.

1. Establish program office framework:
   Objective: Define program vision and goals; organization structure, critical success factors, and implementation framework.
   Output: Program framework and program office setup.
2. Align critical success factors (CSFs) measures and metrics:
   Objective: Align critical success factors to program goals, and establish a shared set of measures and metrics to track program progress and performance.
   Output: Benefits summary, CSF-Measure-Metric mapping.

3. Create program milestone plan and data collection templates:

   Objective: Develop an integrated program milestone plan; identify project linkages and interdependencies, and benefit metrics; create data input, metric collection, and status report templates.

   Output: Benefit tracking model, program status collection templates.

4. Roll out program and conduct reviews:

   Objective: Roll out data collection templates and metrics templates, and start collecting baseline data from projects.

   Output: Program status collection and tracking tool kit.

5. Consolidate, analyze, and report:

   Objective: Assess, consolidate, and align inputs from projects and initiatives to determine program-level status; conduct program status meetings and produce status reports.

   Output: Program status report and dashboard.

6. Operationalize and go live:

   Objective: Establish ongoing communication process and institutionalize the program office as single means of tracking and reporting.

   Output: Communications plan, PMO roles and responsibilities, and project tracking templates.

7. Evolve and expand:

   Objective: Build momentum with early wins, incorporate lessons learned, and expand the program for complete rollout.

   Output: Communication strategy.

Organizations should pay special attention to the following aspects when establishing the program:

- Establish an owner for the program from the executive leadership team consisting of business and technology decision makers.
- Clearly define key roles and responsibilities for all activities associated with the program.
- Secure buy-in and sponsorship from the executive leadership team.
- Assess the information maturity of the new organization to determine the initiatives that can take information as a driver.
- Prioritize the key information management initiatives with participation from all the business functions, and institute an information management framework.
- Develop an operating model that captures the key interactions between the different business functions, integration teams, and support teams, and aligns with the organization's systems development lifecycle (SDLC), which facilitates the operations during and after integration.

Implementing a program management approach that can respond in real time to M&A data challenges is one of the top 10 keys to improving the outcome of a merger or acquisition.

4. Create a Data Domain Prioritization Strategy

In many cases, organizations prematurely focus on rationalization of applications and integration of different platforms that support the business functions, customers, products, and operations. However, organizations stand to realize specific benefits by initially focusing on critical data assets that deliver significant increased business value before embarking on an integration exercise. Understanding the critical data domains and the dependencies that exist between them will allow the organization to plan and prioritize its integration activities. This can help the organization make strategic decisions around an effective data integration approach: data coexistence, data consolidation, or an amalgamation of both approaches. For example, customer data are a critical data domain across most industries, and reporting to customers is a top priority. However, there should be an initial effort to determine all the data elements that are being reported to customers across both entities and the sourcing of these data elements after the merger or acquisition. A classic example is in the investment management space, where customer reporting systems are dependent on feeds from the accounting systems.

Client Case Study: Diversified Financial Services Company

The Challenge: A leading financial services company acquired part of a large bank to obtain a wider footprint in the asset management space. As this was the company's first major acquisition, Wall Street was closely monitoring its ability to complete the acquisition and integration. Based on initial assessments, the entire program was divided into over 110 projects grouped by releases that did not align with the logical flow of business processes in the to-be state. In addition, dependencies were poorly managed between the different projects.

The Approach: A three-month program was initiated to understand the specific requirements and critical data domains. This involved a detailed analysis of different releases, projects, as well as in-flight and new interfaces. Based on an understanding of the critical data domains and the logical flow of business processes in the to-be state, the releases and projects were prioritized based on the following seven steps:

1. **Security data.** Since this was a considerable expansion of existing asset management services, the security master had to be bolstered to intake additional securities that were being traded by the acquired entity.

2. **Accounting data.** Once the security data activities were completed, the back-office technologies (for example, accounting systems) had to be consolidated to streamline customer reporting and provide an integrated view to the customer.
3. **Trade processing.** The majority of the trading desks were distinct due to their presence in different markets. However, to account for the consolidation of a few of the trading platforms, the trade processing systems needed to be upgraded to route trades based on their origins.
4. **Trading data.** The trading platforms were later consolidated into three platforms.
5. **Client data.** Once the integrations of the accounting and trading platforms were completed, customer reporting systems were integrated. Until then, customer reporting was done via distinct systems.

The Result: The company was able to effectively deploy a new end-to-end stack that included three trading systems, four accounting systems, over 1,000 new interfaces, and 175 technology assets from trading to trade processing to accounting, transitioning to business-as-usual operations.

5. Institute an M&A Data Factory Framework

An M&A data factory framework defines a common set of procedures and controls to manage data across different integration projects and work streams to standardize the process across the program. It leverages best practices to manage data across the different work streams. Some of the common work streams include program management, governance, data integration, testing and environment management, and go-live transition. The data factory framework should be used not only in executing tactical integration activities, but also in focusing and delivering the long-term strategic objectives of the merged entity going forward.

The framework incorporates leading practices to manage, deliver, and operate the IM factory. The leading practices constitute tested processes, tools, and accelerators that support effective execution of post-merger integration activities across the lifecycle covering the focus areas of architecture, data, delivery, and operations.

The IM data factory can be implemented by leveraging an operating model that is comprised of manage, deliver, and transition processes built on a common framework.

The use of a well-defined operating model can achieve the following benefits:

- Accountability at each stage of integration, consistent high-quality deliverables, and tracking to expected outcomes.
- Effective management of cross-dependencies and early identification of potential pitfalls.
- Improved cross-team coordination and potential operational synergies across the build, test, and deliver phases.
- Effective go-live and smooth transition to application support teams.

6. Plan and Control Data Integration

Data integration is a real challenge when it comes to M&A. It is the norm to hear about companies storing massive amounts of information in separate data warehouses and data marts for business intelligence and analytical reporting. In addition to this, mergers and acquisitions are more challenging, because large amounts of business data also get generated on a daily basis since the show must go on. There is a push toward starting data integration as soon as possible to integrate quickly and help comply with regulations. However, from our experience with effective mergers and acquisitions, we have realized that sufficient time should be invested early on to define data flows and approaches for data conversion, data migration, test data management, batch window management, interface management, and identifying the big data opportunities early that are integral to an organization's data integration activities. The payback is that data are efficiently integrated and readily available as needed by the new company to support its business operations and reporting requirements.

Some keys to effective data integration include:

- Understand the critical data domains, as doing so is a precursor to data integration activities. To explain this using an example, one common anticipated benefit of a merger transaction is the leverage associated with an integrated customer base.

  Depending on the sophistication and maturity of the acquired company's data structures, its customer data may not easily integrate into the acquiring organization's systems, resulting in delays or costly workaround procedures to integrate the data. If the acquired company has a custom-developed customer database and the acquiring company has a fully integrated customer relationship management system, integrating the data could prove difficult and result in significant delays in moving to a smooth joint operation.
- Establish a common business taxonomy that will drive data integration activities and will capture the correlations between business, data,

application, and reporting requirements, thereby supporting a smooth transition to business continuity and business transformation.

▪ Set up an architecture and governance committee that is responsible for establishing and maintaining controls on data integration activities. This architecture committee will keep track of the data integration activities across the integration program, approve the building and delivery of any additional interfaces, and prioritize work across different work streams. During a merger or acquisition, there is often a tendency to bypass established controls relating to data in order to meet merger milestones. This team needs to make sure to promote adherence to established enterprise standards (for example, templates and deliverables) for data integration.

▪ Establish a single repository to track the intake, build, test, and delivery of interfaces. This repository will be a single location to store pertinent information about all the interfaces built across the integration program among all the individual projects. Information that will be stored about each interface includes data domain, source and target systems, file-level details, and delivery information. This will assist in establishing a single source of truth across the program, facilitate reporting the progress of the data integration efforts, and expedite the decision making during integration.

▪ Apply appropriate tools and methodologies. While many companies may have adequate data conversion processes and procedures, they may still lack the right tools and methodologies to perform a complex data integration effort. Within companies that don't have adequate data integration tools and methodologies, IT personnel are often asked to adapt methodologies normally associated with other IT tasks for the data integration process. While such approaches may suffice, they may also lead to potential control lapses and data integration inefficiencies. To fully address this issue, companies should develop a specific data integration strategy and consider acquiring a data integration software suite as they develop their overall M&A strategy. The benefit of this approach is the establishment of a more effective controls system and, ultimately, greater data integration efficiency.

In summary, sufficient time and focus should be invested on data issues early in the M&A planning cycle to reap available benefits.

7. Set Up an Integrated Testing and Data Management Program

The complexity of mergers and acquisitions makes it difficult for testing and quality leadership to develop an effective test strategy and approach that

Solution Structure

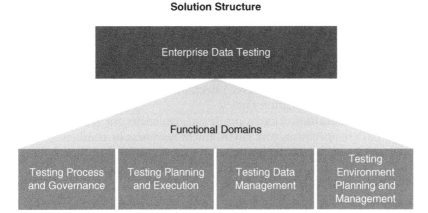

EXHIBIT 24.5 Integrated Enterprise Testing Approach
Source: Deloitte

considers dependencies across critical path projects. An integrated testing program (see Exhibit 24.5) needs to be developed to accomplish four things:

1. Establish a program-level capability to clarify and drive overarching test strategy, approach, interaction model, and cadence for the program.
2. Create a single-pane view of testing to establish and centrally manage the overarching testing schedule to better control test data and mitigate environment conflicts.
3. Raise the talent and capacity bar to provide test leadership and needed resources at release and project levels, provide the necessary capacity, and foster quick adoption of test strategy and approach.
4. Establish and enforce testing standards to manage program risks by creating a consistent testing pattern and rigorously enforcing process expectations.

This integrated testing program should encompass the following:

- **Testing process and governance.** Provide guidelines for test processes, procedures, and documents; enforce standards; and central points of escalation.
- **Testing planning and execution.** Provide resources at the program and project level, a test strategy for projects and releases, and a centralized view of test execution progress and quality.
- **Testing data management.** Guide key interactions with the project teams, enterprise data management, and data providers (source systems or data hub) to better manage and understand data requirements.
- **Testing environment planning and management.** Centralize timeline view, requirement, requests, and governance of environments.

Some of the key benefits that can be realized by establishing an integrated testing program include:

1. Single version of the truth across projects containing milestone detail, dependency detail, and testing phase scope and progress.
2. Establishment of project-level governance to revise test approaches, plans, and risk mitigation tactics.
3. Early identification of cross-project dependencies for testing based on test data requirements and environment readiness or conflicts.
4. Establishment of a standard operating process for test data definition and acquisition that enables the effective management of multiple project usage of data sets.
5. Installation of risk-based approaches in critical project domains, buttoned-up accountability, and decommission of siloed testing efforts.

The benefits of setting up an integrated testing and data management program will outweigh the cost and effort.

8. Develop a Reporting Strategy and Implementation Plan

During all phases of a merger, quality reporting is required to achieve the expected outcome and results. Much has been written regarding the importance of and approaches to financial information analysis during the pre-merger stage. If a target is a U.S. publicly traded company, an acquirer's initial assessment of the potential benefits generally is based on publicly available information. The acquirer usually is able to obtain only limited private information from the target prior to announcing the deal, but then engages in transactional due diligence after signing the acquisition agreement to affirm that the financial reporting warranties made by the target are accurate. Research has shown that low-quality financial reporting increases the likelihood of deal renegotiation and contributes to the probability of a deal going bust. Failed targets are more likely to restate their financial statements after the announcement of the deal, which then results in low-quality financial reporting contributing to the deal being terminated.

The need to implement a broad reporting strategy during the post-merger phase, while intuitively obvious, is less understood. Many organizations focus exclusively on the creation of financial information for regulatory bodies and investors during this phase, but may ignore other critical reporting needs. M&A events provide a specific, different, and particular set of reporting requirements that need to be delivered in a compressed timeframe to different audiences in different formats using different kinds of data with low tolerance for errors and rework. After the transaction, there is a constant pressure from business and leadership for accurate and reliable reports to be delivered on a constant basis. Reporting the benefits to shareholders and stakeholders during the integration is essential to maximizing benefits from the transaction. Therefore, organizations need to focus on developing a strong post-merger reporting framework that transitions them from a reactive view of business to a proactive one.

9. Implement Data Governance

Data governance can be defined as the set of organization structures, processes, and policies that promote and sustain high-quality data across the enterprise. A data governance organization structure is necessary for assigning roles and responsibilities, decision making, accountability, and escalation. Processes describe the standardized execution steps for the definition, creation, and maintenance of critical data assets. Data governance policies dictate the rules that should be enforced throughout the data management lifecycle. The data sets that typically require governance include master data (for example, customers, products, vendor, location), as well as key performance indicators (KPIs).

Post-merger integration can add another degree of complexity to preexisting and often already complex data environments due to increased volume of data and inconsistent data definitions. In addition, there is the constant pressure from business to accomplish a single view of customer, product, operations, and finance across the merged entities as quickly as possible. This unified view presents numerous data challenges, as it entails alignment and synergy of data domains and mapping the data to business processes and functions. This requires organizations to develop a strong data governance framework, focusing on the establishment of key roles and responsibilities for data ownership and stewardship, and establishment of data standards and processes for effective management and reporting of data.

In addition to establishing a data governance framework, organizations should also focus on understanding the data quality issues that can uncover potential integration complexities early in the integration lifecycle. Creating and maintaining high-quality data are not an easy endeavor under the normal course of business operations. Moreover, this is exacerbated in business scenarios where an organization undergoes a merger or an acquisition. The data issues that organizations face under these circumstances are common: unclear business terms and definitions, inaccurate numeric measures, inconsistent hierarchies, and increased data integration fallouts. The business ramifications related to these data quality issues are daunting: inability to up-sell or cross-sell to acquired customers, fines due to reporting inaccuracies, and increased monetary costs to integrate systems. By implementing sound data governance policies and practices, organizations can quickly integrate business processes and systems in order for the M&A to succeed.

The following seven leading governance practices should be considered when an M&A is in play:

1. **Adopt a top-down approach.** Strong executive support and sponsorship are a requirement for data governance to succeed.
2. **Be clear on roles and responsibilities.** The roles will include those for management, business, and IT. The assigned responsibilities should also be measurable.
3. **Communicate regularly.** Frequent communication regarding progress and success stories for consolidating and integrating data are essential.
4. **Establish baseline metrics.** Data quality metrics should be defined and enforced for the combining organizations.
5. **Deploy automated data processes.** By deploying simplified processes and work flow tools, the data maintenance and redundant data entry are minimized.
6. **Define data management policies at the enterprise level.** Common policies that exist in both organizations should be institutionalized; siloed practices should be discontinued.
7. **Operationalize on critical projects.** The need for operationalizing data governance on critical projects does not change in an M&A scenario. Instead, there is an increased need to standardize data management processes and policies on high-visibility projects to demonstrate the business benefits of high-quality data.

Client Case Study: Health Care Provider

The Challenge: A leading health care service provider acquired a competitor and, as a result, faced severe data quality issues: lack of a single version of the truth; inconsistent data definitions and usage across similar functional units; multiple reporting tools; and, most importantly, lack of policies, procedures, and controls to manage data as an enterprise asset. These issues severely hampered employee productivity and inflated operational expenses. To combat these issues and develop a strategy to transform its approach from a concept of information as a business outcome to information as a business driver, the client asked to develop a data governance framework to fast-track data quality as a driver for all integration activities.

The Approach: The data quality framework was defined, and specific processes were designed to fast-track the data integration objectives. This included the design of processes for metadata objectives, change control, issue management, and report sharing to implement the framework. In addition, a data stewardship program was defined and institutionalized to support the creation and maintenance of specific data objects. Finally, a data governance organization structure was designed along with supporting policies and procedures to facilitate the desired level of controls, accountability, and capabilities for promoting the desired level of data quality.

The Result: The solution enabled the client to enhance the integrity and accountability of data by adoption of the data governance and steward framework. In addition, the deliverables also enhanced the data quality capabilities to the business units of both client companies.

10. Build a Platform for Future M&A Management

Finally, a key to effectively achieving ongoing results and objectives is to build all of these keys into a sustainable organizational capability. Strengthening the corporate capacity to take on future M&A opportunities will reduce the risks associated with these transactions and help to squeeze out benefits early and often. For most organizations, data challenges associated with M&A transactions are addressed as an afterthought, frequently resulting in missing Day 1 and longer-term objectives for the merger. Given the critical role that data plays throughout the M&A lifecycle, it is important to set up practices to manage data effectively early in the lifecycle so as to enable a seamless integration. A well-established data management program will provide a solid foundation for companies to meet Day 1 objectives.

In particular, organizations should look to build the following institutional capabilities:

- Leadership and vision from executives who understand the critical nature of data management, including the benefits and risks associated with its implementation during the full cycle of M&A activities.
- Skilled staff who reside in both IT and business units who have awareness, skills, capabilities, and expertise with data and a willingness to build a capacity to take on these transactions.
- Business processes that are purpose-built for M&A and are refined during each M&A.

■ Technology architecture, solutions, and tools that have been implemented and upgraded to support M&A.

Planning for future mergers and acquisitions and building an institutional capability focused on data and information management will increase the organization's ability to benefit from subsequent M&A activities.

WRAPPING IT UP

Conventional technology integration techniques may not achieve the desired or expected post-merger integration business targets. Often, they do not take into account specific information management challenges and opportunities such as data integration planning, data consolidation, and data quality. Effective data management both during and after the merger is critical to managing M&A activities; determining or confirming that consolidated data from multiple systems and the resulting information can be trusted is critical. Through interviews with various clients we have determined that in many cases, the role played by data in a transaction is typically understated, and data's potential to positively impact synergies is not well understood. To help facilitate the achievement of M&A goals and objectives in the information management area, companies should consider using the 10 key ways described in this chapter to aid in delivering the planned benefits from M&A.

CHAPTER 25

Overview of Testing

Angela Mattix

Testing is a critical component in mergers and acquisitions (M&A) projects. In an effort to reduce project duration, this is an area projects are tempted to shortcut; however, the most successful projects include a sufficient number of testing cycles. This chapter reviews the following specific areas:

- Types of testing
- Testing functions and tools
- Test preparation activities

TYPES OF TESTING

Before exploring the tools and key preparation activities required to execute successful testing cycles, you should understand the various types of testing and their objectives:

- Unit
- String
- Integration
- Parallel
- User acceptance testing
- Regression
- Performance and stress or volume
- Disaster and backup recovery
- Dress rehearsal or mock cut-over

Unit Testing

The key objective of unit testing is to validate a discrete piece of functionality or a specific development object. Unit testing is typically started during the end of the design phase and continues into the early stages of the build phase. As mentioned, there are several different types of unit testing:

- **Technical unit testing** is typically conducted by a developer to validate that the code written for a custom developed object meets the key objectives and criteria of the development object.
- **Functional unit testing** typically refers to when a business team member tests a development object to confirm it meets the business objectives that are identified in the functional specification that documents the business needs and rules for the development object.
- **Configuration testing** is typically conducted by the business user and is used to confirm the specific configuration decision to validate that the package performs as expected.
- **Process controls testing** is typically a combination of business and internal audit testing used to validate that the internal and Sarbanes-Oxley (SOX) controls are being met by the system design.
- **Security testing** is typically conducted by the business and internal audit to confirm that package responsibilities do not violate segregation of duties rules.

When defining test scenarios for unit testing, the scenarios should incorporate both positive and negative testing. Positive testing is a scenario in which the system is expected to perform without an error, whereas a negative test is meant to validate that when something is entered incorrectly the appropriate error message will be generated. Examples of a positive test and a negative test are:

- **Positive test.** Create an employee with a valid job position and the employee should be created successfully.
- **Negative test.** Create an employee with an invalid job position and the system should generate an error message.

String Testing

The key objective of string testing is to validate the flow of data within a specific module or subprocess. The following is an example of discrete unit tests that would then be strung together to make up a string test:

- Enter journal entry.
- Approve journal entry.
- Post journal entry.

String testing does not typically include conversions or integration from legacy systems and is therefore not typically a formal testing cycle within an M&A. A subset of string testing might be completed for a specific process area if there is a significant change to an existing process due to the merger.

Integration Testing

The key objective of integration testing is to test end-to-end process scenarios. Not only should integration testing scenarios test the business process, but the test should also validate the responsibilities the user should be using to execute the test script as well as any process or SOX controls and reporting requirements expected as part of the process. A typical M&A project should include a minimum of two rounds of full end-to-end integration testing. The first round of integration testing may not have full security enabled to help facilitate process testing. This makes it easier to determine that any issue is related to the process and not related to security. The second round of integration testing should include full security testing to validate that the roles have access to the forms and reports needed to perform the key functions and activities expected of that role.

Parallel Testing

The key objective of parallel testing is to parallel or mimic production activity, or a particular subset of transactions to validate calculations and allow the users to compare the results between production and the proposed new processes. Parallel testing is typically executed only for payroll and occasionally consolidation process scenarios. Most projects do not have the resource bandwidth or the time needed to perform parallel testing.

User Acceptance Testing

The main objective of user acceptance testing (UAT) is to have key business users validate that the system will perform the critical functions of the business. User acceptance testing is typically a subset of the test scenarios executed during integration testing. This is an important testing cycle to complete; the final validation of the system prior to going live, continue the education of the user community, and help enhance business acceptance of the new system.

Regression Testing

Regression testing is the concept of testing a system after changes have been made to validate that the changes did not impact existing functionality. In the case of mergers and acquisitions, regression testing should be done for the acquiring company's transactions that were not expected to be impacted by the acquisition, to validate that the existing processes were not affected.

Performance and Stress or Volume Testing

Typically performance and stress or volume testing will be combined into a single testing event. Performance testing focuses on the performance of the infrastructure, software application, and network. The primary goal of performance testing is to discover potential performance flaws in the infrastructure and software configurations that can be addressed prior to cut-over into production. Performance testing is focused on the typical volumes and response times from the system.

Another aspect of performance testing is to execute stress and volume testing. The primary focus on stress and volume testing is to push the system to its limits to get a better understanding of the system's breaking point. Stress testing is typically performed at 125 percent to 150 percent of typical volumes of key transactions.

Disaster and Backup Recovery Testing

Another key testing activity that should be performed as part of an M&A project is understanding the disaster recovery and backup recovery process as well as planning and executing testing of this process. First, let's review the backup recovery testing process. As part of the project, a backup strategy should be defined and understood. At periodic points in time during the project, the backup recovery process should be tested. These tests should be planned to identify a specific backup and attempt to create or refresh an environment based on this backup. The testing of the backup strategy can help identify potential issues with the actual backup process and also assists with understanding the timing required to recover an environment based on a backup.

Disaster recovery is a much more extensive recovery and testing process. The primary objective of this testing is to validate that a company has the ability to recover data and get the organization back up and running in a short period of time when a disaster such as a hurricane, tornado, or some other such event might impact the location where the infrastructure of a system is maintained. This test should simulate the production environment being compromised so the disaster recovery procedures and process can be confirmed.

Dress Rehearsal or Mock Cut-Over Testing

Last but not least is what is commonly referred to as dress rehearsal or mock cut-over testing. It is highly recommended to conduct at least two mock cut-overs before the actual production cut-over is executed. These mock cut-overs serve several key purposes:

- Allow the cut-over manager to validate the sequence, dependencies, and timing of all the cut-over activities.
- Educate the cut-over task owners on their responsibility related to the cut-over process.

Now that you have a basic understanding of the various types of testing and their goals, we will review the different types of tools that can be used to help facilitate the testing process.

TESTING FUNCTIONS AND TOOLS

You should have an understanding of a few of the testing tools that can be leveraged, and the various functions that testing activities can be grouped into. The five primary functions are:

1. **Test management** tools assist with the management of tests, scheduling of them through arranging test scripts into logical groupings, as well as facilitating the traceability of tests to defects and test status reporting.
2. **Test execution** tools allow testers to store expected results, log test results, and attach screen shots of test results or errors.
3. **Performance measurement** tools facilitate the simulation of high user test load and analytical information to interpret test performance during volume testing.
4. **Requirement management** tools assist with storing of requirements and linking requirements to test scripts or test cases to facilitate a traceability matrix for audit purposes.
5. **Defect management** tools support categorization, prioritization, and assignment of ownership of various issues or defects that are identified during testing.

TEST PREPARATION ACTIVITIES

Test preparation activities require a significant amount of time from the project team and should be planned for and understood early in the design phase of the project.

Test Strategy and Approach

During the design phase of your project, the test manager should first prepare the overall test strategy and approach, which should cover these general topics:

- Testing overview.
- Types of testing to be executed during the course of the project.
- Identification of the testing tools to be used.
- Testing roles and responsibilities.
- Estimated testing timeline, including number of integrated test cycles to be executed before moving into user acceptance testing.
- Testing scope for each type of testing.
- Defect management process.

Develop Unit Test Scripts

The process team should develop the unit test scripts to validate the standard package functionality as well as any custom processes or interfaces. As mentioned earlier, unit test scripts should include both positive and negative test scripts.

Define End-to-End Scenarios

It is important that the top end-to-end scenarios are defined to confirm that data flow from start to finish. Depending on the scope of processes being impacted by the M&A activity, you should have anywhere between 10 and 30 scenarios defined. Once the scenarios are agreed upon, then there is an exercise to identify the specific unit test scripts that need to be executed to test the end-to-end flow. The test scripts should be sequenced in the appropriate order, and you should identify the resource responsible for executing each test script. The most important thing during end-to-end testing is tracking the transactional data being created in each step of the test scenario. For example, if there is an end-to-end scenario for creating a requisition all the way through posting to general ledger. The tester that creates the requisition should be sure to document the supplier and requisition number used so this can be passed to the purchase order tester. Once the requisition is turned into a purchase order, the purchase order number should be documented in the data sheet and so forth.

Identify and Prepare Test Data

The next step is to understand the type of data needed and any dependencies before each test script can be executed. Data needs should take into consideration any master data requirements as well as transactional data needs. As an example, for a test to enter and approve a purchase requisition, the following information needs must be considered:

- Master data needs:
  - Suppliers and employees converted.
  - Items.
  - Ship-to/bill-to locations.
- Transactional data:
  - Specific supplier to use.
  - Specific item to use for requisition.
  - Approver to whom requisition will be routed for approval.

Prepare the Test Environment There are numerous activities to be considered as part of the environment preparation. These include but are not limited to:

- Configuring the modules.
- Applying patches to the environment.
- Identifying any printers that need to be set up for testing.
- Defining and setting up security.
- Defining testers and setting up access to the system with the appropriate responsibilities.

Developing the Test Plan Once the test scripts and end-to-end scenarios are defined, the next step is to determine the timing, sequence, and dependencies of executing each of the test scripts. This should be a high-level plan used to communicate to testers on when they should expect to execute specific test scripts.

Developing the Requirements Traceability Matrix After the test scripts are defined, they should be mapped back to the business requirements identified during design to use as an audit control to confirm that all business requirements were tested at some point during the testing cycles.

While all these activities are being executed, the project team is also conducting unit testing for configurations and for development objects, and configuring the test environment; therefore, planning for and managing priorities are critical activities.

TIMING OF TESTING

There are typically five standard phases in the software development life cycle: vision/planning, design, build, deliver, and operate. It is important to understand when you should plan to execute the various types of testing referenced earlier. Let's now take a look at a few of the phases (design, build, deliver) and what types of testing activities should be conducted in these phases.

- **Design.** There is typically minimal or no testing conducted during the design phase. Generally, the type of testing conducted at the very end of design is configuration testing. This phase of testing may also occur in the early stages of the build phase.
- **Build.** This is where the majority of the testing activities occur. The typical sequence of testing activities is:
  - **Configuration testing** is executed by the business process team (if not done at the end of design).
  - **Technical unit testing** is executed by the developers responsible for designing any custom development objects.
  - **Functional unit testing** is the process team testing the functionality of the custom development objects that have passed technical unit testing. This is done to validate that the developer designed the custom object to meet the business requirements.
  - **String testing** is primarily performed by the process team to make sure the data within a specific module is flowing correctly. String testing may or may not include any custom development objects. It is not expected that all development objects are executed during string testing. An example of an effective string test would be to enter an accounts payable invoice for a converted supplier, approve the entry, and then pay the invoice. String testing may include some form of limited process controls testing as well.
  - **Integration testing** is primarily performed by the process team with the focus on string as well as end-to-end testing, including all development

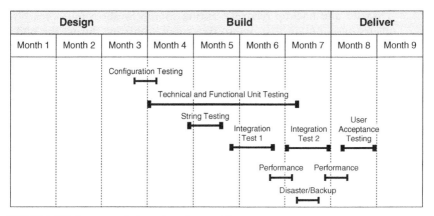

EXHIBIT 25.1 Sample Testing Gantt Chart

objects. Integration test cycles are traditionally planned for anywhere from three to four weeks, depending on the scope of the project. When there is significant development or risk, the test cycle could be planned for up to six weeks. It is common for projects to plan to conduct two full rounds of integration testing. The last round of integration testing should also include the testing of process controls and security testing. Also, regression testing may be incorporated into the final round of integration testing for process areas that were not impacted by the M&A activity, just to make sure there are no negative impacts due to any changes made to accommodate the merger or acquisition.

- **Performance and stress testing** is typically performed by the IT team. However, the project business process team should have input into the processes and service-level agreements on processing time that will be used to evaluate the performance tests. The first round of performance testing is traditionally two to three weeks long and conducted shortly after the first round of integration testing. If adjustments need to be made to improve performance, a second, shorter round of performance testing may be executed to validate that any issues have been resolved.
- **Mock cut-over testing** is typically performed by both IT and the process team to start knowledge transfer of the tasks required to be executed during the production cut-over. These mock cut-overs can be done as stand-alone mini one- to two-week test cycles, or they can be executed as the system preparation activities for a round of integration or UAT test cycles.

- **Disaster and backup recovery testing** should be short one-week test cycles executed at least one to two times sometime during the build phase. There are no dependencies of other test cycles.
- **Deliver.** This is when UAT is conducted, as this is the final round of business testing where you bring in a larger end-user audience to confirm that what has been designed will allow the organization to continue its operations. This round of testing should be a reduced scope of end-to-end test cases focused on core functionality using the security expected to be used in production.

A typical testing timeline is shown in Exhibit 25.1.

WRAPPING IT UP

This chapter has covered a lot of information on testing. Testing is a critical component of any technology project and even more so when executing a merger, acquisition, or divestiture. During the planning phase of the project, it is critical to clearly understand the testing cycles that will be executed during the project. It is essential to reinforce the importance of not scrimping on testing. Testing is a highly effective way to gain confidence that the operations will not be impacted at the time of cut-over.

Conclusion

Why Mergers, Acquisitions, and Divestitures Fail, and Considerations to Help Avoid a Similar Fate

Nikhil Menon

A merger, acquisition, or divestiture project is one of the largest, most complex, and most far-reaching projects an organization undertakes. The principal mergers and acquisitions (M&A) challenge for a company is to capture synergies through initiatives such as functional consolidations, personnel reductions, and cross-selling/up-selling while integrating the different aspects of the two merging companies (such as systems, customers, suppliers, and employees) and building a strategic platform for the new organization without negatively impacting any of its stakeholders (such as regulators, customers, employees, shareholders, and vendors).

When companies undergo a merger or an acquisition, there are typical outcomes they expect going into it. These outcomes include reinventing and redefining the competitive landscape, integrating and rationalizing like operations, capturing synergies rapidly, protecting current customer and user base, and executing an issue-free Day 1.

It is an unfortunate fact that many M&A efforts fail to achieve the business results that were used to justify them. A study of these transactions shows that about 60 percent of acquisitions fail to achieve their stated strategic objectives within the planned time frame.[1] Many are dissolved, often at a loss. Targeted and announced synergies are not achieved in surround 70 percent of the M&A transactions.[2] Productivity of these companies can be reduced by around 50 percent in the first four to eight months after close. Only 23 percent of the acquirers earn their cost of capital, and around 47 percent of executives leave in year 1, 75 percent by year 3. Mergers and acquisitions are, therefore, high-risk undertakings.

Based on our experience, the major cause of M&A failure is ineffective planning and execution. In the excitement of the deal, integration and divestiture planning is sometimes left as an afterthought.

M&A RISKS

There are four groups of risks that impact the results of M&A transactions.

1. **Synergy risk.** This is the probability of meeting the synergy targets that have been set and have been announced to the street. Analysts and investors keep track of this risk, and this tends to affect the stock price of the acquirer. The synergy risks are typically driven by the following:
   - **Quality of financial figures.** How detailed are the financials for each company? Over what time horizon do the companies have financials for? What are the different key performance indicators (KPIs) that the companies have been tracking?
   - **Complexity of synergy goals.** What are the synergy targets by function and cost category? What are the different synergy sources? What are the expected timelines for the synergy achievement?
   - **Execution plan viability.** What are the feasibility and plausibility of the synergy project plan? Are there detailed steps identified and documented for the synergy realization?
2. **Structural risk.** This is the risk originating from the integration of two discrete and different enterprises into one. Structural risk can be classified into:
   - **Organizational and management structure differences.** What are the spans of control for the two different organizations? How are the profit centers and cost centers set up in the two companies? How different are the remunerations for similar roles? What changes need to be made to work flows and approvals?
   - **Business process heterogeneity.** What is the overlap between the two organizations in products, customers, and regions? What changes need to be made to the business processes during the integration?
3. **People risks.** Merger and acquisition transactions are periods of flux for the workforce, as there are significant impacts to the organization of both the acquirer and the target. This can represent a risk to the transaction. People risks typically arise from:
   - **Realignment at the executive level.** What are the redundancies between the two companies? How are the nominations and selections done between the two companies? Are there any external hires required to fill any skill gaps?

- **Changes at a managerial level.** What are the redundancies between the two companies? Will resources be relocated?
- **Extent and direction of downsizing.** What are the redundancies between the two companies? Is the downsizing focused on one of the companies or is it balanced?
- **Cultural compatibility.** What differences exist in the way the two organizations interact internally, with their suppliers and with their customers? Are there disconnects in work-life balance expectations across the two companies?

4. **Project risks.** These are risks in executing the integration and divestiture projects to meet all requirements on time and within budget. The risks can be because of:
   - **Lack of experience.** Do the resources working on the integration or divestiture have prior M&A experience? Do the resources have an understanding of the business processes, people, and systems of their respective companies? Is there access to contractors available with prior M&A experience?
   - **Limited human resource capacity.** Are there enough resources to staff all the integration and divestiture projects? Are the resources incentivized appropriately for an M&A project?

Project risks can result in delay in execution of the integration or divestiture, resulting in pushing out the transaction close date and the achievement of the end state.

COMMON PITFALLS

The companies that fail in mergers, acquisitions, or divestitures are unable to manage some or all of these risks. Here are a few recurring themes that have been observed in the deals where IT has contributed to failures of mergers, acquisitions, and divestitures.

1. Unclear scope and not aligned with business:
   - **Unclear IT scope for the M&A transaction and/or debate on the IT integration or divestiture approach for the transaction.** Multiple companies undergoing mergers, acquisitions, and divestitures have faced timing, resource, and cost issues because there was no clarity of scope for the IT organization. Inability to agree on, communicate, and adopt an IT integration or divestiture approach has resulted in operational issues because of disconnects between different parts of the organization. In order to help articulate and document scope and

approach for IT, set and articulate the IT M&A strategy (guiding principles, nonnegotiable items, etc.) up front; establish a governance and escalation process early on; appoint strong IT leads who can help ensure that IT M&A activities are in line with the IT M&A strategy; and conduct a scoping workshop early on with outputs being clear, concise, documented, and agreed upon.

- **Unaligned business and IT requirements.** The approach to IT is highly dependent on the business approach and must be closely synchronized with it. If IT requirements are not enabling the business requirements, this can result in inefficiencies and also can result in business continuity issues in Day 1 and Day 2 cut-overs. Alignment between business and IT requirements can be achieved by helping ensure that business requirements are documented, vetted, and agreed; conducting joint project kickoff sessions to assess feasibility of requirements; conducting periodic joint design and plan reviews (align business and IT requirements, and identify dependencies); and monitoring cross-functional dependencies.

2. Trying to do a lot in a short period of time:

- **Complex Day 1 scope.** A primary reason for M&A transactions having major issues on Day 1 is because IT and other functions signed up for complex Day 1 scope. Complex scope can result in issues, as typically timelines to Day 1 are tight and ability to execute is limited prior to regulatory approval. Day 1 scope can be made more manageable by using an approach that leverages the existing solution of one or the other organization; by managing, reducing, and controlling the tendency to reengineer solutions; and by focusing only on must-haves for Day 1.

- **Commitment to overly aggressive synergies.** Synergies are critical to realizing the value from an M&A transaction, but committing to overly aggressive synergy targets can result in reduced ability to provide services to the business. Proper synergy targets can be identified and established by performing top-down IT synergy analysis, understanding overall and IT synergy commitments from program leadership, validating the proposed synergies with technical experts, negotiating synergies to achievable levels, and educating leadership that a majority of IT's synergies come with long lead-time items (such as data center consolidation, help desk consolidation, and application consolidation and retirement).

3. Lack of communication or incomplete or inaccurate communication:

- **Information erroneously shared.** There are restrictions on what information can be shared between the two companies prior to transaction close. There could be legal and regulatory implications if these restrictions are not followed. To help ensure that the regulatory restrictions are observed, it is important to get legal counsel involved early in the process to articulate what can and cannot be shared prior to the closing date. Also, if required, it may be necessary to implement a clean team approach to share information confidentially and secure sensitive material.

- **Disconnect between IT communications and overall communications.** Lack of coordinated communications can lead to inefficiencies and confusion throughout the integration or divestiture projects. Companies should coordinate communications through creating a dedicated communications team to confirm that messages are created and delivered to the appropriate audiences, helping ensure coordination with any other communication stakeholders, using the same tools for IT communication as are used by the business communication team, and publishing an IT communications timeline aligned to the overall business communications timeline.

4. Lack of resource and budget:
   - **Overstretched IT team members.** Typically IT initiatives within M&A projects are staffed with existing IT staff. These resources have to deliver the M&A project in addition to working on their existing roles. The pressure on the IT staff can be reduced by documenting IT resource needs early on, prioritizing IT initiatives required for the transaction, off-loading regular jobs where possible to other company personnel, hiring contractors to work with the company's subject matter experts where required, and shutting down in-flight projects where possible.
   - **Lack of clarity on IT budgeting for M&A project.** IT is one of the largest drivers of costs in integrations and divestitures. Hence, it is critical to have a clear line of sight into the IT budget and be able to track these costs throughout the project. IT should involve financial analysts and project controllers early in the project to establish guidelines and processes. They should assist in interpreting budgets and actual cost data.

CRITICAL SUCCESS FACTORS

In an M&A project, the organization frequently is putting its future at stake. It is therefore worthwhile to understand and address the following 10 critical M&A success factors:

1. **Experience.** M&A efforts should be guided by resources with in-depth experience in M&A integration using past lessons learned and repeatable processes.

2. **Coordination.** There should be a coordinated, cross-functional corporate plan supported in a hierarchical fashion by detailed subplans with specific milestones and targets. All functions need to work closely with one another. It is practically impossible to achieve a successful functional integration without considering the integration points with other functions.

3. **Leadership.** Organizations that achieve their desired M&A objectives typically appoint high-level, full-time leaders with the authority and accountability for achieving the M&A goals. Generally, a business executive has overall responsibility for the integration or divestiture, and an IT executive is responsible for the IT aspects.

4. **Clear intent.** In organizations that achieved their desired M&A objectives, the business value to be derived from the deal has been explicitly articulated in measurable terms. In other words, the business intent is clear to everyone involved.

5. **Perseverance.** Organizations that achieve their desired M&A objectives commit themselves to achieving the M&A goals forcefully and consistently for the duration. Merger integration is typically a long process that takes over a year to achieve. It is also important to look for small wins early on in the integration. Although they may not be the most impactful in the scope of the overall deal, checking items off of the long list of to-dos can be great for morale.

6. **Accountability.** The best and the brightest people from both companies are dedicated to the integration or divestiture effort, and their performance criteria are set accordingly. Incentivize resources to meet stretch goals in relation to the integration and divestiture efforts. Identify the key resources for the transaction, and plan for their retention during and after the transaction.

7. **Leverage.** The integration or divestiture efforts are carried out by the same departments or teams who will have to live with and manage the results produced.

8. **Focus.** Organizations that achieve their desired M&A objectives are able to keep a clear distinction between work that is part of the M&A project and work that is required to maintain or evolve the current business. The M&A project is budgeted and tracked without intermingling with other efforts.

9. **Decisiveness.** Organizations that achieve their desired M&A objectives readily make decisions (especially the hard decisions involving people) and move ahead without regrets.

10. **Communications.** Organizations that achieve their desired M&A objectives communicated proactively, comprehensively, and with one voice both internally and externally. This may be the most important of all factors. There is no such thing as overcommunication during a merger,

acquisition, or divestiture. Employee uncertainty can be the silent killer of successful merger integration.

The more an organization can adhere to these critical success factors, the greater are its chances of M&A success. If there is significant departure from these factors, some corrective actions may be warranted before proceeding with the integration or divestiture effort.

WRAPPING IT UP

Mergers, acquisitions, and divestitures are complex projects that have significant impact on the company's operations and financial results. There are multiple risks in play that can impact the results and outcome of the transaction—synergy risks, structural risks, people risks, and project risks. Many companies are unable to mitigate these risks, resulting in significant failure rates.

Since IT plays a major part in these transactions, any failure on IT's part can affect the whole deal. There are a few recurring themes that are seen across transactions that fail because of IT. These can be managed by clearly managing scope and working with the business, not trying to do too much in tight timeframes, timely and appropriate communications, and proper resourcing and budgeting. By focusing on the 10 critical success factors, companies can help improve their probability of achieving the expected and desired value in a merger, acquisition, or divestiture.

Notes

1. "Solving the Merger Mystery: Maximizing the Payoff of Mergers and Acquisitions," Deloitte, 2000.
2. "Conducting Successful Transactions: We Keep the Deal in Swing," Deloitte, 2008.

CHAPTER 27

M&A IT Key Success Factors

Nadia Orawski
Luke Bates

Based on our research and experience, it is widely accepted that many mergers fail to deliver their expected value. Getting IT involved early and often throughout the M&A and divestiture lifecycle is critical to an effective merger or divestiture. This shouldn't be too surprising, as many deal benefits rely heavily on IT systems and infrastructure. Yet, many companies ignore IT during the transaction, putting off the inevitable until the deal is essentially done. By then, it's usually too late. To aid in the effectiveness of the transaction design and execution, we have identified a number of factors that should be front of mind for any IT executive about to embark on a transaction and are applicable to the full gamut of M&A and divestiture activity.

KEY SUCCESS FACTORS

Involve IT Early

It is critical to engage IT early in the deal cycle to maximize M&A benefits and minimize execution risk. Most of the effective M&A efforts we have seen had significant IT involvement in all phases of the M&A lifecycle, from preliminary due diligence to Day 1 and beyond. Through up-front involvement, IT can uncover potential issues, high-cost items, and additional synergies to drive significant value during an M&A deal. It is considered best practice for organizations to assign a senior IT executive to engage in the M&A process as early as possible, to make the CIO (or designee) a key member of the due diligence team, and to keep the IT function involved until all key synergies have been captured.

Facilitate IT Readiness

Identify, at a detailed level, IT requirements before you sign the deal. Insist the due diligence team identify all IT investments that will be needed to achieve the expected short-term and long-term benefits. Although it is generally not possible to define the exact cost and timing of required IT systems and infrastructure (due to the speed of the deal and limited information available during due diligence), it is essential to develop order-of-magnitude estimates for these critical IT projects.

Control the Integration

The IT department, in conjunction with the program management office, can establish a structure that can help to accelerate planning and a framework for other critical business functions to align with. A well-defined IT road map includes specific and clear goals, a detailed approach or methodology for achieving those goals, and a list of all resources and time required to reach the goals. Ideally, companies should work on the road map as part of the pre-merger financial and operational due diligence so they are asking the right questions from the start and are able to provide a structure to which other critical business functions can align.

Minimize Risk

The technology area should proactively assess and mitigate operational, productivity, and service continuity risks. Understanding the business risks includes appreciating IT's relationship with the business, the importance of a business-driven IT strategy, and the value of IT in enabling business operation. When business functions and IT work smoothly together, this understanding drives current and planned IT projects—projects aimed at actualizing the value of the deal.

Manage Cost to Achieve

The IT function is often one of the largest budget line items in any M&A activity, and proactively managing this can drive material value. However, because IT is a secondary focus in most deals, the magnitude, complexity, and cost of these activities are often significantly underestimated.

Enable Key Stakeholder Engagement

Merger and acquisition activity can have a greater chance of achieving the desired execution results when key business and IT stakeholders are engaged in the program's success. Many of the most effectively run M&A programs operate within a structure that actively encourages collaboration and teamwork between IT and the business and functional areas. One way to do this is by staffing key positions on the M&A team with someone from IT and someone from the business to jointly drive planning and execution. This "double boxing" team structure can help foster a strong working relationship and sense of ownership.

Focus on Talent Retention

Most IT professionals know that head count reduction is a common outcome in all M&A activity. Organizations should be prepared to answer common questions such as: Will employees retain their current level of compensation and benefits? Will they lose their stock options? Will the workload double? Will employees have to relocate? And what about that anticipated promotion? If companies are not prepared to act fast to address employee concerns, they risk losing key employees when they are most needed.

WRAPPING IT UP

Regardless of the size and complexity of an integration or a divestiture, the IT team's speed and effectiveness is likely to have a significant impact on whether the deal achieves the expected results. That's why it is beneficial to get the IT function involved early in the deal, to keep IT involved throughout the M&A and divesture lifecycle, and to follow the key success factors contained in this chapter and throughout the book.

CHAPTER 28

M&A IT, Summing It All Up

Habeeb Dihu
Nadia Orawski
Justin Calvin
Luke Bates
Bryce Metro
Eric Niederhelman

The role of IT in business has never been more significant than it is today. Technology is an enabler of virtually every operating element in contemporary organizations and is critical to a successful merger, acquisition, or divestiture for many reasons. The ability to keep one's company on the rails while simultaneously executing a complex merger, acquisition, or divestiture is a skill that should be a part of every technology leader's repertoire. Not only is IT typically a significant driver of opportunity, whether it be synergy or cost reduction, but it can also be one that has the largest cost and takes the longest time to execute. Technology typically underpins the operations of the entire organization, potentially impacting every function. Organizations that embark on an M&A activity without effective IT preparation and input run the very real risk that the incremental deal value could be threatened, potentially resulting in shareholder value destruction.

Throughout this book we have identified and provided tangible ways to embed key success factors into your M&A activity, including:

- Involving IT early.
- Facilitating IT readiness and making sure IT is prepared in advance of any M&A activity.
- Controlling the transaction and putting in place a structured program.
- Focusing on minimizing risk.
- Effectively managing cost.
- Enabling key stakeholders' engagement.
- Focusing on talent retention.

Aligning your guiding principles and decisions to these factors will help to facilitate a more successful M&A outcome. In this chapter, we focus on providing you with a series of best practices, case studies, and lessons learned that are aligned with the key success factors outlined. They are applicable to the full gamut of M&A activity and can enhance an organization's ability to complete current or pending IT M&A or divestiture due diligence, planning, and execution to achieve the desired objectives and to help drive shareholder value creation.

BEST PRACTICES

Each merger or divestiture is unique and will have its own set of challenges, risks, and pitfalls. The best practices outlined here represent experiences that have spanned industries, deal size, and transaction complexity and represent the essence of what makes a good best practice—activities or processes that work across a variety of deals in predictable, repeatable ways. Throughout the deal process, the following best practices should be considered and used as tools to help navigate the complexities that are found in any merger or divestiture. Each stage of the deal contains a different series of tasks, but ultimately they all tie together to form a single, cohesive plan. Utilizing the outlined best practices helps link each phase of the transaction into a continuous process that drives toward a successful merger or divestiture.

The next section aims to provide a framework to assist in planning and completing the merger or divestiture activities. Understanding the dos and don'ts associated with each best practice is a critical aspect to increase the chances of success, as well as to mitigate the risks that can lead to failure. Each best practice described aims to provide a quick reference summary of activities to keep in mind while planning and working through a merger or divestiture.

These best practices are intended to form a guide to steer the transaction in the proper direction, but, like any guide, they cannot cover every unique situation, though the guidance is applicable to the majority of deals.

BEST PRACTICES TO BE CONSIDERED PRIOR TO THE DEAL

Do Not Ignore IT

IT involvement throughout the due diligence and merger or divestiture process is critical to making sure there is a successful Day 1. In addition, high involvement from IT leads to the effective capture of IT-related synergies. Failure to involve IT, especially early in the planning process, can lead to several serious consequences. To mitigate the risks associated with the merger or divestiture process, several items should be considered.

Design IT for the Future Business Strategy   While M&A deals aim to take advantage of synergies between multiple entities, these benefits are significantly reduced when IT is not adequately aligned with the business's goals. An effective IT strategy needs to be constructed and aligned with the business objectives of the future entity(ies) to make sure IT enables the new business and allows synergies to be realized. In many cases, each entity prior to separation or merger may have a fully functional IT department; however, the strategies and principles implemented may not align with the new business objectives and can prevent the business from achieving its future business potential. The IT function needs to be planned and aligned to meet the new strategic direction.

Plan for Additional, Unexpected Costs   Technology can be the largest cost during a merger or divestiture, and thus needs to be treated as a high-impact, high-cost area. Treating IT as a secondary cost can lead to the underestimation of the time, resources, and budget required to successfully merge or separate the IT department(s). Technology-related activities are often more complex than originally anticipated, and without proper due diligence, preparation, and planning, can lead to millions of dollars in additional costs not originally planned for when beginning the merger or separation.

Implement Temporary Solutions Only When Necessary   Technology integration and divestiture activities often have long lead times. To mitigate risks and help ensure deals are closed on schedule, companies frequently develop transition services agreements (TSAs). While this may help meet short-term needs, TSAs should be used only when necessary to bridge gaps, as they can force the company to incur large expenditures to support the IT needs. The IT department should be planned early on to allow adequate time to be stood up and become fully operational in order to avoid costly TSAs to provide support until the transition is completed.

Get IT Involved Early

The majority of businesses today are fully dependent on their IT departments, and thus need to involve IT during the early stages of planning a merger or divestiture. Successful deals keep IT involved throughout the process, reducing issues that arise from lack of alignment between IT and the business. To help ensure IT is involved across all phases of the deal, several methods can be implemented.

Assign a Senior IT Executive to Do Due Diligence Making the CIO (or a designee) a primary member of the due diligence team helps ensure that the IT function will be well represented throughout the process. Keeping the IT function involved during the planning efforts better prepares the business for a successful Day 1. Senior IT involvement provides a valuable perspective and helps make sure IT will be better aligned with the future business.

Encourage Communication between IT and Business Leaders Providing an environment and structure that fosters collaboration between the IT and business areas increases communication between the groups and improves overall alignment across the business. Providing a channel for this discussion increases awareness and discourages functional areas from working in silos. A common method to encourage this collaboration is staffing the IT and functional areas within the M&A team together to complete the planning and execution. An emphasis should be placed on joint ownership and accountability, incentivizing both parties to work together to make sure there is a successful Day 1.

Begin IT Research Before the Deal Is Closed

Although information may not be readily available before the deal is signed, IT planning should occur well before committing to an agreement. Understanding what will be required to successfully stand up the postdeal IT function is an essential component in the valuation. Failure to understand the future IT needs, requirements, and level of effort can lead to large unanticipated future costs.

Gather Requirements Perform due diligence activities prior to finalizing the deal. The key synergies and benefits (qualitative and quantitative) that are identified before the deal closes allow for better planning and understanding of what is required for a successful merger or divestiture. The IT investments that will be needed, both in the short term and in the long term, should be identified and factor into the decision whether to go forward with the deal. Prior to a deal being signed, it is often difficult to gather all of the required information to estimate the IT-related costs; however, this effort is most effective when utilized to deduce an order-of-magnitude estimate for the IT implementation costs required if the deal is signed.

Estimate IT Costs   A preliminary budget should be developed that estimates the necessary costs to stand up a new infrastructure, migrate data, vitiate data, purchase licensing, and create any TSAs that will be in place. This up-front work needs to be factored into the valuation of the deal, as these costs that will require a significant initial capital investment.

Estimate the IT Timeline   Understanding the timeframes required to implement the postdeal IT department is essential to accurately create a budget and to value the deal. Underestimating the timeline can lead to large costs associated with penalties, additional or extended TSAs, or additional contract labor.

Gather as Much Information as Possible   Prior to signing the deal, negotiate access to restricted information that enables most of the IT planning. Building out a detailed IT transition plan prior to closing the deal allows the company to immediately begin work once the deal closes. This reduces the time TSAs need to be in place, ultimately reducing overall costs. The additional planning also provides a better insight into the scope of work that will be required after closing the deal.

Inspire Change within the IT Organization

A merger or divestiture is a great opportunity to alter how IT will operate within the new entity. Utilize the time of change to redesign the department to be more efficient, leaner, simpler, and more effective. Changes may include improvements to the architecture, infrastructure, or application management strategy. The new IT approach should also align with the new business objectives.

M&A IT STRATEGY, APPROACH, AND GOVERNANCE BEST PRACTICES

Align Your Approach with Integration Strategy

Align your approach to each function with your overall integration strategy to prioritize the level and timing of the applications that need to be deployed to each function.

- *Why:* If you don't align your approach to post-merger integration with your overall strategy, the benefits or synergies that were planned have little or no chance of being realized. IT integration may never be the primary driver of a merger or acquisition, but it is almost always listed as one of the key areas for rationalization and review. It takes hard work to make sure IT strategy is aligned with corporate strategy, but it can be a key enabler and positive differentiator in mergers and acquisitions.

▪ *Do:*
- Involve senior leaders from both organizations early and often in setting the priorities for IT integration.
- Have clearly documented decision paths and decision makers assigned so "the buck stops here."

▪ *Don't:*
- Don't choose to adopt any of the legacy systems without understanding what the pros and cons of that system will be for the future of *both* organizations.
- Don't underestimate the resistance to change that people will have. The system changes may be the biggest and most noticeable changes for some of the people in either organization; helping make a positive impression is critical.

Establish a Cross-Deal Program Structure Early in the Process

▪ *Why:* Aligning the deal team with the organizational functions increases communication between functional areas and assigns accountability.

▪ *Do:*
- Align deal teams with organizational functions and other stakeholders.
- Establish a cross-transaction steering committee and reporting process to drive necessary urgency in decision making and issue resolution that is critical to manage multiple parallel deals.
- Extract high-performing internal or external resources; assign resources to transaction-focused roles.

▪ *Don't* allow siloed work environments divided by organizational areas.

Develop Blueprints Up Front for All Deals

▪ *Why:* Considering other potential sales during the blueprinting process can reduce redundant work if a follow-on transaction occurs.

▪ *Do:*
- Start preparation for potential sales across all functional areas (for example, HR, IT, sourcing, sales, and marketing) before units are even considered for sale.

- Use a blueprinting process (six to eight weeks) to develop comprehensive service and asset inventories at the start of the transaction process.
- Develop standard transaction milestones and supporting processes to drive repeatability and efficiency.
- *Don't:*
- Don't wait until a deal is announced to begin preparation.
- Don't assume all follow-on transactions will occur at the same time.

Assess Transaction Characteristics and Context Early in the Process to Establish a Proper Understanding of Due Diligence Scope and Priorities

Proper understanding of key transaction characteristics, such as deal type, buyer type, IT landscape, and post-merger objectives, is critical to correctly evaluating due diligence project requirements (e.g., key areas of investigation, level of effort, resource needs, and mix).

- *Why:*
  - It can facilitate efforts to have the right mix of resources available to conduct the work.
  - It can facilitate efforts to have people available and ready to support the due diligence activities.
  - It can foster an effective and desired alignment between the deal team and the IT team.
- *Do:*
  - Conduct this analysis as early as possible in the M&A process.
  - Confirm with the deal team the business rationale, transaction objectives, and diligence priorities.
  - Pick the right IT team (based on transaction context and priorities), and set expectations up front with both the IT due diligence team and the deal team.
  - Tailor due diligence approach, scope, and standard artifacts to align with transaction context and due diligence priorities.
- *Don't:*
  - Don't simply apply a predefined standard due diligence approach and scope. You should adapt to the specific transaction context.
  - Don't assume people will be responsive and find time to conduct due diligence work. You need to clearly set expectations and confirm availability and flexibility of key required resources.

Take into Account Not Only Pure IT Source of Information but Also Potential Sources of Hidden IT Information

In the due diligence data room, sources of hidden information include finance (IT budgets, IT expenses, assets inventory, audit controls); HR (IT organization charts, employee locations, job responsibilities); legal or procurement (IT contracts, intellectual property inventory); or real estate (data center locations).

- *Why:* It is critical to make sure all-important data are analyzed and the due diligence process covers all required areas of investigation.
- *Do:*
  - Anticipate by developing a data request to make sure expected data and inputs are clearly documented.
  - Go beyond IT folders to look for potential missing IT-related information.
  - Coordinate with other functions involved in the due diligence to make sure information is shared across the board, and develop a collaborative working style.
- *Don't:*
  - Don't assume all IT-related information will be documented in the IT folders only.
  - Don't hesitate to ask questions to management on key areas where information is missing.

Focus the Effort on Critical Areas of Investigation While Making Sure There Is No Gap in the Performed Assessment

During the initiation and planning phase, clearly identify areas of investigation, and then progressively focus on potential issues identified throughout the due diligence process.

- *Why:* Preparation is critical to the effectiveness of an IT due diligence process, but it is impossible to anticipate everything. Therefore, being flexible during the due diligence phase can help ensure you get the most of the available resources and address as many areas of investigation as required to get to a careful, final recommendation to the leadership team.

- *Do:*
  - Develop initially a clear map of areas of investigation.
  - Be flexible and adapt the effort as you go through the due diligence analysis and identify potential issues that need to be further investigated.
  - Make sure the full IT scope is covered by following a strict approach and having a team in charge of making sure the analysis is performed in a consistent and exhaustive manner.
  - Consult subject matter advisers to address specific areas that need to be clarified.
- *Don't:*
  - Don't remain rigid in your approach by refusing to adapt anticipated priorities and level of effort.
  - Don't let the whole team be pulled into analyzing specific issues that would put at risk the full scope of analysis to be performed. Keep a balanced approach.

Manage and Clearly Define Transition Service Agreements

- *Why:* Transition services agreements (TSAs) that are not clearly defined can cause ambiguity as to what services will be provided in the future, exposing the transaction to additional risk.
- *Do:*
  - Establish a TSA management structure.
  - Map services to provider and user, including cost, systems, and resources needed.
- *Don't:*
  - Don't agree to more TSAs than are necessary as a risk mitigation strategy.
  - Don't sign a TSA that is not fully understood or not well defined.

Effectively Negotiate Deal Terms

- *Why:* A deal should be completed when it mutually benefits all parties involved; effective negotiations make sure all parties have their concerns addressed prior to finalization of the deal.
- *Do:*
  - Address separation costs, identifying recurring and one-time costs.
  - Design standard boilerplate TSAs, associated legal terms, and pricing, and clearly establish boundaries of what will *not* be provided as interim services.

- Set expectations up front to reduce prolonged negotiations and unnecessary rework.
- *Don't:*
  - Don't be afraid to negotiate changes to the TSA as more details become available.
  - Don't overlook the concerns of the other party.

M&A IT SECURITY AND PRIVACY IMPLICATIONS BEST PRACTICES

Conduct IT risk and control self-assessments.

- *Why:* To gain an understanding of current-state operations and identify any issues that could introduce security and privacy implications into the environment.
- *Do:* Base the IT risks and controls library on industry standards. Make sure that compliance requirements (legal, regulatory, SOX, etc.) are included in the assessment.
- *Don't* conduct assessments too late into the M&A transaction.

Employ Strong User Access Provisioning and Certification Practices

- *Why:* To reduce the likelihood of granting improper access to new infrastructure, systems, and applications that can introduce new threats during the M&A transaction.
- *Do:* Choose the type of access to provision (direct versus indirect). Perform certifications as necessary and depending on the timeframe required (full certifications, delta certifications, or event-based certifications).
- *Don't* grant unnecessary access or rubber-stamp access requests.

Implement Data Management Controls

- *Why:* To protect sensitive information from threats beyond those caused by improper access.
- *Do:* Create and review data protection plans for all infrastructure, systems, and applications. Conduct security reviews for the highest-risk areas.
- *Don't* assume that the IT risk and control self-assessments identify all technical issues.

Review, Approve, and Prioritize Change Management Requests

- *Why:* To appropriately plan for changes occurring in the environment and to implement controls to minimize security and privacy risks during these changes.
- *Do:* Review and approve change requests, using stakeholders from across the business where possible. Prioritize the changes with the highest impact that are easiest to implement first.
- *Don't* rubber-stamp requests.

M&A IT AND SYNERGIES BEST PRACTICES

Leverage ongoing restructuring work stream to identify expected stranded cost opportunity.

- *Why:* Restructuring is one of the preferred times to redefine operating processes and implement cost reduction initiatives.
- *Do:*
  - Analyze capacity and staffing requirements.
  - Implement cost reduction initiatives according to ease of implementation and amount of cost savings.
  - Capture operating efficiencies through process improvement to become more competitive.
- *Don't:*
  - Don't stray from the original business strategy.
  - Don't allow initiatives to interfere with the underlying transaction.

M&A IT CONTRACTS BEST PRACTICES

Capture business intent for third-party IT products early. Business intent is how the business functions of the seller wish to hand over a product or service used by the sold entity and provided by a third-party supplier under a contract to the buyer. The objective of identifying business intent is threefold:

1. Help make sure continuity of business operations on Day 1.
2. Request rights from suppliers as appropriate to make sure of contractual compliance on Day 1.
3. Minimize cost impact associated with third-party products and services due to the transaction.

- *Why:*
  - Suppliers need lead time of up to six months to grant required contractual rights.
  - Not providing enough lead time may lead to a situation where contractual compliance may be compromised on Day 1.
  - Suppliers may have leverage to extract a higher fee if it realizes that the transaction won't go through without its consent.
- *Do:* Know that if a provision is silent in the contract, a notification to the supplier might be sufficient in most cases.
- *Don't:*
  - Don't let contract provisions drive business intent.
  - Don't assume new rights can't be negotiated—with enough notice, it is generally feasible to do so.

Know Your Suppliers and Contracts Well

Document all the third-party suppliers and related contracts impacted by a transaction. Documentation should include the contract provisions associated with Day 1 requirements.

- *Why:* There are precedents where supplier contract noncompliance has resulted in penalties to the tune of millions of dollars for the seller.
- *Do:*
  - Start the documentation process as early as possible in the transaction cycle.
  - Automate the documentation process as much as possible.
- *Don't:*
  - Don't commit to provide specific contractual provisions associated with Day 1 requirements to buyer prior to Legal Day 1.
  - Don't assume that a contractual provision cannot be negotiated with supplier to meet Day 1 requirements.
  - Don't document contracts impacted by the transaction based solely on the master service agreements without considering all amendments and schedules.

Control Communication with Suppliers

Restrict business functions' communications with the suppliers to business as usual. Allow only certain individuals or a specific function to talk to the suppliers regarding the impacts from the transaction.

▪ *Why:* Certain information may allow the supplier to gain better leverage to extract fees and higher pricing from both buyer and seller.
▪ *Do:* Set up guiding principles for supplier communication early in the transaction cycle for business functions, procurement, and deal teams.
▪ *Don't* encourage the buyer to speak to the supplier directly without involving the seller.

M&A IT ORGANIZATIONAL IMPLICATIONS BEST PRACTICES

Design the IT organization for success. Define and configure elements of the IT organization to achieve business, customer, and employee outcomes. Design the IT structure for the newly combined companies.

▪ *Why:* Aligning IT structure to business objectives (building a structure that will better enable you to meet business needs):
  ● Balances workload, head count, and budget.
  ● Creates efficiencies.
  ● Drives accountabilities.
  ● Clarifies roles and responsibilities for IT professionals (especially important after a merger).
  ● Defines how the IT organization will interact with other functions across the business.
▪ *Do:*
  ● Begin with the end in mind. Be clear about end state and vision. Start with the strategy and any specific synergy or efficiency targets you're trying to achieve.
  ● Eliminate redundant or overlapping responsibilities. Create clear charters for IT subgroups.
▪ *Don't* draw boxes too soon. Allow form to follow function and reflect new business processes.

Communicate with Employees

Share merger-related information and updates with IT leaders and employees.

▪ *Why:*
  ● Helps control rumors.
  ● Builds confidence and trust in IT leadership team.

- Answers people's questions, and helps them stay focused on their jobs.
- *Do:*
  - Have specific employee messaging and communications ready for announcement and Day 1.
  - Be open and honest with people. Tell them what you know when you know it.
- *Don't:*
  - Don't sugarcoat it. Acknowledge that change will be difficult.
  - Don't wait until you have all the answers. Communicate early and often.
  - Don't make promises you can't keep. If you don't know something, tell people when you will know.

Identify and Retain Talent

Determine the required skills and capabilities to support the new operating model and IT structure.

- *Why:*
  - Identification of IT capabilities to support the new model in achieving synergy targets and business benefits quickly identifies skill gaps, head count gaps, or overlaps.
  - Provides better alignment to customer needs and requirements.
  - Drives efficiency and productivity.
  - Creates a plan for retaining critical skill needs.
- *Do:*
  - Understand requirements of IT to support the new business model.
  - Clarify vision for IT with employees.
- *Don't* wait until after the close to determine your skill requirements.

Create an Employee Experience That Facilitates a Successful People Transition

- *Why:* Making sure there is a smooth people transition reduces the risk of employee opposition and allows the business to continue with minimal interruptions.
- *Do:*
  - Align leadership on the employee value proposition associated with each entity.

- Customize divestiture messages across employees, customers, and other stakeholders to reduce uncertainty.
- Develop retention strategies for key employees.
- *Don't:*
- Don't assume all employees support the transition.
- Don't keep the employees in the dark about the changes to come.

BEST PRACTICES TO CONSIDER IN ORDER TO EXECUTE THE DEAL

Stand Up a Well-Defined Program Management Office

A merger or divestiture consists of many parallel threads of work, many with dependencies that span the organization. In order to manage the various simultaneous projects, a well-structured program management office (PMO) should be implemented to manage and oversee the merger or divestiture. Having a single PMO with insight into each team's activities allows for increased alignment across functional areas and provides a single point of contact for program-level issues, risks, decisions, and action items.

Determine Project Milestones   Identifying the essential milestones of the project provides a key metric in tracking the project's process. It is important to have multiple dates to manage toward, not just the ultimate Day 1 milestone. Having multiple key milestones throughout the process provides early indicators of the project status, and allows delays to be caught earlier in the process where they are easier to mitigate.

Identify the Critical Path   After the key milestones are defined, the tasks essential to reach each milestone should be identified and sequenced. The critical path view should include only items that are necessary to meet a specific milestone. Critical path items include physical activities such as standing up a data center, implementing core software (e-mail, document server, etc.), and installing business critical applications, and process activities such as defining a records retention policy, determining an application migration strategy, and signing contracts with equipment and service providers.

Determine Dependencies   In most scenarios, not all tasks can be completed in parallel due to software or hardware needs, resource constraints, or legal requirements. Identifying the key dependencies between tasks allows for proper sequencing and provides insight into which tasks should be prioritized in order to prevent delays in the subsequent tasks. The dependency mapping also assists in determining estimated completion dates for key milestones, and quickly demonstrates the impact of tasks not completing on time.

Assign Accountability   Assigning ownership to action items, decisions, and tasks provides a single party who is held responsible for making sure the item is completed. If an owner is not assigned, there is a risk that no party will fulfill the required task, as everyone assumes someone else is responsible. Providing a single name also incentivizes that person to complete each task assigned, as he or she is directly linked to its success or failure. Assigning accountability to a group or multiple people should be avoided when possible, as no single party is then held responsible. Although some tasks will need to be completed by multiple parties, a single point of contact and accountability should be assigned.

Provide Visibility   Whenever several parallel threads of work are in flight simultaneously, there is a risk that each may not see, or understand, what the other threads are working on or how issues impact other groups. A well-organized PMO is able to provide relevant information to each team without burdening their workloads. This empowers each team to make decisions that consider the impacts on other threads of work.

In addition to providing visibility across the work threads, the PMO should distill relevant information and surface key issues and decisions to executive leadership as necessary. This process prevents leadership from becoming overwhelmed with unnecessary requests from the various work streams. The PMO is also able to prioritize key items that need to be surfaced to leadership, as well as providing relevant program-level information around the items.

Implement a Well-Defined Process   Creating standard processes to follow can reduce ambiguity and increase the visibility of critical items. The consistency allows for easier management of key items. Another key role of the PMO is to communicate the standard processes implemented to all users who may be affected by the change.

LESSONS LEARNED

Best practices are intended to provide a series of thought-provoking items to consider throughout the M&A IT process. They offer insight into ways to potentially mitigate risk and increase the probability for success. Each item should be interpreted and adjusted to match the specifics of the current transaction. The best practices should not be viewed as rules or a rigid methodology by which every transaction can be run, but rather as a loose framework that should be adapted to the specifics of the engagement and implemented where applicable.

Understanding the underlying principles behind each best practice is paramount for success. The strategy and planning efforts should take into account the fundamental drivers of each best practice, and be built to align with those ideas.

Ultimately the goal of the best practices is to make sure a continuous vision exists throughout the transaction, increasing the odds for success. No two transactions are identical, and therefore it is impossible to develop a uniform process for successfully completing an M&A transaction; however, best practices provide the guidance necessary to improve the strategy, planning, and execution phases of the transaction.

Presented in Exhibit 28.1 are key lessons learned for both buy-side and sell-side M&A activities in five impact areas. Understanding how these lessons, which have been compiled over the course of many transactions, influence the buy side and sell side by impact area is critical to increasing the chances of success, as well as mitigating the risks that can lead to failure.

The lessons learned in Exhibit 28.1 are intended to highlight the common pitfalls and key success areas by impact area.

WRAPPING IT UP

An M&A or divestiture event is the fastest way to materially change the fundamental structure of an organization. IT is at the center of this change and will play a major role in the success of this transformation. We hope this book has provided you with a guiding framework as you embark on an M&A or divestiture event. Once the transaction begins to materialize and the impacts crystalize, we hope the best practices, case studies, and lessons learned included within the book will provide you with a point of reference to tap and provide you with invaluable insights into real-world examples accumulated over the design and execution of many transactions.

Last, here are a few case studies for you to review vis-à-vis the summaries presented in this chapter.

EXHIBIT 28.1 Lessons Learned for Buy-Side and Sell-Side by Impact Area

Impact Area	Lessons Learned	Buy-Side	Sell-Side
Program Management Office (PMO)	Establish a cross-deal program structure early in the process. Design a cross-transaction program structure that aligns deal teams with organizational functions and other stakeholders against a deal-focused accountability structure and shared guidelines. Establish a cross-transaction steering committee and reporting process to drive necessary urgency in decision making and issue resolution that is critical to manage multiple parallel deals as well as change management.	The buy-side program management office should provide governance, communication standards, program templates, and other necessary program oversight required to represent buy-side obligations to the cross-company sell side, paying particular attention to making sure the reconciliation of assets or services received meets the necessary transition services agreements. Focus should be on making sure of the assets/services being received, not on the separation deadlines of the sell side. Oversight should be governed throughout the entire lifecycle of the merger or divestiture.	The sell-side program management office should provide governance, communication standards, program templates, and other necessary program oversight required to represent sell-side obligations to the cross-company buy side, paying particular attention to making sure of the transition of its assets (i.e., people, processes, technology, etc.) in order to meet the necessary legal obligations and separation deadlines. Focus should be on managing toward the separation deadlines and scope.
Costs (TSA, Synergies, Sourcing, and Procurement)	Manage costs and invoices.	Invoices will begin to be submitted after Day 1. The service receiver should develop a structure that proactively enables the auditing and approval/denial of all invoices and other related charges associated to the merger or divestiture. This should be in alignment with the PMO governance structure. (Note: Reference PMO lessons learned.)	Key focus should remain on managing requests to increase scope outside the merger/divestiture activities. Reduce service-enhancement requests as much as possible. (Note: Reference TSA lessons learned.) Careful organization and traceability need to occur in order to track project requests outside the transition services agreements. All cost increases outside of the TSAs should go through the governance structure between both organizations.

EXHIBIT 28.1 (_Continued_)

Impact Area	Lessons Learned	Buy-Side	Sell-Side
	Manage contracts and commercial agreements.	Jump-start divestiture-related contract review, assignment, and securing of required TSA license permissions. Classify contract risks and develop mitigation plan. Identify minimum purchase guarantees and dates. Negotiate most favorable rates for revised volumes. Dedicate resources to obtain the right to use and secure applicable new software licenses at the lowest cost possible. Renegotiate reduction of licenses and fees. Proactively identify commercial agreement requirements, and work with the related parties to secure them.	Provide proficient staff to conduct due diligence with vendor management contracts in order to eliminate or reduce early termination charges wherever possible. Service provider focus should be on aggressively managing against stranded costs when defining terms, conditions, and contract termination dates.
	Facilitate careful vendor management and planning.	Assess opportunities to reduce vendor base, cancel contracts with multiple suppliers, and consolidate requirements to regain volume advantages. This can help the receiver manage supplier services in the marketplace.	Involve suppliers, and communicate proactively to help ensure little or no disruption for direct or indirect materials during transition.
	Manage the inspection, quality, and operational performance during transition.	Service receiver needs to make sure deliveries and commitments stipulated within performance-level objectives or performance-level agreements are not affected at the time of transition through careful Day 1 planning. Service receiver should monitor performance so that receiving services do not fall below the target service-level agreements (SLAs).	Service provider should maintain day-to-day operations as normal. Focus should be on monitoring SLAs against agreed-upon negotiated TSA terms and conditions. Maintain thorough documentation on root cause analysis of incidents and performance effects throughout the separation in order to manage service liability.

EXHIBIT 28.1 (*Continued*)

Impact Area	Lessons Learned	Buy-Side	Sell-Side
Organization/ Workforce	Take proactive steps to acquire and retain resources.	Be a part of the employee acquisition process, working with service providers to attain key resources that will manage the service delivery after the merger or divestiture. Focus on how to interact and negotiate with target company resources; how to identify and avoid common integration pitfalls; and how to accelerate integration planning, execution, and synergy capture through the use of clean teams (sequestered teams of subject-matter specialists who are allowed to access and analyze restricted information before the deal is approved).	Overconsumption of departmentalized resources with project-based separation work associated to the merger/divestiture is inevitable. Implement retention programs early in the integration process in order to reduce attrition for key resources. Establish bonus plans for key integration executives that are performance-based, measurable, and back-end loaded.
	Only final organization charts should be distributed, and timing to release is critical to reducing conflicts of interest from conveying resources.	Make sure organizational charts do not contain names until after agreement is reached among executives concerning the overall structure, and until conceptual views of the structure have been distributed. Increases the chance of service receiver department leads reaching out to service provider resources prior to conveyance to conduct service optimization tasks. By previewing conceptual views of the to-be structure, internal resources will not be caught off guard about new job assignments.	Take steps to make sure organizational charts do not contain names until after agreement is reached among executives concerning the overall structure, and until conceptual views of the structure have been distributed. Disseminating organizational charts prematurely creates unnecessary employee contention and increases the opportunity for conflicts of interest for resources conveying to the service receiver.

EXHIBIT 28.1 (*Continued*)

Impact Area	Lessons Learned	Buy-Side	Sell-Side
Functional (Security/Privacy, Application, Infrastructure, Data/Security)	Security and Privacy—Special attention must be placed on maintaining security, controls, and regulatory compliance throughout the transition. Due to the complexity of deals, proactive focus on maintaining security, controls, and regulatory compliance throughout the transition will be critical.	Service receiver is responsible and accountable for making sure there is compliance with regulations during the transition. Risk of receiving noncompliant infrastructure will impact service receiver brand name. Privacy—Make sure risk-based privacy programs are in place and monitored to protect consumer, employee, vendor, and partner data enterprise-wide during and after the transition. Identity Management—Take steps to make sure processes and systems to manage organizations identities across multiple applications are in place and monitored. Include role-based access control, directory and directory integration, provisioning, and access management.	Process Controls—Make sure all internal controls related to the business processes, including application configuration controls, security controls, reports, control procedures, and policies, are monitored and managed throughout the transition. Application Security—Make sure appropriate application security for the business processes, application infrastructure, reports, interfaces, and business intelligence is maintained. Make sure security setup, maintenance, administration, and operations policies and procedures are in place for all environments: development, QA, training, and production. Interface and Data Migration Controls—Make sure controls are in place to manage the accuracy and completeness of interfaces and data conversions between legacy applications, new applications, and third-party software.

(*continued*)

EXHIBIT 28.1 (*Continued*)

Impact Area	Lessons Learned	Buy-Side	Sell-Side
			Information Technology Controls—Make sure controls that provide for the reliability, availability, and recoverability of the IT infrastructure, such as change control, backup and recovery, job scheduling, problem management, database and operating system administration, are in place and operational throughout the transition process.
			Infrastructure Security—Make sure overall security infrastructure is in place to address overall enterprise security architecture, including logging, monitoring and reporting, intrusion detection, incident response, network security, encryption, messaging, and availability.
			Privacy—Make sure risk-based privacy programs are in place and monitored to protect consumer, employee, vendor, and partner data enterprise-wide during and after the transition.
			Identity Management—Ensure processes and systems to manage organizations' identities across multiple applications are in place and monitored. Include role-based access control, directory and directory integration, provisioning, and access management.
Network (Data and Voice)		Service receiver should focus primarily on the transition of the network infrastructure from the service provider, but keep a sharp secondary focus on adapting the design infrastructure to service receiver environment. This maintains consistency with the service receiver's compliance obligations.	This is an area that service receivers typically enhance during transition. The service provider should focus on managing additional scope and costs outside of the TSA. (Note: Reference effectively negotiate deal terms lesson learned.)

EXHIBIT 28.1 (*Continued*)

Impact Area	Lessons Learned	Buy-Side	Sell-Side
		Avoid substituting time to deliver for quality in the delivery. The service receiver will inherit the solution long-term and be responsible for service operations and accountable for security and compliance after the transition. (Note: Reference the minimize and clearly define transition services agreements, effectively negotiate deal terms, and security and privacy lessons learned sections.)	Plan early for Day 1 firewall implementation. It will be a security requirement to provide cross-company access during transition. Order dedicated circuits and firewalls as early as possible. Design integrated network firewall infrastructure across global locations to leverage combination of firewalls and secure VPN tunnels to hub firewalls. Establish centralized firewall rule database and rule collection effort to manage massive identification effort. Schedule the weekend firewall testing plan early and confirm business user participation. Prepare for a long testing process—late discovery is a reality of firewall cut-over process. Establish and test interface connectivity early on, then leave interfaces in a shutdown state until transition. Document onetime costs for separation in TSA—who pays this cost will depend on the deal structure. (Note: Reference cost and invoice management lessons learned.) Understand buyer Day 1 connection requirements. Buyers may want to establish back-to-back firewall, and most buyers need to establish network link to RemainCo for IT access. A common way to facilitate the data transfer process is to clone and operate parallel network infrastructures.

EXHIBIT 28.1   (*Continued*)

Impact Area	Lessons Learned	Buy-Side	Sell-Side
	Data and Asset Migration Management	M&A IT is not business as usual—This statement is particularly true prior to the deal close. During this period, numerous legal and regulatory restrictions make sharing design documentation, data, and key subject matter information extremely difficult. Engage service provider early after Day 1 to evaluate the overall data and technical architecture. Assess the complexity and develop work plans accordingly in order to separate as much of the data and assets as early as possible prior to the transition. The service receiver will be responsible for legal and regulatory data retention requirements after transition. It should work through the PMO governance structure to gain access to any archived data repositories that were unable to transition from the service provider by the separation deadline. The service receiver will be responsible for approving the completion of the transitioned data and assets. Focus should remain on having a reconciliation process in place to validate the receipt of the data and assets. Engage the service provider early in the process to build consensus on a process to sign off that data and assets transitioned meet the TSA terms and conditions.	It is uncommon for service providers to have a robust asset management solution in place to track commissioning/ decommissioning of company assets. Cycles are often spent and wasted trying to solidify and integrate various spreadsheets to conduct this exercise during a merger or divestiture. Understanding the current state of the inventory landscape is increasingly important, depending on the size of the merger or divestiture. It is the responsibility of the service provider to have a understanding of its asset inventory. Service providers should conduct a cost-benefit analysis of instituting an asset management solution versus a last-minute scramble to gather company-owned asset information. Key focus should be on protecting data integrity during transition and ensuring that only required assets and data transition to the service receiver.

EXHIBIT 28.1 (*Continued*)

Impact Area	Lessons Learned	Buy-Side	Sell-Side
	Active Directory (AD) Migration	Assess service provider's security guidelines for provision of access to current AD after Day 1; most companies require senior-level risk acceptance to provide the service receiver with access to current mail environment. Secure and eliminate user authentication through firewall by establishing domain controllers on service receiver side of network. This solution option reduces risk.	Engage service receiver early to understand the target AD environment. Migration tools such as Quest need domain-level access to the service provider AD; this may result in the service provider performing the migration on the buyer's behalf.
	Application Services/Mainframe and Server Hosting	Assess the mainframe LPAR level separation; logical separation of LPARs may be required to provide TSA access (this is a significant effort). Understand early firewall access requirements for applications; some applications that use "dangerous ports" such as FTP (21) and Telnet (23) may need to be remediated to meet security guidelines. Establish reverse TSAs for any applications that service provider needs to provide to the service receiver to fulfill post-Day 1 obligations. Financial and comptroller application access usually needs to be provided 60 to 90 days after close. Review all contractual implications related to applications, including license transfers and contract terminations.	Evaluate each requested application TSA against security guidelines to help ensure permissions and data are separated from RemainCo users. Review all user account permissions; the scope of access may need to be reduced.

EXHIBIT 28.1 (*Continued*)

Impact Area	Lessons Learned	Buy-Side	Sell-Side
Transition Services Agreements (TSAs)	Minimize and clearly define transition service agreements.	Receiver should own its destiny and begin planning the TSA exit while crafting TSA services. Receiver, not the provider, should take ownership of the exit. Set expectations up front with the seller to define exactly what services will transition.	Establish TSA management structure. Create content, processes, and terms of TSAs. Map services to provider and user, including cost, systems, and resources needed. Set expectations up front with the buyer to reduce prolonged negotiations and unnecessary rework.
	Effectively negotiate deal terms. Address separation costs, identifying recurring and one-time costs. Design standard boilerplate TSAs, associated legal terms and pricing, and clearly establish boundaries of what will *not* be provided as interim services to buyers.	Consider marking up costs by 30 to 50 percent to incentivize quick exit from TSA services and avoid the identified risks and issues if a larger markup was not put in place: Encourages service receiver to complete the terms of the TSA in order to modify service delivery. Service receiver should pay special attention to potential double-charge scenarios in TSA terms and incorporate preventive measures wherever possible. Default to fixed-price-based pricing wherever possible when developing TSA costs. Post-Day 1 TSA billing and invoicing are easier for both parties when using fixed prices. Audit requirements need to justify volumes if significantly less than fixed price.	"What you get today is what you get tomorrow." Service provider is not burdened to enhance the service. Allows service provider to focus on separation deadlines. Consider marking up costs by 30 to 50 percent to incentivize quick exit from TSA services and avoid the identified risks and issues if a larger markup was not put in place: TSA owners are required to be more precise in estimating the costs of services, resulting in delays to the budgeting cycle. Service providers are put at greater risk of eating costs due to overruns. Management of TSAs post-Day 1 are more complex given all the calculations required to the base.

Case Study 1: Incomplete Due Diligence

A large, global manufacturer purchased—and attempted to integrate —a division of another large, global conglomerate.

Role of IT   IT was not involved in due diligence and did not participate in integration planning until after the deal was announced and closed.

Outcomes

- IT-related integration costs exceeded due diligence estimates by more than $100 million.
- IT issues caused significant operational problems after the cut-over.
- The TSA had to be extended because the buyer wasn't ready to operate independently.

Case Study 2: IT Integration Planning Done Right

A company acquired a smaller competitor in order to improve its market position. The company expected to achieve $100 million per year in synergy benefits. Day 1 was set to occur just 90 days after the deal closed.

Role of IT   The aggressive merger targets were feasible because the company had done extensive IT integration planning during the due diligence phase. It had mapped out an IT integration strategy and identified the major IT integration issues. In addition, the company used clean teams to get a head start on planning and execution before the deal was finalized. Key IT integration tasks included combining the companies' ERP applications, IT infrastructures, and voice/data networks. One of the main challenges identified during due diligence was that the two companies were running on different versions of their ERP systems, which meant that one of the ERP systems had to be upgraded before the integration could be completed.

Outcomes

- The ERP upgrade and subsequent integration were completed on time and at minimum expense, largely due to the company's advanced IT planning.
- IT integration was completed in only eight months, less than half the time typically required for a large-scale merger.
- Throughout the integration process, people from IT and business operations worked side by side to achieve the desired results.

Case Study 3: Making the Most of a Difficult Situation

This merger involved two large insurance companies, each built from a series of prior acquisitions that had not been fully integrated. In addition to the integration challenges, the merger was touch and go for a long time due to an extensive and prolonged regulatory approval process.

Role of IT IT was involved in predeal due diligence, as well as extensive preclose planning and preparation. Operational efficiency comparisons revealed significant improvement potential and a compelling business case to fundamentally change the IT infrastructure delivery model. Savings opportunities ranged as high as 60 percent for various technology components, with a total IT synergy target of $75 million.

Throughout the process, the CIO remained deeply committed to transforming IT and meeting or exceeding the synergy target, even when regulators initially rejected the deal and it appeared as if the merger might fall through.

Outcomes

- The merger ultimately was approved and completed.
- Annual IT savings of $189.5 million were identified (well above the $75 million target).
- An issue-free Day 1 was achieved.
- The combined organization effectively shifted to an outsourced IT infrastructure.

M&A IT Playbook Overview

Joseph Joy
Shalva Nolen
Simon Singh
Nikhil Uppal

Chief information officers (CIOs) and chief technology officers (CTOs) in organizations anticipating multiple merger, acquisition, and/or divestiture transactions can proactively prepare to execute the necessary information technology (IT) activities by developing an M&A IT playbook. An M&A IT playbook is a prescriptive guide documenting the tasks needed to effectively and efficiently execute an IT integration or divesture based on the parameters of the deal. The M&A IT playbook does not look to answer every single question associated with IT during a deal; rather, it is intended as a practical guide that can be adapted to address most integration or divesture situations across the M&A lifecycle, including due diligence, Day 1, and Day 2. Since technology does not operate in a vacuum, ideally the organization would develop an M&A playbook, and the M&A IT playbook would align to the overall corporate strategy.

The M&A IT playbook is typically tailored to the specific aspects of each organization and provides answers to common questions such as:

- Who does it?
- When does it start?
- What are the dependencies?
- How long might it take (if appropriate)?

Typically, an M&A IT playbook is intended to be mandatory reading for IT senior management and recommended reading for all IT team members involved with M&A transactions.

SCOPE OF THE PLAYBOOK

The scope of the playbooks can vary from concentrating on a particular phase of the integration or divesture (e.g., due diligence, IT separation planning and execution) to the complete M&A lifecycle. Most playbooks focus on one or all of the following themes:

- Acquisitions and divestitures can be large, complex undertakings that should be planned and managed in a top-down hierarchical manner with a business executive leading the effort.
- An M&A effort in any company is not a stand-alone project, but is a subset of the overall business/M&A effort and should be planned and executed accordingly.
- Acquisitions and divestitures are projects, albeit large and complex ones, and should employ the company's standard project management methods and practices (for example, approval gates, issue resolution, resource balancing, acceptance testing).
- Playbooks can only provide guidance, ideas, and suggestions. A playbook should not be a substitute for experience, critical thinking, and common sense.
- Every deal is different: all plans, templates, tools, and the like should be tailored to the circumstances, and the playbook should continually evolve.
- People issues can be the most challenging. Therefore, it is critical for the playbook to address this specific aspect of the deal.

M&A PLAYBOOKS SHOULD BE ALIVE

No two deals are alike. Although an M&A IT playbook can cover a variety of situations, it cannot address every permutation. Most companies typically focus on acquisitions when developing M&A playbooks, but as companies diversify there may be opportunities to divest pieces of the business that no longer fit the business strategy. Thus, in many cases, it may make sense to create an IT divestiture playbook or consider including sections on divestitures in the M&A IT playbook itself. Furthermore, with each deal comes further modification and learning. As a result, the M&A playbook should be treated as a living and breathing document that is constantly evolving as the organization matures.

A sample table of contents for an M&A IT playbook whose scope covers the M&A lifecycle from predeal due diligence through integration or divestiture execution follows, and an illustrative example of an acquisition framework for a playbook is at the end of the chapter.

1. Executive Summary
2. Overview of Mergers, Acquisitions, and Divestitures
3. Introduction to M&A IT Playbook
   3.1 Playbook Objectives
   3.2 Playbook Scope
   3.3 Playbook Assumptions
   3.4 Maintenance and Update of the Playbook
4. Due Diligence
5. IT Integration Planning
   5.1 Establish the IT Integration Management Office
   5.2 Discover Current State
   5.3 Design Future State
   5.4 Define Gap-Closing Initiatives
   5.5 Create IT Integration Plan
6. IT Divestiture Planning
   6.1 Establish the IT Separation Management Office
   6.2 Assess Current State
   6.3 Develop IT Transition Services Agreements
   6.4 Design Future State
   6.5 Define Gap-Closing Initiatives
   6.6 Create IT Separation Plan
7. M&A Project Execution
   7.1 Make and Communicate Staffing Decisions
   7.2 Execute Detailed Work Plans
8. Appendix: Supporting Material
   8.1 Tools, Templates, and Samples
   8.2 Glossary

VARIATION IN M&A IT PLAYBOOK CONSIDERATIONS DUE TO DIFFERENCES IN TYPES OF M&A DEALS

Although an M&A IT playbook cannot anticipate every transaction scenario that may occur, it can be adapted or extended to address a variety of situations. Some of the common variations that should be taken into consideration when developing a playbook include the deal type, the buyer type, the deal size, and the target type. All are discussed in this section.

Deal Type—Integrations

There are several factors that generally impact an M&A transaction and affect the considerations made in developing an M&A IT integration playbook. Some of these factors include the type of buyer, target type, deal size, and complexity of the business architecture. Incorporating these nuances into the M&A IT playbook is essential to helping the playbook users capture the full value of the deal, regardless of the details of the deal.

Buyer Type (Financial versus Strategic Buyers)

Financial buyers include private equity firms (also known as financial sponsors), venture capital firms, hedge funds, family investment offices and ultra-high-net-worth individuals. These buyers are in the business of making investments in companies and realizing a return on their investments. Their goal is to identify private companies with attractive future growth opportunities and durable competitive advantages, invest capital, and realize a return on their investment with a sale or an initial public offering (IPO). Financial buyers typically have an investment time horizon of four to seven years. Financial buyers generally need the target business's back-end infra-structure to endure, and as a result will need to develop playbooks focused less on integration with existing systems and more on the development of TSAs and use of outsourcers to fulfill IT service delivery. For example, an M&A IT playbook for a financial buyer would focus on how to evaluate the target's systems during due diligence or how to stand up the infrastructure and applications to support an acquisition when the target does not have adequate systems to support the stand-alone company.

In contrast, strategic buyers operate companies that provide products or services and are often competitors, suppliers, or customers of the acquisition target. They can also be unrelated to the target company, but looking to grow in that market to diversify their revenue sources. Their goal is to identify companies whose products or services can synergistically integrate with their existing product line to create incremental long-term shareholder value. Strategic buyers are going to focus less on the strength of the target company's existing back-office infrastructure (IT, human resources, payables, legal, etc.), as these functions will often be eliminated during the post-transaction integration phase. The M&A IT playbook developed for a strategic buyer will focus on identifying the synergies to be achieved when consolidating systems and on how the target's data would be migrated to the buyer's systems. The playbook may outline methodologies for consistently identifying and reporting against synergies in line with the overall integration program.

Deal Size and Business Complexity

The size of the deal plays a significant role in deciding the buyer's future-state operating model and therefore dictates considerations that will need to be addressed in the M&A IT playbook. Some of these considerations are:

- If the target is small, the future-state operating model may be very close to the acquiring unit's current state. As a result of smaller size, it would be easier for the buyer to move all IT-related operations of the acquired unit to the buyer's systems. In this case, the key consideration of the M&A IT playbook would be how to plan the migration of the acquired systems and processes to the buyer's systems and processes while minimizing the impact on the business.
- Even though the target may be relatively small in total revenue, it may involve significant business complexity if the target is active in multiple business segments, in multiple legal entities, or in multiple countries, or if it operates on multiple platforms. Furthermore, integration complexity can be high if the target has a significantly different business model than the acquirer has. In such a case an adoption of the buyer's systems and processes may not work. The IT integration team will have to evaluate each individual business model and the role technology plays in it before it can decide what should be the future state. These considerations should also be addressed in the M&A IT playbook.
- If the target is very large, the integration planning team will likely also be very large, and the resulting future state may be quite different from the buyer's current state. In such a scenario a detailed as-is analysis is done, followed by an options analysis as to which future state would best meet the needs of the combined future business. For example, if the buyer and the target use different enterprise resource planning (ERP) tools, then a detailed analysis of both tools and other competing tools should be conducted to understand which tool will most effectively service the business needs, will involve the least risk to business continuity and functioning, and would be the most cost-effective. The playbook should provide frameworks and methodologies to effectively conduct the as-is analysis followed by the product/application assessment.
- The IT playbook's considerations are also impacted by how the business decides to integrate the target. Each of the four most common integration approaches has implications for IT that should be discussed in the M&A IT playbook. Some of the common integration approaches are described in Exhibit A.1.

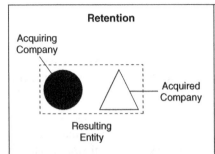

Retention

In the retention model, the acquired company is left to operate independently with minimal standardization except for contracts consolidation and a financial reporting roll-up. From an IT perspective, file transmissions or interfaces may need to be established to support the consolidated financial reporting. These IT considerations should be made a part of the playbook.

Assimilation

In the assimilation model, one organization, typically the target, adopts the other organization's strategy, structure, processes, and systems in order to achieve aggressive synergy targets rapidly. This model would plan to convert the target's IT processes and systems to those of the acquiring company quickly, and the playbook would need to have considerations to assess the current state, the future integration methodology, and ways to mitigate the risk during the transition.

Transformation

In the transformation model, the organization and technology from the acquiring company and acquired company are synthesized into a new, combined company. From an IT perspective, a new architecture is defined, resulting in a significant technology impact, along with the major impacts to the people and processes. A significant planning effort is required to achieve the desired execution objectives, and the resulting new organization should be prepared to handle the complex change management characteristics of such a deal. All of these considerations should make their way into the playbook to help ensure a smooth IT integration.

Metamorphosis

In this approach, for each system and process, a determination is made as to whether the parent company's or the acquired company's is preferred. Then those preferred systems and processes are adopted to form an improved operating model. The IT function does need proficiency in synthesizing disparate systems and technologies. The playbook in this approach will have frameworks and templates to identify the disparate systems, would have leading practices around integrating disparate systems and ways to mitigate the risks involved in integrations.

EXHIBIT A.1   Classic Approaches to Integration

Target Type (Entire Company or Selected Assets)

The integration complexity can increase significantly when the buyer is purchasing a target that is a carved-out piece of the seller's business instead of an existing stand-alone company. Carved-out acquisitions present particular challenges because they involve the carving out of the acquired assets, as well as their integration into buyer's operations. Some of the challenges in integrating a carved-out business that the M&A IT playbook should address include the following:

- In the case of an acquisition of a stand-alone company, the M&A IT playbook would focus on methods of integration, potential synergy opportunities, and reduction in cost, whereas in the case of a selected asset, the playbook would focus on all those along with the key dependencies in terms of both hardware and software, potential overlap that might exist with the buyer's organization, and ways to integrate the new asset into the existing ecosystem of the buyer.
- In case of the acquisition of selected assets, the playbook would also look at the supporting applications such as financial systems, HR payroll, intranet facilities, and so on that the new asset would require to run its operations successfully once carved out of the parent company.

DEAL TYPE—IT DIVESTURES

Most of the areas that an M&A IT playbook should address during a divestiture are similar to those that should be addressed in integration but with a slightly different focus. For instance, in the predeal due diligence phase, just as the M&A IT integration playbook would lay out the steps a buyer would take to assess a target company's IT function, an M&A IT divestiture playbook should lay out the steps the team supporting due diligence at the seller would take to assess its current IT function, and address any areas and issues in order to increase the perceived value to potential buyers. The IT divestiture playbook would also provide the guidelines to document the seller's current IT function and extract the information about the portion of the business to be divested to share with potential buyers.

Similarly, just as the M&A IT integration playbook would discuss the process for integration planning depending on the integration approach, the M&A IT divestiture playbook would document the guidelines and approach to IT separation planning.

Some of the key considerations of an M&A IT playbook during a divesture are transition services agreements (TSAs), data migration strategies, and the divestiture approach.

Transition Services Agreements

Divestitures are usually tricky to pull off, particularly when the affected people, processes, and systems are deeply integrated within the seller's business or when services and infrastructure are shared across multiple business units. Added to this complexity is the time constraint that is an inherent feature of all M&A deals. Transition services agreements (TSAs) can address these challenges and facilitate a smooth separation. If TSAs are included as part of the deal, the IT divestiture playbook should provide guidelines on how to map business TSAs to IT TSAs and work with the legal team to develop the IT TSAs. It is critical that IT be involved in the TSA development so that IT is not obligated to provide support it cannot deliver. The IT divestiture playbook should also include recommendations on what services typically would be provided to a buyer and whether a service is dependent on a third party for delivery, duration of TSA period for each service, clearly defined service metrics, penalties for not achieving TSA performance levels, incentives for exceeding TSA performance levels, TSA management, costs for each service, and basis on which costs are derived. The IT divestiture playbook should also include recommendations on penalties if the divested business is unable to exit the TSA when the defined term is complete. The playbook may describe how to structure a TSA, its governance, and a clear plan on how to exit from the TSA.

One significant advantage of including the recommendations on TSAs in the playbook is that IT is forced to consider these TSA-related items and determine guidelines and recommendations without the time pressure that usually accompanies an M&A transaction. Critical items are less likely to be overlooked, and the process of developing the IT TSAs can be accelerated. (See Chapters 14 and 16 for additional information on TSAs.)

Data Migration Considerations

During a divesture, the seller and buyer have different intentions when it comes to the shared data. The seller, frequently selling the business to a competitor, wants to minimize the data migration so that the proprietary data does not end up in the possession of the buyer. However, the seller does need to make sure that it provides the data required to continue to run the business. The M&A IT playbook will have key divestiture considerations and leading practices around data separation and data migration.

Divesture Approach

Based on the divesture approach, the deal and hence the M&A IT playbook would vary substantially. Three of the leading divesture approaches and their respective impacts on the M&A IT playbook are described next.

Clone, Cleanse, and Go   In the clone, cleanse, and go approach, the parent company production system is copied into separate production instances for the divested entity and the sensitive data is deleted or masked. (See Exhibit A.2.)

The major consideration of the M&A IT playbook during this approach is to find a way to identify the data that is required by the carved-out unit, designing the appropriate script to delete or mask data not relevant to the divested business unit. Done incorrectly, the divested business could end up with a system that is not functional due to data dependencies that were not maintained, or the parent company could be at risk when sensitive data was not properly deleted or masked and is now potentially accessible by a competitor. Another consideration in the M&A IT playbook regarding this approach is how testing is approached to validate that the divested business unit's systems are still operational but do not have access to sensitive parent company data.

Extract and Load   With the extract and load approach, the divested business unit's master data and open transactional data are extracted from the parent company's systems and loaded into a new instance for the divested business. (See Exhibit A.3.)

The key considerations on which the M&A IT playbook focuses in this approach are a detailed plan for the developers and testers to validate that conversion programs are successful and ways to identify and isolate the data specific to the divested business unit while maintaining data dependencies and data integrity.

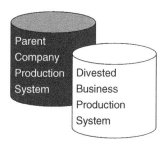

EXHIBIT A.2   Clone, Cleanse, and Go Approach

Configuration

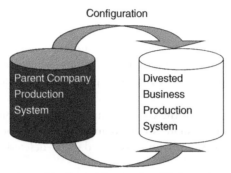

Master and Transactional Data

EXHIBIT A.3   Extract and Load Approach

EXHIBIT A.4   New Build Approach

New Build   With the new build approach, a key consideration of the M&A IT playbook is around the new systems that will be developed for the divested business unit, which may involve the selection of a new platform and may require the redesign of business processes and the conversion of data required for the divested business to function independently. (See Exhibit A.4.)

TOOLS AND TEMPLATES

In addition to the guidelines around the IT activities in an M&A effort, the M&A IT playbook should include an accompanying set of tools, templates, and samples to enrich the material and help expedite the IT activities during an M&A transaction. The tools and templates will also have to be adapted to individual deal circumstances, but including them in the playbook can accelerate the IT activities, as the IT team will not have to reinvent the wheel and create a whole set of new templates for each deal. Typical tools and templates to include with the playbook are:

- Generic work plans for executing IT due diligence, IT integration or divestiture planning, IT integration or divestiture transition.
- IT due diligence checklist.
- IT security questionnaire.
- Tool to model cost estimates during due diligence.
- Synergy tracking tool.
- IT TSA checklist.
- IT integration and divestiture Day 1 readiness checklists.
- List of lessons learned aggregated from previous M&A deals and updated after each new transaction.

The relevant project management templates currently used in the organization should also be included in the playbook and modified as necessary for M&A transactions.

Including sample material from previous M&A transactions with the M&A IT playbook can also help accelerate the planning and execution of the M&A-related IT activities, such as:

- Sample due diligence report.
- Sample IT integration/divestiture program kickoff deck.
- Sample due diligence, IT integration, and IT divestiture project plans.
- Sample IT integration test plan.
- Sample IT divestiture test plan.
- Sample communication plan.
- Sample Day 1 user experience document.
- Sample IT integration cut-over plan.
- Sample IT divestiture cut-over plan.

The tools, templates, and samples can bring significant value to the transaction team and jump-start its work.

WRAPPING IT UP

Each M&A transaction is different, and although an M&A IT playbook cannot cover every situation, it can provide general guidance on the IT activities during a deal and reduce the level of ad hoc project planning that often occurs with each M&A project. M&A IT integrations and divestitures do require thoughtful planning and consideration. Although an M&A IT playbook can provide a detailed, prescriptive procedure to follow, it should not be blindly followed down a path that is not appropriate for the intricacies of a given deal. Playbook users still need to bring experience, critical thinking, and common sense to the table.

Exploratory	Due Diligence	Day 0 (Preclose)	Day 1–30 (Postclose)	Day 30–60 (90, 120)[a] (Business Integration)	Execution (ERP Migration)	Sustain
Lead— Business Development Manager	*Lead— Business Development Manager*	*Leads— Business Development Manager, Integration Manager*	*Leads— Integration Manager, Integration Functional Leads*	*Leads— Integration Functional Leads (Business and IT)*	*Leads— Integration IT Functional Leads*	*Business Owners*

Project Management

	1. Identify relevant functional teams.	1. Request that functional leads update Day 1 through Day 30 critical checklist. 2. Request that functional leads update data requests list. 3. Confirm Day 1 readiness with functional leads. 4. Create transition team collaboration. 5. Finalize Day 1 issues management process. 6. Create IT project request shell. 7. Prepare draft IT project charter.	1. Publish Day 1 communications. 2. Submit team-specific high-level transition plan for Day 30–120.[a] 3. Submit data request to seller. 4. Publish Day 1 issues log to integration functional leads. 5. Monitor Day 1 checklist progress. 6. Distribute data requests received from seller to integration functional leads.	1. Update IT project request. 2. Update project charter. 3. Identify key decisions needed, critical issues, and escalation items. 4. Submit transition weekly status reports to IMO. 5. Gather weekly status reports from IT functional leads. 6. Complete project scope and high-level mid- and long-term project plan.	1. Complete baseline detailed IT project plans for each functional stream. 2. Refine weekly IT functional leads status report templates as necessary. 3. Submit IT weekly status reports for integration team meetings (IMOs). 4. Identify key decisions needed, critical issues, escalation items. 5. Issue weekly status report formats to IT functional leads. 6. Establish IT KPIs— development, communication, testing, training.	

Governance

	2. Define cross-functional due diligence team roles and responsibilities. 3. Launch cross-functional due diligence core team. 4. Complete nondisclosure agreement (NDA) forms for due diligence team. 5. Define meeting cadence.	8. Mobilize integration transition team. 9. Establish expanded cross-functional integration team leads organization structure (IMO). 10. Distribute and obtain signatures for nondisclosure agreement (NDA) form.	7. Implement Day 1 issues escalation management process. 8. Begin meeting cadence with integration functional leads. 9. Adjust IT integration team meeting cadence (as necessary).	7. Document and resolve key decisions. 8. Document business cases (as needed for additional scope).	7. Adjust IT integration team meeting cadence as necessary. 8. Implement IT change request process. 9. Resolve escalation issues via IT integration leads meetings, IT steering committee, or executive steering committee.	

EXHIBIT A.5 Example of an Acquisition Framework for a Playbook.

		11. Identify IT PMO team. 12. Establish/execute meeting cadence.	10. Mobilize Tier 2 functional leads. 11. Define IT transition team roles and responsibilities. 12. Define IT escalation and approval process.			
Change Management and Communications	6. Define operating model for HR organization. 7. Conduct high-level culture and management of change assessment.	13. Develop detailed management of change plan (global, local, and function specific). 14. Define stakeholder management plan (RACI matrix). 15. Launch communications team. 16. Define communications strategy. 17. Develop communications road map, by audience (newsletter, poster, video, flyer, leadership team bulletin, targeted communications). 18. Develop Day 1 readiness materials.	13. Execute communications and management of change plans. 14. Capture and respond to stakeholder feedback. 15. Define super user strategy. 16. Onboard super users. 17. Change management team kickoff. 18. Conduct end-user change readiness assessment.[b]	9. Conduct business design review.[b] 10. Obtain change impact sign-offs.[b]		
TSA Management	8. Begin estimated TSA timeline and cost (based on due diligence info received).	19. Finalize TSA. 20. Establish TSA management process. 21. Communicate TSA tracking process to functional leads. 22. Communicate target TSA exit dates and scope to functional leads for joint approval.		11. Communicate target TSA exit dates and scope to integration functional leads for joint approval. 12. Monitor TSA exits.		

EXHIBIT A.5 *(Continued)*

		23. Coordinate IT systems and applications transition dates with transition manager. 24. Monitor TSA exits.			
Budget Management	9. Complete high-level budget estimation template based on due diligence info received.	25. Refine budgets across functional areas. 26. Request capital approval. 27. Manage and track the budget. 28. Provide monthly budget versus actual report.	13. Gather IT internal and external resource estimates for ERP migration. 14. Provide monthly budget versus actual report. 15. Submit IT external resource request form.		
IT Blueprinting and Design	10. Gather target systems and application landscapes through due diligence data request process. 11. Build initial IT high-level systems transition strategy.	29. Assess interim systems application and infrastructure requirements. 30. Perform high-level systems and application mapping. 31. Define IT road map. 32. Complete clustering strategy by defining as-is and to-be IT systems landscape. 33. Project longer-term systems migration timing. 34. Conduct high-level systems and process flow design workshop with business partners. 35. Identify end-to-end open questions for seller. 36. Conduct end-to-end systems and process flow kickoff with seller.	16. Conduct IT end-to-end detailed systems and process flows workshop. 17. Identify business change impacts— roles, processes, organizational. 18. Conduct business design review. 19. Obtain business sign-offs on design (including change impact sign-offs[b]).		

EXHIBIT A.5 (*Continued*)

<table>
<tr><td rowspan="2" style="writing-mode:vertical">Key Process and Activities</td><td></td><td></td><td>37. Incorporate seller's responses into IT systems and process landscapes.
38. Refine IT high-level systems transition strategy.
39. Develop IT midlevel systems and process flow design.</td><td></td><td></td><td></td></tr>
<tr>
<td>1. Perform target screening process.
2. Analyze risks and mitigations for targets.
3. Publish business case.
4. Obtain approval from executive steering committee via business case.</td>
<td>12. Present deal overview document to due diligence team.
13. Create functional due diligence data request/ questionnaire for target.
14. Prepare functional due diligence reports from target data received.
15. Complete functional high-level synergy estimates.
16. Consolidate final due diligence report summary.
17. Obtain approval to begin negotiations.</td>
<td>40. Define clean room process.
41. Define and communicate Day 1.
42. Establish escalation process within (acquirer) transition team and with seller.
43. Establish communication flow process with seller.
44. Execute Day 1 fast close plan.
45. Confirm critical tasks flagged in Day 1 checklist are completed.
46. Conduct IT enterprise resource planning (ERP) migration kickoff meeting.
47. Refine strategy for IT systems and processes landscapes.
48. Refine IT high-level systems transition strategy.
49. Refine IT road map.</td>
<td></td>
<td></td>
<td>1. Transition open stabilization issues to regular issues management process.
2. Measure operational KPIs.
3. Define production change control process.
4. Execute systems and applications decommissioning plan.</td>
</tr>
</table>

EXHIBIT A.5 *(Continued)*

		50. Communicate.				
		51. Develop and configure.				
		52. Test.				
		53. Train.				
		54. Infrastructure.				
		55. Allocate security/roles.				
		56. Assess readiness.				
		57. Cut-over planning and execution.				
		58. Go live.				
		59. Post go-live stabilization.				
		60. Close project.				

a, the timeline can be adjusted depending on the integration scope; b, this activity is also part of blueprinting and design work.

EXHIBIT A.5   (*Continued*)

The M&A IT playbook should never be considered final. It is a living document that should continually be adapted to the changing business environment and regularly refined based on the experiences of its users. Users should be encouraged to submit suggestions for modifications, and an updated playbook version should be issued as appropriate (for example, following each M&A transaction).

For companies anticipating multiple M&A deals, developing an M&A IT playbook can prepare an organization to jump-start its IT integration or divestiture activities. The development of the playbook and the accompanying library of customized tools and templates can lead to improved flexibility and scalability to handle different-size deals or even multiple simultaneous deals. Ultimately, this could reduce the time and the costs of IT integration and divestiture activities. (See Exhibit A.5.)

Sample M&A IT Checklists

Shalva Nolen
Sreekanth Gopinathan
Devi Aradada

The checklists in this appendix can serve as a guide to a CIO and his or her team in preparing for M&A events, including conducting due diligence, crafting and implementing an information technology (IT) integration or divestiture plan, improving synergies, and preparing for future mergers. The right set of capabilities, knowledge, processes, tools, and experience can help prepare an IT organization to effectively support the business's M&A goals. The checklist examples that follow are tools that can be tailored to an organization's needs and included in its M&A tool kit and playbook.

IT DUE DILIGENCE

An IT due diligence checklist can be used by a potential buyer when assessing a target during the due diligence phase. The potential buyer may use a checklist to validate that none of the critical areas of a target's IT function have been inadvertently overlooked during the due diligence period.

The IT due diligence checklist can also be used when preparing for a divestiture. Prior to engaging potential buyers, the seller can use the checklist to evaluate its IT function and identify any areas where there are issues or risks that might impact the sale. The seller can then address any issues discovered during this predeal time or determine a course of action to mitigate the risks and increase the IT function's perceived value. Moreover, the areas in the checklist can be used by the seller to support the detailed due diligence effort by helping the seller determine the information it might have to pull together for the data room and by helping the seller identify what documentation it may need to create if it is not readily accessible.

See Exhibit B.1 for a sample IT due diligence checklist that can be used by either the seller or the buyer.

EXHIBIT B.1   IT Due Diligence Checklist

IT Area	Checklist Item

Applications	❑ Enterprise applications
	  ❑ Enterprise resource planning (ERP)
	  ❑ Finance and accounting
	  ❑ Customer relationship management (CRM)
	  ❑ Supply chain management (SCM)
	  ❑ Business intelligence (BI)
	  ❑ Enterprise content management (ECM)
	  ❑ Business process management (BPM)
	  ❑ Product lifecycle management (PLM)
	  ❑ Human resources management system (HRMS)
	❑ Specialized applications (industry-specific)
	  ❑ Proprietary
	  ❑ Open source
	❑ Office productivity applications
	  ❑ E-mail and calendaring
	  ❑ Instant messaging
	  ❑ Collaboration software
	  ❑ Office and personal productivity

Infrastructure	❑ Hardware
	  ❑ Mainframes
	  ❑ Servers
	  ❑ Storage
	  ❑ End-user devices (e.g., desktops/laptops, phones, personal digital assistants [PDAs])
	❑ Network and telecommunications
	  ❑ Data
	  ❑ Voice
	  ❑ Mobile service
	❑ Infrastructure software
	  ❑ Operating systems
	  ❑ Application development
	  ❑ Middleware
	  ❑ Data management
	  ❑ Storage management
	  ❑ Security systems
	  ❑ IT operations
	  ❑ Compliance
	❑ Databases

Organization	❑ Size and structure ❑ Capabilities ❑ Tenure ❑ Training (IT staff and end users) ❑ Outsourcing ❑ Staff location ❑ Compensation

EXHIBIT B.1 (*Continued*)

IT Area	Checklist Item

Suppliers/Vendor Management (Hardware, Software, and Services)	❑ Vendor viability
	❑ Licenses
	    ❑ Terms and conditions
	    ❑ Transfer or relicensing fees
	❑ Contract termination fees

IT Culture	❑ History ❑ Governance ❑ Mission ❑ Innovation ❑ Adaptability ❑ Compensation structure ❑ Communication
IT Operations	❑ IT operating and capital budgets ❑ Security and risk management ❑ Disaster recovery and business continuity ❑ IT service portfolio (including the associated service level agreements [SLAs]) ❑ Current and planned project portfolio ❑ Help desk ❑ Desk side services ❑ Regulatory compliance ❑ Data center facilities

Source: Pavel Krumkachev, Indira Gillingham, and Shalva Nolen, "The Importance of IT Due Diligence during a Merger or Acquisition," in *IT Best Practices for Financial Managers*, ed. Janice M. Roehl-Anderson (Hoboken, NJ: John Wiley & Sons, 2010), 212–213.

IT INTEGRATION READINESS

The sample IT integration checklist provided in Exhibit B.2 is an accelerator to help CIOs and their teams in planning their activities during an integration event. The checklist includes key items an IT organization should consider to help facilitate an issue-free Day 1 and minimize the impact to key stakeholders inside and outside the organization.

IT DIVESTITURE READINESS

The sample IT divestiture checklist in Exhibit B.3 provides practical guidelines on activities to ease the separation from the parent company and help

EXHIBIT B.2   IT Integration Checklist

Program Strategy and Planning
❏ Review merger/acquisition agreement and outline high-level IT requirements.
❏ Determine integration program management structure, roles and responsibilities, and timeline.
❏ Review merger/acquisition rationale and understand go-forward IT strategy for the new entity.
❏ Establish communication link between two organizations for information sharing.
❏ Document inventory of assets, source code, and intellectual property to be transferred.
❏ Conduct periodic management status reviews.

IT Application and Infrastructure Integration Strategy
❏ Select IT applications and systems leads for individual functions:
   ❏ Finance
   ❏ Human resources
   ❏ Sales and marketing
   ❏ Operations and service delivery
   ❏ Logistics
   ❏ Customer service and CRM
   ❏ Quality and regulatory
   ❏ Corporate real estate and facilities
   ❏ Risk management and risk operations
   ❏ Compliance
   ❏ Legal
   ❏ Fraud and security
   ❏ Procurement
   ❏ Communications and corporate affairs
❏ Develop application and systems inventory.
❏ Develop hardware inventory.
❏ Document infrastructure landscape:
   ❏ Computing platforms (for example, mainframe hardware, server hardware, mainframe operating system, and server operating system).
   ❏ Storage (for example, storage area network, network-attached storage, direct attached storage, tape libraries, server backup).
   ❏ Hosting (for example, data center facility, disaster recovery, and maintenance services).
   ❏ End-user computing (for example, client hardware, client operating system, and terminal emulation).
   ❏ Personal productivity (for example, e-mail, handheld devices, office automation, imaging, and collaboration).
   ❏ Security (for example, audit and compliance tools, authentication, directory services, encryption, network security, and virus protection).
   ❏ Systems management (for example, configuration management, asset management, change management, service/help desk, network management, performance monitoring, capacity planning, and software distribution).
   ❏ Telecommunications (for example, firewall, wireless, voice, data, Internet protocol [IP] services, and other protocols).
❏ Assess hardware and software standards of target organization and compare to the acquirer.

EXHIBIT B.2 (*Continued*)

❑ Identify mission-critical applications and infrastructure components.
❑ Identify required Day 1 applications and infrastructure modifications and changes.
❑ Establish project prioritization criteria for application rationalization process.
❑ Develop high-level IT applications and infrastructure carve-out strategy.
❑ Schedule IT applications and Infrastructure kickoff and check-in meetings.

Pre-Day 1 Activities

❑ Staff IT functional implementation team.
❑ Conduct IT functional kickoff meeting and schedule periodic review sessions.
❑ Document as-is functional application and infrastructure landscape. Illustrative list includes:
  ❑ Finance
  ❑ Human resources
  ❑ Sales and marketing
  ❑ Operations and service delivery
  ❑ Logistics
  ❑ Customer service and CRM
  ❑ Procurement
  ❑ Corporate real estate and facilities
  ❑ Legal
❑ Develop and document detailed IT functional integration strategy.
❑ Document Day 1 to-be functional application and infrastructure landscape per integration strategy.
❑ Develop detailed work plans to implement detailed IT functional integration strategy.
❑ Develop high-level functional project cost estimate, and track costs.
❑ Identify hardware and software requirements, and order hardware and software to support integration strategies.
❑ Review detailed integration strategy and work plans across functional teams to determine if any disconnects exist, and update strategy/work plans (if required).
❑ Develop functional issues log and management process.
❑ Modify third-party agreements, service contracts, lease agreements, and the like related to desktops and end-user computing needs.
❑ Determine data extract, migration, and archive activities, and complete them (if required).
❑ Put in place agreements with all vendors for licenses to be transferred, and transfer contracts when applicable.
❑ Develop required transition services agreements (TSAs).
❑ Determine development and data conversion requirements for Day 1, and set up development program and related staffing.
❑ Determine system testing requirements, and set up testing program and associated staffing.
❑ Conduct detailed security assessments to identify vulnerabilities, and develop mitigation strategies and contingency plans for problem areas.
❑ Conduct detailed risk assessment, and develop risk mitigation strategies and contingency plans for risk areas.
❑ Determine help-desk procedures, and create documentation defining how to handle cross-help-desk calls.
❑ Finalize post-Day 1 business continuity/disaster recovery plan and IT contingency plan.

(*continued*)

EXHIBIT B.2 (*Continued*)

⊔ Develop detailed cut-over requirements and plan:
  ⊔ Complete and distribute Day 1 cut-over plan.
  ⊔ Finalize required ID and user access (re)provisioning to various systems and platforms (e.g., Unix, Windows, mainframe, remote, etc.).
  ⊔ Finalize key communications to customers, vendors, and business partners.
  ⊔ Finalize key communications to end users and internal customers.
  ⊔ Validate that resources have been lined up for Day 1 activities.
⊔ Implement integration strategies.

Post-Day 1 Activities

⊔ Complete shutdown activities where appropriate:
  ⊔ Terminate user access on IT systems.
  ⊔ Shut down applications.
  ⊔ Shut down interfaces.
  ⊔ Decommission servers.
  ⊔ Terminate contracts with third parties.
⊔ Develop post-Day 1 support process:
  ⊔ Develop issues escalation process.
⊔ Establish meeting cadence to assess TSA performance (if required).
⊔ Conduct postmortem and document the lessons learned.

achieve the divestiture goals. The checklist covers keys aspects of management, strategy, and pre- and post-Day 1 activities that the IT organization should consider to effectively achieve an issue-free transition.

IT TRANSITION SERVICES AGREEMENTS (TSAS)

Transition services agreements (TSAs) are one of the crucial elements of a divestiture, and an effective TSA can help both buyer and seller accomplish their respective goals. The sample IT TSA checklist in Exhibit B.4 provides an overview of factors to consider when creating and managing an effective TSA to help execute a rapid and smooth separation. (See Chapters 14 and 16 for more detailed discussion of TSAs.)

DATA REQUIREMENTS

Managing data during an integration or a divestiture is important, and IT plays a crucial role in effectively planning for and managing the risks and impacts associated with data integrations. The sample data requirements

EXHIBIT B.3 IT Divestiture Checklist

Program Strategy and Planning
- ❏ Review divestiture agreement and outline high-level IT requirements.
- ❏ Determine divestiture program management structure, roles and responsibilities, and timeline.
- ❏ Review divestiture rationale and understand acquirer's go-forward IT strategy.
- ❏ Establish communication link between two organizations for information sharing.
- ❏ Document inventory of assets, source code, and intellectual property to be transferred.
- ❏ Schedule periodic management status reviews.

IT Application and Infrastructure Separation Strategy
- ❏ Select IT applications and systems leads for individual functions:
  - ❏ Finance
  - ❏ Human resources
  - ❏ Sales and marketing
  - ❏ Operations and service delivery
  - ❏ Logistics
  - ❏ Customer service and CRM
  - ❏ Quality and regulatory
  - ❏ Corporate real estate and facilities
  - ❏ Risk management and risk operations
  - ❏ Compliance
  - ❏ Legal
  - ❏ Fraud and security
  - ❏ Procurement
  - ❏ Communications and corporate affairs
- ❏ Develop application and systems inventory.
- ❏ Develop hardware inventory.
- ❏ Document infrastructure landscape:
  - ❏ Computing platforms (for example, mainframe hardware, server hardware, mainframe operating system, and server operating system).
  - ❏ Storage (for example, storage area network, network-attached storage, direct attached storage, server backup).
  - ❏ Hosting (for example, data center facility, disaster recovery, and maintenance services).
  - ❏ End-user computing (for example, client hardware, client operating system, and terminal emulation).
  - ❏ Personal productivity (for example, e-mail, handheld devices, office automation, imaging, and collaboration).
  - ❏ Security (for example, audit and compliance tools, authentication, directory services, encryption, network security, and virus protection).
  - ❏ Systems management (for example, configuration management, asset management, change management, service/help desk, network management, performance monitoring, capacity planning, and software distribution).
  - ❏ Telecommunications (for example, firewall, wireless, voice, data, Internet protocol [IP] services, and other protocols).
- ❏ Identify mission-critical applications and infrastructure components.
- ❏ Identify required Day 1 applications and infrastructure modifications.
- ❏ Establish project prioritization criteria for application rationalization process.
- ❏ Develop high-level IT applications and infrastructure carve-out strategy.
- ❏ Schedule IT applications and infrastructure kickoff and weekly check-in meetings.

(continued)

EXHIBIT B.3   (*Continued*)

Pre-Day 1 Activities
- ❏ Staff IT functional implementation team.
- ❏ Schedule IT functional kickoff meeting and periodic review sessions.
- ❏ Document as-is functional application and infrastructure landscape. Typical list includes applications for the following:
  - ❏ Finance
  - ❏ Human resources
  - ❏ Sales and marketing
  - ❏ Operations and service delivery
  - ❏ Logistics
  - ❏ Customer service and CRM
  - ❏ Procurement
  - ❏ Corporate real estate and facilities
  - ❏ Legal
- ❏ Develop and document detailed IT functional carve-out strategy.
- ❏ Document Day 1 to-be functional application and infrastructure landscape per carve-out strategy.
- ❏ Develop detailed work plans to implement detailed IT functional carve-out strategy.
- ❏ Develop high-level functional project cost estimate, and track costs.
- ❏ Identify hardware and software requirements, and order hardware and software to support carve-out strategies.
- ❏ Review detailed carve-out strategy and work plans across functional teams to determine if any disconnects exist, and update strategy and work plans (if required).
- ❏ Develop functional issues log and management process.
- ❏ Modify third-party agreements, service contracts, lease agreements, and so on related to desktops and end-user computing needs.
- ❏ Determine required data extract, migration, and archive activities, and complete them.
- ❏ Put in place agreements with all vendors for licenses to be transferred, and transfer contracts when applicable.
- ❏ Develop required TSAs:
  - ❏ Complete negotiations with third parties to support delivery.
  - ❏ Put in place infrastructure to support TSAs.
  - ❏ Develop performance metrics.
  - ❏ Put in place performance tracking process.
  - ❏ Finalize TSA costing and billing model and process.
- ❏ Determine development and modification requirements for Day 1, and set up development program and associated staffing.
- ❏ Determine system testing requirements, and set up testing program and associated staffing.
- ❏ Conduct detailed risk assessment, and develop risk mitigation strategies and contingency plans for risk areas.
- ❏ Determine help-desk procedures, and create documentation defining how to handle cross-help-desk calls.
- ❏ Update post-Day 1 business continuity and disaster recovery plan and IT contingency plan.
- ❏ Develop detailed cut-over requirements and plan:
  - ❏ Complete and distribute Day 1 cut-over plan and command center playbook.
  - ❏ Finalize required ID and user access re-provisioning to various systems and platforms (e.g., UNIX, Windows, mainframe, remote, etc.).

EXHIBIT B.3 (*Continued*)

❑ Finalize key communications to customers, vendors, and business partners.
❑ Finalize key communications to internal customers and end users.
❑ Make sure resources across work streams have been lined up for Day 1 activities.
  Implement carve-out strategies.
  Schedule regular status meetings.

Post-Day 1 Activities

❑ Complete shutdown activities where appropriate:
  ❑ Terminate user access on IT systems.
  ❑ Shut down applications.
  ❑ Shut down interfaces.
  ❑ Decommission servers.
  ❑ Terminate contracts with third parties.
❑ Develop post-Day 1 support process:
  ❑ Put in place infrastructure and staff to support command center.
  ❑ Develop issues escalation process.
❑ Conduct postmortem for lessons learned.

EXHIBIT B.4 IT TSA Checklist

❑ Identify services that will be provided at each stage of TSA period.
❑ Provide a complete description of service to be provided. Clearly specify process and subprocess detail involved in executing delivery of TSA services.
❑ Provide a description of services not provided.
❑ Typical services include:
  ❑ Enterprise application support
  ❑ Application enhancement and application development
  ❑ Network services
  ❑ Service management center
  ❑ Server and storage hosting service
  ❑ Mainframe infrastructure services
  ❑ Backup and recovery
  ❑ E-mail/messaging and collaboration
  ❑ Corporate application support
  ❑ Desktop services
  ❑ Help desk
  ❑ Identity and access management
  ❑ Remote access
  ❑ Voice and video service
  ❑ Telecommunication services
  ❑ File and print services
❑ Determine whether TSA is dependent on third-party delivery (common for IT TSAs), and complete negotiations to agree to the provision of service.
❑ Determine how often the service is provided (for example, daily, weekly, as-needed basis, or 24/7 support).

(*continued*)

EXHIBIT B.4 (*Continued*)

☐ Determine what resources will provide the services:
  ☐ Identify types of resources (for example, specific names or job descriptions) required to adequately provide services, especially if the service requires special expertise.
☐ Determine length of the TSA period. All TSA schedule items must have a defined end date (either a specific date or a period of time measured from transaction closing).
  ☐ Create clearly defined TSA exit plans with proposed timing and extension request process.
☐ Define the process to add, delete, or change the services provided under TSA.
  ☐ Procedure to add services—creation of new TSAs.
  ☐ Procedure to exit services—termination of TSAs.
  ☐ Procedure to modify existing services—amendment to TSAs.
☐ Define what all parties own at the end of the TSA period:
  ☐ Operating versus capital lease principals—simple rental or does transfer of ownership occur?
  ☐ Identification of specific assets (copiers, printers, etc.).
☐ Define TSA review process and issue resolution path:
  ☐ Joint periodic review is important to maintain relationship and resolve issues quickly.
  ☐ Issue escalation path that is specific about how issues are resolved.
  ☐ Progress updates on a regular basis until all services are exited.
☐ Define service metrics.
☐ Define penalties or incentives for TSA performance levels.
☐ Establish TSA management:
  ☐ Identify individual TSA owners to manage day-to-day functionality.
☐ Define financial arrangements:
  ☐ Payment terms (i.e., how services will be paid).
  ☐ Basis on which costs are derived (one-time costs versus recurring costs).
  ☐ Process to review costs.
  ☐ Handling of changes in payments (for example, discounts or incentive payments based on performance).
  ☐ Identify how costs will behave when exiting TSAs.
☐ Identify any dependencies with other TSAs.
☐ Identify key TSA risks, issues, and mitigation strategies.

checklist in Exhibit B.5 provides an overview of activities that should be considered for data conversion, archiving, and retention during an integration divestiture event.

WRAPPING IT UP

During an M&A transaction, IT is under tremendous pressure to deliver, and numerous things have the potential to go wrong. Merger, acquisition, and divestiture deals are complex, and effectively tackling them is part art and part science. A properly structured approach to dealing with the various aspects of the IT integration or divestiture can provide practical

EXHIBIT B.5 Data Requirements Checklist

Data Conversion, Archiving, and Retention

- ❏ Identify the areas that will need to be part of the conversion and archival strategy. Illustrative list includes the following:
  - ❏ Finance (monthly balances, corporate asset data, tax book asset data, depreciation methods, accounts payable [A/P] open invoices, A/P recurring invoices, accounts receivable [A/R] open invoices, A/R recurring invoices, collections history).
  - ❏ Operations (master supplier list, items, bills of materials [BOMs], open unpaid purchase orders, open blanket purchase orders, price lists, modifiers, inventory balances, open sales orders).
  - ❏ CRM (installed base, service contracts, customer master).
  - ❏ Sales (leads/pipeline, sales quotas, and sales territory).
- ❏ Identify data details such as transaction volumes, source application, target application, and complexity assessments for each conversion. Gather the physical volumes for each ancillary system from the application owner.
- ❏ Identify the list of systems that will be converted and the systems that will receive the data via data warehouse, tape, and so on.
- ❏ Identify the list of systems to be archived.
- ❏ Identify systems for decommission and how they interact with other systems.
- ❏ Determine the roles and responsibilities of the data conversion and archival team.
- ❏ Determine the nature of the data for each system and subsystem—sensitive or nonsensitive.
- ❏ Identify dependencies, both internal and external, to the customer and application. Examples of external dependencies include vendor licenses, support for converted or decommissioned systems, and legal requirements for data.
- ❏ Evaluate rules and dependencies for the acquirer's systems. Apply the rules and criteria developed by the conversion team to the new data being converted.
- ❏ Identify the types of data storage devices (for example, tape, data warehouse, file, and so on) to assist in implementing a tiered storage design.
- ❏ Set the sequencing of the conversions or export programs.
- ❏ Identify the retention periods and formats for each set of data.
- ❏ Identify and institute the clean room guidelines, policies, and roles as they relate to data accessed. Some of the data elements that may require protection on Day 1 are:
  - ❏ Customer terms and conditions (for example, customer contracts).
  - ❏ Customer-specific pricing (for example, price catalogs, bids, quotes, data warehouse).
  - ❏ Product costs, margins (for example, material master, quotes, data warehouse).
  - ❏ Sales forecast, revenue views, demand plan, revenue reports.
  - ❏ Customer-specific sensitive information (for example, customer install base).
  - ❏ Customer issue management (e.g., case/ticket).
  - ❏ Financial transactional data (revenue, A/R, deferred revenue) (for example, ERP applications, decision support tools).
  - ❏ Revenue recognition policies and methodology (for example, revenue recognition white papers, recognition rule sets, spreadsheets).
  - ❏ Product development lifecycle information (for example, product road maps, development plans of record).
  - ❏ Product information (for example, R&D apps, product data management (PDM) apps, data warehouse).
- ❏ Identify the strategy for future data archival mechanisms, including the tools and archiving run times from different systems and the archive utility. (The run times will assist in cut-over planning for conversion metrics.)
- ❏ Develop detailed work plans and blueprints for the execution of the data conversion, archival, and retention strategy.

insights and help proactively identify the risks and issues that can prevent the organization from achieving its short-term and long-term goals related to the transaction. The checklists documented in this appendix can prove to be very valuable tools for facilitating effective and efficient IT participation in the merger, acquisition, or divestiture. Following this path will not ensure that the expected benefits are achieved, because nothing is guaranteed. However, proper planning and execution of pre- and post-Day 1 activities related to IT integration and divestiture can make the process easier and more effective, and can increase the likelihood of achieving the expected benefits.

M&A IT Sample Case Studies

Manish Laad
Abhishek Mathur
Prasanna Rajappa

INTRODUCTION

Whether you're taking a company apart or putting one together, M&A and restructuring tend to take place in the glare of the spotlight. These are high-visibility endeavors that come loaded with risk. If approaches are adopted that have already been tested, revenue and cost synergies can be expanded and accelerated, transaction risk can be significantly reduced, and transition of the workforce can be achieved in a smooth, structured manner even as the business, its operating model, and/or its capital model undergo fundamental changes.

In the current digital age, businesses have a critical dependency on IT systems; hence the success of any merger integration or divestiture transaction partially depends on the efficient and fast execution of the integration or separation of the business-critical IT systems. In addition to loss of cost synergies, integration or separation delays can lead to major business disruption, loss in value and revenue, reputational risk, and loss of key human capital. Additionally, not performing the IT systems transformation right can lead to a whole new set of problems, such as errors in business-critical operational data, regulatory compliance, and reporting. To make matters worse, IT executives and operations personnel are often brought into the due diligence process very late or not at all. This situation prevents them from providing valuable input on what the integration or separation drivers are and how to address them from an IT perspective. Consequently, the IT group is faced with the formidable task of executing on an ambiguous scope within an unreasonable timeframe dictated by the business.

The challenging task of M&A IT integration or separation requires an accelerated but organized, systematic, and well-coordinated approach for current-state IT blueprinting and target-state IT planning and execution.

A well-defined set of tools, accelerators, and playbooks is vital to the outcome and results of the IT transformation to support the new business operating model.

CASE STUDIES

This appendix contains three recent M&A-related case studies. They are intended to highlight the IT integration or separation challenges faced and the approaches utilized to overcome those challenges and complete the transition process effectively.

Large Oil and Gas Company Merger

Abstract   Two large North American oil and gas companies decided to undergo a merger, making the new company one of the largest oil companies in North America. While one company needed to find a way to finance its megaprojects in the days of erratic oil prices, the other was searching for a way to demonstrate to shareholders it was more valuable than its market valuation. The merger of the two companies combined one company's extensive retail gasoline and refining business and its international operations with the other's extensive operations in oil sands.

The synergies of the merger, based on plans and spending, included obtaining annual operating expenditure reductions in excess of $300 million from efficiencies in overlapping operations, streamlining business practices, and improving logistics. Additionally, capital efficiencies of $1 billion per year were forecasted due to elimination of redundant spending and realigning capital budgets with high-return and near-term projects.

The companies had to work through significant cultural differences. One company was an erstwhile public-sector company and known to be risk averse, whereas the other was known to be a more aggressive company.

The Challenge   One of the biggest issues facing the new merged entity was the consolidation of the two existing enterprise resource planning (ERP) systems, their ancillary ecosystems, and related functional processes. The objective was to deliver an ERP system for the merged entity with functional work processes to enable legacy systems from both the companies to drive to the new unified operating model and to realize the ERP consolidation synergy business case. Where appropriate, upgrades to take advantage of new ERP functionality were also to be performed. A precursor to the ERP and business process integration was the merged entity's data center infrastructure consolidation, which also called for rationalization and consolidation. Critical success factors for the transaction from an IT perspective were:

- The ability for both legacy organizations to be able to conduct business with the unified environment.
- Minimal business disruption to either organization.
- Successful deployment to international and offshore operations.

Approach An assimilation approach was chosen for the vast majority of the IT systems in the merger. This also meant that the business process of the acquiring company would extend to the company being acquired. In some cases, some legacy retail systems from the acquired company were retained due to material gaps or deficiencies in the acquirer's systems. An initiation and detailed planning phase followed by a postclose readiness phase were used to perform detailed planning for the overall integration. Best practices for functional and technical blueprinting, "walk-the-wall" sessions, and applications portfolio rationalization were extensively leveraged to provide an accelerated plan. (See Chapter 12 for an overview of the applications portfolio rationalization approach.)

The execution of the project took place over four simultaneous releases. Each release had five overlapping phases, namely, planning, design, build, deployment, and operation.

- **Release 1** included a broad revamp of the infrastructure that supported the ERP systems, including the move to a new data center, platform migration from one environment to another environment, implementing new networks, and other new technology components such as server load balancing and middleware. The technology components included in Release 1 supported the scaling of the integrated system, which hosted all new business processes and the 12,000 users in North America, Europe, and the Middle East.
- **Release 2** included upgrades of the core ERP platform, supplier relationship management (SRM) module, and customer relationship management (CRM) module. The release was primarily technical in nature, but due to the enhanced capabilities of SRM and CRM, some process and user interface changes were incorporated as well.
- **Release 3** (multistage deployment) was the most complex release, with the deployment of refining and marketing functionality, including marketing and distribution; the lubricants plant, people, and processes; and major refineries along with their staff. This release integrated all the downstream business functions onto a common set of processes and a single ERP platform. The business process scope included the upgrade

and integration of software applications across modules involving major technical and functional teams.

■ **Release 4** was the final deployment of the merged entity's processes and included the deployment of the company's international and offshore businesses. The merged entities' entire upstream international and offshore functions were also integrated into one consistent system and process in this release.

Results An integrated team approach was adopted whereby change management, communications, training, deployment, and super users worked together as the M&A team for planning and execution. Detailed plans were developed and implemented in an integrated manner, helping to facilitate an effective change effort for end users. Site-specific plans were tailored to each location, making sure the site-specific change risks, issues, and challenges were identified early. Change impacts were identified and understood by function and by business unit.

Based on strong planning and credible execution, the ERP integration and consolidation were effectively planned and executed. The transformation scale was formidable. Business process scope was detailed and included core processes in finance; supply chain management (SCM); project management; marketing and distribution (M&D); production, sales, and supply planning (PSSP); and CRM.

Financial Services Divestiture

Abstract A large financial services organization in the United States with assets totaling more than $350 billion committed to a multiyear program focused on improving alignment with its parent's global business model and vision: to become the leading international bank. To achieve this goal, the North American entity launched an aggressive transformation program inclusive of a number of restructuring and cost-reduction initiatives and targeted divestitures. The client's business transformation team was interested in devising a playbook for executing the divestitures in a structured and consistent manner while preserving quality and minimizing business disruption to both its divested businesses and the core banking and wealth management business.

The Challenge The organization was completely unprepared for the onslaught of divestiture activities that needed to be executed. There was no governance, process, or methodology in place to guide the multiple divestiture efforts. There was also a lack of divestiture experience within the organization. Additionally, there was a strong potential for multiple divestitures to be executed in parallel, which placed a very heavy strain on the business transformation team and other shared services teams in IT, such as infrastructure, IT applications, contract management, IT quality assurance and testing, information risk, and security. Significant gaps in both the capacity and the capabilities of internal staff were quickly recognized. To further complicate matters, the expedited timeline required the early divestiture execution of complex transactions. The first in the string of many divestitures was already in progress and was one of the largest and most complex, especially from an IT systems standpoint, where the lack of a structured approach, tools, and templates was already causing severe delays on the large majority of separation work.

Critical success factors for the transaction from an IT perspective were:

- Development of an efficient IT resources deployment model for key IT resources in light of multiple concurrent transactions.
- Establishment of a clear set of transition services agreements (TSAs) along with an effective TSA governance model.
- Successful logical or physical separation of commingled data between the divested entities and the remaining organization, with no disruption to either organization.

Approach In order to address the large and complex nature of this transformation, a multifaceted approach had to be used to mobilize and gain control over the planning and execution of this large business transformation. At the very core of the transformation, a governance model and a detailed divestiture playbook were developed by leveraging accelerators, best practices, and previous divestiture experiences. This provided the structure for the execution of the rest of the transactions using a tested methodology and approach. Above all, this structure had to remain flexible to provide execution support as deal timelines continued to accelerate significantly. Templates, tools, and data sharing electronic rooms were established to provide uniformity and consistency where possible. A set of teams was set up to provide cross-transactional support for the separation management office (SMO) functions, contract separation offices (CSOs), and transition services agreements (TSAs).

For the transaction that was already in progress, there was a lack of transparency as to the scope and status of the work, and what issues and risks were halting overall progress. The IT systems scope of work was clearly structured into a set of approximately 200 separation projects, broadly distributed across the IT infrastructure, mission-critical applications, end-user computing, and access management. Clear roles and accountability were established for each of the separation projects, with a designated project manager providing overall leadership by project.

A level of oversight was established at the IT work stream level by having a SWAT team of field agents in each of the work streams. The role of the field agents was to provide work-stream-level oversight and guidance to the project managers. A weekly set of one-on-one meetings were established between the IT field agents and each of the project managers in that work stream. The objectives of these meetings were to quickly gather the status of the project, proactively mitigate any risks to the schedule, and help resolve showstopper issues in an expedited manner.

The field agents, staffed with experienced IT personnel with a focus on divestitures, were also able to provide guidance on developing an execution approach and determine what scope items could be descoped or deferred from a Day 1 standpoint in the interest of preserving overall program timelines.

Detailed approaches were developed for programwide system testing, user acceptance testing, cut-over, and command centers during the cut-over. Due to criticality of timelines, these activities were managed very closely under the purview of the IT SMO in order to ensure adherence to plan and to proactively mitigate any defects or roadblocks.

Results Leveraging the IT SMO oversight and management approach, the transaction was effectively completed for Day 1. All Day 1 IT projects in the applications, infrastructure, end-user computing, and access provisioning spaces were tested, completed, and delivered, leading to a problem-free Day 1.

For IT infrastructure, all data center and infrastructure separation activities for Day 1 were completed on time. However, a large scope of activities was identified and preplanned for post-Day 1, including complex projects like full network separation, active directory cut-over, and full data center separation, relocation, and migration.

In the applications space, mission-critical applications' changes in scope for the transaction were completed, tested, and cut over during the Day 1 activities. Applications went through different changes depending on business requirements. Either applications were decommissioned, data segregation was accomplished between the remaining entity (RemainCo) and the sold entity (SellCo), or applications were transferred over to SellCo. Similar to the infrastructure space, preliminary planning for the post-Day 1 project was also completed in order to get a clear understanding of the post-Day 1 scope of work.

Access provisioning was also completed for Day 1 across all applications and IT infrastructure and end-user computing objects, leading to a high-quality end-user experience for business users.

Close to 10,000 end-user computing objects, which included a collection of MS access databases, mainframe data sets, and other desktop objects, were carefully analyzed, classified, assigned a disposition, and completed for Day 1, including transition to the sold entity where applicable. Transition services agreements were negotiated between the two companies where RemainCo would continue to provide key services and support to the SellCo entity. Also, a disposition was developed and executed for IT contracts. Additionally, the RemainCo organization exploited an opportunity to reduce approximately $800 million in third-party supplier spend using the divestiture program as a catalyst.

Manufacturing Divestiture

Abstract A leading provider of enterprise network equipment that designs, manufactures, and sells Internet protocol (IP)–based networking and other products related to the communications and information technology industry worldwide was selling its set-top box manufacturing facility in Mexico to one of its contract manufacturers based in China, one of the world's leading electronic devices manufacturers. The set-top business was the seller's only business unit that used a specific ERP system to power its business, while the rest of the seller's business was based on another ERP solution.

The Challenge As the deal was being finalized, an aggressive timeline of four months was envisioned to separate IT systems, including IT applications and infrastructure. While the seller was divesting the manufacturing plant based in Mexico, it would continue to manage the design, product development, sales and distribution, marketing, and all other intellectual property for the set-top products. The seller also wanted to retain a high level of transparency into the supply chain for the set-top products since it would continue to play a large part in the negotiation and pricing for raw materials with direct vendors, even though the buyer would be directly procuring the raw material on its own. Additionally, the seller would be one of the buyer's primary customers and would continue to have a stake in the success of the buyer during the transition of this manufacturing plant. In addition to a complex, tightly integrated ERP environment and a set of boundary applications that were integrally tied into it, the manufacturing operations were in a free trade zone or *maquiladora*, where factories import material and equipment on a duty-free and tariff-free basis for assembly, processing, or manufacturing and then export the assembled, processed, and/or manufactured products, sometimes back to the raw materials' country of origin, in this case the United States. Negotiation and careful construction of a transition services agreement were also required for effective transition.

In addition to the technical challenges, the IT team was also constrained due to late engagement of internal business resources as well as the business and IT resources from the buyer. This led to a significant delay in the finalization of business and IT requirements and the subsequent design in an already aggressive schedule.

Archaic systems and infrastructure caused further limitation of the original ERP system and related boundary applications. Security roles were modularized yet deeply integrated, and use of point-to-point and nonstandardized messaging interfaces between applications further led to complications throughout the separation process.

On the business front, the absence of current-state documentation and the presence of conflicting stakeholder views on business process flows led to confusion in development of the future-state blueprints. Deep supply chain functional and ERP technical knowledge and experience were required to spin off instances in the different plants.

Critical success factors for the transaction from an IT perspective were:

- Design and development of an ERP model that allowed for successful operation of the plant on Day 1, while preserving the tight timeline available for the transaction.
- Clear disposition and transition of all physical infrastructure and boundary applications.
- Establishment of clear transition services agreements and an associated governance model.
- Confidence in data boundaries and security between the separated entity and the parent organization.

Approach   The approach was divided into three separate work streams: IT infrastructure, the core ERP work stream, and the boundary applications.

For the core ERP and the boundary applications work streams, detailed blueprinting sessions were conducted at the functional and the technical levels internally in order to document the current state and the target state after separation. Different approaches were considered for the ERP separation, ranging from using the same instance between both companies all the way to having completely mutually exclusive ERP instances. After a careful evaluation and analysis of different options, having different ERP company codes within the same instance was finalized to be the balanced approach for separation between extremely aggressive Day 1 timelines and data privacy requirements between the entities (in lieu of a separate ERP instance). Multiple demonstrations of this approach were conducted with the buyer to demonstrate that data privacy requirements could be met.

The boundary applications had similar challenges to the ERP environment, in terms of not having a good infrastructure and documentation during the blueprinting phase. These applications were analyzed and each was given an individual disposition based on whether the buyer wanted to transition the application, share it with the seller along with a transitional services agreement, or demise the application altogether. A significant amount of current-state analysis and documentation was completed as a part of the transaction before the future-state disposition could be arrived at and the application could be successfully transitioned.

Changes to the infrastructure layer were in the form of physical separation of infrastructure, logical separation of networks, changes to end-user access, and the development of a secure network barrier between the two companies following the transition.

Results The complex separation of ERP and the effective integration of the two supply chains was achieved on time and led to an issue-free Day 1, enabling the plant to come back on line and resume manufacturing under the new company immediately after the short cut-over.

WRAPPING IT UP

Mergers, acquisitions, and divestitures can be a vital part of a company's strategy. All of the strategic initiatives behind a transaction frequently rely on IT. Organizations and businesses can no longer minimize IT or view it as a back-office function if they want to achieve the strategic benefits behind a merger, acquisition, or divestiture. An effective transition of the technology landscape is now a centerpiece of any M&A deal and critical to the outcome and results of the transition.

Early identification and execution of the technology changes required for a transaction can be very complex and require an in-depth understanding and analysis of the applications enabling the business, the underlying infrastructure that supports these applications, and the data with which these applications work. The case studies in this appendix demonstrate the tight integration between the successful technology transformation and the success of the broader M&A transaction.

ABOUT THE EDITOR

Janice M. Roehl-Anderson is a Principal at Deloitte Consulting LLP and the lead for key components of the M&A IT-related service area. She has led the successful implementation of numerous enterprise resource planning (ERP) packages and has worked in a variety of industries, including high-technology manufacturing, media and entertainment, and retail. She has been responsible for leading some of Deloitte Consulting's most complex global mergers, acquisitions, divestitures, and initial public offering projects from a technology perspective. Roehl-Anderson has computer security, custom-system, and extensive ERP implementation experience. She has written several books on controllership and information technology and has successfully passed the CPA exam.

ABOUT THE WEBSITE

Please visit www.wiley.com/go/maitbestpractices and enter the password *bestpractices123* to access additional resources to use alongside this book, including:

- **Sample M&A IT Checklists:** Mergers, acquisitions, and divestitures are complex, and effectively tackling them is part art and part science. A properly structured approach to dealing with the various aspects of the IT integration or divestiture can provide practical insights and help to proactively identify the risks and issues that can prevent the organization from achieving its goals related to the transaction. A well-thought-out checklist can be a valuable tool for facilitating effective and efficient IT participation in the merger, acquisition, or divestiture. This document provides checklists useful for the IT organization in some of the key areas of M&A: IT due diligence, IT integration readiness, IT divestiture readiness, IT transition service agreements, and data requirements.
- **M&A IT Playbook Overview:** Managing the technology components of a merger, acquisition, or divestiture can be the key differentiator between potential and realized synergies. Therefore, managers who are planning multiple merger, acquisition, or divestiture transactions can proactively prepare to execute the necessary IT activities by developing an M&A IT playbook. This document provides an overview of M&A IT playbooks and a sample table of contents. Developing an M&A IT playbook can help an organization jump-start its IT integration or divestiture activities and can lead to improved flexibility to handle different size deals or even multiple simultaneous deals.

Index

Access, user, 101, 259, 293–296, 472
Accountability, 195, 456, 478
Accounting, 51–53, 340, 383–385
Active directory migration, 94, 97, 99, 488
Active program management, 419, 424–428
Active validation, transition services agreements, 240–241
Ad hoc tools, due diligence investigations, 74
Administration role, CIOs, 307, 309
Adopt and go decision making criteria, 43
Alignment, with business objectives, 35–45
  best practices, 467–468
  blueprints and, 38–43
  CFOs role in achieving, 329
  critical success factors, 45
  decision making and, 43
  in due diligence, 44
  elements of, 150–151
  of enterprise IM strategy with M&A strategy, 420–423
  integration models and, 29–30, 36–37
  introduction, 35–36
  IT strategy and, 146
  lack of as deal failure risk, 454
Announcement day, 349, 366
Applications
  administration of, 64
  cloud suitability, 161
  Day 1 migration solution options, 94
  divestitures, 188–193
  drivers for streamlining footprint, 175, 176

due diligence investigations, 72, 74, 75, 89
emerging trends, 193–194
IT's role in direction for, 121
lessons learned, 488
long-term planning, 382–383
rationalization, 175–188, 194–197
support strategy, 64
synergy opportunities, 138
synergy planning and road map process, 127
transition from current state to target state approach, 179
transition plans, 100, 101
See also Business processes
Applications rationalization, 175–188
  best practices, 194–197, 198
  cost synergies through, 178–182
  drivers contributing to, 175, 176
  elements of, 178
  financials consolidation, 187
  four Cs of, 177
  function of, 175
  objectives of, 178
  operational synergies through, 182–188
Architecture diagrams, 108, 109–110
Architecture plans, 62–63. *See also* Enterprise architecture, "M&A-aware"
Archiving, data, 168–169
As-is access, 101
Assessments
  data quality, 170–171
  employee performance, 60, 360–361
  risk, 286, 291–292

Assets
  CFO's role in protecting, 337–342
  identification of, 169
  migration, 487
  utilization metrics, 124
Audits, regulatory requirements,
  290–291
Authoritarian leadership style, 32
Automated contract review, 209–210

Backup recovery testing, 442, 448
Balance sheets, 255
Banks, 218–219
Benchmarks, 81, 124
Benefits, employee, 58, 126–128
Best-of-breed approach, 62
Best practices, 464–479
  applications rationalization,
    194–197, 198
  for deal execution, 477–478
  organizational implications,
    475–477
  prior to deal, 464–467
  security and privacy implications,
    472–473
  strategy, approach, and governance,
    467–472
  synergies, 473
  third-party contracts, 473–475
  See also Critical success factors
    (CSFs)
Bias, in synergies analysis, 111
Blueprints
  alignment of IT with business
    objectives, 38–43, 150
  applications portfolio, 183–187,
    196
  best practices, 468–469
  critical success factors, 42
  definition of, 38
  design execution, 16–18
  infrastructure, 91–93
  IT's role in functional blueprint
    preparation, 39–43
  phases of, 10
  role of, 10, 38–39

  sample of, 13
  transition services agreements, 227
Bottom-up synergy commitments, 13
Brainstorming, 112
Budgeting, 53, 89, 148, 455
Bundling of transition services, 242, 247
Business-aligned integration models,
  36–38
Business case, for long-term business
  process integration, 380–381, 389
Business continuity, temporary, 295
Business intelligence (BI) systems, 57
Business intent, 207–208, 222
Business objectives, integration
  approach and, 29–30. See also
  Alignment, with business objectives
Business processes, 373–389
  building business case for, 380–381,
    389
  building phase, 385–386
  business requirement details, 381
  Day 1 integration requirements,
    376–380, 389
  deployment, 387
  design phase, 381–385
  diagrams, 106, 107
  due diligence and, 72–74, 89
  flow diagrams, 106, 107
  long-term integration requirements,
    380–388, 389
  long-term support, 387–388
  pre-Day 1 planning road map,
    373–376, 388–389
  testing, 433
  See also Applications

Capability maturity models (CMMs),
  310, 311
Carve out and hand off (COHO) teams,
  228
Carve-outs
  divestitures, 143–144
  due diligence, 71, 78, 87
  process, 143
  time constraints, 265
  See also Divestitures

Case studies
  data domain prioritization, 429–430
  difficult situations, 490–491
  divestitures at multinational bank,
    218–219
  incomplete due diligence, 490
  integration planning, 490
  merger between two energy
    companies, 219–221
Cash management, 54
Catalyst, CFO as, 323, 329–332, 342
Centralized organization structure, 356
CEOs (chief executive officers), role of,
    374
Certification, access, 296
CFO's (chief financial officers),
    321–344
  business process role, 374
  as catalyst, 323, 329–332, 342
  collaboration with CIOs, 343
  cross-functional collaboration,
    321–323
  Four Faces Framework, 323–324
  as operator, 332–338, 341–343
  as steward, 338–342
  as strategist, 323, 324–329, 342
Change management, 277, 293,
    297–298, 363–370
Change requests, 397, 473
Charge-backs, 269
Chart of accounts (COA), 340–341
Checklists, 128, 130
CIOs (chief information officers),
    305–320
  alignment, of business and IT
    strategy, 146
  business process role, 374
  challenge of multiple roles, 305–307
  collaboration with CFOs, 343
  external role, 314–317
  internal role, 307–313
  involvement of, 22
  lessons learned, 317–319
  models of, 306
Clean rooms, 168, 331
Clean teams, 7–8, 331

CLM (contract lifecycle management)
    system, 55
Clone, vitiate, and go separation model,
    12, 101
Clone and go separation model, 12,
    101, 143
Closure, financial, 339, 343, 375
Cloud computing, 157–165
  benefits, 158, 159
  critical success factors, 164–165
  emerging trends, 193–194
  integration opportunities, 158–159
  migration timing, 160–162
  by operating model, 159–160
  provider evaluation, 163–164
  strategy for, 162–163
  suitability for, 160, 161
  types of systems, 157–158
CMD (customer master data), 57
CMMs (capability maturity models),
    310, 311
COHO (carve out and hand off) teams,
    228
Collaboration, 321–323, 343,
    399–401, 427
Combination integration model
  alignment of IT with business
    objectives, 37
  critical success factors, 31
  definition of, 29
  execution priorities, 30
  features of, 11, 142
  leadership style, 32
  M&A failure causes, 31
Commercial applications, 74. *See also*
    Applications
Commercial diligence, 326
Communication
  by CFO, 335
  challenges, 350
  for change management, 363
  control over, 402–403
  Day 1 priorities, 254, 261–262,
    351
  deal failure themes, 454–455
  with employees, 346–352, 475–476

Communication (*Continued*)
  of employee transition plans,
    366–367
  information management office's
    role, 395, 402–403
  between IT and business leaders, 466
  with IT leadership, 111, 363–366
  M&A critical success factor,
    456–457
  by merger stage, 348–351
  plan for, 346–352
  procurement division, 211, 214–215
  for rumor control, 346
  with suppliers, 210–211, 223,
    474–475
  of synergy road map, 128
Communications systems, 64–65
Compensation, 58, 377–378
Competitive advantage, 292
Compliance, 102, 277–278, 294
Confidentiality. *See* Privacy and
    confidentiality
Configuration testing, 440, 446
Consolidation integration model
  alignment of IT with business
    objectives, 37
  cloud solution considerations, 160
  critical success factors, 31, 142
  definition of, 28
  execution priorities, 30
  features of, 11
  leadership styles, 32
  for M&A-aware enterprise
    architecture, 142–143
  M&A failure causes, 31
Consultants, 112, 149, 150
Continuous improvement, 388
Contract lifecycle management (CLM)
    system, 55
Contracts. *See* Third-party contracts
COO, role of, 374
Copy, configure, and load separation
    model, 12
Cost(s)
  baseline for, 13

due diligence valuations, 7, 87
  estimates of, 28
  lessons learned, 480–482
  M&A IT, 3
  planning for unexpected, 465
  reduction opportunities, 25, 178–182
  stranded, 206, 249–250, 279–280
  synergy opportunities, 119–120,
    331
  third-party contracts, 205–206
  transition services agreements,
    267–269
Cost benefit analysis, 119–120
Cost escalation technique, 233
Cost management
  cloud computing benefits, 159
  as critical success factor, 460
  third-party contracts, 205–206,
    212–215
Cost plus technique, 233
Cost reduction, 25, 178–182
Cost-saving integration model,
    141–142, 160
Critical success factors (CSFs), 459–461
  alignment with business objectives,
    45
  blueprints, 42
  cloud computing, 164–165
  cost management, 460
  due diligence, 28, 33
  early IT involvement, 459
  information management, 419–438
  by integration model, 31
  IT readiness, 460
  risk management, 460
  road maps, 460
  stakeholder engagement, 461
  talent retention, 461
  top 10, 455–457
  See also Best practices
CRM (customer relationship
    management), 47, 56–57, 66
Cross-deal program structure, 468, 480
Cross-fertilization, 23, 25
CSFs. *See* Critical success factors (CSFs)

Culture, organizational, 30–32,
131–133, 367–369
Current-state systems architecture
diagram, 108, 109
Custom-developed applications, 74.
See also Applications
Customer data, 172–173, 187–188,
291–292
Customer master data (CMD), 57
Customer relationship management
(CRM), 47, 56–57, 66

Dashboards, 19
Data
archiving of, 168–169
assets, identification of, 169
customer, 57, 172–173, 187–188,
291–292
due diligence preparation, 72
ownership, 167–168, 170
protection, 168, 294, 299–300
segregation, 254, 260–261
supplier, 187–188
Data architecture diagrams, 106
Databases, 62–63
Data centers, 76, 95, 138
Data cleansing, 172, 255–256
Data coexistence, 418
Data consolidation, 417
Data dictionaries, 170
Data domain prioritization strategy,
429–430
Data extraction, 188, 210
Data factory framework, 430
Data governance, 167–168, 435–437
Data integration planning, 417,
431–432
Data management, 167–173
archiving, 168–169
controls, 472
customer data, 172–173
data protection, 168
governance and organizational issues,
167–168
importance of, 167

lessons learned, 487
master data management, 57, 319
road map for, 169–172
testing, 433
See also Information management
(IM)
Data mapping, 171, 195
Data migration, 141, 142, 280–281
Data quality, 170–171, 418
Data readiness, 418
Data relationship model (DRM), 187
Data requests, 82–83
Data requirements definition, 171
Data room reviews, 83–84
Data sheets, synergy capture, 132
Day 0 (announcement day), 6, 349, 366
Day 1, 253–263
blueprinting and, 10, 13
business process changes and
integration, 376–380
communication, 254, 261–262, 351
data segregation, 254, 260–261
defined, 112
e-mail, 254, 261–262
financial separation, 253–256
human resource separation, 254,
256–257
infrastructure planning, 93–99
integration and separation execution,
17
integration and separation planning,
9
in M&A lifecycle, 5, 6
network connectivity, 254, 258–259
priorities, 113, 253–263
rebranding strategy, 254, 257–258
risk management, 301
scope of, 454
synergy planning and road map
process, 127
third-party contracts, 216–217
transition services agreements and,
15, 20, 254, 259–261
Day 1 Complete, 216–217
Day 1 Ready, 216

Day 2
  communication, 351
  defined, 113
  synergy planning and road map
    process, 127, 152
Deal closed. *See* Day 1
Decentralized organization structure,
  356
Decision making, 43, 401–402, 456
Defect management tools, 443
Demand planning, 56
Demand-to-results management, 316
Dependencies, determination of,
  477–478
Deployment, of business process,
  387
Disaster recovery, 442–443, 448
Distribution, 56
Divestitures
  applications management, 188–193
  challenges of, 265
  costs of, 5
  data archiving, 169
  data requirements definition, 171
  data solutions implementation, 172
  due diligence, 152–153
  enterprise architecture frameworks
    and, 143–144
  infrastructure issues, 91
  IT integration issues, 61
  risks of, 285
  Sarbanes-Oxley requirements, 288
  separation planning, 153–154
  synergy opportunities, 138
  third-party contracts, 200, 218–219
  See also Transition services
    agreements (TSAs)
Documentation, 197, 230–231, 401
Dress rehearsals, 443
DRM (data relationship model),
  187
Due diligence
  alignment of IT with business
    objectives, 44
  areas of investigation, 72–76
  benchmarks, 81

best practices, 469–471
case studies, 490–491
CFO's role, 326–327
CIO's role, 314
complexity of, 70–72
confidentiality issues, 83, 85
cost, 7, 87
critical success factors, 28, 33
deal context, 80–81
definition of, 24
divestitures, 152–153
expectations for, 81
final report, 86–87
hidden information sources, 470
importance of, 6, 27–28, 88
objectives of, 6–8, 70, 149–150
other IT assessments vs., 69
planning considerations, 79–81
post-transaction activities and, 88,
  89–90
preparation for, 79
process, 82–86
proprietary or product
  technology-driven, 76–77
scope of, 469
for strategic vs. financial buyers,
  78–79
team member selection, 80
transaction type impact, 77–78
unpredictability of, 79
DuPont Model, 113, 124

Early IT involvement, 459, 465–466
EBAM (electronic bank account
  management), 54
Economies of scale, 23, 25
E-discovery, 210
Efficiency metrics, 125
Electronic bank account management
  (eBAM), 54
E-mail
  Day 1 migration solution options, 94,
    97, 98
  Day 1 priorities, 254, 261–262
  impact of changes on, 47, 66
  integration issues, 65

Employees
  access to technology, 319
  assessments, 60, 360–361
  benefits, 58, 256–257, 377–378
  communication with, 346–352,
      475–476
  compensation, 58, 377–378
  morale, 311–312
  recruitment, 59
  retention, 59–60, 121, 300–301,
      362–363, 461, 476, 482
  selection, 361–362
  training, 280
  transition plans, 366–368, 476–477
End state, 10, 92–93, 196
End-to-end scenarios, 444–445
Energy companies, 219–221
Enterprise architecture, "M&A-aware,"
    137–144
  divestitures and, 143–144
  for integration support, 146–147
  models, 139–143
  synergy sources, 137–138
Enterprise blueprints, 38–39
Enterprise resource planning (ERP)
    system
  applications rationalization, 197
  consolidation issues, 318–319
  finance department's role in decision
      making, 323, 326
  financial consolidation in, 51–52
  impact of changes on, 47, 66
  manufacturing and supply chain, 55
  operations, 55
Enterprise Value Map (EVM),
    113–115, 116
Entity relationship diagrams, 106
ERP. *See* Enterprise resource planning
    (ERP) system
Errors, 293, 380, 387
EVM (Enterprise Value Map),
    113–115, 116
Exception management, 298
Exit management, 20
Exit planning, transition services
    agreements, 247–249, 272–273,
    277, 278–281

Experience, M&A critical success
    factor, 455
External role, CIOs, 314–317
Extract and go separation model, 12,
    101

Facilities, transition schedule, 100–102
Failure of deals, 451–457
  causes of, 452
  common patterns, 453–455
  critical success factors, 455–457
  risk factors, 452–453
  statistics, 451
Finance department
  integration issues, 49, 51–54
  integration or divestiture priorities,
      332–333
  integration teams, 334
  performance metrics, 125
Financial buyers, 78–79, 225
Financial closure, 339, 343, 375
Financial planning and analysis
    (FP&A), 53
Financial policies and procedures, 52
Financials
  consolidation of, 51–52, 53, 187,
      340–342
  Day 1 priorities, 253–256, 376–377
  due diligence, 327
  statutory requirements, 53
Financial services industry, 289
Financial systems, selection and
    integration of, 375–380
Firewalls, 93
Focus, M&A critical success factor, 456
Forecasting, 53
Forward transition services agreements,
    265–266, 267
Four Faces Framework, 323–324
Full integration, 48
Functional areas, integration
    components, 47–66
  alignment with overall integration
      strategy, 48–49, 66
  coordination of, 66
  finance, 49, 51–54

Functional areas, integration
  components (*Continued*)
  governance, 50–51
  human resources, 57–60
  introduction, 47–48
  IT, 60–65
  operations, 54–57
  timing matrix, 49–50
Functional blueprints, 39–43, 183–187
Functional redundancy, 106
Functional unit testing, 440, 446
Funding, streamlining of IT, 148
Future, planning for, 437–438, 465
Future-systems architecture diagram,
  108, 110

General ledger, 255, 376, 377
Geographic coverage changes, 315
Give and go separation model, 12, 101
Globalization, 399
Governance, 405–415
  best practices, 467–472
  CFO's role, 334, 342–343
  CIO's role, 314–315
  collaborative project management
    tools, 401
  data, 167–168, 435–437
  example of, 18, 407
  four pillars of, 314–315
  importance of, 50
  information management office's
    role, 395
  plan execution, 413–415
  program management office
    establishment, 408–413
  roles and responsibilities, 408
  streamlining processes, 148
  structure for, 18, 50–51, 405–408
  testing, 433
  transition services agreements,
    235–247, 273–278

Hacking, 293
Hardware, synergy opportunities, 138
Hardware maintenance agreements,
  102

Hart-Scott-Rodino Antitrust
  Improvements (HSR) Act, 398
HCM (human capital management), 47,
  66
Health care industry, 289, 436–437
Health insurance, 58
Holding companies, integration
  strategy, 48
Human capital management (HCM),
  47, 66
Human error, 293
Human resources (HR)
  Day 1 priorities, 254, 256–257
  integration issues, 57–60
  performance metrics, 125
  priorities, 345–346
  risk management, 301
  See also Employees; People
    management
Hybrid organization structure,
  356–357
Hybrid separation model, 12

IaaS (infrastructure as a service),
  157–158, 163
ICFR (internal control over financial
  reporting), 288–289
IMOs. *See* Integration management
  offices (IMOs)
Information gaps, third-party contracts,
  209
Information management (IM),
  417–438
  active program management, 419,
    424–428
  alignment of strategy with M&A
    strategy, 420–423
  challenges and opportunities,
    417–419
  critical success factors, 419–438
  data domain prioritization strategy,
    429–430
  data governance implementation,
    435–437
  data integration plans and control,
    431–432

for future M&A deals, 437–438
integrated testing, 432–434
M&A data factory framework,
    430
reporting strategy, 434–435
road map for, 423–424, 425, 426
See also Data management
Information rationalization, 418
Information technology (IT)
    communication plans, 346–352
    complexity of, 35
    contract management, 216
    dependency areas, 42
    functional blueprint preparation,
        39–43
    governance structure, 18
    job families, 358, 359
    M&A impact on, 47
    managers, 365–366
    M&A objectives, 35
    M&A role, 4–6, 45
    organization structure, 313, 352–358
    performance metrics, 125
    sources of "hidden" information,
        83–84
    staff, 7, 111
    supervisors, 365–366
    synergy capture team role, 120–122
    synergy metric establishment, 127
    synergy planning, 127–128
    See also specific index headings
Information Technology Infrastructure
    Library (ITIL), 307, 308
Information technology (IT) leadership
    communication, 111, 363–366
    due diligence assignment, 466
    identification of, 373–374
    IT system selection influence, 374
    readiness for M&A deals, 148
    summit or working session for,
        363–364
    synergies identification analysis,
        111
    synergy capture team membership,
        122
    understanding risks, 284–293

Infrastructure
    blueprinting, 91–93
    components of, 91, 92
    dependencies, 100–102
    diagrams, 106
    due diligence investigations, 72, 74,
        76, 90
    IT's role in decision making, 122
    management, 76
    planning, 62–63, 93–99
    prioritization vs. deferral to
        transitional period, 93, 94–95
Infrastructure as a service (IaaS),
    157–158, 163
Inspirational leadership, 32
Instance management, 63
Integrated testing, 432–434
Integration
    business processes, 376–388
    cloud opportunities, 158–159
    costs of, 5
    critical success factors, 32, 33
    customer data, 172–173
    data management tools, 171–172
    definition of, 24
    framework, 19
    importance of, 32–33
    inadequate, 24–26
    management issues, 30–32
    models, 11, 28–30, 36–38, 139–143
    monitoring process, 369–370
    priorities, 16–20, 30
    risks of, 284–285
    road maps for, 126–128, 129
    synergies from, 23
    testing, 441, 446–448
    timing, 50
    See also Functional areas, integration
        components
Integration management offices (IMOs),
    393–404
    best practices for deal management,
        399–403
    challenges, 398–399
    key activities, 395–397
    roles and responsibilities, 393–395

Integration models
  alignment of IT with business
    objectives, 29–30, 36–38
  changing over time, 38
  choosing, 139
  features of, 11, 28–29
  for M&A-aware enterprise
    architecture, 139–143
  review of, 139
  use of multiple models, 36
Integration planning
  case studies, 490
  complexity of, 27
  components of, 151
  critical success factors, 30, 33
  definition of, 24
  by functional area, 49–50
  importance of, 32–33
  inadequate, 24–26
  objectives of, 150–151
  priorities, 8–15
  timing matrix, 49
Integration strategy
  critical success factors, 27, 33
  definition of, 24
  development of, 150
  enterprise architecture design,
    146–147
  governance structure and, 50
  types of, 48–49
Intellectual property protection and
  exposure, 197
Interactive voice response (IVR),
  65
Internal control
  due diligence investigations, 73, 89
  key practices, 293–301
  understanding current state of,
    283–293
Internal control over financial reporting
  (ICFR), 288–289
Internal role, CIOs, 307–313
Intervention, manual, 108
Interviews, due diligence process,
  84–86
Invoicing, 242–244, 277

Issue escalation, transition services
  agreements, 236, 239
IT. *See* Information technology (IT)
ITIL (Information Technology
    Infrastructure Library), 307, 308
IVR (interactive voice response), 65

Job families, 358, 359
Joint ventures, 71, 78, 87

Key performance indicators (KPIs)
  establishment for each value driver,
    134–135
  integration program performance,
    427
  synergy opportunities, 117, 119, 124
  system stability measurement, 387
Kickoff meetings, 411–413

Launches. *See* Day 1
Laws and legislation, 288, 398–399
Leadership, 32, 60, 456. *See also*
    Information technology (IT)
    leadership
Leaks of information, 291–292, 350,
    399
Legal department, 216, 327
Lessons learned, summary of, 480–489
Letter of intent (LOI), 5
Leverage, M&A critical success factor,
    456
Licenses, 102. *See also* Third-party
    contracts
LOI (letter of intent), 5

Mainframes, 95
Managers, 30–32, 60, 365–366
Manufacturing, 55–56
Mapping, 171, 195, 267
Marketing and sales, 56–57, 257–258,
    378
Market share, 25
Master data management (MDM), 57,
    319
Master services agreements (MSAs),
    205, 215, 269

MDM (master data management), 57, 319

Media, leaks to, 291–292, 350, 399

Meetings
  due diligence interviews, 84–86
  kickoff, 411–413
  status, 409–411

Mergers and acquisitions (M&A)
  cost of, 3
  of equally sized organizations, 318
  failure to create shareholder value, 23
  four pillars of, 24, 33
  introduction, 3–4
  IT impact, 47
  IT's role in, 4–6, 45
  lifecycle, 5–6, 20–22, 421
  motivations for, 27, 29–30, 35
  See also specific index headings

Messaging services, 94, 97, 98

Metrics
  applications rationalization, 195, 196–197
  performance, 331
  for progress against plan, 414
  for synergy tracking, 124–126, 134–135
  system stability, 387

Middleware technology, 319

Migration costs, 233

Minimal integration, 48

Minimum fee technique, 233

Mock cut-over testing, 443, 447

Momentum, CFO's role in maintaining, 337–338

Monitoring, 300, 369–370

Morale, 311–312

MSAs (master services agreements), 205, 215, 269

Negative tests, 440

Negotiation, 471–472

Networks and networking
  capacity, 63
  Day 1 migration solution options, 93, 94, 96
  Day 1 priorities, 254, 258–259
  due diligence investigations, 76
  integration process, 63
  lessons learned, 485–486
  synergy opportunities, 138

New builds, application access, 101

New market creation and entry, 25

Offshore outsourcing, 356

Operational role, CIOs, 307, 310

Operations
  costs, 206
  defined, 54–55
  due diligence, 73, 326–327
  integration issues, 23, 25, 54–57
  IT integration benefits, 25
  synergies, 23, 182–188

Operator, CFO as, 332–338, 342–343

Organizational culture, 30–32, 131–133, 367–369

Organization structure, 147–148, 352–358, 393–394, 483

Output tracking, 210

Outsourcing, 143, 148, 317, 356

Overcontrolled processing, 108

Overhead, shared, 23, 25

PaaS (platform as a service), 157–158, 159

Parallel testing, 441

Partial integration, 48

Payment processing, 378–379

Payroll, 52, 58, 256–257

People
  deal failure themes, 455
  due diligence area, 72–74
  risks associated with, 452–453
  See also Employees

People management, 345–371
  change management, 363–370
  communication plans, 346–352
  organization structure design, 352–358
  priorities, overview of, 345–346
  talent assessment and selection, 358–363
  See also Human resources (HR)

Performance and stress testing, 442, 447
Performance management, 244–247, 276, 312
Performance measurement tools, 443
Performance metrics, 125, 331
Phased approach, 334–335, 336
Plan to make (PTM), 56
Platform as a service (PaaS), 157–158, 159
Playbooks, 195
PMI (post-merger integration) steering committee, 50
PMOs. *See* Program management offices (PMOs)
Portals, 65, 257
Portfolio integration model, 140, 160
Positive tests, 440
Post-merger integration (PMI) steering committee, 50
Preannouncement, communication during, 348–349
Preservation integration model
    alignment of IT with business objectives, 37
    critical success factors, 31
    definition of, 29
    execution priorities, 30
    features of, 11
    leadership style, 32
    M&A failure causes, 31
Pricing, of transition services, 231–235
Prioritization mechanism, third-party contracts, 209
Privacy and confidentiality
    best practices, 472–473
    data protection requirements, 168
    due diligence process and, 83, 85
    lessons learned, 483–485
Private clouds, 157
Private equity firms, 14, 193–194
Process controls testing, 440
Processes. *See* Business processes
Procurement
    business intent as driver of, 207
    communication, 211, 214–215
    contract management, 216
    contract ownership, 204
    integration, 378–379
    involvement in transaction, 213
    volume goals, 209
Procure to pay (PTP), 55
Production planning and optimization, 56
Product technology-drive due diligence, 76–77
Program management offices (PMOs)
    applications rationalization, 194
    communication plans, 111
    establishment, 16, 408–413, 427–428, 477–478
    integration and separation execution role, 20–22
    kickoff meetings, 411–413
    lessons learned, 480
    project direction and control, 409
    project plans, 411, 413–415
    reporting, 414
    status meetings, 409–411
    third-party contracts, 215–217
Project management tools, 400–401
Project risks, 453
Proprietary due diligence, 76–77
PTM (plan to make), 56
Public clouds, 157

Quality, data, 170–171, 418
Quality reporting, 434–435

RACI (responsible, accountable, consulted, and informed) matrix, 402
Rationalization, 64, 175–188, 418
Readiness
    facilitation, 460
    factors, 147–148
    metrics, 125
    transition services agreements, 236, 240–241
Real estate, transition schedule, 100–102
Rebranding strategy, 254, 257–258

Recruitment, employee, 59
Regression testing, 442
Regulatory issues
  CIO's understanding of, 315
  data segregation, 261
  Sarbanes-Oxley requirements,
    288–289
  transition plans, 102
  understanding, 287–291
Relationship management, transition
  services agreements, 276
Remediation, 286–287
Repetitive cycles, 108
Reports and reporting
  due diligence, 86–87
  errors, 380
  information management, 434–435
  program management office,
    414–415
  regulatory requirements, 53,
    290–291
  of synergy achievements, 128–131
  See also Financials
Requirement management tools, 443
Requirements traceability matrix,
  446
Research, initial on target company, 82,
  466–467
Restricted access, 101
Restructuring, 352–358
Retention, of employees, 59–60, 121,
  300–301, 362–363, 461, 476,
  482
Retention of documents, 197
Return on equity (ROE), 113
Return on investment (ROI), 142, 319,
  418
Revenue capture integration model,
  140–141, 144, 160
Revenue recognition, 378
Reverse transition services agreements,
  266, 267
Right to use (RTU) clauses, 102
Risk
  identification of (*See* Due diligence)
  synergy opportunities, 119–120

third-party contracts, 202, 204–205,
  206–212
understanding current state of,
  283–293
Risk assessments, 286, 291–292
Risk governance, 285–286
Risk management
  collaborative project management
    tools, 400–401
  as critical success factor, 460
  IT areas, 285
  key practices, 293–301
  third-party contracts, 206–212
  transition services agreements,
    277–278
Risk response phase, 286–287
Road maps
  applications, 196
  business processes, 373–376,
    388–389
  critical success factors, 460
  data management, 169–172
  integration, 126–128, 129
ROE (return on equity), 113
ROI (return on investment), 142, 319,
  418
RTU (right to use) clauses, 102
Rumors, 346

SaaS (software as a service), 157–158,
  159, 163, 193–194
Sales and marketing, 56–57, 257–258,
  378
Sarbanes-Oxley Act (SOx), 288
Scope of M&A transaction,
  453–454
Security
  best practices, 472–473
  data management issues, 168
  Day 1 solution options, 95
  HR role, 59
  key practices, 293–301
  lessons learned, 483–485
  migration planning, 93
  testing, 440
  transition plans, 102

Security (*Continued*)
    understanding current state of,
        283–293
    See also Privacy and confidentiality
Self-validation, transition services
    agreements, 240, 241
Senior executives, due diligence role, 7
Separation
    execution priorities, 16–20
    models of, 10, 12
    objectives of, 154
    planning, 8–15, 153–154
Servers, 63, 76, 138, 488
Service-level agreements (SLAs),
    244–245, 246
Service levels, CIO's role in
    maintaining, 312
Service Organization Controls (SOC)
    No. 1, 288
Shareholder value, 112, 113–115
Sherman Antitrust Act, 398
SLAs (service-level agreements),
    244–245, 246
SMAs (subject matter advisers), 80
Software, 52, 102, 138. *See also*
    Third-party contracts
Software as a service (SaaS), 157–158,
    159, 163, 193–194
SOW (statement of work), 277
Spending, as due diligence area, 72–74
Spreadsheets, financial consolidation in,
    52
    AE (Statement on Standards for
    Attestation Engagements) No.D
    16, 288
Stakeholder support and participation,
    121, 300–301, 461
Standards, 121–122, 178, 380
Statement of work (SOW), 277
Statement on Standards for Attestation
    Engagements (SSAE) No. 16, 288
Status meetings, 409–411
Status report template, 396
Statutory reporting and compliance, 53
Steering committees, 215, 393–394
Steward, CFO as, 338–342

Stranded costs, 206, 249–250,
    279–280
Strategic buyers, 78–79, 225
Strategy, 145–155
    alignment with business goals, 146
    building capabilities to support and
        execute M&A deals, 149
    CFO's role, 324–329, 342
    components, overview, 145
    divestiture approach, 152–154
    enterprise architecture design to
        support integration, 146–147
    funding process, 148
    governance process, 148
    integration approach, 149–152
    readiness for M&A deals, 147–148
    See also Integration strategy
String testing, 440–441, 446
Structural risk, 452
Subject matter advisers (SMAs), 80
Success factors. *See* Critical success
    factors (CSFs)
Succession planning, 60
Supplier data, 187–188
Suppliers
    analysis of, 214
    communication with, 210–211, 223,
        474–475
    knowledge of, 208–209, 222, 474
    prioritization mechanism, 209
    See also Third-party contracts
Supply chain, integration issues, 55–56
Support, for new business processes,
    387–388
SWIFT connectivity, 54
Synergies
    applications rationalization,
        196–197
    benefits of, 24, 25
    best practices, 473
    CFO's role in development and
        tracking of, 329–332
    cost benefit analysis, 119–120
    definition of, 13, 24
    examples of, 23
    identification of, 49, 105–118

opportunity templates, 118
overly aggressive targets and deal
   failure, 454
planning, 111–120
risks of, 284, 452
road map for, 126–128, 129
sources of, 13, 137–138
valuation of, 123–126, 131–135
Synergy analysis planning, 13–14
Synergy capture
   checklist, 128, 130
   data sheets, 132
   failure of, 24–26
   IT's role, 45, 105–111, 120–122
   planning, 123–135
   tracking and management, 18–19,
     128–135, 332
Synergy identification
   analysis of, 105–111
   external assistance, 112
   by functional area, 49
   IT as partner in, 111–112
   structured approach for, 112–115
   workshops, 116–118
Synthesis of capabilities, 25
System architecture diagrams, 106
System owners, synergy capture team
   membership, 122

Talent. *See* Employees
Taxes, 53
Taxonomy, establishment of, 431
Teamwork
   due diligence, 7, 80
   integration planning, 151
   synergy capture, 120–122, 131–133,
     134
Technical security reviews and scans,
   299–300
Technical unit testing, 440, 446
Telecommunications, due diligence
   investigations, 76
Telephony, 65
Testing, 439–448
   importance of, 386
   integrated program for, 432–434

preparation activities, 444–446
timing of, 446–447, 448
tools, 443
types of, 172
Text mining, 210
Third-party contracts, 199–223
   best practices, 473–475
   case studies, 218–221
   contract lifecycle management
     system, 55
   costs and cost management,
     205–206, 212–215
   Day 1 solution options, 95
   due diligence investigations, 73, 89
   lessons learned, 221–223, 481
   management plans, 203, 215–217
   during mergers vs. divestitures, 200
   program management office role,
     215–217
   risks and risk management,
     204–205, 206–212
   situation of buyers vs. sellers,
     200–204
   suppliers' leverage, 199–200, 202
   transition plans, 102, 278
Timing matrix, by functional area, 49
Top-down synergy target setting, 13
Traceability, synergy value, 133–134
Tracking
   collaborative project management
     tools, 400
   IMO's role, 395
   output, 210
   synergy capture, 18–19, 124–126,
     128–135, 332
   transition services agreements, 20
   value, 131–135
Training, 280
Transaction costs, third-party contracts
   and, 202, 206
Transaction type, 77–78, 120
Transformation integration model
   alignment of IT with business
     objectives, 37
   critical success factors, 31
   definition of, 29

Transformation integration model
(*Continued*)
execution priorities, 30
features of, 11
leadership style, 32
M&A failure causes, 31
Transition phase, 151–152, 154. *See
also* Day 1
Transition plans, employees, 366–368,
476–477
Transition services agreements (TSAs),
225–251, 265–281
alignment of legal agreement with
exhibits, 229–230
applications management, 189–191
architecture supporting, 266–267
benefits of, 267, 268
best practices, 471
components of, 229
costs, understanding and defining,
267–269
Day 1 priorities, 254, 259–261
definition of, 14, 225–226, 265–266
disadvantages of, 5
documentation requirements,
230–231
drafting tips, 267–270
execution and management, 20, 21,
61, 271–273, 471
exit planning, 247–249, 272–273,
277, 278–281
functional area input, 61
governance structure, 235–247,
273–278
infrastructure, 91
lessons learned, 489
planning, 14–15, 227–228
pricing services, 231–235
resources dedicated to, 228–229
roles and responsibilities, 238
secure access to services, 259
stranded costs, 249–250
structure of, 270–271

talent identification and selection,
358–360
timeline, 15, 266
types of, 265–267
use of, 465
Transition services coordinators, 271
Treasury, integration issues, 54
TSAs. *See* Transition services
agreements (TSAs)

Unionization, 317, 377–378
Unit testing, 386, 439–440, 444
Upgrades, 383
User acceptance testing (UAT), 441, 448
User access, 101, 259, 293–296, 472

Value and valuation
Enterprise Value Map, 113–115, 116
of synergies, 123–126, 131–135
tracking, 131–135
Vendor clouds, 157–158
Vendor management
Day 1 solution options, 95
due diligence investigations, 73, 89
lessons learned, 481
Vendor sourcing, 122
Virtual desktop infrastructure (VDI)
solution, 295
Vision, 317
Volume goal, 209
Volume testing, 442

Warehousing, 56
Websites, 65, 257
What-if-analysis, 112
Workforce services, 319
Work plans, 128
Workshops, 40, 116–118, 128
Workstations, 76
Work stream, 134

XML format, 54

Printed and bound by CPI Group (UK) Ltd, Croydon, CR0 4YY

16/04/2025

14658369-0005